Winning in the New Global Business Landscape

"A masterfully written, incisive and highly engaging assessment of today's complex international business environment in this era of global turbulence, transition, and transformation."

—Deborah Wince-Smith, *President and CEO, Council on Competitiveness*

"*Winning in the New Global Business Landscape* is a brilliantly written, highly original and thought-provoking opus that will captivate scholars and practitioners alike."

—Claudio Muruzabal, *IT thought leader & board member, former Chief Business Officer, SAP*

"A clear, strategic and actionable blueprint for navigating the complexities of today's fast-paced and interconnected global business arena."

—Christoph Klein, *Director of Business Development, Porsche Latin America*

Jerry Haar · Ricardo Ernst · Santiago Gutierrez

Winning in the New Global Business Landscape

Integrating Technology, Infrastructure, Geopolitics, and Harnessed Talent

Jerry Haar
College of Business
Florida International University
Miami, FL, USA

Ricardo Ernst
McDonough School of Business
Georgetown University
Washington, DC, USA

Santiago Gutierrez
Latin Trade
Bogotá, Colombia

ISBN 978-3-031-95969-1   ISBN 978-3-031-95970-7 (eBook)
https://doi.org/10.1007/978-3-031-95970-7

© The Editor(s) (if applicable) and The Author(s), under exclusive license to Springer Nature Switzerland AG 2025

This work is subject to copyright. All rights are solely and exclusively licensed by the Publisher, whether the whole or part of the material is concerned, specifically the rights of translation, reprinting, reuse of illustrations, recitation, broadcasting, reproduction on microfilms or in any other physical way, and transmission or information storage and retrieval, electronic adaptation, computer software, or by similar or dissimilar methodology now known or hereafter developed.

The use of general descriptive names, registered names, trademarks, service marks, etc. in this publication does not imply, even in the absence of a specific statement, that such names are exempt from the relevant protective laws and regulations and therefore free for general use.

The publisher, the authors and the editors are safe to assume that the advice and information in this book are believed to be true and accurate at the date of publication. Neither the publisher nor the authors or the editors give a warranty, expressed or implied, with respect to the material contained herein or for any errors or omissions that may have been made. The publisher remains neutral with regard to jurisdictional claims in published maps and institutional affiliations.

Cover credit: eStudio Calamar

This Palgrave Macmillan imprint is published by the registered company Springer Nature Switzerland AG
The registered company address is: Gewerbestrasse 11, 6330 Cham, Switzerland

If disposing of this product, please recycle the paper.

To the companies, traders, financiers, and entrepreneurs who work arduously to triumph in the new global economy.

Foreword

In the first three decades of the twenty-first century, we are witnessing an accelerating pace of change in science, technology, and even geopolitics. We are at the cusp of the AI revolution, which holds great promise but equal risk. At the same time, the internet has disrupted mass media and politics, and we watch nationalism, populism, and protectionism on the rise in many countries. In such a turbulent environment, traditional frameworks that assume ever-greater globalization and frictionless trade are often no longer relevant and may, in fact, lead businesses astray, potentially losing access to their supply chains, markets, or consumer preferences as a result. To be able to prosper and avoid such pitfalls in this ever more complex environment, it is imperative that business leaders find new frameworks to properly evaluate future opportunities and risks.

To address this problem, Messrs. Haar, Ernst, and Gutierrez have developed a clear and practical framework for navigating today's volatile environment. Within that framework, they identify four key drivers: technology, infrastructure, geopolitics, and harnessed talent.

As President and CEO of AES, a Fortune 500 Company and one of the leading clean energy technology companies in the world, I can attest that these drivers impact our strategic business decisions and help determine our ability to meet our financial and environmental goals, such as doubling our renewable energy fleet by 2030 and achieving net-zero carbon emissions from electricity generation by 2040. In times of great disruptions, great opportunities may arise, but only for those with the clarity of vision and analytical tools that give them a competitive advantage. This book can be a valuable guide for business leaders striving toward that end.

Andres Ricardo Gluski
President and CEO of the AES
Corporation
Arlington, VA, USA

Chairman of the Council
of the Americas/Americas Society
New York, NY, USA

Preface

The worldwide pandemic and its aftermath have altered the business landscape broadly and profoundly. However, the seeds of change were planted before the global health crisis. During the last decade, the geography of accelerated economic growth potential has changed and is moving forward at an even faster pace and will continue to do so over the next ten years. Geopolitics has overtaken purely economic issues, as witnessed by the conflict between Russia and Ukraine, Gaza and Israel, ethnic-religious tensions in India, the rise of populism and authoritarianism in many regions of the world, increased inflation and fiscal deficits, public safety and anti-foreigner manifestations are impacting nations—their public and private sectors as well as consumers and citizens at large.

Four key drivers are altering today's global business landscape—technology, infrastructure, geopolitics, and harnessed talent. The acronym we apply here is TIGHT (technology, infrastructure, geopolitics and harnessed talent) and we refer to it as the TIGHT Framework. Individually and collectively, they are producing dramatic impacts on how nations and companies compete. To illustrate, geopolitics in the form of deteriorating US-China relations are motivating American companies that operate in and source from China to consider nearshoring. New technologies in artificial intelligence and machine learning are accelerating innovation and productivity in both manufacturing and service firms. Public-private partnerships in infrastructure, such as ports and roadways, are producing efficient and cost-effective solutions to both domestic and foreign commerce, while the quest for talent presents an overwhelming and continuous challenge for corporations of all sizes.

The aim of our book is twofold: (1) assess how four game-changing factors, as embodied in the TIGHT Framework, are altering today's global business landscape; and (2) examine how one important "living laboratory"—new emerging markets—is faring vis-à-vis the framework.

In the first instance, we will do a deep dive into each driver and present the challenges and impediments, opportunities and prospects, and evaluation to date of how, when, and where each driver is achieving results. Their interdependence is the most critical part of our focus and message; for it is the dynamic nature of the interrelationship that makes a difference. In the second instance, we intend to zero in on six of the new emerging markets—the fastest growing segment of global commerce—to apply our TIGHT framework.[1]

Among the important questions we address are: How well does the TIGHT framework fit in explaining the new global business landscape? How can the drivers collectively be better positioned to confront the challenges in the global business landscape? How well does the TIGHT framework explain the key business-related developments in the six markets we have selected as case examples?

A unique and extremely important feature of the book is the symbiotic relationship among and between technology, infrastructure, geopolitics, and harnessed talent. Evaluating technology, infrastructure, geopolitics, and harnessed talent as a cohesive framework is essential for gaining a comprehensive understanding of today's global business landscape. These four interconnected elements provide a holistic perspective that helps businesses navigate the complexities and challenges of operating in an increasingly interconnected world. Here's why evaluating them as a unified block is crucial. Not evaluating technology, infrastructure, geopolitics, and harnessed talent as a cohesive framework can lead to a significant misunderstanding of today's global business landscape. Some reasons why neglecting this integrated approach can be a mistake include incomplete insights, risked of blind spots, missed opportunities, and inefficient resource allocation. The Framework illustrates that a TIGHTer position (better marks on the four key drivers) facilitates the engagement and to capitalize on the opportunities offered by the new global business landscape.

---

[1] In referring to "emerging markets" one tends to immediately think of the BRICS—an acronym for five leading emerging economies: Brazil, Russia, India, China, and South Africa. The first four were initially grouped as "BRIC" (or "the BRICs") in 2001 by Goldman Sachs economist Jim O'Neill, who coined the term to describe fast-growing economies that would collectively dominate the global economy by 2050. The "new" emerging markets are the next wave, especially since the original BRICs, except for India, have not been faring well.

We believe the proposed book is both timely, highly relevant, and unique. We make the case for each of the drivers we have selected and employ as case studies, six new emerging markets that are rapidly growing in importance yet under-represented in both the academic and practitioner-oriented literature: Turkey, Saudi Arabia, Mexico, Poland, Nigeria, and Vietnam. In terms of intended audience, our book targets government policymakers, the corporate community, policy analysts, and the media. The book can also be used for classroom instruction at the graduate level and hopefully inspire academic researchers toward further investigation.

The book is divided into seven chapters. The first presents the TIGHT framework, introducing the four key drivers impacting business, highlighting the relevance and importance of these drivers to both public policy formation and corporate planning and operations. We also explain and define the meaning of a TIGHTer position. Every Chapter includes specific examples to illustrate the meaning of the key variable and the context to explain advantages and disadvantages of having a TIGHTer approach.

One of the most important drivers of a nation's economic health and competitiveness is technology; and this is the focus of Chapter 2. The technology driver refers to the collection of tools, systems, techniques, methods, and processes designed to solve problems, improve efficiency, and achieve specific goals. It includes cutting edge developments and applications in artificial intelligence, the Internet of Things, blockchain, big data, the cloud, and augmented reality.

The infrastructure driver addressed in Chapter 3 covers the status and needs, including current and required investment, in infrastructure such as telecom, IT, transportation, ports, bridges, and electrical grids along with alternative energy. Infrastructure includes both hard and soft elements. All are introduced in the context of the TIGHT Framework.

Current challenges and conflicts, whether domestic politics across nations, where populism looms large, as well as Russian and Chinese expansionism, cannot be overlooked. This is addressed in Chapter 4. Whether populism, nationalism-protectionism, the Ukrainian-Russian conflict, or trade tensions, cross-border issues of political, economic, and territorial natures impact the business environment and affect both governance and economics.

The last of the drivers in the new business environment is harnessed talent. The subject of Chapter 5 harnessed talent refers to the process of effectively utilizing and channeling the abilities, skills, and potential of individuals in a purposeful and organized manner. It involves taking advantage of the talents people possess and directing them toward specific goals, tasks, or projects.

When talent is harnessed, it's not just about recognizing individual capabilities, but also creating an environment or system that maximizes the impact of those talents for the benefit of a particular endeavor or the larger context in which it operates.

Having covered the TIGHT framework, the volume proceeds to provide in Chapter 6 case studies drawn from six dynamic new emerging markets. This chapter reiterates the reason for the selection of emerging markets, particularly newer ones, to analyze and assess how the TIGHT framework with its four key drivers impact high growth countries. We present the rationale selecting each country and illustrate the TIGHT framework in each nation and highlight which variable is making the greater impact and why.

In our conclusion (Chapter 7), we summarize the key points from all previous chapters. We then do some crystal ball gazing to suggest possible future outcomes—specifically what both policymakers and companies should be most concerned about and how they may wish to proceed to shape new policies and initiatives that can maximize the benefits using the TIGHT Framework.

Finally, we wish to provide our sincere thanks and deep appreciation to Audrey He of Georgetown's McDonough School of Business for her invaluable research assistance, FIU EMBA Cohort 29 for their contribution to the country case studies, and Professors David Doyle of the University of Oxford and Steven Levitsky of Harvard University for their support. We also are grateful to Marcus Ballenger and Ashika Joycell of Palgrave for their guidance and support throughout the book production process.

Jerry Haar
Florida International University
Miami, FL, USA

Ricardo Ernst
Baratta Chair in Global Business
Georgetown University
Washington, DC, USA

Santiago Gutierrez
Executive Editor
Latin Trade
Bogotá, Colombia

Contents

1	**Introduction**	1
	Globalization vs Globalism: Defining the New Global Landscape	1
	The 'China' Conversation	2
	An Era of Globalization Without Globalism	3
	Genesis of a New World	4
	The COVID-19 Pandemic	4
	Russian-Ukrainian Conflict	6
	Israel – Gaza	7
	Risk Hedging and Navigating Complexity	9
	Four Key Drivers in the New Business Landscape	12
	Utilizing the TIGHT Framework in Business	14
2	**The Technology Driver**	17
	Technology: The Basis of the Modern World	17
	Technology and the Development of the Global Business Landscape: A Flurry of Technological Shapes, Sizes, and Functionalities	18
	Measuring the Technology Driver	25
	Technology Within the TIGHT Framework	27
	Technology and Infrastructure	28
	Technology and Geopolitics	33

	Technology and Harnessed Talent	36
	Conclusion: Technology Within Today's Business Landscape Is a Catalyst	39
3	**The Infrastructure Driver**	41
	Infrastructure: The Great Enabler	41
	The Two Types of Infrastructure and Their Effect on the Development of the Global Business Landscape	42
	Infrastructure as a Connector: The Future of Global Business	44
	Measuring the Infrastructure Driver	48
	Infrastructure Within the TIGHT Framework	52
	Infrastructure and Technology	53
	Infrastructure and Geopolitics	57
	Infrastructure and Harnessed Talent	60
	Conclusion: Infrastructure Is the Foundation of all Possibility	63
4	**The Geopolitical Driver**	65
	Geopolitics: The Mandate of Resilience	65
	The Trade Story: Integration of Geo and Politics	66
	Governability: The Key to Understanding Geopolitics	68
	Measuring Geopolitical Factors	71
	Geopolitics Within the TIGHT Framework	76
	Geopolitics and Technology	76
	Geopolitics and Infrastructure	80
	Geopolitics and Harnessed Talent	84
	Conclusion: Geopolitics Is the Matchbox That Incites All	88
5	**The Harnessed Talent Driver**	89
	Harnessed Talent: The Prerequisite for Success	89
	Changes to Harnessed Talent: A New Digital Transformation	90
	Availability and the Challenge with Harnessed Talent	94
	Measuring Harnessed Talent	97
	Harnessed Talent Within the TIGHT Framework	99
	Harnessed Talent and Technology	100
	Harnessed Talent and Infrastructure	104
	Harnessed Talent and Geopolitics	108
	Conclusion: Harnessed Talent Is the Driving Force Behind Corporate Expansion	111
6	**Case Studies**	115
	Introduction	115
	Mexico	118

Business Environment	120
Technology	122
Infrastructure	126
Geopolitics	129
Talent	136
Key Drivers	139
Country Outlook	140
Nigeria	142
Technology	147
Infrastructure	149
Geopolitics	154
Talent	157
Key Drivers	160
Country Outlook	166
Poland	168
Technology	174
Infrastructure	177
Geopolitics	179
Talent	183
Key Drivers	185
Country Outlook	188
Saudi Arabia	189
Business Environment	191
Technology	194
Infrastructure	197
Geopolitics	202
Talent	208
Key Drivers	211
Country Outlook	214
Turkey	214
Technology	220
Infrastructure	223
Geopolitics	226
Talent	230
Key Drivers	233
Country Outlook	237
Vietnam	238
Technology	245
Infrastructure	247
Geopolitics	251

Talent	255
Key Drivers	258
Country Outlook	261
7 Conclusion	263
Index	279

About the Authors

Jerry Haar is a professor of international business at Florida International University, a visiting faculty fellow at Georgetown University's Baratta Center on Global Business and a senior fellow of the Council on Competitiveness.

Ricardo Ernst is the Baratta Chair in Global Business and Professor of Operations and Supply Chain Management at Georgetown University.

Santiago Gutierrez is the Executive Editor of Latin Trade and a lecturer at Universidad de los Andes in Bogotá, Colombia.

List of Figures

Fig. 1.1	Change in the share of US imports 2017–2023 (*Source* US Census Bureau, F. Guerrera, Breakingviews, October 13, 2023)	2
Fig. 1.2	Eras of globalization (Sum of exports and imports as a percentage of GDP) (*Sources* PIIE, Jorda-Schularick-Taylor Macrohistory Database. Penn World Data (10,0) World Bank, and IMF staff calculations)	4
Fig. 1.3	Annual real GDP percentage change since January 2006 (*Source* Office for National Statistics)	5
Fig. 1.4	Russia in the world economy (2024) (*Source* Oxford Economics/Haver Analytics/World Bank/Eurostat)	7
Fig. 1.5	Tourism receipts are at risk amid travel concerns (*Source* Haver Analytics and IMF staff calculations)	8
Fig. 1.6	Impact on energy prices (index: Oct-6th, 2023 = 100) (*Source* Bloomberg Finance L.P.)	9
Fig. 1.7	Which of the following resilience dimensions have you decided to take action on in the short term (within the next 2 years) and in the mid to long term (next 2 to 5 years)? (*Source* McKinsey Global Resilience Survey, July 2023, $n = 331$)	10
Fig. 1.8	Likelihood and impact of top 2024 geopolitical risks (*Source* S&P Global Research Insights- Geopolitical Risk)	11
Fig. 1.9	Corporate attention to geopolitics (*Source* BofA Global Research Call: 2024 "The Year of the Landing")	12

Fig. 1.10	TIGHT: Technology, Infrastructure, Geopolitics, Harnessed Talent	13
Fig. 2.1	Worldwide upward trend in information technology spending (*Source* Gartner, Statista 2024)	20
Fig. 2.2	Renewable energy is projected to grow significantly (*Source* Allied Market Research, Newswire: accessed through Statista)	21
Fig. 2.3	Rise of US Fintech (*Source* Grand View Research)	22
Fig. 2.4	IOT applications in operations management (*Source* Futurism Technologies)	23
Fig. 2.5	Supply chain of Boeing (*Source* Business Insider—*Dreamliner Structures*)	24
Fig. 2.6	Rise of Chinese e-commerce (*Note* The top line represents revenue growth, and bottom line represents YoY percent change. *Source* Insider Intelligence: EMarketer)	27
Fig. 2.7	Projected growth of 5G (*Source* Insight Software: Mekko Graphics)	30
Fig. 2.8	Rise of smart cities (*Source* Global Market Insights)	32
Fig. 2.9	The evolution of crypto (*Source* Gartner, Statista. 2024)	35
Fig. 3.1	Social spending from highest to lowest (*Source* Statista and the OECD)	45
Fig. 3.2	Internet usage over time (*Source* S&P Global Research)	50
Fig. 3.3	Road quality and connectivity (*Source* Statista with World Economic Forum Data)	54
Fig. 3.4	Renewable energy investments in the U.S. (*Source* Bloomberg NEF)	55
Fig. 3.5	Deployment of 5G technology (*Source* Statista from GSA 5G data)	56
Fig. 3.6	Reviving the Silk Road (*Source* Reuters and the Mercator Institute for China Studies)	59
Fig. 3.7	OECD health expenditures as a share of GDP (*Source* Statista Data)	62
Fig. 4.1	U.S.-China trade over time (*Source* Council on Foreign Relations [cfr.org])	67
Fig. 4.2	Countries with the highest political stability (*Source* Statista)	72
Fig. 4.3	Trade as a percentage of GDP of Afghanistan, the Bahamas, Germany, Japan, the UAE, and the United States (*Source* World Bank Data)	73
Fig. 4.4	Global military expenditure (*Source* Stockholm International Peace Research Institute)	75
Fig. 4.5	Rise in cybercrime rates (*Source* Statista Data)	79
Fig. 4.6	The cap on H-1B visas (*Source* American Immigration Council)	85
Fig. 4.7	Effect of Brexit on education (*Source* Statista)	87
Fig. 5.1	US digital market growth YoY (*Source* Grand View Research)	91

List of Figures   xxi

Fig. 5.2	Growth in STEM occupations (*Source* Bureau of Labor Statistics Projections)	93
Fig. 5.3	Illustration of how harnessed talent fits within the TIGHT framework	100
Fig. 5.4	Growth of generative AI (*Source* Market.us)	103
Fig. 5.5	The growth of Chinese railways (*Source* China Daily)	107
Fig. 5.6	Growth of talent across OECD and G20 (*Source* Statista)	112
Fig. 6.1	Mexico and neighbors—GDP per capita (current $) (*Source* The World Bank)	118
Fig. 6.2	Mexico—exports to the world ($ billion) (*Source* Intracen)	130
Fig. 6.3	Mexico—imports from the U.S. and China ($ billions) (*Source* Intracen)	131
Fig. 6.4	Mexico—investment and savings (Gross capital formation and domestic savings—current $) (*Source* The World Bank)	133
Fig. 6.5	Mexico—foreign direct investment inflows (Current $ billions) (*Source* The World Bank)	134
Fig. 6.6	Mexico—migrant population to the U.S. (millions) (*Source* BBVA Research)	138
Fig. 6.7	Nigeria—price of oil and GDP growth (Current $ and %) (*Source* IMF, World Bank)	144
Fig. 6.8	Nigeria—production of petroleum and other liquids (thousands of barrels per day) (*Source* EIA)	153
Fig. 6.9	Nigeria—capital imports (billions of $) (*Source* Nigeria's National Bureau of Statistics)	161
Fig. 6.10	Nigeria—foreign direct investment and Official Development Assistance and aid (Current billion $) (*Source* The World Bank)	162
Fig. 6.11	Nigeria—foreign direct investment net outflows (Current $) (*Source* The World Bank)	162
Fig. 6.12	Nigeria—Corruption Perception Index (2012–2023) (*Source* Transparency International)	164
Fig. 6.13	Nigeria and Africa (select countries)—change in total factor productivity (%) (*Source* The Conference Board)	166
Fig. 6.14	Poland—growth of total factor productivity (%) (*Source* The Conference Board, https://www.conference-board.org/retrievefile.cfm?filename=TED_SummaryTables_Charts_may20241.pdf&type=subsite)	173
Fig. 6.15	Poland—savings and investment (% of GDP) (*Source* World Bank, https://databank.worldbank.org/source/world-development-indicators)	186
Fig. 6.16	Poland—foreign direct investment, net (BoP, current $ and trend) (*Source* World Bank, https://databank.worldbank.org/source/world-development-indicators)	187

Fig. 6.17	Poland and EU—exports of goods and services (% of GDP) (*Source* World Bank, https://databank.worldbank.org/source/world-development-indicators)	188
Fig. 6.18	Poland—real effective exchange rate index (2010 = 100) (*Source* World Bank, https://databank.worldbank.org/source/world-development-indicators)	188
Fig. 6.19	Saudi Arabia—Corruption Perception Index 2012–2023 (Score 1 = poor, 100 = excellent) (*Source* Transparency International)	194
Fig. 6.20	Saudi Arabia—exports (Current billions $) (*Source* Intracen)	203
Fig. 6.21	Saudi Arabia—foreign direct investment inflows and outflows (Current $) (*Source* The World Bank)	205
Fig. 6.22	Turkey—GDP and manufacturing value added growth 1999–2023 (Annual % growth) (*Source* World Bank, https://databank.worldbank.org/source/world-development-indicators)	217
Fig. 6.23	World—GDP growth volatility (horizontal axis) and manufacturing value added as a percentage of GDP 1999 to 2023 (*Source* Latin Trade, The World Bank data, https://databank.worldbank.org/source/world-development-indicators)	218
Fig. 6.24	Turkey—Economic Complexity Index (*Source* Harvard Growth Lab, https://atlas.cid.harvard.edu/rankings)	234
Fig. 6.25	Turkey—Total Factor Productivity (TFP) 1996–2024. Change in the natural log (*Source* The Conference Board, https://www.conference-board.org/retrievefile.cfm?filename=TED_SummaryTables_Charts_may20241.pdf&type=subsite)	236
Fig. 6.26	Vietnam—GDP per capita (Current US$) (*Source* World Bank, https://databank.worldbank.org/source/world-development-indicators)	239
Fig. 6.27	Vietnam—Poverty headcount. Poverty headcount ratio at $6.85 a day (2017 PPP) (% of population) (*Source* The World Bank, https://databank.worldbank.org/source/world-development-indicators)	241
Fig. 6.28	Vietnam—Total Factor Productivity (TFP) 1971–2024. Change in the natural log (*Source* The Conference Board, https://www.conference-board.org/retrievefile.cfm?filename=TED_SummaryTables_Charts_may20241.pdf&type=subsite)	260
Fig. 7.1	The TIGHT conundrum and four key drivers	264

1

Introduction

Globalization vs Globalism: Defining the New Global Landscape

A seemingly pressing term in the media and the modern psyche, de-globalization refers to the process of reducing global integration, primarily via the imposition of trade barriers, protectionist policies, and a retreat from international cooperation. However, despite hundreds of sensationalized media reports predicting the end of this era of globalization, the world is more interdependent and interconnected than ever before. Put simply, de-globalization is not the reality in which we currently reside. So, what *is* our new global business reality?

Taking a step back, what does globalization *really* mean? Globalization is the interconnectedness and integration of economies, cultures, and societies worldwide through the exchange of goods, services, information, and ideas. Globalization's definition is the identity of the twenty-first century. Today, no region is close to being self-sufficient. Every single modern economy relies on imports for more than 25% of at least one important type of goods, even export powerhouses such as China, Germany, and the Netherlands. Thus, globalization's erasure is not only technically impossible; to the modern consumer or corporation, it is unimaginable.

The reality is that globalization is here to stay. It is a process that, while often impacted by external factors such as pandemics, natural disasters, climate change, and civil unrest, is agile and incredibly resilient. In fact, in the past three decades, world trade volume has expanded by 4%, while world trade value has expanded by 6%. Trade in services, an aspect of GDP excluded in global trade reporting, now exceeds $6.1 trillion USD, while the global aggregate in Foreign Direct Investment (FDI) now exceeds $1.37 trillion USD, according to a UNCTAD report published in 2024.

* * *

The 'China' Conversation

Any discussion of trade invariably brings up U.S.-China trade and the notion of "decoupling." To be sure, a gradual and ongoing diminution of commerce between the two nations has ushered in a new trade reality. According to the US Census Bureau, between 2017 and 2023, Chinese products as a fraction of US imports fell by 8.1%, marking the beginning of an era of slow decline in trade partnership between the two nations (see Fig. 1.1). Meanwhile, regions in Latin America, including Monterey, Mexico, and other nations in east and Southeast Asia, including South Korea, Taiwan, and Singapore, have stepped in to fill the void.

Be that as it may, China remains a crucial subject in this book, because its influence in the global trade landscape is simply too big to ignore. In the past five years, rather than decreasing, Chinese exports have actually increased significantly across the globe, and the nation's influence on the global business landscape has continued to grow as China expands its network

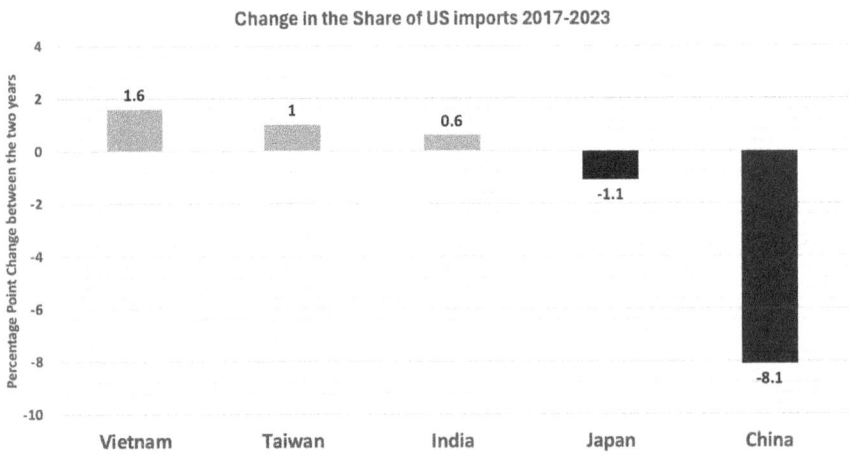

Fig. 1.1 Change in the share of US imports 2017–2023 (*Source* US Census Bureau, F. Guerrera, Breakingviews, October 13, 2023)

of trade alliances in emerging markets through the Belt and Road Initiative. For instance, ASEAN states continue to see China as an essential ally in addressing development and associated challenges because prioritizing job creation, economic growth, and stability maintenance are paramount for ruling elites striving to uphold domestic legitimacy. As of 2024, China makes up nearly 30% of the total global output for manufacturing. The world as it is currently simply cannot survive without Chinese trade and investment—living proof of the incredible chokehold that globalization holds on the modern world economy.

* * *

Unquestionably, the era of globalization will not end anytime soon. The real subject of attack– the concept that our world *will* soon do without, is *globalism*. In the nineteenth century, the prosperity brought about by globalization led to an ideological belief in the absoluteness of international economic cooperation. Globalism is the ideology of free trade between borders. It insists that the movement of people, capital, services, and goods across nations should be unfettered and facilitated by trade agreements, such as the 40 the EU currently has in place. As is apparent by the common dialogue of this decade, as a result of nationalistic world leaders and increasing geopolitical tensions, globalism as an ideology is dead. We, as a species, have killed it.

As such, our world must now navigate our new reality: globalization in the absence of globalism. Rather than de-globalization, as was feared and predicted by the media, we are witnessing a *re*-globalization. The first suggests that global business is "ending," while the second advocates for a new type of globalization (i.e., regionalization, nearshoring, friendshoring, etc.). (Figure 1.2 illustrates the different eras of globalization.) This new pattern is defined by the search for a different or alternative commitment to global integration, emphasizing interconnected economies, cross-border collaboration, and shared solutions to unprecedented global challenges. The USMCA, successor to NAFTA, strives toward this goal through encouraging international trade, cooperation, and the free flow of goods and services.

An Era of Globalization Without Globalism

In today's world, there is no doubt that new geopolitical tensions, trade disruptors, and economic challenges are emerging every single day. *Resilience* is the new strategic mandate, but resilience does not mean the reduction of globalization and trade; it means increasing networks of potential suppliers.

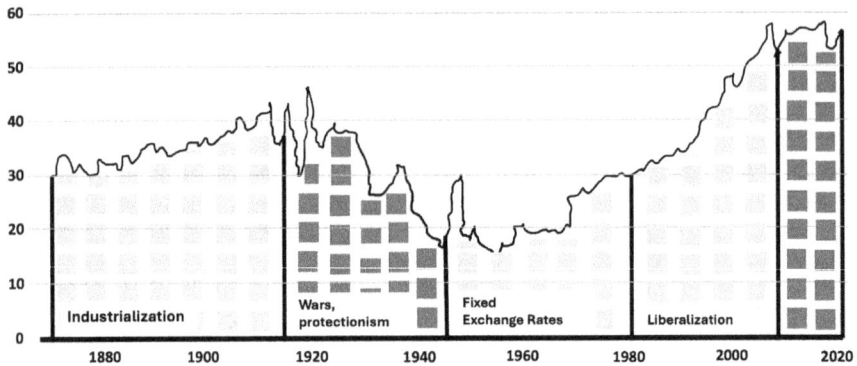

Fig. 1.2 Eras of globalization (Sum of exports and imports as a percentage of GDP) (*Sources* PIIE, Jorda-Schularick-Taylor Macrohistory Database. Penn World Data (10,0) World Bank, and IMF staff calculations)

For example, in the automotive industry, it would mean greater integration between Germany and Poland through firms such as BASF, Bosch, and Continental. Resilience means increasing intercultural understanding and expanding global awareness. This means that we must redefine globalization and the way we evaluate performance in the global business landscape.

Our previous book, *Globalization, Competitiveness and Governability* introduced the foundation of potential interactions among the three title variables, recognizing that globalization and competitiveness are the result of market forces while governability describes the policies that can help or hinder how countries, companies, and individuals take advantage of the opportunities presented. In *this* book, we will introduce a new framework that can be used to analyze the significant changes the global business landscape is facing and help you define what it means for companies hoping to build resilience.

Genesis of a New World

The necessity of a new framework with which to assess our world comes at a point of extraordinary turmoil and change. In the past four years, the world of trade and global business has been reshaped by an unprecedented series of shocks.

The COVID-19 Pandemic

On March 15, 2020, the first major shock struck the United States and, over the course of two years, permanently altered human life and the global landscape. The COVID-19 pandemic disrupted the entire global economy, exposed vulnerabilities in public health infrastructure, and re-highlighted the topic of international cooperation.

In this period of mass strife and uncertainty, geopolitical tensions arose as nations scrambled for scapegoats. Globalization became increasingly scrutinized and condemned, and protectionist sentiment began spreading, even in countries such as the U.S. and the United Kingdom, which have historically championed an open approach to markets and benefitted substantially from the world's increased connectedness (see Fig. 1.3).

Meanwhile, the U.S.-China trade war placed significant pressure across nearly every company's entire supply chain network, as sanctions closed many possibilities for cooperation and importation. China threatened to sell US Treasury bonds, and the US blacklisted some Chinese technology companies, causing mass corporate panic on both sides. In February 2021, stock markets across the world began to crash, triggering a chain of unfavorable, self-perpetuating economic conditions characterized by perilous price fluctuations, inflation, and bank failings.

During the pandemic, travel restrictions and supply chain disruptions reshaped global trade, emphasizing the need for resilience; remote work became widespread, transforming long-held workplace culture; socioeconomic inequalities were exacerbated; widespread mental health concerns rose; and governments implemented unprecedented fiscal measures. For

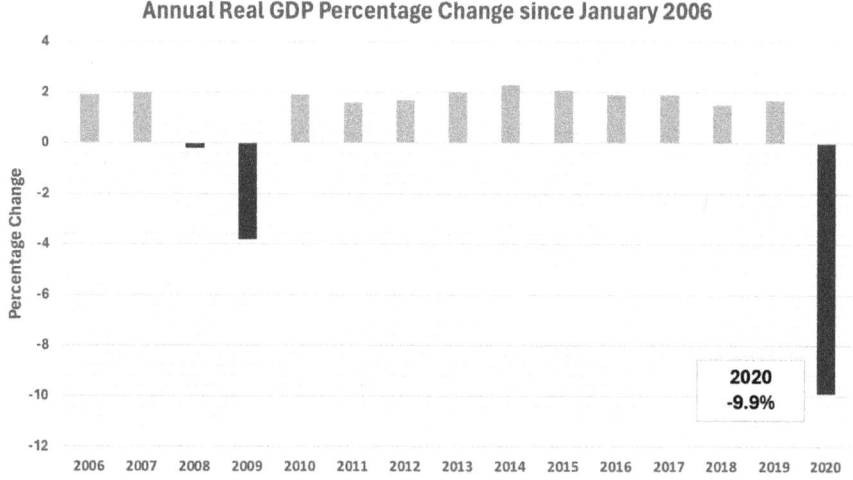

Fig. 1.3 Annual real GDP percentage change since January 2006 (*Source* Office for National Statistics)

instance, in Albania, the government implemented a series of three fiscal stimulus packages that, as reported by the IMF, totaled nearly 3% of their entire GDP and issued a mass tax policy that allowed all non-financial institutions to defer payment of income taxes for an entire year. Meanwhile, in Spain, unemployment soared to nearly double the rate of bordering EU nations due to its relatively high share of family-owned and small-scale businesses that were forced to close.

Meanwhile, vaccine development and later distribution also showcased the power of scientific collaboration and the necessity and potential of international coordination in the face of existential threat. The creation of the mRNA vaccine required the cooperation of scientists, laboratories, and testing agencies across 25 countries, while later distribution called for trade agreements between nearly every member of the 164 nations within the WTO.

The pandemic was the first to force us to reevaluate modern international priorities and underscore the interconnectedness of nations and the extent of our globalization, even in an age where globalism had met its end.

Russian-Ukrainian Conflict

The second major disruptor was the Russian invasion of Ukraine, which marked the first time in recent memory that a major world power instigated and directly involved itself in a large-scale conflict.

The Russia-Ukraine conflict has always had significant global repercussions, as it has escalated tensions between Russia and Western nations. Historically, the annexation of Crimea in 2014 and ongoing territorial disputes had already triggered sanctions that damaged global trade and diplomatic relations. However, in February 2022, Russia's direct invasion signified a new phase in the conflict (Fig. 1.4).

NATO reinforced its eastern flank, altering European security dynamics, while straining Russia's ties with the EU and the US, shaping geopolitics. As a result of this, trade routes, key supply chain manufacturers, and global export dynamics have been semi-permanently disrupted. For instance, prior to the escalation, Russia accounted for 41% of EU imports of natural gas. Today, due to trade embargoes and increasing geopolitical complexity surrounding alliances in NATO, that number is nearly halved. In addition, Ukraine has long been a major exporter of seed oils, grains, and other agricultural products, but due to the recent escalation, has been largely unable to maintain the same trade volume on the world market, causing a hike in prices in US and European markets.

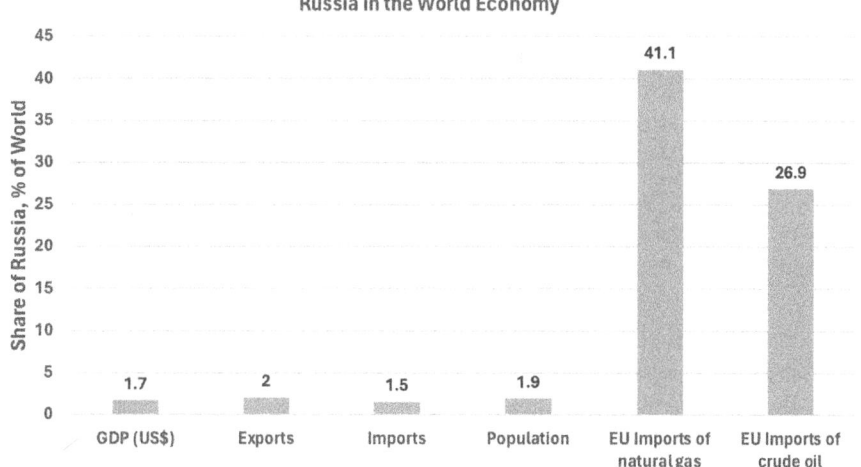

Fig. 1.4 Russia in the world economy (2024) (*Source* Oxford Economics/Haver Analytics/World Bank/Eurostat)

As of 2024, one of Ukraine's largest "imports" is weapons and war supplies from countries within NATO and the EU. This change in trade dynamic has created tighter alliances and steadier economic policies on some fronts while increasing tensions and instability within others, making conducting a multinational or international business increasingly complex. For instance, the spike in newfound demand and market niches for specific supplies have been filled by weapons manufacturing corporations, such as Sweden's SAAB and BAE Systems, while the copper and uranium mining industries have experienced wild volatility in both supply and demand as a result of trade complexity within eastern Europe.

Overall, the war also fueled concerns about the erosion of international norms, because the twenty-first century's expectations of a major world power have largely centered around seeking peace or conducting itself with a certain degree of diplomacy and adherence to the soft power of NATO and the EU.

Israel – Gaza

A final shock came in October of 2023. The prolonged conflict in Gaza has caused immense human suffering and rippling impacts on the geopolitical and economic landscape as a whole. Both Israelis and Palestinians have been hugely impacted by the conflict.

Most directly, neighboring countries like Egypt, Jordan, and Lebanon are already enduring economic reverberations as visitors cancel travel to the region (see Fig. 1.5). This sudden hard hit on tourism, which serves as a critical source of foreign exchange, economic development, and employment in the region, has already lowered the standard of living and future potential for economic growth in the nation. In tourism-dependent Lebanon, hotel occupancy rates fell by 45% in October 2023 compared to the previous year.

The oil economy, already crippled by the previous conflict in Ukraine, is facing immense risk, as the Middle East accounts for nearly 30% of global oil production. In our modern shipping economy, oil prices have severe effects on day-to-day life and are factored into the prices of nearly every consumer product and commodity on the market. This means that sky-rocketing in oil prices would have severe ramifications across the entire global economy and create a dangerously risky and unprofitable global landscape for many businesses (Fig. 1.6).

Although commodity prices have thus far been contained, experts say that the probable prolonged escalation of the conflict will push commodity markets into uncharted territory—the first time the world has endured shocks in two major energy-producing regions within a short period.

As international efforts rally to de-escalate the situation, the western developed world has never been quite as divided as it is now, and American soft power has never been weaker. Damaged roads, conflict zones, and sanctions

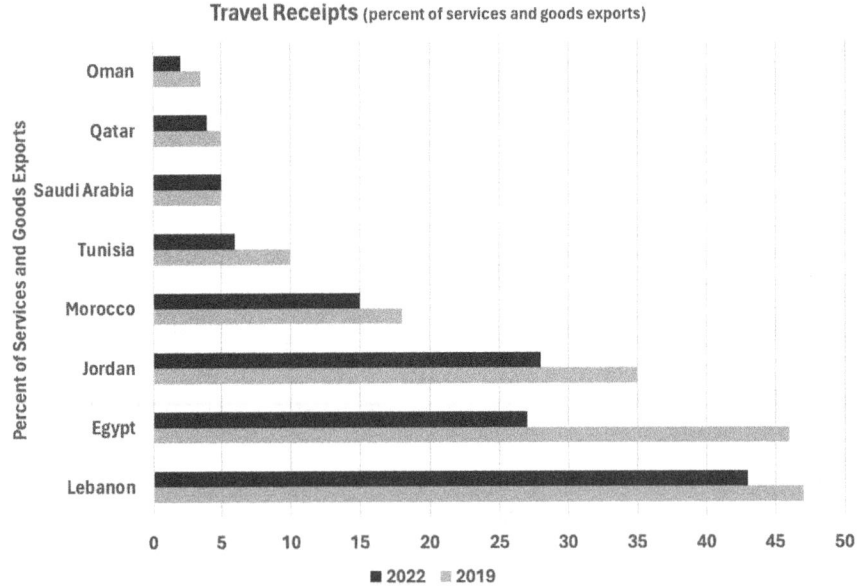

Fig. 1.5 Tourism receipts are at risk amid travel concerns (*Source* Haver Analytics and IMF staff calculations)

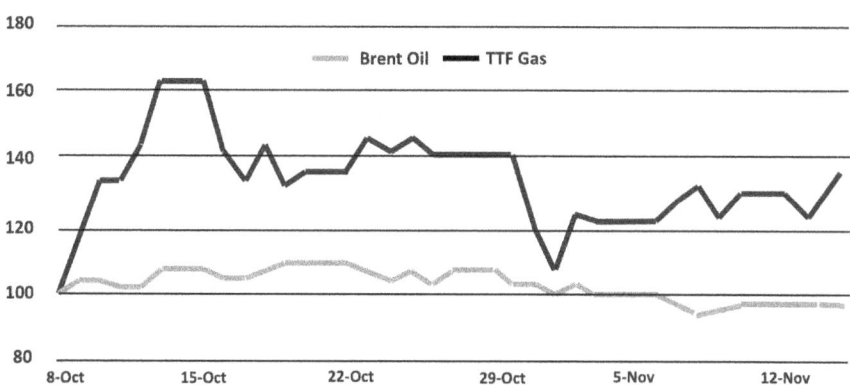

Fig. 1.6 Impact on energy prices (index: Oct-6th, 2023 = 100) (*Source* Bloomberg Finance L.P.)

have disrupted supply chains, disagreements between developed nations have led to tensions in international trade, and uncertainty surrounding the possibility of escalation or US direct involvement has led many companies to halt investment or expansion in the region entirely.

This situation has led to a business environment in which hedging risk and navigating complexity in a conflict-ridden world have created daunting challenges for companies.

Risk Hedging and Navigating Complexity

Hedging, an act described as a corporation's proactive approach to managing financial risk through various strategies, allows for greater predictability and protection against unforeseen market events. Common precedents in hedging instruments included futures contracts, options, and derivatives. By hedging, individuals and organizations aim to minimize exposure to market volatility, ensuring a level of financial stability and safeguarding against adverse movements in asset prices or exchange rates.

In the past, two types of hedging have dominated corporate conversations—*financial and operational hedging*. Financial Hedging involves using financial instruments or strategies to mitigate or offset the risks associated with price fluctuations, currency exchange rates, or market uncertainties. This is the most traditional form of hedging and often involves financial firms, strategic investments, and futures contracts. Meanwhile, operational hedging involves managing operational risks within a business to enhance resilience and flexibility. It goes beyond financial instruments, focusing on strategies like diversification, flexible production processes, and geographic dispersion. By adapting operational activities, companies can mitigate the impact of uncertainties such as supply chain disruptions, currency fluctuations, and regulatory changes. For the past two decades, supply chain network design, offshoring, and inventory concerns have been at the core of operational hedging. Figure 1.7 illustrates executive views with respect to financial, operational, and organizational resilience.

In this new reality, however, risk hedging has been forced to evolve from financial and operational hedging to geopolitical hedging. Geopolitical hedging, a wide-ranging term which includes all aspects of a region, including involving innovation, technology, and demographic changes, is a strategic approach where entities diversify and adjust operations to navigate geopolitical uncertainties. Businesses and investors employ this strategy to mitigate risks arising from political instability, trade tensions, or regulatory changes in different regions. Figure 1.8 illustrates the likelihood and impact of geopolitical risks today.

Geopolitical hedging involves diversifying supply chains, identifying alternative markets, and staying informed about geopolitical developments. To illustrate, Cyberattacks are a growing geopolitical risk, and many corporations

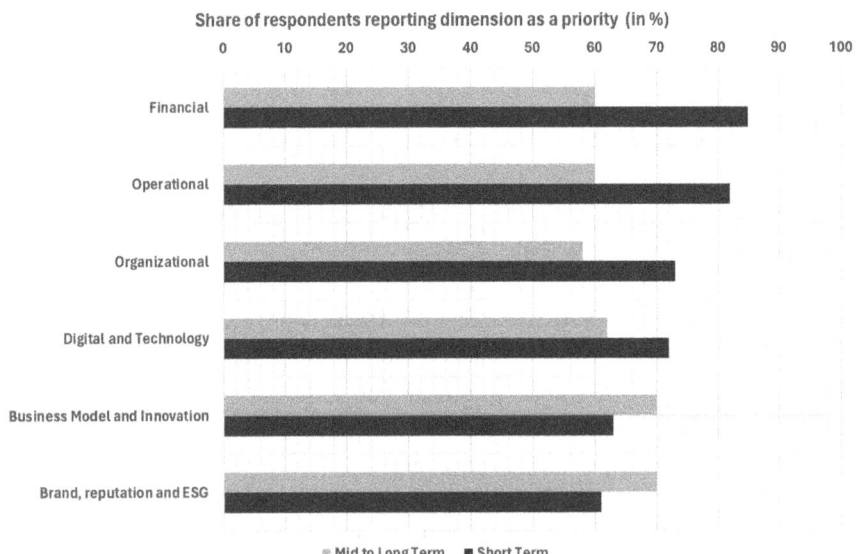

Fig. 1.7 Which of the following resilience dimensions have you decided to take action on in the short term (within the next 2 years) and in the mid to long term (next 2 to 5 years)? (*Source* McKinsey Global Resilience Survey, July 2023, $n = 331$)

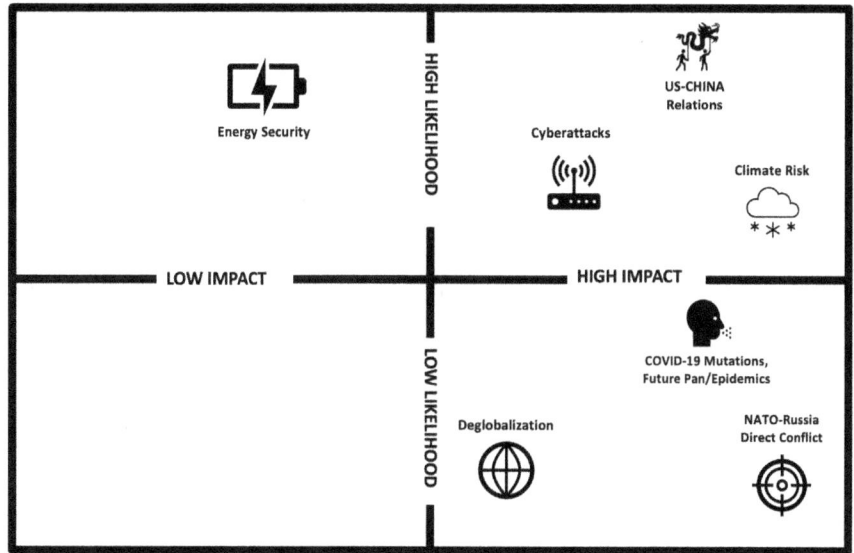

Fig. 1.8 Likelihood and impact of top 2024 geopolitical risks (*Source* S&P Global Research Insights- Geopolitical Risk)

have begun strengthening network security and developing global protocols for potential attacks as a form of geopolitical hedging. Firms such as Palo Alto Networks, Brazil's Apura, and India's Qualysec are among the myriad technology enterprises engaged in cyber security.

By adopting a proactive stance, organizations aim to minimize the impact of geopolitical events on their operations, ensuring resilience in the face of shifting international dynamics. This form of hedging is thus crucial for safeguarding assets and maintaining stability in an ever-changing global political landscape.

Geopolitical hedging is fundamentally different from the other two in that it requires the use of variables that might not be measurable (e.g., trade barriers impact global trade, but the actual metric to be used is difficult to determine). Most drivers and variables are quantifiable (i.e., big/small, high/low), but not all are measurable. At the same time, geopolitical hedging requires a sense of urgency that challenges traditional planning horizons, forcing the decision process to move from tactical to strategic (i.e., supply chains are now evaluated as strategic alternatives).

Unfortunately, as illustrated in Fig. 1.9, corporate attention to geopolitics has waned in recent times despite political risk remaining elevated. The present business landscape can best be described as VUCA—an acronym

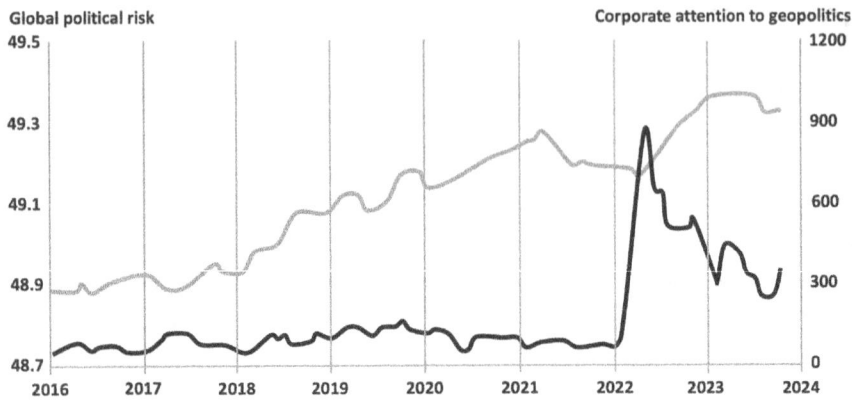

Fig. 1.9 Corporate attention to geopolitics (*Source* BofA Global Research Call: 2024 "The Year of the Landing")

signifying Volatile, Uncertain, Complex, and Ambiguous.[1] While these are good environmental descriptors, the follow-up question is: What are the drivers of the new business landscape?

Four Key Drivers in the New Business Landscape

In this book, we will introduce the four drivers we have identified as crucial to a structured approach to evaluating the challenges of the new landscape. While other more specific factors exist, we believe that Technology, Infrastructure, Geopolitics, and Harnessed Talent accurately encapsulate an all-encompassing view of 21st-century business economics. They are the foundation of the TIGHT Framework, the framework we propose to win in the new global business landscape (Fig. 1.10).

Technology is the application of scientific knowledge for practical purposes. In the business world, it has enabled new forms of communication and transportation, created new industries, and changed the nature of work. Significant contemporary developments in technology include the implementation of supply chain overhead monitoring software, the substitution of physical offices for virtual co-working spaces, and, most recently, the widespread use of AI. Firms such as FreightPOP and Shipedge are leaders in supply chain software.

---

[1] VUCA was coined by management theorists Warren Bennis and Burt Nanus in 1987 and has gained prominence ever since among both academics and practitioners.

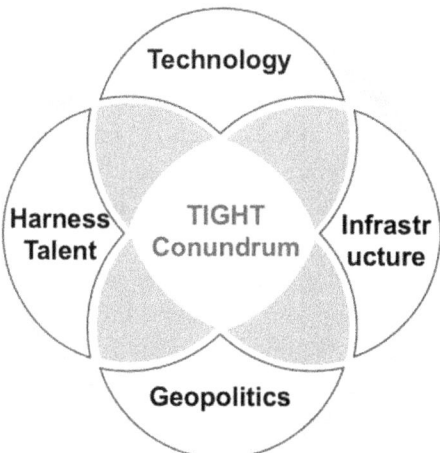

Fig. 1.10 TIGHT: Technology, Infrastructure, Geopolitics, Harnessed Talent

Infrastructure refers to the physical and organizational structures and facilities needed for the operation of a society or enterprise. Infrastructure within the context of business and international trade includes the availability of transportation systems, energy networks, and communication systems. Significant contemporary developments include fiber-optic cables for increased communication, 5G connectivity, and the modern shipping industry. To illustrate, NexGen and Atom are the most comprehensive crane rental management software solutions on the market.

Geopolitics refers to the study of international relations, the distribution of resources, and the influence of geography on political and economic systems. In the contemporary world, stable and desirable geopolitics can attract FDI, boost economic growth, and propel the formation of new industries in emerging markets. Costa Rica is a prime example. Since Intel decided to make a major investment in the nation decades ago, ICT companies have flocked to Central American nations, presently home to 450 ICT companies. A favorable political, economic, legal, and social environment has made Costa Rica a magnet for foreign direct investment.

Harnessed Talent is, in essence, human capital, and it refers to the skills, knowledge, and abilities of individuals. Talent is developed through investment in educational infrastructure and is critical to the success of organizations and societies as it enables innovation and productivity. In the contemporary world, the most significant example of success through Harnessed Talent is known widely as the East Asian Miracle– the rapid-fire development of Japan, South Korea, Taiwan, Hong Kong, Singapore, etc. Firms such as TSMC, Samsung, Rakuten, and Lenovo glean the very best technology talent through both college recruitment and headhunting from competitors.

Evaluating **Technology, Infrastructure, Geopolitics,** and **Harnessed Talent** as a cohesive framework is essential for gaining a comprehensive understanding of today's global economic landscape. These four interconnected and interdependent drivers provide a holistic perspective that helps navigate the complexities and challenges of operating in a rapidly changing world.

When considering entering a new market, businesses must evaluate political stability, technological readiness, infrastructure capabilities, and availability of skilled talent. Evaluating all four components together allows for more accurate and comprehensive risk assessment and unveils unique business opportunities that may harness *local* talent while fulfilling *global* needs.

Utilizing the TIGHT Framework in Business

The new business landscape is poised with uncertainties that require a structured evaluation to come with a set of appropriate strategies. A conundrum is a perplexing problem or puzzle, often characterized by complexity and difficulty in finding a solution, leading to a state of confusion or uncertainty. The *TIGHT* Conundrum is our framework for explaining what companies are better prepared to win in the new business landscape.

Each of the four drivers can be quantified to determine the level at which it impacts the microeconomic situation within a given region. For example, a country such as the USA with a high level of Technology availability (e.g., internet access for all), a solid Infrastructure (e.g., good ports and highways), strong Geopolitical position (e.g., political stability), and available Talent in different fronts (e.g., good education system) is in a better position than countries such as Russia where any of the drivers are lacking. Thus, a TIGHTer position offers a solid opportunity to take advantage of the new business landscape.

Within the framework, geopolitical changes have, in recent times, been the main disruptor in the new business landscape. They force businesses to create new paradigms surrounding long-standing existing challenges, requiring the development of new public policies and, consequently, new corporate operations. For instance, the historical evolution of business began with an emphasis on manufacturing and operations. Optimization methodologies were developed to minimize total cost. From Ford's production system, which

Toyota adapted, to the sweeping organizational changes implemented by GE under Jack Welch, systems to increase efficiency, improve quality, and decrease costs have been the key drivers of change.

Not to be excluded from the dynamics of change, marketing emerged as the functional area in charge of increasing the other side of the profit equation, i.e., revenues. Later, supply chain management emerged as a need to orchestrate the tradeoff between operations and marketing by aligning product availability, production efficiency, and distribution with market demand. However, in this changing geopolitical landscape where trade routes have become increasingly unpredictable and extreme delays in shipping times have become the norm, traditional ideas in operation management, such as Just-In-Time, Lean Manufacturing, and Total Quality Control, are being rendered obsolete. While **efficiency** continues to be a main operational objective, **effectiveness** is gaining more importance.

An accurate assessment of a TIGHT position requires a proper understanding of how geopolitics affects the other three variables–a relationship that is often complex and multifaceted. Geopolitical decisions can influence technology access, talent migration, infrastructure development, and vice versa.

For instance, geopolitics can influence technology in several ways. Geopolitical tensions and conflicts can lead to the development of new technologies, such as advanced weapons systems, or the expansion of existing technologies into new domains such as space. Meanwhile, governments may use technology to gain a competitive advantage or achieve strategic objectives, including investing in research and development of new technologies (e.g., AI), restricting the export of sensitive technologies, or using technology to support military operations in the cases of Ukraine and Israel. The opposite may also be true of geopolitical influence. In Argentina, for example, suboptimal economic policy leadership continuously and repeatedly led to economic crises and driven away foreign direct investment. Examples are Argentina's tax on exports and bans on foreign investment in aviation and media.

At the same time, *technology* can also impact geopolitics. The development and spread of digital technologies have enabled new forms of communication and collaboration across borders, creating new opportunities for economic and cultural exchange, while technological innovations such as automation and artificial intelligence are disrupting traditional economic models and destroying previous supply–demand equilibriums. Oxford University researchers contended as early as 2013 that advances in technology would almost inevitably, within two decades, replace 47% of US workers through automation. This trend could potentially lead to mass unemployment, changes in labor force demographics, and even political instability, thus leading to significant changes in the global workforce and job markets.

Thus, as seen by the relevance of just two of the variables interacting with one another within the TIGHT-framework, in the modern business landscape, businesses that can navigate the interplay of geopolitics, technology, infrastructure, and human talent gain a competitive advantage. They are better positioned to capitalize on emerging trends, anticipate challenges, and adapt to changing conditions.

In today's world, businesses have to navigate complex regulatory environments and geopolitical risks to access new markets and technologies. This book will be our guide to finding countries with TIGHT positions. Different chapters will delve into the details of each one of the drivers. We will start by defining what exactly is included in the scope of each driver, followed by the impact it has on the other drivers and the symbiotic relationships between each variable. Then, using examples and case studies, we will illustrate the symbiotic relationships between each variable and the impacts of each driver on the others. Finally, we will dedicate an entire chapter to developing case studies of six new emerging markets (NEM) that demonstrate the specific applicability of the TIGHT Framework.

2

The Technology Driver

Technology: The Basis of the Modern World

From the Gutenberg Bible to the steam engine, nuclear power, and artificial intelligence, it is difficult to find a simple, true definition of technology. While the Oxford Dictionary defines technology as "the branch of knowledge dealing with the mechanical arts and applied sciences; the study of this and the application of such knowledge for practical purposes, esp. in industry, manufacturing, etc.," this clinical definition hardly seems satisfactory in light of technology's scope and daily impact on our economic and personal well-being.

Despite the difficulty in definition, we all intrinsically understand the meaning and connotations behind the word technology, as we are all exposed to it constantly. Modern humans interact with hundreds of forms of technology on a daily basis. Life in the developed world would be unimaginable without it. For instance, the first thing one does in the morning upon waking up is to check one's mobile phone. Your breakfast is made by a toaster. Then, you drive to work in a car while listening to the radio. If you work at an office job, you'll spend the next eight hours of your life staring at a computer screen that contains all of the world's presently available knowledge. Finally, what is the last thing you do before going to bed? Checking your phone again.

The uses and effects of technology are everywhere, not only in our private lives but also in the modern geopolitical and business landscape. We are surrounded by thousands of types and forms of technology, and learning to understand, assess, and navigate technology as a factor on the geographical scale is crucial for effective business leadership.

Technology and the Development of the Global Business Landscape: A Flurry of Technological Shapes, Sizes, and Functionalities

For the sake of clarity and backstory, we will begin by discussing the forms and broad categories that define the term as we intend to use it. Technology can be categorized into various types based on its nature and application. While the relevance of categories such as agricultural and biological technology (e.g., crop sensors, gene therapy, etc.) certainly cannot be understated, especially in a post-pandemic world, for our purposes within this book, we will limit ourselves to ranking and discussing five of the most relevant, disruptive, and overarching categories of technology as they pertain to the *business* and *operations* world.

This myriad of technologies has dramatically reshaped not only borders and international policy but also the business landscape in particular, by impacting operations, customer engagement, and competition. Some of the most promising and impactful are presented below.

Firstly, Artificial Intelligence (AI). OpenAI released an early version of ChatGPT on November 30, 2022, and the chatbot quickly went viral on social media as examples of what it could do began populating the internet. Within five days, the chatbot attracted over one million users, and today, the startup OpenAI has gained a market cap of $29 billion. Artificial Intelligence is, essentially, a simulation of human intelligence, including learning, reasoning, problem-solving, perception, decision-making processes, and most recently, word processing by machines and computers. In the business world, AI holds immense potential implications due to its ability to enhance operational efficiency and productivity. Automation of routine tasks, language, and mathematical AI programs free up human resources for more strategic and creative endeavors, leading to cost savings and improved competitiveness, while AI-powered data analytics also enables businesses to derive valuable insights from vast amounts of data, facilitating better decision-making and driving innovation. As a result, early adoption and investment in artificial intelligence has proven itself an exponentially lucrative endeavor. For instance, according to McKinsey research conducted in 2022, early adopters of AI in the supply chain space have seen their logistics costs decrease by more than 15%.

In addition, AI-driven personalization enhances customer experiences by delivering tailored products and services, thus fostering stronger customer loyalty and increasing revenues. For instance, to showcase the benefit of using AI in creating and targeting ad copies, in a test conducted by Kroger,

AI-optimized versions of advertisements were tested against a randomized control group on various social media platforms. For AI-optimized versions of their ads, Kroger saw a 259% increase in their target key performance indicators (KPI), which sensed user engagement, clickthrough rate, and profitability. More recently, in May 2023, Meta began a rollout of AI-generated advertisements that would adjust themselves to each individual viewer (larger font for older users, etc.), using their now commercially available technology, Sandbox. This rollout has, according to Meta leadership, dramatically increased clickthrough rates on Facebook ads.

Secondly, Information Technology (IT) refers to the use of computers, software, networks, and other electronic devices to store, retrieve, transmit, and manipulate data for communication, decision-making, and automation. In the business world, information technology plays a crucial role in erasing borders and making the world "flatter," driving innovation, enhancing productivity, and enabling competitive advantage. IT infrastructure such as enterprise software systems, communication networks, and cloud computing services enables businesses like Amazon and Apple to streamline global operations, improve efficiency and customer communication, and reduce costs. Global IT spending on devices, including PCs, tablets, mobile phones, printers, as well as data center systems, enterprise software, and communications services, came to $4.7 trillion U in 2023. As indicated in Fig. 2.1, one should note that the upward trend line has continued uninterrupted since 2017. By 2024, IT spending increased to a staggering $5 trillion worldwide.

It has had an indispensable role in the creation of all of the twenty-first century's truly globe-spanning companies, with Amazon estimating that a single sales representative will answer over 900 phone calls in a week. Complex supply chains and border-defying businesses can leverage data analytics and business intelligence tools to gain actionable insights from large datasets, enabling informed decision-making and strategic planning. Additionally, IT facilitates communication and collaboration among employees, customers, and stakeholders, regardless of geographical location, fostering greater agility and responsiveness to market dynamics. E-commerce platforms and digital marketing tools empower businesses to reach a global audience, expand market reach, and personalize customer experiences, driving revenue growth and market share.

Third, Green Energy Technology. In 2023, following the enactment of the previous year's Inflation Reduction Act, a study by Deloitte noted that companies had announced over 200 new manufacturing projects, including US$9.6 billion in 38 solar projects—investments totaling US$91 billion.

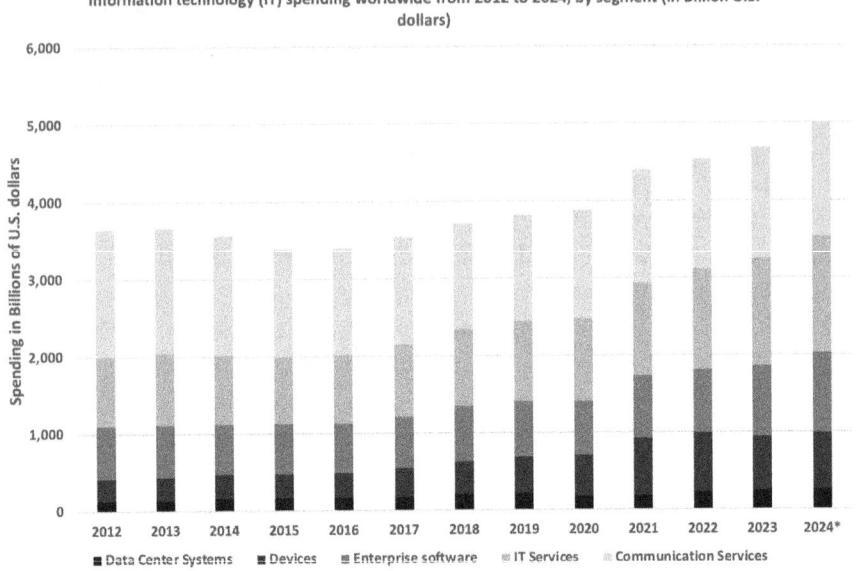

Fig. 2.1 Worldwide upward trend in information technology spending (*Source* Gartner, Statista 2024)

Green Energy refers to renewable energy sources and sustainable practices that minimize environmental impact while meeting energy needs. Exemplified by companies such as NextEra Energy (wind and solar generation plants) and General Electric (fuel and energy-efficient engines, turbines, etc.) and encompassing solar power, wind energy, hydroelectric power, biomass, and geothermal energy, as well as energy-efficient solutions like smart grids and energy storage systems, the renewable energy market is projected to reach $2.15 trillion worldwide in 2025 according to analyst projections. As noted in Fig. 2.2, this is an eight-year growth rate of 68%.

In the business world, green energy technology holds significant implications for disruption and reevaluation of the status quo. In October 2020, shares of solar companies worldwide had more than doubled in value from December 2019, and this trend has largely continued throughout the last four years.

With the modern socio-political landscape, adopting renewable energy sources not only helps companies mitigate the risks associated with climate change but also enhances their brand reputation and attractiveness to environmentally conscious consumers and investors. Moreover, investing in green energy technology can lead to long-term cost savings by reducing dependence on fossil fuels and volatile energy markets. For instance, the world's

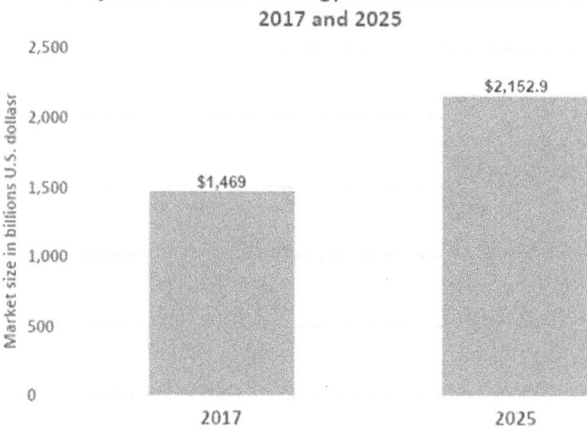

Fig. 2.2 Renewable energy is projected to grow significantly (*Source* Allied Market Research, Newswire: accessed through Statista)

largest furniture retailer, IKEA 2012, set a goal to produce as much renewable energy as it consumes by 2020. Through investments in wind and solar energy projects, IKEA has achieved this goal, thus significantly reducing its carbon footprint and showcasing a commitment to sustainability that has attracted a wave of environmentally conscious consumers while also allegedly saving the company millions in energy costs.

Additionally, the growing demand for green technologies presents lucrative opportunities for innovation and market expansion. While the transition to green energy may require significant upfront investment and organizational changes, posing challenges for some businesses, companies that develop and implement cutting-edge green energy solutions stand to gain a competitive edge in emerging sectors such as clean energy infrastructure, electric mobility, and energy-efficient technologies. For instance, Airbus, the European aerospace manufacturer, has invested nearly a billion dollars in the creation of a zero-emission hydrogen-powered plane engine that is set to become available in 2035. Meanwhile, companies such as Tesla have reached market caps of hundreds of billions ($524.61 billion in Tesla's case) from their innovation and work in the renewable energy sector, while fossil fuel companies have faced criticism, bearish investors, and shrinking market share in the energy sector.

Fourth, Financial Technology (FinTech). In 2002, Elon Musk allegedly earned upwards of $175 million following his foray into the financial technology sector through his acquisition of PayPal. A lucrative industry, FinTech refers to the financial service sector and encapsulates everything from banking apps to new ways of analyzing securities and trades. This means that Fintech can be anything from programs managing inventory levels to apps helping consumers access their bank accounts to software optimizing cash flow for better investment opportunities. Fintech, exemplified by companies such as Block Inc, Paypal, and Venmo, is contributing to a far more dynamic and competitive global business environment by introducing new offerings that are often accessible through user-friendly mobile apps and challenge the dominance of traditional financial institutions. According to 2022's World Retail Banking Report (WRBR): "75% of customers surveyed are attracted to FinTech's cost-effective and seamless services, [a new statistic which] significantly raises their digital banking expectations." Essentially, the development of the financial technology sector not only benefits consumers with a wider range of options but also pushes established players to adapt and improve their offerings. The U.S. as a FinTech service market, including payments, loans, and funds transfers, is illustrated in Fig. 2.3.

In the business world, by leveraging technologies like big data and cloud computing, cloud-based accounting software companies such as Xero or QuickBooks enable businesses to make informed decisions faster, streamline processes and automate tasks, and significantly reduce operational costs for businesses. For instance, a study done by Forrester concluded that the average market Return On Investment (ROI) of QuickBooks was 488%, as routine financial tasks were automated and became 30% more efficient

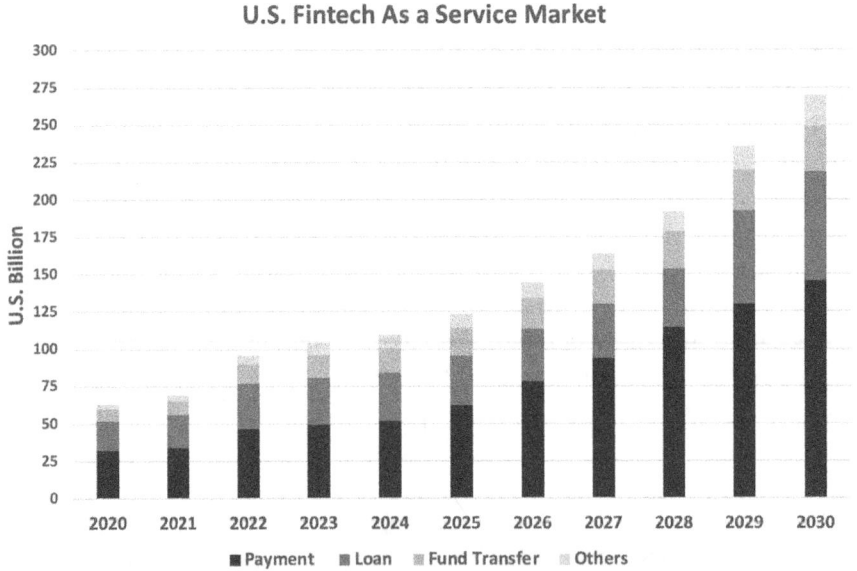

Fig. 2.3 Rise of US Fintech (*Source* Grand View Research)

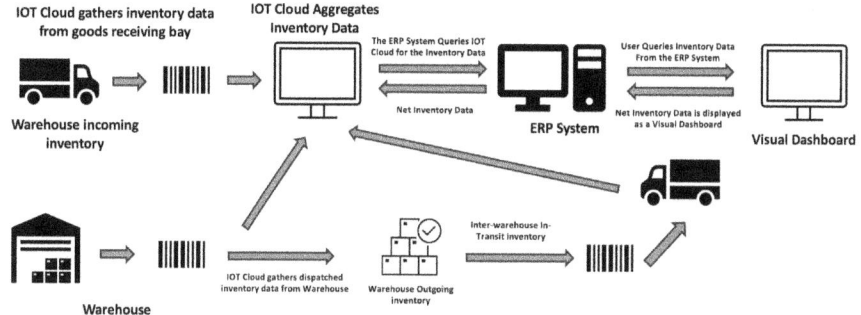

Fig. 2.4 IOT applications in operations management (*Source* Futurism Technologies)

on average. This streamlining enabled by the financial technology sector has allowed businesses to reallocate resources and focus on core competencies.

Fifth, there is the Internet of Things (IoT). As illustrated in Fig. 2.4, IoT describes a vast network of everyday objects infused with sensors, software, and internet connectivity.

These "smart devices," ranging from thermostats, Google Home, and Amazon Alexa devices to factory robots, collect and exchange data, enabling them to automate tasks and respond intelligently. This web of interconnected devices is poised to revolutionize global business.

Businesses can leverage IoT to optimize processes, improve efficiency, and gain valuable insights from real-time data. Imagine factories where machines self-diagnose maintenance needs or warehouses where inventory automatically tracks itself. Additionally, IoT data can provide businesses with a deeper understanding of customer behavior and preferences, enabling them to personalize experiences and develop targeted marketing strategies. For instance, retailers such as Target are already using IoT to create a more personalized shopping experience. In 2024, stores across North America were equipped with smart shelves that have embedded weight sensors that automatically track inventory, thus preventing the extremely costly possibility of being out-of-stock from ever occurring.

It is no exaggeration to say that *Artificial Intelligence, Financial Technology, Green Energy, Information Technology*, and the *Internet of Things* have changed the course of business history going forward. From supply chain management to customer service, these technologies streamline processes through automation, optimized workflows, and reduced costs, allowing businesses to operate leaner and more effectively.

Technology has also created modern, extreme examples of interconnected global supply chains, as illustrated in Fig. 2.5. The availability of vast amounts of data has empowered businesses to make more informed decisions. Data

Fig. 2.5 Supply chain of Boeing (*Source* Business Insider—*Dreamliner Structures*)

analytics tools allow companies to extract valuable insights from customer behavior, market trends, and operational processes, while advanced logistics and tracking systems, along with real-time communication tools, facilitate smoother cross-border trade and reduced delivery times, rendering the idea of traditional constraints nonexistent.

In recent times, the COVID-19 pandemic has also normalized and drastically accelerated corporate adoption of remote work and virtual tools like Zoom, Google Meet, and Slack. Businesses have become more open to distributed teams, remote offices, and flexible work arrangements, allowing them to tap into global talent pools. In the past, technology erased borders for physical products as shipping and logistics became easier, but today, physical distance has become largely irrelevant in human capital as well. Educational institutions like Johns Hopkins University grant virtual degrees and increase the education level of a hundred-odd countries across the globe, while investment banks such as Barclays have implemented remote work programs that allow them to source their teams' talent from everywhere.

Perhaps more importantly, these five technological sectors have also democratized entrepreneurship and lowered barriers to entry for new players, allowing innovative ideas to flourish and giving room for startups and disruptors to challenge established industries. This has enabled startups and small businesses to compete on a global scale. For instance, the rise of e-commerce platforms and online marketplaces has transformed how goods and services are bought and sold. Platform-based business models, like those of Uber, Airbnb, and Amazon, mean that businesses can now reach global markets, and consumers can shop from anywhere, leading to increased competition and new market opportunities that have eliminated hundreds of previously well-established players.

This technological revolution, which will only continue to accelerate in the age of AI, means that businesses must adapt quickly, investing in cybersecurity measures, complying with regulations, and bridging the digital skills gap to fully leverage the benefits of technology. Understanding the future of technology in this new business landscape and how this driver interacts with the world around it by influencing infrastructure, geopolitics, and harnessed talent is essential for globe-spanning businesses to thrive in an increasingly digital world.

Measuring the Technology Driver

Measuring the status of technology in a country involves assessing various indicators that reflect the level of technological advancement, infrastructure, and capability. Four key indicators to consider are research and development expenditure, the number of patent applications, the availability of technological infrastructure, and the rate and percentage of technological adoption within the population.

Firstly, Research and Development (R&D) Expenditure: The amount of money a country invests in research and development is a primary indicator of its commitment to technological progress. High R&D spending is often correlated with innovative outputs, such as patents, new technologies, and advancements in various scientific and technological fields. This reflects a nation's commitment to progress. High R&D spending signifies that a nation is initiating a strong push for innovation, while low R&D spending signifies lower capacity or willingness to innovate. According to the World Bank, in the US, R&D spending as a percentage of gross domestic product (GDP) rose to 3.40% in 2021, while in France, that number lies around 2.2%, and in the African nation of Togo, that number is closer to 0.2%.

Secondly, Patent Applications: The number of patent applications filed and granted can be a measure of a country's innovative activity. Patents are a direct outcome of research and development efforts and indicate a country's ability to generate new ideas, inventions, and technologies. For example, if a country files 100,000 patent applications in a year, with 60% being in technology sectors such as electronics, biotechnology, and software, this high volume and focus on technology sectors suggest a vibrant innovation ecosystem. In the United States, 418,262 patent filings were made in 2023, with a majority of them being in pharmaceutical and technological sectors, signaling the widespread trust of the rule of law within the US patent office, a population who are willing and able to innovate, and a national focus on entrepreneurship.

Next is the availability of *Technology Infrastructure*, including internet connectivity, telecommunications networks, and digital services, which are crucial for a country's technological status. Infrastructure enables the dissemination and application of technology across industries and communities. This widespread access to advanced telecommunications infrastructure is essential for supporting a technologically advanced society, and indicating to business executives and foreign investors that a country is viable for expansion, supply chain involvement, or foreign direct investment. As of 2023, GQII, a nonprofit global infrastructure research group, ranks Germany as the number one most well-developed nation in terms of technological infrastructure, with Brazil falling in 17th place, and Taiwan falling into 60th place.

Finally, *Technological Adoption and Integration* is the extent to which new technologies are adopted and integrated into everyday life and business operations. This includes the use of digital technologies, automation, artificial intelligence, and the digital economy's overall size relative to the country's GDP. For example, if e-commerce transactions make up 15% of all retail sales in a hypothetical country, over 50% of the population uses mobile payment solutions regularly, and the country has a 40% adoption rate for industrial automation technologies in manufacturing, this would mean that this nation shows an extremely high level of technological integration into both consumer and industrial sectors.

In China, for instance, as noted in Fig. 2.6, e-commerce makes up more than half of all retail sales, and an overwhelming majority of citizens below retirement age use mobile payment solutions such as AliPay regularly. As such, the degree of technological adoption and integration within the Chinese economy shows that the nation is technologically highly advanced, with a population that is willing and able to continuously adapt to changing financial technologies and infrastructure that can support such widespread adoption of technology.

These numerical indicators are only a few examples of metrics that can be used to measure the technology sector within a country. They are interrelated and collectively provide an overview of a country's technological landscape, illustrating not just the scale of investment and innovation but also the degree to which technology is embedded in the economy and society, and helping to identify strengths, weaknesses, and opportunities for growth in the modern business environment.

Fig. 2.6 Rise of Chinese e-commerce (*Note* The top line represents revenue growth, and bottom line represents YoY percent change. *Source* Insider Intelligence: EMarketer)

Technology Within the TIGHT Framework

Innovations in technology push the boundaries of what's possible, enabling new products, services, and solutions, such as cybernetically-enhanced robotic surgery. As new technologies emerge, they necessitate updates or expansions in infrastructure to be fully utilized (e.g., broadband for internet access, and charging stations for electric vehicles). Technological superiority offers strategic advantages, influencing global power dynamics. Nations vie for leadership in key technological domains like AI, quantum computing, and biotechnology. Cutting-edge technology sectors attract skilled professionals and researchers, fostering a cycle of innovation.

The cycle begins with technology as the driving force that advances infrastructure, which in turn, underpins further technological development. Both technology and infrastructure shape and are shaped by geopolitics, as nations such as the US leverage these assets for global influence and security, by building missiles, fighter jets, and military bases. Across all these dimensions, harnessed talent plays a crucial role in innovation and execution, driving the cycle forward. Nations and organizations that effectively integrate these components—leveraging technology, building and maintaining infrastructure, navigating geopolitical landscapes, and nurturing talent—will be better positioned to lead in the twenty-first century.

The deployment of 5G technology requires a comprehensive infrastructure of cell towers and fiber-optic cables, which then enables a wide array of smart city applications, improving urban living and operational efficiency.

The global race for AI dominance reflects how technological leadership is viewed as crucial to national security and economic power. Countries are investing heavily in AI research and development, recognizing its potential to transform military capabilities, economic structures, and social governance. Silicon Valley's success as a global tech hub is attributed not only to its innovative companies and technologies but also to its ability to attract and nurture talented individuals from around the world, creating a cycle of innovation and growth.

This cycle highlights the interconnectedness of technology, infrastructure, geopolitics, and talent, demonstrating how advancements in one area can stimulate progress across others, contributing to a nation's or organization's competitiveness and strategic positioning on the global stage.

In this section of the chapter, we want to highlight the interrelationship that exists between the technology driver and the other three drivers within the TIGHT Framework. It is important to emphasize that each chapter will address the relationship from the perspective of the driver introduced. In this chapter, rather than discuss the impact the other drivers have on technology, we emphasize the impact that technology has had on Infrastructure, Geopolitics, and harnessed talent.

Technology and Infrastructure

The availability of infrastructure is crucial for a business considering expanding or moving parts of its supply chain to a new country. Reliable roads, bridges, airports, and ports are essential for moving goods efficiently and cheaply. Poor infrastructure leads to delays, damage, and higher transportation costs, hurting a company's bottom line. Additionally, a steady and reliable supply of electricity is vital for most businesses; unreliable power can disrupt production, damage equipment, and lead to lost revenue. For instance, Henry Ford, in 1928, famously attempted to move a crucial part of his supply chain—the rubber for his tires—to Brazil, founding a factory town that he dubbed "Fordlandia." Yet, a lack of reliable transportation and electricity, among other factors, in 1945 led to a loss of over $20 million (equivalent to $338 million in 2023) and heralded the end of Fordlandia. Perhaps just as important as electricity, a modern business's logistics depend on the availability of communication infrastructure because high-speed internet and reliable telecommunications services are essential for seamless communication between suppliers, manufacturers, distributors, and retailers. A well-developed network of warehouses, distribution centers, and transportation options allows for the efficient movement of goods throughout the supply chain, while a lack of communication through a value chain will mean that the company will face challenges in managing inventory, meeting customer demands, and staying competitive. By carefully evaluating a country's infrastructure, a business can make informed decisions about expansion. Strong infrastructure reduces costs, improves efficiency, and minimizes risks, while weak infrastructure can make expansion a costly challenge.

Technological advancements and infrastructure development possess a circular relationship, as technology has a significant impact on the planning, design, construction, and operation of infrastructure, while infrastructure development provides the foundation and support for the deployment and utilization of various technologies. A clear example of the relationship is how technological advancements can create demand for new infrastructure or improvements to existing infrastructure. Innovations in materials, construction techniques, and engineering practices enable the creation of more efficient, sustainable, and resilient infrastructure systems. For instance, in China, new bridge-building methods have allowed the city of Chongqing to construct a series of vertically overlapping and interconnected highways and overpasses that have dramatically improved transportation speed and efficiency.

Next, as stated above, in the modern business landscape, one of the most important requirements for cross-border expansion is that country's capacity for telecommunications. A country's telecommunications infrastructure acts as the digital nervous system, shaping its participation in the global business landscape because limited internet and mobile connectivity restricts a country's ability to participate in e-commerce, online services, and global supply chains.

Yet, the advancement of technology has the potential to completely redefine communications infrastructure to be faster, more widespread, and more defiant of physical distances or borders. For instance, Low Earth Orbit (LEO) satellite networks like Starlink promise to bring high-speed internet to remote and underserved areas, meaning that new countries may soon be entering the realm of possibilities for businesses looking to expand. More immediately, in a more familiar example, 5G promises to revolutionize global business with its ultra-fast speeds and high bandwidth. The rollout of 5G technology in modern, developed economies is already enhancing mobile internet speed and reliability, enabling new applications in remote work, telemedicine, and the Internet of Things (IoT). Yet, by 2024, 5G networks are expected to cover one-third of the world's population. As illustrated in Fig. 2.7, the six-year projected growth rate of 5G will surge from nearly 8 billion subscribers to almost 9 billion.

A second, more quiet consideration of equal importance in assessing the business potential of a nation lies in water and waste management. Many industries rely heavily on water for manufacturing processes, such as pulp and paper, forestry, and aluminum. Limited access to clean water can restrict operations and hinder production capacity. Meanwhile, businesses need to comply with environmental regulations regarding waste disposal. Inefficient waste management infrastructure in a country can make it difficult or impossible for a company to dispose of industrial waste safely and compliantly, leading to fines or even operational shutdowns that can damage a company's reputation and brand image. Examples include BP, Coca-Cola, ALDI, and IKEA.

Yet, advancements in technologies such as rainwater harvesting, greywater recycling, and small-scale wastewater treatment plants are creating new geographical and economic possibilities for entire value chains. For instance, smart water management systems use sensors and real-time data analytics to detect leaks, manage water resources more efficiently, and reduce waste. In 2022, faced with a severe drought, The City of Los Angeles Department of

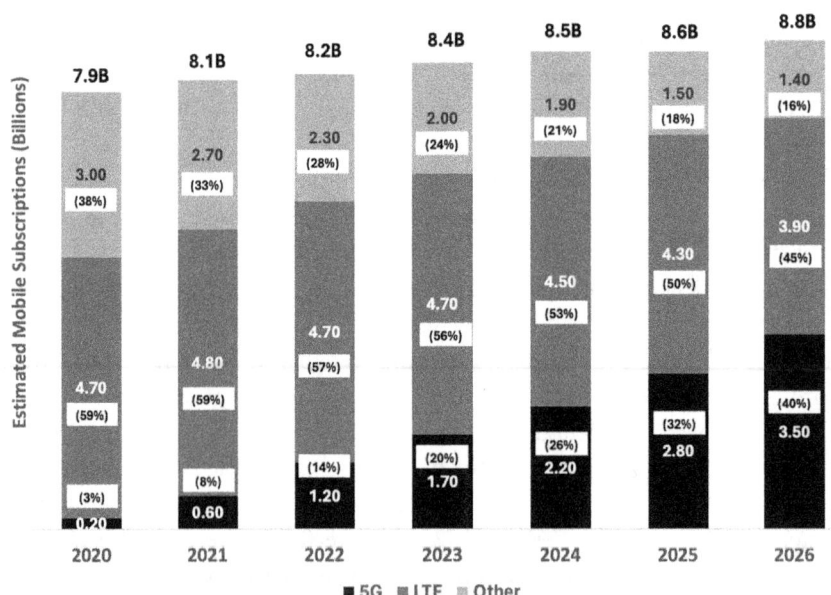

Fig. 2.7 Projected growth of 5G (*Source* Insight Software: Mekko Graphics)

Water and Power (LADWP) partnered with a company called Sensus (now part of Xylem Inc.) to implement a smart water metering system across the city. Before the smart system, leaks could go undetected for weeks or even months. The system collected data that has helped LADWP optimize water distribution and target conservation efforts more effectively while also identifying and fixing leaks much faster, leading to significant water conservation. The global smart water management market was valued at approximately $11.7 billion in 2019 and is expected to grow to $21.4 billion by 2024 at a CAGR of 12.9%.

A more contemporary factor to consider is green energy infrastructure. The current decade's many extreme fluctuations in global oil and gas prices have significantly impacted many businesses' bottom lines. Green energy sources offer greater price stability and protection from these market fluctuations. Additionally, regulations around carbon emissions and environmental impact are becoming increasingly stringent and many businesses are setting ambitious sustainability goals and facing pressure from consumers and investors to reduce their environmental footprint. As such, locating the company's value chain in areas with green energy infrastructure—or simply establishing the infrastructure itself—allows a company to demonstrate its commitment to sustainability and enhance its brand reputation while also protecting itself from future risks in the energy market.

The advancement of technology is poised to revolutionize green energy and energy infrastructure, making it more diverse, distributed, and economically viable. Solar and wind energy technologies have dramatically reduced the cost of producing electricity, making renewable sources more competitive with fossil fuels. According to the International Renewable Energy Agency (IRENA), the cost of solar photovoltaic (PV) electricity has fallen by 89% from 2010 to 2020, making it the cheapest electricity in history in some regions, while development of efficient and cost-effective energy storage solutions like advanced batteries and pumped hydro storage will allow for greater integration of renewable energy sources that are variable by nature (like solar and wind).

Finally, a factor of the infrastructure driver that encapsulates all of the ideas presented above is Smart Cities such as Singapore, Helsinki, Zurich, and Auckland. Advancements in 3D printing, robotics, and modular construction techniques have the potential to revolutionize the way buildings and other structures are constructed, leading to faster, cost-effective, and environmentally friendly projects, while existing technology such as IoT also continues to increase in popularity across the world, bettering lives and a nation's economic prospects.

The global smart cities market is expected to grow tenfold from 2022 to 2032 (see Fig. 2.8). For instance, already in effect is Singapore's Smart Nation initiative, which uses sensors and IoT devices across their capital city to optimize traffic flow, reduce energy consumption, and improve public safety and health services.

These examples underscore the profound impact of technology on infrastructure development and how this driver can influence the viability of global business expansion within a certain region. Properly interpreted within a TIGHT context, the relationship between technology and infrastructure has the potential to transform industries, enhance efficiency, and improve the quality of life in various domains, including transportation, energy, telecommunications, and urban development. The impressively rising numbers reflect the growing investment and rapid adoption of these technologies across various sectors, highlighting the ongoing evolution of our physical and digital worlds. In the twenty-first century, businesses that recognize the available infrastructure within a region are a step closer to winning in the business landscape.

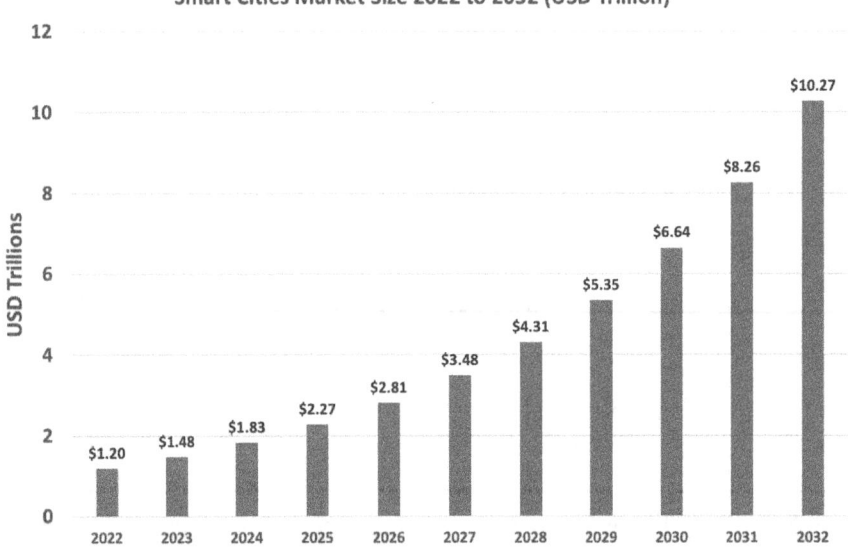

Fig. 2.8 Rise of smart cities (*Source* Global Market Insights)

Technology and Geopolitics

The relationship between technology and geopolitics is intricate and multifaceted, influencing global power dynamics, national security, economic competitiveness, and societal norms. Technology can be a tool for geopolitical power. A good example of the influence of technology on national security is Israel's deployment of the "Iron Dome" to protect the nation from incoming missiles from hostile nations and their proxies.

As technology advances, it becomes a pivotal element in shaping geopolitical landscapes, with nations leveraging technological innovations to assert dominance, protect sovereignty, and negotiate international relations, thus enhancing their nation's economic, military, and cultural power. In the twenty-first century, countries such as the United States that are leaders in technology innovation and development often have stronger political influence.

More importantly, technology can be a driver of geopolitical change, creating new opportunities and challenges for countries, which can influence their geopolitical position. For example, the rise of e-commerce and the digital economy have disrupted traditional trade patterns and created new opportunities for countries such as India, Mexico, and Bermuda that can leverage technological capacity. Similarly, emerging technologies such as artificial intelligence and blockchain have the potential to reshape the geopolitical landscape by creating new industries and changing the nature of work. The race for technological leadership in areas like 5G, AI, and semiconductors is tied to economic prosperity, military capabilities, and global influence. The U.S. and China are leading the global race in AI. China partnered with companies like Huawei and Tencent and plans to become the world leader in AI by 2030, aiming for the AI industry to be worth 1 trillion yuan (USD 147.80 billion), while The U.S. Department of Defense's 2020 budget request included approximately $927 million for AI and machine learning technologies, highlighting the strategic importance of technological superiority.

This large increase in technological investment ultimately has geopolitical roots, as the rise of cyber warfare, code-breaking, and espionage marks a turning point in international conflict, transforming the battleground from physical to digital. Nation-states are wielding cyberattacks as potent weapons, capable of crippling a country's infrastructure, stealing intellectual property that fuels economic growth, and even manipulating elections to influence global power dynamics. Examples like alleged Russian interference in the 2016 U.S. elections and cyber assaults on Ukrainian infrastructure highlight this new reality. The financial stakes are staggering, with Cybersecurity Ventures predicting a 15% annual increase in global cybercrime costs, reaching a staggering $10.5 trillion by 2025, compared to $3 trillion in 2015. This exponential growth underscores how cyber threats have become a paramount national security concern, prompting nations to invest heavily in fortifying their digital defenses.

On a more internal scale, for businesses looking to expand their operations overseas, the digital age brings with it questions of privacy and data security as supercomputers, analysis software, and AI blur the lines between national security and individual, private corporate liberties, creating new geopolitical tensions in the business world. Governments are increasingly deploying advanced surveillance technologies like facial recognition and data mining under the banner of national security and crime prevention. In Washington, DC, for instance, Closed Circuit TV cameras in Reagan National Airport with AI-powered facial recognition software were implemented in January of 2024. However, such measures raise critical questions about individual privacy and the potential for authoritarian control and pose a genuine threat to the concept of free markets. As American companies continuously move out of the Far East and seek other regions and continents for key parts of their supply chain, China's vast network of over 200 million CCTV cameras exemplifies this trend, with its "Safe City" initiative raising concerns about social control and a chilling effect on dissent. This extensive use of technology for surveillance has significant implications beyond China's borders, impacting international perceptions of governance and potentially creating an unfair advantage for Chinese businesses operating in countries with stricter privacy regulations.

Moving even more into the realms of economics and global businesses, the rise of digital currencies and blockchain technology could redefine the global financial system, affecting currency dominance, international sanctions, and economic independence while disrupting traditional geopolitical power structures and impacting the business world on a global scale. The global blockchain technology market in the banking and financial services industry was valued at around $1.9 billion in 2019 and is expected to grow to more than $22.5 billion by 2026, at a CAGR of approximately 44.5%.

As illustrated in Fig. 2.9, the total number of cryptocurrencies and their overall market capitalization have been dramatic. Cryptocurrencies, arguably, destabilize the need for the trading power of the US dollar and introduce significant unknown variables in the global financial and investment markets. In November 2021, the market capitalization of cryptocurrencies saw an unprecedented increase, reaching an all-time high of approximately $2.9 trillion. This shift has economic implications beyond just currency itself. Digital currencies could render international sanctions less effective, impacting a nation's ability to exert economic pressure. Additionally, widespread adoption of blockchain technology, such as that currently underway in El Salvador, could empower countries by streamlining financial transactions, reducing (or perhaps increasing) fraud, and fostering economic independence. These developments create a complex geopolitical landscape for businesses, forcing them to adapt to a new financial ecosystem with potentially altered power dynamics.

Most relevantly, the relationship between technology and geopolitics in a business context lies in supply chains in the technology industry. The rise of large-scale data analytics technology is forcing private businesses to walk a tightrope between efficiency and geopolitics within their supply chains. Blockchain technology can track goods throughout the supply chain,

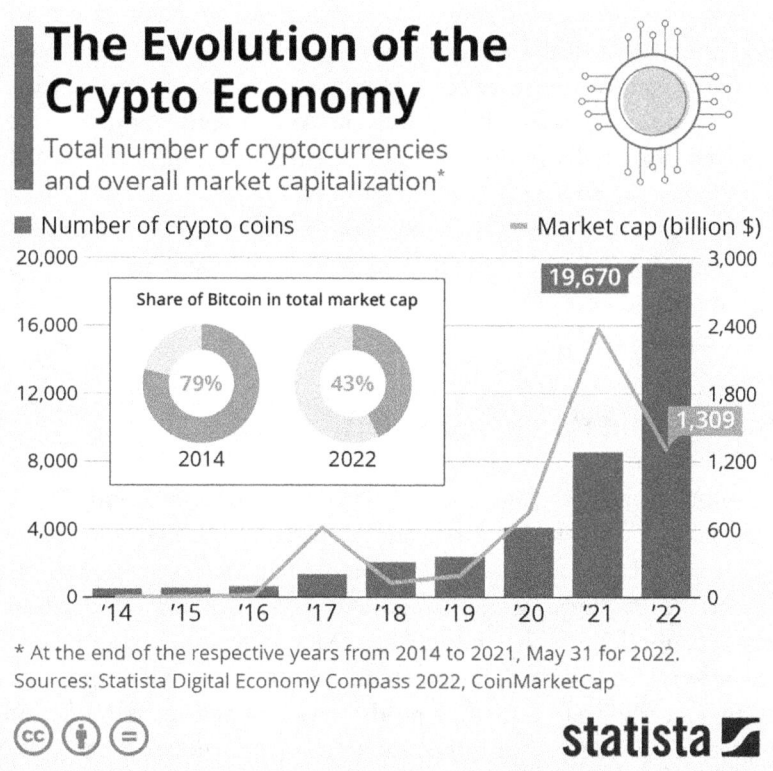

Fig. 2.9 The evolution of crypto (*Source* Gartner, Statista. 2024)

reducing fraud and ensuring ethical sourcing. This fosters trust and eases collaboration in large-scale value networks such as the ones run by Apple and Boeing that span the globe. While the global market for blockchain technology in supply chains is expected to surge from $253 million in 2020 to a staggering $3.2 billion by 2026, highlighting its potential to improve transparency and security, this digital transformation also exposes vulnerabilities. Cybersecurity breaches in logistics, averaging a hefty $3.5 million according to IBM's 2020 report, demonstrate the potential for financial losses and reputational damage. For instance, Expeditors International, a global logistics shipping company, faced losses of over $65 million following a cybersecurity breach that disrupted their entire network and forced partial shutdowns along their operations. Caught between the need for efficiency and the ever-present risk of geopolitical tensions disrupting access to critical components—like the recent global chip shortage caused by U.S. restrictions on China—businesses must navigate this complex landscape by embracing secure technologies like blockchain while simultaneously fortifying their defenses against cyber threats.

As shown by the examples given above, technology has become a major player in the geopolitical arena, which in turn affects a country's viability as a potential expansion territory for a business or its supply chain. Countries are vying for dominance in critical areas like AI and semiconductors, creating tensions and potentially leading to trade restrictions. Additionally, technologies like cyber warfare and data manipulation can be used as weapons, disrupting economies and influencing elections. This new tech-driven landscape forces nations *and* companies to constantly adapt their strategies to both compete and cooperate in a world increasingly shaped by technological advancements.

Technology and Harnessed Talent

In the global business landscape, harnessed talent is among the most important considerations for expansion. A thriving business and technology ecosystem requires a continuous supply of skilled professionals, and talent is also essential for unlocking the full potential of technology to drive societal progress, economic growth, and global competitiveness. Thus, the relationship between technology and harnessed talent is complex and dynamic, influencing nearly every aspect of modern society and the global economy. This interplay is crucial for innovation, economic development, and the continuous evolution of both technological landscapes and workforce skills. Technological advancements create new demands for talent, while talented individuals drive innovation and shape the development and application of technology. For instance, the creation of AI created a wholly new industry sector in need of individuals with high human capital, while those very same individuals were the ones who led us toward a digital revolution and developed the necessary hardware and software.

While harnessed talent has a clear impact on technology, as talented individuals, including scientists, engineers, developers, and researchers, are essential for technological innovation, technology also acts as a catalyst for the growth of human capital and harnessed talent. From online learning platforms that equip individuals with in-demand skills to remote work opportunities that expand the talent pool, technology empowers people to develop and contribute. Communication tools enable seamless collaboration across borders, maximizing the potential of diverse teams. Furthermore, technology democratizes access to information, fostering a culture of continuous learning and innovation. However, challenges remain. Unequal access to technology can exacerbate existing inequalities, and the focus on automation necessitates investment in nurturing essential human skills like critical thinking and problem-solving. Overall, technology presents a remarkable opportunity to cultivate a skilled, adaptable, and innovative global workforce, but harnessing its full potential requires careful navigation of the geopolitics and infrastructure of the region.

Perhaps the best example of technology and harnessed talent in the business world is the explosion of telecommunications and cloud-based solutions. These advancements have facilitated the mass outsourcing of call centers and back-office operations to regions like Latin America and Asia. For instance, Apple has placed many of its call centers in Indonesia and Asia, while companies such as Avis and Coca-Cola have shifted their call centers to English-speaking countries in Latin America, and the Caribbean such as Jamaica. This shift presents a wealth of opportunities and challenges for both developed and developing nations. For businesses in developed economies, this global talent pool translates to significant cost advantages and access to a wider range of skilled professionals. Companies can leverage this to enhance their competitiveness on the international stage. For individuals in these developing regions, outsourcing creates pathways to gain valuable experience in the global economy, potentially leading to higher wages and career advancement and fostering a more inclusive and interconnected business landscape.

As such, the global business landscape is experiencing a surge in potential new expansions and supply chain links, particularly in regions with strong

IT talent. The rapid evolution of software development, coupled with a fast-paced, competitive technology market, necessitates a continuous upskilling of the workforce. To remain at the forefront of these advancements, companies like Google, Microsoft, and Amazon are investing heavily in employee training programs. This focus on continuous learning is reflected in the booming IT training market, which is expected to reach a staggering $92.2 billion by 2028. This presents a significant opportunity for new regions of the world. The global IT training market, valued at $68.9 billion in 2021 and projected to grow at over 5% annually, highlights the demand for skilled IT professionals. Google, Microsoft, and Amazon recognizing this potential, are already investing heavily in employee training programs to develop their global workforces, signifying a shift toward a more geographically diverse talent pool, where regions with a strong focus on IT training can become hubs for innovation.

Additionally, the rise of artificial-intelligence and machine learning (ML) within the global business landscape is dramatically reshaping human capital demands. These fields, at the forefront of technological innovation, require a specialized talent pool capable of developing and implementing these powerful tools. OpenAI's development of groundbreaking GPT models exemplifies this—a fusion of cutting-edge research and individuals skilled in complex machine learning algorithms. This is not a singular case. The number of AI jobs listed on platforms like Indeed has skyrocketed by nearly 30% in just a year, highlighting the ever-growing demand for AI talent. This trend underscores the crucial role technology plays in shaping human capital across the global business landscape. As AI and ML continue their rapid evolution, fostering and attracting this workforce will be paramount for businesses to thrive in the years to come.

Most interestingly, the global push toward new technology that harnesses renewable energy sources such as solar and wind power is also creating a significant shift in the human capital landscape. This transition demands a new generation of engineers, technicians, and scientists with specialized knowledge in these burgeoning technologies. Companies like Tesla and Vestas, at the forefront of innovation and large-scale deployment of renewable solutions, rely heavily on these talented individuals. The rapid growth in this sector is evident in the U.S. solar industry alone, where employment has surged by a staggering 167% in the last decade—five times faster than the overall U.S. job market. This surge underscores how technology, in this case, the drive for clean energy, is not only transforming our environment but also reshaping human capital on a global scale. Businesses that can adapt and attract this specialized workforce will be well positioned to capitalize on the opportunities presented by the renewable energy revolution.

These examples and numbers underscore the critical relationship between technology and harnessed talent. As technology advances, it creates new opportunities and demands for skilled professionals. In turn, the innovations driven by this talent pave the way for further technological advancements, creating a cycle of growth and innovation that drives industries forward.

The relationship between technology and harnessed talent is deeply synergistic, with each driving the evolution and effectiveness of the other. For instance, experts in artificial intelligence development would not be necessary or relevant without the existence of the necessary semiconductors and hardware to build their programs. This interplay is crucial across industries, from information technology and biotech to renewable energy and beyond. Technological advancements create new demands for talent, while talented individuals drive innovation and shape the development and application of technology. A thriving technology ecosystem requires a continuous supply of skilled professionals, and talent is essential for unlocking the full potential of technology to drive societal progress, economic growth, and global competitiveness.

Conclusion: Technology Within Today's Business Landscape Is a Catalyst

As shown by our analysis of the TIGHT framework, in today's business landscape, technology acts as a transformative accelerant, unlocking a new era of possibility across geopolitics, infrastructure development, and talent acquisition. On the geopolitical front, technology fosters collaboration and innovation, chipping away at geographical barriers. Blockchain technology, for instance, is being explored by countries like China and Australia to create secure and transparent trade corridors, reducing friction and boosting trust. This paves the way for a more interconnected global network where businesses can navigate complex international landscapes with greater confidence.

Furthermore, advancements in areas like AI and automation are revolutionizing infrastructure development. Companies like Siemens in Germany are utilizing digital twins—virtual replicas of physical infrastructure—to optimize construction projects and streamline maintenance, ensuring faster completion times and improved efficiency. This not only benefits developed nations but also empowers developing countries to leapfrog traditional methods and build critical infrastructure at an accelerated pace.

Technology's impact extends beyond physical infrastructure to the human capital that powers it. Communication and collaboration tools empower companies to tap into a global pool of talent, fostering diversity and maximizing human potential. Imagine a Bangalore-based software engineer collaborating seamlessly with a design team in San Francisco—this is the reality enabled by technology. However, to fully harness this potential, addressing the digital divide is crucial. Initiatives by companies like Microsoft to provide subsidized internet access in underserved communities are a step in the right direction. By investing in equitable access to technology, businesses can cultivate a global workforce brimming with potential, ready to tackle the challenges and opportunities of the future.

Technology's influence within today's business landscape is undeniable. It fosters collaboration across borders, accelerates infrastructure development, and unlocks a global pool of talent. By embracing these advancements and addressing the challenges that come with them, businesses have the potential to unlock a future brimming with possibility.

3

The Infrastructure Driver

Infrastructure: The Great Enabler

From transportation to healthcare and power transmission to highways and schools, infrastructure is essentially all the man-made structures and services that surround modern life. On a daily basis, we drive down roads, make phone calls, surf the internet, and rely on stable electricity to do our jobs and heat our homes. As with the Technology driver, modern humans interact with hundreds of forms of infrastructure daily. Life in the developed world would be unimaginable without it.

It is no exaggeration to say that infrastructure is essential for economic development, social progress, and the functioning of modern societies. Roads and highways facilitate trade, hospitals ensure the health of the working population, and underground internet and telephone wiring enable efficient communication. Infrastructure sets the stage for all possibilities within technology, positively correlates with stable governance, and can shape a nation's population into strong human capital.

Without stable infrastructure, companies would struggle to establish clear lines of communication, find physical and digital supply chain operations near-impossible, and struggle with the day-to-day revenue-generating operations of their business. As such, investment in infrastructure is a critical consideration for governments, businesses, and communities seeking to ensure sustainable growth and development, and for companies seeking to invest or expand overseas, understanding, measuring, and evaluating international infrastructure is a key determinant of success.

The Two Types of Infrastructure and Their Effect on the Development of the Global Business Landscape

What exactly is included when talking about infrastructure? From our perspective, the infrastructure driver should be interpreted as "hardware," while the previously described technology driver is "software." They are both closely interrelated and often work in sync. However, in this analogy, technology (software) specifically comprises the digital tools, applications, and systems that process data, manage operations, and enable innovation. Infrastructure (hardware) represents the physical components—buildings, networks, and transportation—that support and enable these technological functions.

For our purposes in this book, there are two broadly defined categories of infrastructure: Physical and social. Both help shape the viability (or nonviability) of a nation for foreign companies to expand into and invest in.

Firstly, *Physical Infrastructure*: This type of infrastructure consists of tangible and visible elements that provide essential services and enable various functions. Physical infrastructure forms the backbone of a society, providing essential services and enabling the functions that keep everything running. This includes (1) transportation networks like roads, bridges, and railways that move people and goods; (2) energy infrastructure such as power plants, grids, and storage facilities that keep the lights on and power our lives; (3) water treatment plants, dams, pipes, plumbing, and waste management systems that ensure water sanitation and a stable water supply; (4) a web of digital infrastructure, including data centers, telecommunication networks, internet cables, and cell towers that enable modern communication and fuel our digital world; and (5) housing and shelter.

One of the most cutting-edge, macro-level infrastructure developments in recent decades has been "smart cities." These include Singapore, Helsinki, Amsterdam, Oslo, Seoul, Zurich, and New York. A smart city uses information and communication technology (ICT) to improve operational efficiency, share information with the public, and provide better quality government service and citizen welfare.

For the private sector, sound physical infrastructure is the lifeblood of any business, and this is especially true for a global business. For a major car manufacturer like Toyota, efficient production relies on a robust transportation network of highways and ports to receive raw materials and deliver finished vehicles. As of 2024, Toyota collaborates with twelve US trading ports and nine inland distribution centers to move their cars. Disruptions at any point in the chain, from congested roads delaying parts to an unreliable power grid hindering factory operations, can significantly impact production schedules and delivery times. Similarly, with its vast e-commerce reach, a company like Amazon thrives on a well-maintained communication infrastructure. Reliable internet cables, data centers, and cell towers ensure seamless online transactions and timely deliveries, keeping customers satisfied. According to Sortlist, with over a million active users, Amazon's AWS, responsible for around 16–17% of their total revenue, powers thousands of businesses in 245 countries and territories.

Even a seemingly mundane element like water infrastructure plays a vital role. A chip manufacturer like TSMC (Taiwan Semiconductor Manufacturing Company), whose intricate processes require ultrapure water, would be crippled by an unreliable water supply. According to Statista, in 2022, TSMC consumed around 97 million metric tons of water. In short, from efficient transportation of goods to uninterrupted power for production and robust communication for global collaboration, strong physical infrastructure is the foundation upon which successful global businesses operate.

Secondly, *Social Infrastructure*: this type of infrastructure refers to facilities and services that support the quality of life of individuals and communities. Social infrastructure acts as a community's safety net and enrichment system, fostering its residents' well-being. This type of infrastructure includes: (1) educational facilities that provide knowledge and skills; (2) healthcare infrastructure, with hospitals and clinics that ensure access to medical care; (3) cultural and recreational spaces like libraries, parks, and museums; and (5) public safety infrastructure, encompassing police, fire, and emergency response centers that safeguard the community and prevent crime.

Social infrastructure is critical in fostering a skilled and engaged workforce, the backbone of any thriving business in today's globalized world. A well-funded educational system, like those in countries like Finland and Singapore, equips individuals with the necessary knowledge and skills to compete in the modern job market. This directly benefits companies like Google, which relies heavily on a talent pool of over 182,502 well-trained engineers, computer scientists, and other staff members in over 30 countries. Similarly, a robust healthcare infrastructure, as seen in nations with universal healthcare, such as Japan, Austria, and Canada, ensures a healthy and productive workforce. Furthermore, cultural and recreational facilities provide employee well-being and social interaction opportunities. Companies like Microsoft, known for its focus on employee wellness, emphasize that access to gyms, healthy foods, support systems, and recreational facilities fosters a happier and more engaged workforce, ultimately driving innovation and business success. By investing in social infrastructure, governments create an environment that fosters a skilled and healthy workforce, a critical asset for any company operating in the global business landscape.

As a driver for the TIGHT framework, we use the most comprehensive interpretation of the word infrastructure. As such, *infrastructure* refers to the fundamental physical and organizational systems, facilities, and structures necessary for the functioning and development of societies, economies, and communities. It forms the backbone of modern civilization and includes both physical and virtual components that support various activities and services. Figure 3.1 illustrates social spending on infrastructure for a sample of leading countries.

Infrastructure as a Connector: The Future of Global Business

Infrastructure is the foundational framework of society, and within that domain, technology is the great connector, serving as the bridge between people, places, and corporations.

One of the pillars of the Global Competitiveness Index developed by the World Bank, a metric indicating the macro and microeconomic competitiveness of a global economy, is *infrastructure*. For instance, safe transportation infrastructure, a term encompassing highways, railways, airports, and ports, connects cities and countries, enables the movement of people and goods, and connects much of the world in terms of physical distance. Transportation infrastructure in the modern day has increasing relevance to business as The World Bank estimates that efficient logistics can lower trade costs by up to 9% in low-income countries and about 6% in middle-income countries, underscoring the importance of transportation infrastructure in global trade, and highlighting an important factor for businesses to consider prior to investment or expansion. One notable example of this improvement is Vietnam, where the expansion of deep-water seaports, such as the Cai Mep-Thi Vai Port near Ho Chi Minh City, has improved Vietnam's ability to handle larger container ships, led to lower costs for international shipping, and made Vietnamese exports such as plastic products and textiles more competitive globally.

As such, infrastructure plays a pivotal role as a key driver for preparedness in this new global business landscape, marked by rapid technological advancements, environmental challenges, and evolving economic patterns.

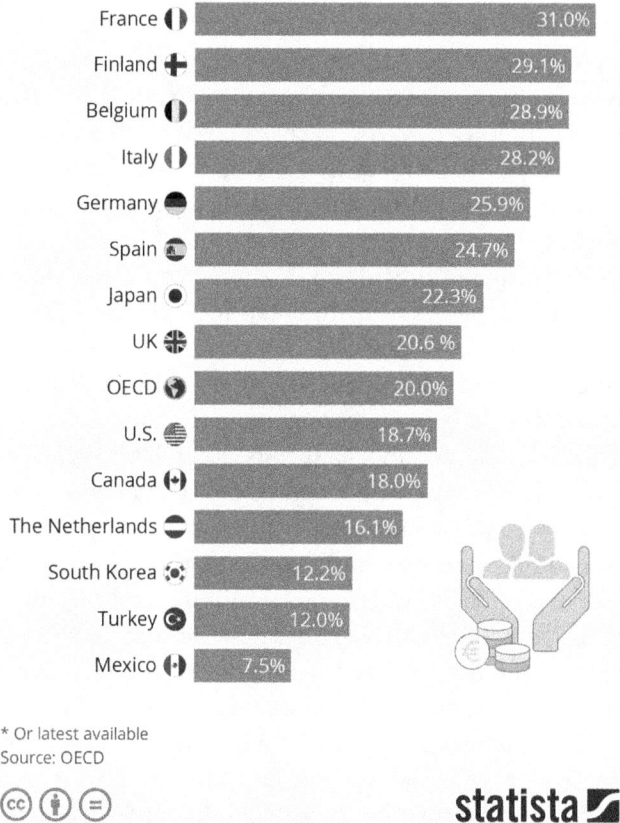

Fig. 3.1 Social spending from highest to lowest (*Source* Statista and the OECD)

In today's world, high-quality infrastructure's role in connecting people underpins readiness and resilience; it helps companies attain a competitive advantage by facilitating the current digital transformation, enhancing supply chain resilience, promoting innovation, and addressing environmental and social challenges. In other words, infrastructure will enable businesses to successfully step into the future.

For one, robust *digital* infrastructure, including high-speed internet and telecommunications networks, is crucial for businesses to engage in e-commerce, leverage cloud computing, and utilize big data analytics. This connectivity enables companies to operate globally, reach new markets, and implement remote working models, which have become increasingly important. For instance, in post-pandemic 2023, more than 20% of Google's employees reported working from home full-time, and more than half reported that they spent at least a few days of each workweek working remotely. As such, for companies wishing to expand their offices overseas, the availability of Internet connections has become a true necessity for operation. As an example to the contrary, India's rural internet connectivity challenges have served as a deterrent for companies expanding into certain areas for years. Even today, internet penetration in India's rural regions remains limited, making it difficult for e-commerce and streaming giants like Amazon, YouTube, and Flipkart to fully tap into the most populous market on earth.

Additionally, the connectivity enabled by digital and physical infrastructure makes it possible for companies operating or manufacturing in emerging markets to enhance their supply chain resistance. With high-speed internet, advanced tracking and forecasting technologies integrated into supply chain infrastructure become possible, enabling businesses to anticipate disruptions, manage risks, and maintain inventory levels, thus ensuring operational continuity. Maersk, one of the world's largest shipping and logistics companies, for example, has integrated advanced tracking and forecasting technologies into its supply chain infrastructure, using a Remote Container Management (RCM) system to track and monitor the status of shipping containers in real-time, and implementing predictive analytics and artificial intelligence (AI) to forecast potential disruptions in the supply chain. Meanwhile, efficient transportation networks (roads, railways, ports, and airports) and logistics infrastructure (warehousing and distribution centers) ensure the smooth operation of global supply chains. Improvements in this area enhance resilience to disruptions, such as those experienced during the COVID-19 pandemic.

More than just maintaining regular operations, the infrastructure supporting research and innovation, including research and development facilities, laboratories, and online databases, drives business competitiveness by fostering new product development and process improvements. In addition, well-designed and maintained infrastructure allows companies to increase efficiency and competitiveness. Access to educational infrastructure and vocational training facilities helps businesses train employees, hire skilled workers, and address skill gaps in their workforce, ensuring they have the talent necessary to adapt to new technologies and market demands. For example, Grupo Bimbo, one of the world's largest bakery companies, with operations across Latin America, Europe, and the United States, once faced the challenge of ensuring a skilled workforce to sustain its large-scale production and distribution processes. To address this, Grupo Bimbo collaborated with various vocational education institutions, including the Technical University of Mexico (UTEC) and other technical schools in Latin America, to offer tailored vocational training programs to train technicians capable of maintaining and troubleshooting complex machinery. Through this, Bimbo developed a pool of skilled technicians who could ensure that their production lines ran smoothly and downtime was minimized.

Finally, in the modern age of social consciousness and sustainability initiatives, it has become important for businesses to assess a new venture's environmental and societal effects before investment and to seek to continuously decrease their negative footprint on our planet. The connectivity brought about by advances in infrastructure allows companies to better care for their employees and achieve their ESG goals. Some outstanding examples are AB InBev, ASML, and Colgate-Palmolive. For instance, in terms of physical infrastructure, sustainable water, and waste management systems, including modernized taps, pipes, and filtration, decrease the amount of water needed in manufacturing/ production by a significant margin and mitigate the environmental impact of wastewater. Meanwhile, regarding social infrastructure, investments in healthcare, housing, and community services improve quality of life, which is crucial for attracting and retaining a skilled workforce, especially in regions experiencing rapid industrial growth. This is why certain frontier economies, such as Jordan, that are not as advanced as emerging markets but possess an illiquid stock exchange and a weak legal system are viable for foreign investment while others struggle. For instance, in nations like Uruguay that are actively participating in the creation of new reliable health infrastructure, FDI amounts to USD 3.8 billion in 2022, while in nations such as Senegal, which has around five times their population, this source of investment is more challenging, with FDI only amounting to $2.58 billion in 2022.

In the new global business landscape, infrastructure's role extends beyond traditional considerations of efficiency and cost-effectiveness. From Morroco's Noor Solar Plant in Ouarzazate, one of the largest concentrated solar power plants in the world and the contributing factor to Morocco's goals of reducing reliance on fossil fuels, to Netherlands' Port of Rotterdam's smart infrastructure that integrates IoT sensors, AI, and data analytics to optimize logistics, reduce carbon emissions, and enhance supply chain resilience by predicting delays and rerouting ships, it encompasses enabling digital transformation, promoting sustainability, enhancing supply chain resilience, fostering innovation, and addressing broader environmental and social challenges. As a result, forward-thinking businesses and policymakers must prioritize strategic investments in infrastructure to successfully navigate the complexities of the twenty-first century's economic environment.

These examples and numbers illustrate the pivotal role of infrastructure in connecting and supporting various facets of modern life, from economic activities and essential services to social interaction. Investments in infrastructure are crucial for a nation's ability to enhance connectivity, resilience, and overall development and for a corporation's ability to stay competitive in the new global business landscape.

Measuring the Infrastructure Driver

Measuring infrastructure within a region helps businesses make informed decisions regarding supply chain sourcing, operational expansion, and future investment. It involves assessing various dimensions such as availability, quality, capacity, and resilience. These metrics provide insights into the nation's infrastructure's efficiency, effectiveness, and impact on economic and social outcomes. Here are some key metrics and examples for evaluating the different types of infrastructure that are most relevant to companies looking to develop in the global business landscape:

Firstly, *High Road Density and Public Transport Accessibility*: High road density can indicate a well-developed transportation network facilitating the efficient movement of goods and people, which is key to hundreds of industries, including mining (transport of goods out of the mine), restaurants, and the food industry (transport of fresh produce), and the commodities market (inventory maintenance and supply chains). A lack of reliable roads and transportation networks can cause stagnation in a region's economy and lead to unsuccessful business ventures. For instance, in regions of Africa, including Zambia and the Congo, there are enormous copper deposits that could account for more than 10% of the world's supply.

Yet, foreign investments in industrial mining in the region are few because, once deposits are mined, there are no safe and reliable roads to transport the goods out of the country and toward shipping ports on the African coastline. Thus, road density, measured in kilometers of road per 100 square km of land area, is a key metric for a business to consider before entering a new market.

Another metric relevant to transportation is Public Transport Accessibility. A lack of access to public transportation, exemplified by regions like Alaska and the American Midwest, where more than 70% of people are forced to drive, walk, or cycle to work, limits the talent pool that companies can draw from during the hiring process because people are less able to travel freely for work. As such, a reliable measure of public transport accessibility would be the percentage of the population living within a certain distance (e.g., 500 meters) of public transportation stops.

Secondly, *Electrification Rate*: A reliable energy grid is crucial for a majority of all modern business operations, powering everything from office lights and computers to complex manufacturing machinery, mining equipment, and logistics programs that ensure smooth production and efficient service delivery. Without consistent access to electricity, businesses face disruptions, delays, and potential data loss, hindering productivity and impacting their bottom line. Thus, a crucial metric to consider when evaluating a region for business plausibility is the electrification rate, which is the percentage of households with access to electricity, where higher rates indicate better energy infrastructure and better investment prospects. For instance, in the USA, the electrification rate is 100%, according to the World Bank's development forum, whereas, in Tanzania, only about 15.3% of the general population had access to electricity as of 2023. This indicates that, unsurprisingly, companies may find it easier to expand into the USA successfully when compared to Tanzania, just by the sheer resources available.

Thirdly, *Internet Penetration Rate and Average Upload Speeds*: Digital infrastructure acts as the nervous system of a modern business. It connects employees, facilitates customer communication, and enables critical operations like data analysis and e-commerce. For a company like Amazon, which has over 1.5 million employees in more than a dozen countries across the world, disruptions to this infrastructure can cripple internal communication and logistics, hinder sales, and stall top-down decision-making, leading to billions in lost revenue and a competitive disadvantage.

Important metrics in digital infrastructure include the Internet Penetration Rate, a metric measuring digital inclusivity through the percentage of the population with access to the Internet, and Average Broadband Speeds (Mbps), a metric measuring the quality and capacity of the available digital infrastructure through average download and upload speeds. For instance, in Singapore, the median internet upload speed was 284 Mbps, and over 99% of the population can access a reliable internet connection. In comparison, its neighbor South Korea's median internet upload speed was only 133.7 Mbps. As such, compared to a measured global average of 93.65 Mbps and

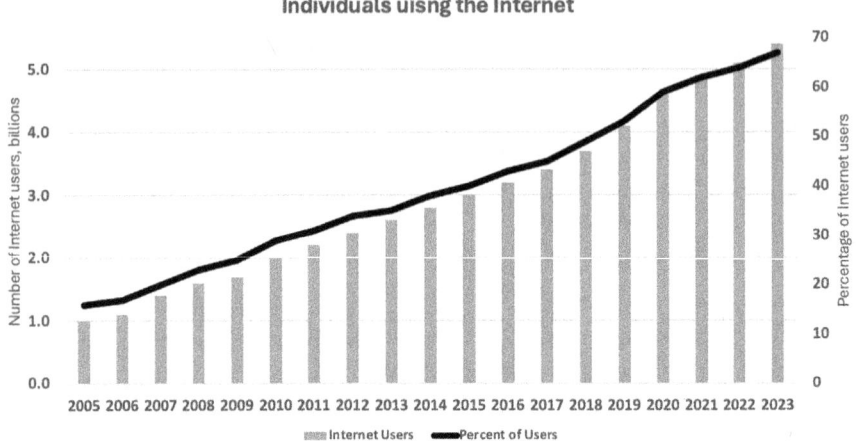

Fig. 3.2 Internet usage over time (*Source* S&P Global Research)

66% of the population with internet connectivity, we see the context behind Singapore's relatively high economic growth capacity and prosperity when compared not only to its regional cousins but the rest of the world. Figure 3.2 portrays the trend line of individual use of the Internet.

Fourthly, *Hospital Beds and Clean Water Availability*: Healthcare, water, and sanitation infrastructure are not only crucial to the operational needs of certain industries, such as the food services and pharmaceutical industries but are also crucial to the attainment and maintenance of a healthy, skilled workforce for any industry. Studies by the World Economic Forum show that healthier workers, as exemplified by the general population in wealthy Western nations, are comparatively more productive and generate higher returns for their employers. For example, Anglo American, a multinational mining company operating in Southern Africa, faced a significant challenge in the early 2000s as HIV/AIDS and tuberculosis (TB) epidemics severely impacted the health of its workforce in South Africa. These health issues led to high absenteeism, increased medical costs, and reduced productivity in its mining operations, where healthy, skilled labor is essential for safety and efficiency. Anglo American implemented a comprehensive HIV/AIDS and TB management program, offering free antiretroviral therapy (ART) to infected employees, as well as widespread health education, testing, and treatment initiatives. The company partnered with local healthcare providers and NGOs to deliver these services on-site and in the communities where its employees lived. By directly addressing the health crises, Anglo American significantly reduced absenteeism and improved the overall health of its workforce, leading to fewer disruptions in operations, better productivity, and enhanced workplace safety. As another example of the direct correlation between workplace productivity and healthcare, in the least economically productive country in the world, the nation of Burundi (whose labor productivity is forecasted to be only $0.29 in 2024), only about 60% of households have access to a source of clean drinking water within 30 minutes of their homes. As such, two important metrics to consider in terms of metropolitan geography for expansion are hospital beds per 1000 People, which is a measure of healthcare capacity that indicates the general availability of medical services, and the percentage of the population with access to clean water sources, such as piped or filtered water or protected wells, both of which help to indicate general population health.

Finally, *Secondary or Tertiary Degrees and National Literacy Rates*: In today's knowledge-driven economy, a strong educational infrastructure acts as the launchpad for a nation's workforce. Well-funded schools and universities equip individuals with the technical skills needed for specific jobs, as well as the critical thinking, problem-solving abilities, and learning capacity crucial for navigating complex technologies. Thus, educational infrastructure is a crucial metric for any business seeking to expand its operations and pool of human capital geographically. This type of infrastructure can be measured using the percentage of the population with a college degree, the number of secondary or tertiary schools in the region, and national literacy rates.

One of the most shocking correlations, if not causations, that demonstrate the importance of educational infrastructure is the relationship between a nation's minimum wage, productivity per capita, and their peoples' average education levels. In developed countries like The Netherlands, where around half of all people have a tertiary degree or higher (university or vocational degree), the minimum wage is $1825.59 per month, and GDP per working hour is $69.78. Meanwhile, in developing countries such as El Salvador, where only 82% of children make it to 9th grade, the minimum wage is about $2 an hour, and GDP per working hour is only $9.70 as of 2023. This data shows that access to higher education fosters a talent pool that can help businesses be more productive, drive innovation, generate higher returns and revenue, and propel businesses forward in the global marketplace.

Measuring infrastructure is a vital indicator of preparedness for the new global business landscape because it highlights areas needing investment or improvement. It ensures that transportation, digital connectivity, and energy systems can support economic growth, innovation, business expansion, and resilience. It enables strategic planning, risk management, and sustainability efforts, essential for navigating future challenges and opportunities. A comprehensive infrastructure measurement offers a clear lens to compare readiness and potential for thriving in the ever-evolving global business landscape.

As a whole, these metrics that measure the five key factors within infrastructure in the context of global business (transportation, electricity, digital connectivity, sanitation, and education) offer a comprehensive view of the state and effectiveness of infrastructure within a region and provide a clear image of whether a location is suitable for direct investment. By evaluating these dimensions, corporations can identify areas of strength and opportunities for improvement, guiding strategic investments and policies to enhance infrastructure development and services.

Infrastructure Within the TIGHT Framework

More than just being the universal connector, infrastructure forms the invisible scaffolding upon which our world functions. It shapes the way we develop technologies, influences the dynamics of global power, and ultimately cultivates the talent pool that drives human progress. From the reliable flow of electricity that powers cutting-edge AI research to the internet cables that connect doctors in remote areas to their patients, physical and digital infrastructure underpins innovation and economic growth. It's a complex web with far-reaching consequences, silently yet actively influencing the trajectory of human progress.

A hypothetical but exemplary cycle of infrastructure's role in the TIGHT framework would play out as such: a new development in digital infrastructure allows a remote community to access the internet. With this access to the internet, more children from this community begin attending school virtually and developing new skills, increasing the pool of human talent. This, in turn, increases the demand for technology and eventually leads to a generation of entrepreneurs who will create businesses, attract investment, and invent new minor technologies adapted to their specific community needs. This transforms underserved regions economically and leads to increased prosperity, which, in turn, facilitates increased political power—thus shaping geopolitics.

It is undisputed that infrastructure shapes technology, geopolitics, and harnessed talent, ultimately influencing the trajectory of our interconnected world. As in the preceding chapter, we only wish to highlight the interrelationship between the infrastructure driver and the other three drivers within the TIGHT Framework.

Infrastructure and Technology

Imagine the research behind groundbreaking AI struggling without a robust power grid to fuel data centers. Or envision the limitations of telemedicine without a high-speed internet infrastructure connecting doctors in remote areas to their patients. These scenarios illustrate how physical and digital infrastructures underpin innovation and economic growth in the technological realm. Reliable power grids, high-bandwidth communication networks, and data storage facilities are all crucial for fostering the development and deployment of new technologies. As technology advances, it creates new demands on infrastructure, necessitating upgrades and expansions to keep pace. The deployment of 5G technology, for instance, requires a comprehensive network of cell towers and fiber-optic cables, which then enables a wide array of smart city applications, improving urban living and operational efficiency. This cyclical relationship between technology and infrastructure ensures continual progress. In essence, infrastructure serves as the backbone upon which technology is developed, deployed, and enhanced, while technology, in turn, offers ways to improve infrastructure efficiency, sustainability, and resilience.

At the core lies physical infrastructure. Reliable electricity grids provide the lifeblood for data centers and research facilities. Extensive transportation networks ensure the seamless movement of materials and personnel crucial for technological advancements. A case in point is China's high-speed rail network, facilitating collaboration between research institutions and manufacturing hubs, accelerating technological innovation across various sectors. Figure 3.3 illustrates road quality and connectivity among a sample of nations across the globe.

Existing infrastructure, often viewed as foundational but static, can serve as a springboard for significant technological advancements with far-reaching implications for the global business landscape. For example, water supply and sewage treatment facilities are essential for public health but can be dramatically enhanced through technology integration.

Advanced water purification technologies provide cleaner water for consumption and industrial processes, which are critical factors for businesses operating in regions with water scarcity. Additionally, smart irrigation systems and leak detection sensors promote water efficiency and conservation, reducing costs for municipalities and businesses that rely on a steady water supply for production. This isn't solely an environmental benefit; the World Bank estimates that smart water management technologies can reduce

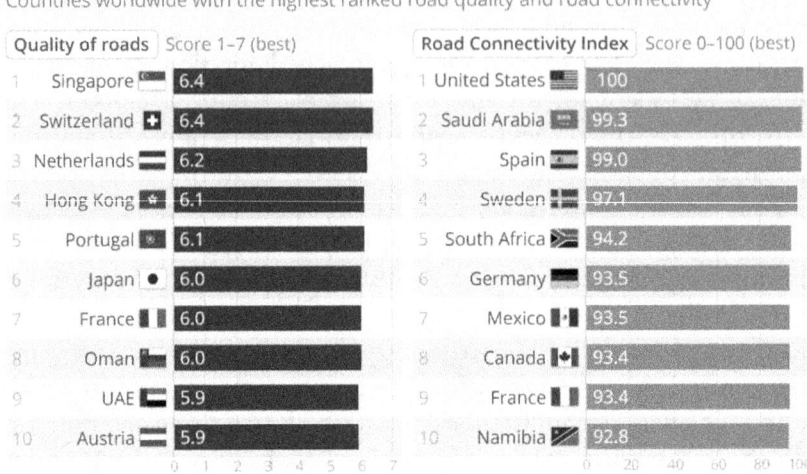

Fig. 3.3 Road quality and connectivity (*Source* Statista with World Economic Forum Data)

water management costs by up to 30%, a significant saving for businesses of all sizes.

Additionally, in recent times, some of the most influential technological developments in physical infrastructure have all centered around renewable energy and energy infrastructure, specifically power generation and distribution systems. These new advances in renewable energy technologies, such as solar photovoltaics and wind turbines, coupled with smart grid technologies, allow for more efficient distribution and management of energy, reducing reliance on fossil fuels. In fact, according to the International Energy Agency (IEA), global renewable electricity capacity is forecasted to increase by over 60% from 2020 levels to reach 4800 GW by 2026, thus illustrating the rapid integration of technology into energy infrastructure. Nations that are in the process of or have successfully implemented such strategies, such as the US, Canada, Mexico, Brazil, the EU's many member states, Japan, Korea, Australia, India, and China, make their nation more capable of stepping into the inevitable renewable future, thus making them more attractive and reliable for foreign companies to expand into and invest. These investments in smart energy infrastructure also drive economic growth in their technology sector, increasing the number of available jobs and promoting innovation. Renewable energy investments in the U.S. are illustrated in Fig. 3.4.

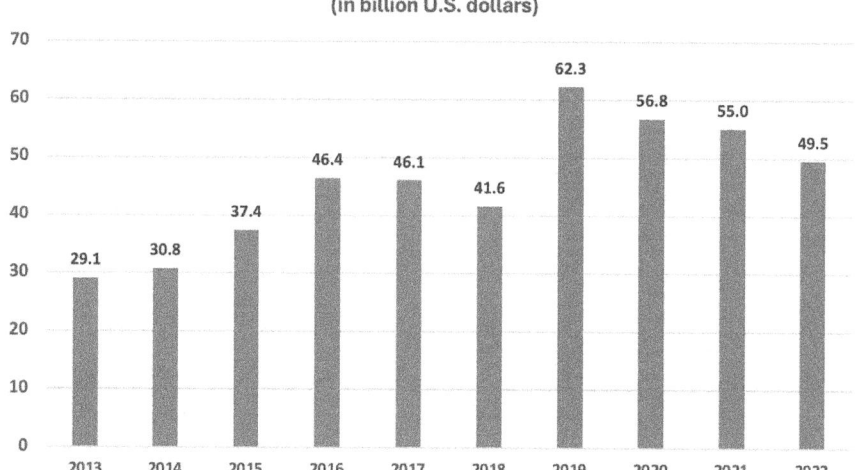

Fig. 3.4 Renewable energy investments in the U.S. (*Source* Bloomberg NEF)

Digital infrastructure plays an equally critical role as physical infrastructure. High-bandwidth internet connectivity allows for seamless communication and collaboration among researchers across the globe. Imagine a world-class research lab dedicated to groundbreaking medical discoveries but crippled by an unreliable cloud system and poor internet connection that leads to frequent data loss. Or picture a business brimming with talented entrepreneurs yearning to create the next big innovation yet hindered by a lack of high-speed internet access to collaborate with global partners. Both situations would be absurdly difficult to navigate and largely unthinkable to the modern CEO.

As a result, digital infrastructure has become critical. Cloud storage facilities offer secure and scalable platforms for data analysis, a cornerstone of many technological breakthroughs. For instance, in early 2022, Netflix leveraged cloud storage through Amazon Web Services (AWS) to store and analyze vast amounts of customer data. By using cloud-based analytics, Netflix improved its recommendation algorithms, personalized content offerings, and enhanced user engagement, leading to higher subscription retention rates and growth in its global user base. Additionally, the rise of AI has also only been made possible through cloud storage and digital infrastructure. The development of complex AI models requires massive datasets and computing power, both of which are heavily reliant on robust digital infrastructure. Telecommunications infrastructure, for instance, including broadband networks, mobile networks, and satellite systems, is rapidly developing to support and encourage such advancements. 5G technology and fiber-optic cables enhance digital communications' speed, capacity, and reliability, facilitating advancements in telemedicine, remote work, and online education. With 5G infrastructure, internet speeds are expected to be about 100 times faster than 4G, providing the infrastructure backbone for a range of technological innovations and applications. Figure 3.5 displays 5G technology deployment around the world.

These examples in water management systems, green energy, and enhanced digital connectivity illustrate how infrastructure acts as the foundation for technological advancements, enabling the deployment of innovative solutions that enhance the efficiency, sustainability, and resilience of critical systems. The integration of technology into infrastructure projects not only addresses current challenges but also prepares societies for future demands, driving economic growth and improving quality of life.

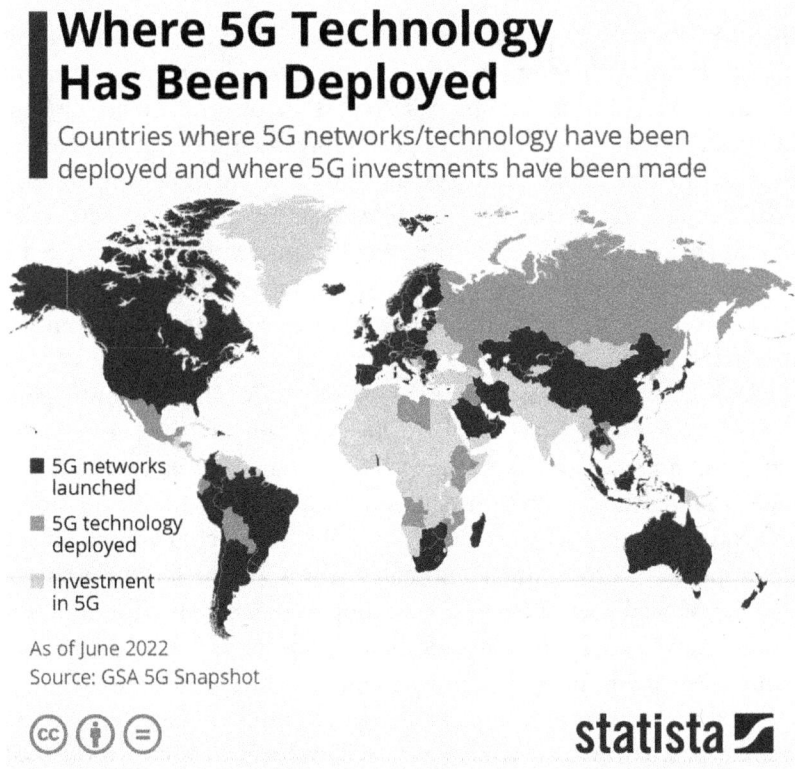

Fig. 3.5 Deployment of 5G technology (*Source* Statista from GSA 5G data)

In today's interconnected world, a nation's technological capabilities directly impact its attractiveness for global businesses. Companies seeking to develop and manufacture cutting-edge products prioritize locations with strong infrastructure. This ensures efficient production processes, seamless communication with international partners, and access to a skilled workforce equipped to handle advanced technologies. By investing in infrastructure, nations foster domestic innovation and position themselves as strong contenders in the global marketplace.

Infrastructure and Geopolitics

In geopolitics, infrastructure is a powerful tool on the global chessboard. Infrastructure and geopolitics are deeply intertwined, with infrastructure projects often reflecting and influencing geopolitical strategies, power dynamics, and economic relationships between nations. Countries with sophisticated infrastructure hold a significant advantage, attracting businesses, fostering innovation, and enhancing their economic competitiveness. Conversely, nations with underdeveloped infrastructure face challenges in attracting foreign investment and developing their domestic economies. Infrastructure serves as a fundamental tool for countries to assert their influence, secure their interests, and foster cooperation or competition on the global stage. Control over key infrastructure assets, such as seaports or communication channels, can give a nation leverage in international relations. The global race for leadership in crucial technological domains like AI, quantum computing, and biotechnology is just one example of how infrastructure superiority influences global power dynamics. This race can lead to competition and conflict as countries vie for dominance in strategic infrastructure development.

As a result, large-scale projects like energy pipelines can become powerful tools that cross international borders, representing strategic assets with the potential to significantly influence global business landscapes. For instance, the Nord Stream 2 project transporting natural gas from Russia directly to Germany is a highly controversial project that has been criticized by some European nations and the United States for potentially increasing European reliance on Russian energy and undermining regional security, creating energy dependence, economic conflict, and potential instability. The pipeline is designed to double the existing Nord Stream pipeline's capacity, carrying 55 billion cubic meters of gas per year directly to Germany.

By relying heavily on Russian gas delivered through this pipeline, Germany becomes vulnerable to potential supply disruptions influenced by political tensions. This can translate into economic leverage for Russia, as they could use the gas supply as a bargaining chip in international relations. These dynamics caused by Nord Stream 2 directly impact the global business landscape. Businesses operating in regions where energy security is heavily influenced by such a pipeline face potential risks. Unexpected supply disruptions due to geopolitical tensions can disrupt production processes and lead to higher energy costs. Furthermore, businesses may hesitate to invest in regions where energy dependence on a single supplier creates uncertainty. Therefore, how infrastructure projects like pipelines are navigated on the geopolitical stage has a ripple effect, impacting the stability and attractiveness of a region for global business operations.

Another example of infrastructure projects being wielded as a powerful geopolitical tool is China's ambitious Belt and Road Initiative (BRI). The BRI was a colossal infrastructure development strategy spanning Asia, Europe, Africa, and beyond. This web of roads, railways, ports, and other infrastructure projects is not purely economic, as China leverages the BRI to expand its influence in several ways, aiming to enhance trade routes, foster economic ties, and potentially create new markets for Chinese goods.

Additionally, the BRI helps China secure energy supplies by building pipelines and ports that facilitate resource transportation while strengthening diplomatic relations with participating countries, allowing strategic Chinese military presence along BRI routes, and expanding China's sphere of influence. Beyond physical routes, as part of the broader BRI, a Digital Silk Road is being created, focused on building digital infrastructure, including fiber-optic cables, 5G networks, and satellite navigation systems, across multiple countries. The DSR aims to extend China's technological reach and standards globally, influencing the digital economy's future landscape and potentially shifting the balance of cyber and technological power.

While specific numbers for the DSR are hard to quantify, they are part of the broader BRI efforts, with China having signed cooperation agreements with over 16 countries to promote the construction of a global information superhighway. As a result of both the digital and physical components of the initiative, critics raise concerns about the BRI's geopolitical implications, including its facilitation of passive militarization, its lack of transparency in data and information sharing, and its creation of unsustainable debt burdens for developing nations, all of which combine to give China considerable economic and geopolitical leverage.

These geopolitical considerations have a significant impact on the global business landscape. Businesses operating in regions touched by the BRI must navigate this complex web of interests. On the one hand, the improved infrastructure can lead to reduced trade barriers, opening new markets and facilitating the movement of goods. On the other hand, potential debt burdens and geopolitical tensions can create instability and uncertainty. Businesses must carefully weigh these factors when making investment decisions in BRI-linked regions. Ultimately, the way infrastructure projects like the BRI are used on the geopolitical stage shapes the global business environment, influencing the opportunities and risks businesses encounter. Reviving the Silk Road is well illustrated in Fig. 3.6.

Finally, in a perhaps less conventional example, beyond traditional ground-based infrastructure, space exploration itself has become a fascinating case study of infrastructure's effect on geopolitics and the global business landscape beyond traditional ground-based infrastructure. The International Space Station (ISS), a marvel of international collaboration, is a prime example. This orbiting scientific hub, co-managed by the space agencies of the United States, Russia, Japan, Europe, and Canada, transcends national

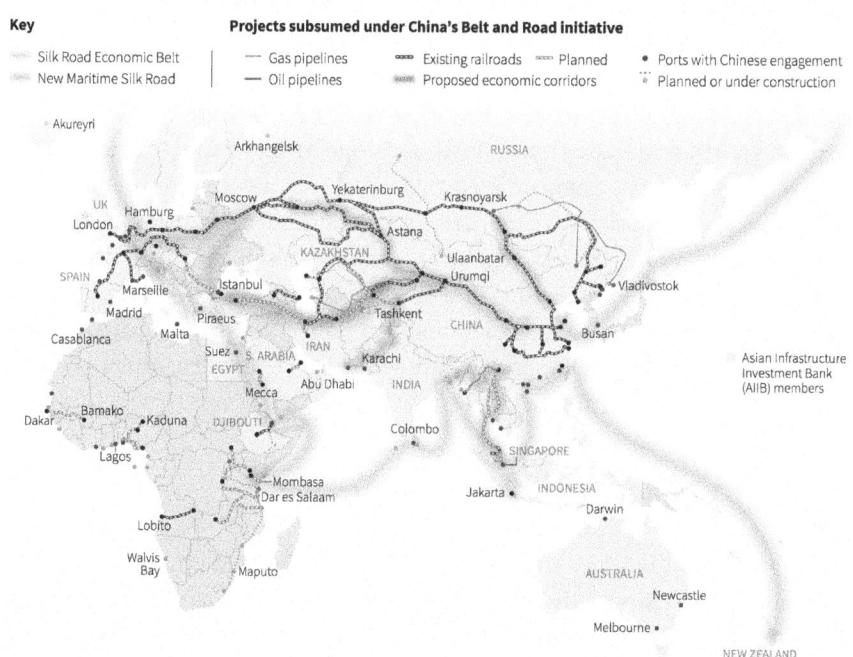

Fig. 3.6 Reviving the Silk Road (*Source* Reuters and the Mercator Institute for China Studies)

boundaries for the sake of scientific advancement. It fosters international cooperation in a strategically sensitive sector, space exploration. This collaboration pushes the boundaries of scientific discovery and demonstrates a spirit of shared goals and mutual benefit. However, the geopolitical landscape around the ISS is not without its complexities. The ongoing tensions between the US and Russia occasionally cast a shadow on the project's future, raising concerns about potential disruptions to its operations. This has led to discussions about alternative space stations or independent space programs, potentially fracturing the current collaborative infrastructure.

These dynamics directly influence the burgeoning spacefaring business sector. Businesses involved in space tourism, satellite communication, or even asteroid mining rely on a stable space environment with clear regulations and international cooperation. Uncertainty surrounding the future of the ISS, or the emergence of competing space stations driven by geopolitical agendas, could create instability and hinder the growth of this exciting new frontier for global business. Therefore, maintaining and fostering international cooperation in space infrastructure like the ISS is crucial for scientific progress and ensuring a predictable and secure environment for the burgeoning space business landscape.

Together, these examples demonstrate how infrastructure is far more than concrete and steel; it's a powerful political tool that shapes the world stage. From pipelines dictating energy security to initiatives like the Belt and Road Initiative shaping trade routes, infrastructure projects are woven into the fabric of international relations. Businesses operating in a world crisscrossed by these projects must navigate a complex web of interests. While improved infrastructure can unlock new markets and streamline operations, geopolitical tensions and potential debt burdens can create instability. Understanding the interplay between infrastructure and geopolitics equips businesses to make informed decisions, navigate risks, and capitalize on opportunities within this ever-evolving global landscape, allowing for a modern global business to survive and thrive in the new TIGHT landscape.

Infrastructure and Harnessed Talent

The relationship between infrastructure and harnessed talent is foundational to economic development, innovation, and societal progress. High-quality infrastructure not only attracts and retains talent but also enables these individuals to maximize their potential, drive growth, and contribute to society's well-being. Essentially, a society's infrastructure directly impacts the quality of its human talent pool.

For instance, a robust educational system, supported by well-equipped schools and accessible libraries, fosters a skilled workforce capable of adapting to the demands of a changing technological landscape. This is especially crucial in today's knowledge-based economy, where innovation and problem-solving are paramount. Access to modern, well-equipped schools, universities, and vocational training centers plays a critical role in developing the talent pool that businesses rely on, and countries that prioritize investment in their educational infrastructure reap significant benefits.

Take Finland and Singapore, for example. These nations consistently top global education rankings and produce highly skilled graduates who are readily employable in the global marketplace. This success can be attributed in part to their well-developed educational infrastructure. Finland, a country that is known for its innovative teaching methods and focus on student well-being, boasts high-quality schools with technology integration and small class sizes. Similarly, Singapore, which invests a staggering 20% of its national budget in education, has established itself as a global leader in educational outcomes and talent development. This investment translates into a workforce equipped with the skills and knowledge necessary to thrive in today's dynamic business environment. The impact on global business is undeniable. Companies seeking highly skilled professionals are naturally drawn to regions with strong educational infrastructure. This creates a virtuous cycle—a skilled workforce attracts businesses, which in turn fuels further investment in education and talent development. This dynamic ensures a steady stream of talent for businesses, fostering innovation and driving economic growth within that region.

Beyond education, other forms of social infrastructure, including healthcare, ensure a healthy and productive workforce. When people have access to preventative care and quality medical services, they can reach their full potential, contributing significantly to a nation's economic and technological advancement. Countries like Germany and Canada invest heavily in hospitals, clinics, and health research institutions. This translates not only into better health outcomes for their citizens but also into a more stable and efficient workforce. Canada, for example, invests nearly 11% of its GDP in healthcare contributing to its high life expectancy and impressive workforce productivity levels. A healthy workforce experiences fewer sick days, leading to increased operational efficiency, long-term productivity, and lower costs for businesses. Figure 3.7 depicts the health expenditures of OECD countries as a share of GDP.

Reliable transportation infrastructure also plays a role in human talent development. In today's "flat" world, geography no longer presents the same

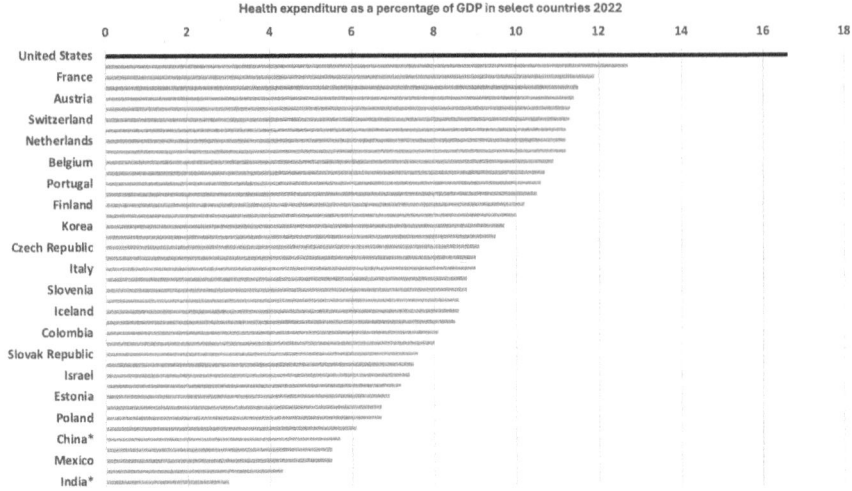

Fig. 3.7 OECD health expenditures as a share of GDP (*Source* Statista Data)

limitations for talent acquisition, fostering a more mobile and diverse workforce. Businesses compete fiercely to attract the best and brightest minds, and a key factor in this competition is a region's infrastructure, particularly its transportation network. Efficient transportation infrastructure plays a critical role in fostering labor mobility and attracting skilled professionals.

Cities with well-developed transportation systems offer a significant advantage. Take Tokyo and Paris, for example. Both boast advanced public transportation networks that reduce commute times, connect residents to job opportunities across the city, and contribute to a high quality of life. This is reflected in their high rankings on global livability and talent attraction indices. A well-connected city allows individuals to access a wider range of job opportunities, regardless of location. This flexibility attracts a more diverse and skilled talent pool, fostering innovation and dynamism within the local economy. For instance, the Greater Paris Express, a massive €35 billion project to expand the city's metro system. This ambitious undertaking is expected to significantly improve connectivity within the region, not only enhancing the quality of life for residents but also supporting economic and talent development. By facilitating easier commutes and opening up new job opportunities, this project will make Paris an even more attractive destination for skilled professionals, propelling the city's growth and competitiveness in the global marketplace.

These examples underscore how infrastructure across various sectors supports the attraction, development, and retention of talent. By providing the necessary facilities and services, infrastructure lays the groundwork for individuals to learn, innovate, and contribute effectively to their fields, driving economic growth and societal advancement. From fostering a skilled workforce through robust educational systems, ensuring a healthy and productive population with quality healthcare, and facilitating talent mobility through efficient transportation networks, infrastructure shapes the foundation of a competitive workforce. By prioritizing investment in these areas, governments create an environment that empowers individuals, attracts and retains skilled professionals, and ultimately positions their nation as a hub for innovation and economic prosperity in the ever-evolving global business landscape.

Conclusion: Infrastructure Is the Foundation of all Possibility

As shown by our analysis of the TIGHT framework, in today's business landscape, Infrastructure serves as the foundation on which all economic possibilities are built. It facilitates the development of new groundbreaking technologies, redefines a region's entire geopolitical landscape, and accelerates the progress of improvements in harnessed talent through education.

For example, infrastructure provides the physical and organizational foundations for technological innovation and deployment. The development of 5G networks requires substantial investments in telecommunications infrastructure, including cell towers and fiber-optic cables. As of 2021, global spending on 5G network infrastructure was projected to reach $8 billion, highlighting the critical role of infrastructure in enabling the next wave of digital transformation.

Regarding geopolitics, the deployment of infrastructure projects can significantly impact geopolitical relationships, affecting everything from economic dominance to national security. For instance, China's decades-long Belt and Road Initiative (BRI), with its emphasis on infrastructure development across Asia, Africa, and Europe, is a prime example of infrastructure's role in geopolitics.

Finally, infrastructure creates and facilitates environments that attract, develop, and retain talent, especially in sectors critical to national interests and a nation's economic competitiveness– factors that indicate a region's viability for investment. Perhaps this is best exemplified by the ongoing global race for technological superiority, particularly in AI and renewable energy, that has led countries to invest heavily in educational and research infrastructure. The European Union's Horizon 2020 program, with a nearly

€80 billion budget, is designed to support research and innovation projects, including those in technology and sustainable development.

This cyclical relationship between infrastructure and each of the drivers highlights infrastructure's central role in the TIGHT framework structure. Infrastructure acts as a launching pad, preparing countries and companies for the new global business landscape by enabling technological innovations, influencing geopolitical strategies, attracting skilled talent, and fostering economic resilience.

By accurately assessing and embracing nations and investments with suitably well-developed infrastructure specific to their firm's needs, companies unlock the potential to tap into dozens of emerging and frontier economies, creating a future of global business that is increasingly unlimited in scope.

4

The Geopolitical Driver

Geopolitics: The Mandate of Resilience

Amidst Russia's new tentative ally-hood with North Korea, an unending decade of US tensions with China, and the multiplying tragedies in the Middle East, "geopolitics" seems to be the keyword of the early twenty-first century.

Two decades ago, if you had asked CEOs of major global corporations about their primary concerns for the future, their answers would have been clear: they were focused on fears of financial and macroeconomic instability. To address these concerns, they employed financial hedging, using instruments like futures, options, and swaps to mitigate exposure to risks related to currency, interest rates, and commodities. A decade later, the focus shifted. When asked the same question, CEOs highlighted supply chain issues and operational hedging. They focused on diversifying production locations, sourcing strategies, and markets to reduce dependency on any single economy or supply chain, ensuring business continuity and risk mitigation across global operations.

Today, when asking industry leaders about their main preoccupation, geopolitical risk ranks as the highest concern, and, as such, geopolitical hedging is the new challenge—one that is significantly more complicated than anything that came before. With the world in considerable turmoil yet more interconnected than ever before, companies seeking to survive must conduct geopolitical hedging. They must implement factors of both financial *and* operational hedging by diversifying investments and operations across multiple regions to mitigate risks from political instability, building flexible supply chains, establishing partnerships in politically stable countries, and leveraging regional trade agreements while also preparing the company for new sub-concepts in geopolitical hedging such as "nearshoring" and "friendshoring."

Only by fully understanding how to analyze and assess geopolitical dynamics, can businesses make strategic decisions, identify growth opportunities, and build resilience against potential disruptions, ensuring long-term success in an interconnected global economy.

The Trade Story: Integration of Geo and Politics

Geopolitical factors defined here refer to the influences that geography and politics have on international relations, global dynamics, and strategic decisions within states or across regions.

Geopolitical factors essentially entail the intersection where geographic considerations directly inform or influence political decisions and vice versa. For instance, a country's geographic vulnerabilities might necessitate forming political and military alliances for security reasons, like the ones that the US shares with NATO and Panama or the open alliances shared by the European Union. These geopolitical factors are increasingly affecting the new business landscape due to the interconnectedness of global economies, advancements in technology, and rising trade tensions. For instance, one of the more pressing concerns is rising nationalism and protectionism, which have affected international trade and investment flows, compelling businesses to adapt to more fragmented markets. As an example, Brexit has led to significant changes in trade and regulatory frameworks for businesses operating in and out of the UK, with costs estimated in billions for the UK economy due to increased trade barriers.

Today, businesses operate on a global scale, making them more susceptible to geopolitical shifts like trade wars, sanctions, and regulatory changes. This is largely because, in a world where the value of global merchandise trade has exceeded $25.3 trillion dollars annually, geopolitics has become synonymous with trade and global business. As such, any new deviations in these landscapes, as exemplified by the U.S.-China trade war in 2018, have significant impacts on global supply chains (see Fig. 4.1). Tariffs imposed by both countries during the trade war have affected roughly $450 billion in bilateral trade, prompting companies to rethink their supply chain strategies. US tariffs affected around 18% of its imports, equivalent to 2.6% of its GDP,

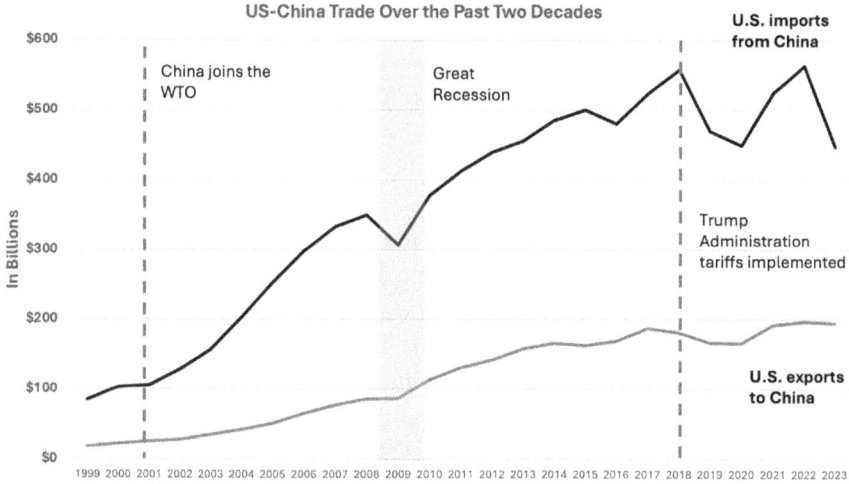

Fig. 4.1 U.S.-China trade over time (*Source* Council on Foreign Relations [cfr.org])

while China's retaliation impacted 11% of its imports, equivalent to 3.6% of its GDP. These tariffs affected multiple industries in both countries and increased costs for about two-thirds of products in the US.

Additionally, on the corporate decision-making side, friendshoring, nearshoring, and diversification have been key geopolitical topics in recent years. The rise of emerging markets has introduced new dynamics in global power structures, with businesses gaining access to new pools of raw materials and human labor. For example, companies like Samsung and Nike have expanded their operations in Vietnam, benefiting from its cheap, skilled labor pool. This has enabled the country to challenge established manufacturing powerhouses like China, alter global production dynamics, and influence traditional trade flows. As such, with geopolitical tensions in recent years highlighting vulnerabilities in global supply chains, the need for resilience and diversification is growing increasingly clear. For instance, the COVID-19 pandemic, while primarily a health crisis, exposed supply chain weaknesses and created new geopolitical considerations between the East and the West, leading investors and CEOs to call for reshoring or nearshoring manufacturing. In fact, a survey by Gartner found that 33% of supply chain leaders had moved sourcing and manufacturing activities out of China or planned to do so by 2023.

Beyond traditional trade, the digital economy's growth has made the trade of information technology and the issue of cybersecurity critical in understanding modern geopolitics. State-sponsored cyberattacks can target infrastructure and corporate data, and corporate espionage and international sabotage along traditional lines of tension can lead to massive overhauls for businesses operating across borders. For instance, the NotPetya cyberattack in 2017, attributed to Russia and targeted at Ukraine, inadvertently caused worldwide corporate losses in France, Germany, Italy, Poland, Russia, the United Kingdom, the United States, and Australia, including an estimated $300 million loss for shipping giant Maersk.

In essence, in other words, in the modern business landscape, geopolitics is almost always uttered in the same sentence as "trade" (as referring to both physical products and information) or "supply chain" issues. Businesses hoping to operate globally today must navigate a complex environment, factoring in potential sanctions and export controls, identifying cybersecurity risks, and diversifying their supply chains. While these challenges can be significant, they also present opportunities in the form of market inefficiencies for companies that are able to adapt and navigate the shifting geopolitical landscape to exploit.

Governability: The Key to Understanding Geopolitics

In our previous work, *Globalization, Competitiveness, and Governability*, we highlighted how governability plays a crucial role in shaping how countries engage with globalization and enhance their competitiveness. Governability, a key aspect of geopolitics and the visible hand of government policies and regulatory frameworks, critically influences a country's ability to leverage globalization for economic growth and development. Here, we wish to explore the intricate relationship between geopolitical factors and governability, examining how various elements can either foster or impede a country's integration into the global economy.

Governability, or the capacity of a government to effectively implement policies, execute new projects, and maintain regulatory frameworks, is essential for countries navigating the complexities of globalization. Although over-governance can lead to excessive regulations and bureaucracy that stifle growth and create countries that are protectionist and slow to adapt to new changes, the effective governance of a nation allows it to rapidly pivot to new opportunities and foster innovation, build efficient infrastructure and attract investment, and sustain economic growth through mass educational improvements.

Investment in infrastructure is a prime example of how governability can enhance a country's global competitiveness. Singapore's government, for instance, has heavily invested in state-of-the-art infrastructure projects such as Changi Airport and its port facilities. This world-class infrastructure and efficient goods market has made it one of the most competitive economies globally and allows it to consistently rank at the top in the World Economic Forum's Global Competitiveness Report.

Additionally, governments that prioritize education and workforce development can significantly boost their country's technological capabilities and competitiveness. South Korea's focus on education and R&D has propelled it to the forefront of global innovation, particularly in electronics and automobiles. With R&D expenditures reaching 4.81% of its GDP in 2018, South Korea exemplifies how strategic investment in human capital can drive global competitiveness. Finally, coherent trade policies, effective governance and rule of law in international trade, and economic openness are vital for enhancing global competitiveness. The European Union's Single Market, which promotes the free movement of goods, services, capital, and labor within the member states, is a testament to this, as the EU's internal trade constitutes more than one-fifth of its total economic activity and has allowed many member states to become global powerhouses.

Overall, governability is a critical factor in determining how effectively a country can engage with globalization and enhance its competitiveness; effective governance, characterized by strategic investments in infrastructure, education, and open economic policies, can significantly boost a country's global standing. For example, following the Korean War, South Korea was one of the poorest countries in the world, yet through effective governance, it transformed into a global economic powerhouse. The South Korean government invested heavily in education, and the expansion of universal primary and secondary education and the establishment of top-tier universities, such as KAIST (Korea Advanced Institute of Science and Technology), produced a highly educated workforce that continues to drive innovation and industrialization. In addition, the South Korean government embraced export-led growth through open economic policies that welcomed foreign investment and focused on developing globally competitive industries; major industries, such as electronics (Samsung, LG) and automobiles (Hyundai, Kia), were supported by the state through targeted industrial policies and incentives for R&D. Through simple, effective governance, South Korea has become the 10th-largest economy in the world and a leader in high standards of living for middle-class families. However, despite this, geopolitical factors that are outside of a nation's direct control can significantly influence a country's governability, affecting political stability, policy effectiveness, and overall governance capacity.

For instance, geopolitical tensions, such as border disputes or regional conflicts, can strain a government's resources and focus, potentially leading to internal instability. For example, ongoing conflicts in the Middle East have severely impacted the region's stability and governance, making it challenging for governments to maintain order and security. Additionally, global economic dynamics, influenced by factors like sanctions, trade agreements, or commodity prices, dictate national economic policies. Governments must navigate these dynamics to ensure economic stability and growth, which directly impacts their ability to govern effectively. The U.S.-China trade war, marked by reciprocal tariffs, disrupted global supply chains and impacted the competitiveness of companies both in and outside of those countries, highlighting the effect of geopolitical factors on economic policies.

Beyond this, access to and control over natural resources, often a central geopolitical concern, directly impacts a government's ability to meet its population's needs and invest in critical infrastructure. Countries rich in natural resources, such as Saudi Arabia, often have enormous streams of wealth derived from these resources but are often also condemned to the "resource curse," which causes constant government upheaval, instability, and poor rule of law and democracy. This, in turn, can also affect the population's perception of how well the government manages geopolitical challenges and can undermine public trust and legitimacy, crucial components of governability. As a case study, Peru's current administration, perceived by many of its own citizens as illegitimate and undemocratic, has caused some of the worst riots in modern South American history. These riots, triggered in part by regional geopolitics and wherein the Peruvian people have claimed a failure of institutional government and a breach of their constitution, have resulted in 50 civilians dead, one policeman casualty, and over 1400 injuries, thus showing that effective handling of geopolitical issues can bolster public confidence in the government, while perceived failures can lead to unrest and decreased governability.

In terms of global business, the governability of a nation significantly impacts its economic landscape, particularly influencing foreign business operations and supply chains. Stable and effective governance fosters a conducive environment for investment and ensures consistent regulatory frameworks, strong legal systems, and efficient infrastructure, which are essential for seamless business operations.

Measuring Geopolitical Factors

Measuring geopolitical factors within a region can help businesses discover safe overseas investments, improve their supply chain resiliency, and protect their business against sanctions and consumer boycotts. It requires a multi-dimensional approach, given the complexity of various elements such as political stability, economic conditions, security issues, and international relations. The following key metrics provide critical insights for businesses, policymakers, and investors navigating the global landscape.

First, *Political Stability*: In today's globalized business landscape, high political stability within operating countries is crucial for business efficacy, steady revenue streams, and quality long-term investments, as it reduces the risk of sudden policy changes or conflicts that can disrupt operations. For the most part, unstable nations experiencing coups, corruption, and frequent economic policy changes can severely decrease the revenue and effectiveness of a business. For instance, Venezuela has faced severe political instability for over a decade, characterized by governmental mismanagement, widespread corruption, and intense political conflicts, and the country's political crisis has had catastrophic effects on its economy and society. Venezuela has suffered from hyperinflation, with inflation rates reaching over 1,000,000% in 2018. This extreme economic instability has eroded savings, reduced purchasing power, and plunged millions into poverty. Thousands of businesses operating in Venezuela went bankrupt during this time, and foreign investors either fled or lost a majority of their capital.

In stark contrast, Singapore has maintained a high degree of political stability since its independence in 1965, underpinned by strong governance, the rule of law, and consistent policies. Singapore's political stability and pro-business policies have made it a prime destination for foreign direct investment. Major multinational corporations have all established regional headquarters in Singapore, and billions of dollars worth of investment capital have generated some of the most stable returns within Asia. As such, properly measuring political stability holds the key to successful operation in the modern era, and there are dozens of metrics that may be combined for an accurate, industry-relevant assessment. For instance, a study analyzing the World Bank's World Development Indicators dataset found that metrics including high degrees of internet access, protection of legal rights, tax revenue, and fertility rates are all significant predictors of political stability. Additionally, indices such as the Political Stability Index assesses the likelihood of government instability or overthrow based on political, economic, and social indicators, and organizations like The Economist Intelligence Unit

Fig. 4.2 Countries with the highest political stability (*Source* Statista)

(EIU) and the World Bank provide rankings and reports that help decode political stability (Fig. 4.2).

Second, *Trade Dependency and Economic Sanctions*. Companies expand across borders to improve their supply chain resiliency and diversify their assets to decrease risk. However, expansions into the wrong nations can have just the opposite effect. A nation's level of trade dependency reveals its potential economic reliance on international markets that make it vulnerable to geopolitical shifts and trade disruptions. High trade dependency can amplify the impact of global political tensions on domestic industries by exposing countries to risks from trade disputes and sanctions, thus affecting supply chains, market access, and overall economic stability. The Trade Dependency Ratio measures the degree to which a country's economy relies on international trade, indicating its vulnerability to geopolitical shifts affecting global trade, while data from the World Bank and national statistical agencies show trade as a percentage of GDP, highlighting regions heavily dependent on global trade networks (see Fig. 4.3). Businesses can use these metrics to evaluate the stability of supply chains and market access in different regions.

Another tool for businesses to use to evaluate the trade landscape of a country is sanction lists. Sanctions are essentially a reflection of underlying geopolitical tensions and conflicts. Understanding sanctions and being able to accurately forecast their implementation through evaluating an overarching geopolitical landscape of shifting relationships greatly helps modern businesses mitigate risks associated with international trade and investment. It would, for example, have been disastrous for an American company, BP, to shift their entire supply chain for oil and gas to Russia on January 1st of

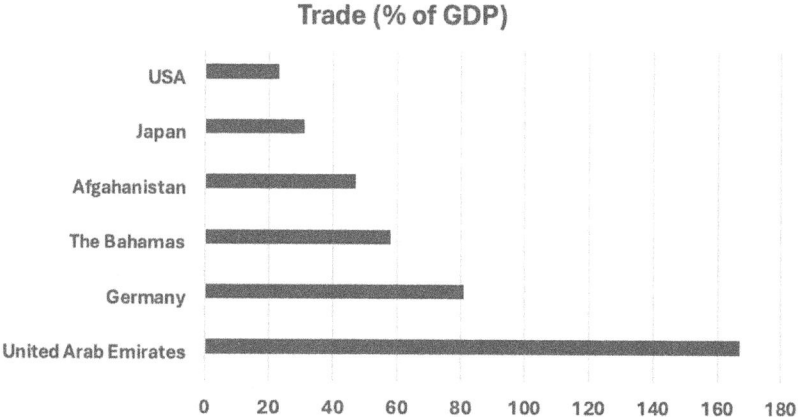

Fig. 4.3 Trade as a percentage of GDP of Afghanistan, the Bahamas, Germany, Japan, the UAE, and the United States (*Source* World Bank Data)

2022, a little more than a month before Russia invaded Ukraine but well after the US and EU had already threatened sanctions for that very action.

Investors today have to be able to quickly navigate the implications of sanctions and international tensions or face significant financial volatility and economic instability. Luckily, information is more accessible than ever before, and clearly defined Economic Sanction Lists track countries, entities, and individuals subjected to economic sanctions by various nations and allies. These lists, maintained by bodies like the US Department of the Treasury's Office of Foreign Assets Control (OFAC), offer insights into regions with heightened geopolitical risks and can greatly help a burgeoning international company navigate its way through the legalities and complications of international expansion.

Third, *Peace and Military Spending*: When a country is at peace, it minimizes the risks associated with political and social unrest, which can disrupt supply chains, inflate costs, and jeopardize the safety of employees and assets. Stable and peaceful nations are more likely to have strong institutions, effective governance, and consistent regulatory frameworks, all of which are crucial for fostering investor confidence and facilitating long-term business planning. Moreover, peace enhances the overall quality of life, leading to a more productive workforce and creating a favorable market for goods and services.

The importance of geopolitical peace for global business operations can be illustrated by comparing Syria and Japan. Syria, experiencing prolonged civil war and political upheaval, has seen its business environment decimated. The conflict has led to the destruction of infrastructure, massive displacement of the population, and severe disruptions in daily economic activities. Foreign businesses have largely withdrawn, and local enterprises struggle to survive amidst the instability. The ongoing conflict has deterred investment, halted industrial production, and caused significant economic contraction, leading to a paltry GDP per capita of $420.62.

In contrast, a nation like Japan, which has enjoyed more than seven decades of enduring peace and stability, has fostered a thriving business environment. The country's stable government, robust legal system, and consistent regulatory policies have made it a global leader in technology, manufacturing, and finance. Companies like Toyota, Sony, and Mitsubishi thrive in this secure environment, benefiting from a predictable market with plenty of foreign direct investment and strong consumer confidence and contributing to Japan's extremely high GDP per capita of $33,823.57.

The Global Peace Index (GPI), published annually by the Institute for Economics & Peace (IEP), measures the relative peacefulness of nations based on domestic and international conflicts, safety and security, and militarization and can help businesses assess and understand the levels of peace within an expansion or investment candidate. High GPI scores indicate stable environments conducive to business operations, while low scores highlight regions with potential risks; as such, businesses can use GPI data to assess market entry risks and develop strategies to operate in or avoid high-risk areas. Additionally, another metric, military expenditure, also reflects a country's potential geopolitical ambitions or security concerns. The Stockholm International Peace Research Institute (SIPRI) compiles data on global military spending, offering insights into countries' geopolitical priorities (see Fig. 4.4). High military spending can indicate potential regional conflicts or a focus on defense rather than consumer prosperity, impacting business operations and investment decisions. Understanding military expenditure patterns helps businesses assess risks related to security and geopolitical tensions.

Fourth, *Foreign Direct Investment (FDI) Flows*. Examining the modern business landscape, High Foreign Direct Investment (FDI) flows indicate investor confidence and perceptions of geopolitical safety in a region. The United Nations Conference on Trade and Development (UNCTAD) provides data and analysis on global FDI flows, showing how geopolitical tensions influence investment decisions. For instance, the emerging markets where large companies such as Apple and Proctor and Gamble have regional headquarters are also those with the highest level of FDI. Nations with high influxes of foreign capital, such as China, Singapore, Brazil, and India, all show other signs of favorable market conditions, such as the presence of the

The Share of World Military Expenditure of the 15 Countries with the Highest Spending in 2022

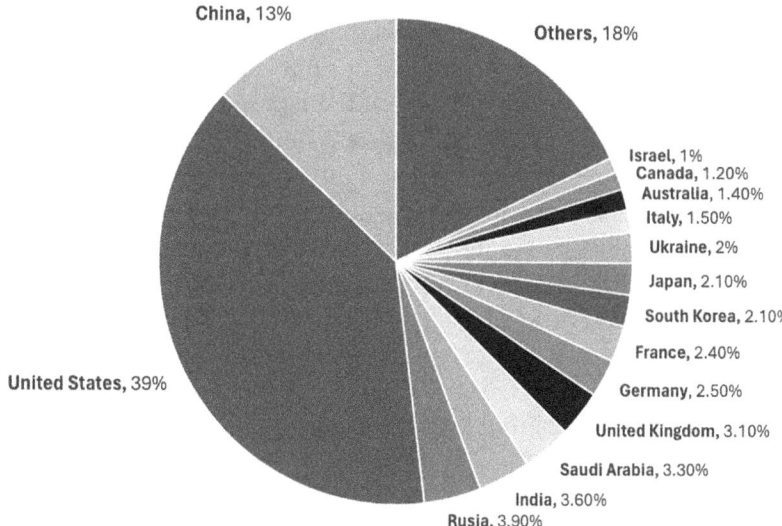

Fig. 4.4 Global military expenditure (*Source* Stockholm International Peace Research Institute)

rule of law, a steady source of talent, and strong consumer demand. Meanwhile, nations with the lowest levels of foreign investment, such as Niger, Lao, and Tanzania, are all described by the UN Council for Trade and Development (UNCTAD) as "structurally weak, vulnerable, and small economies." As such, analyzing FDI flows helps businesses understand investment climates and identify regions with favorable or unfavorable conditions for expansion.

Finally, *Human Rights Protections*. No modern global corporation wants to be boycotted, sanctioned, and featured on the front page of the *New York Times* for violations of overseas employees' rights and safety, just as no modern corporation wishes to send their current employees to nations where their safety may be compromised. Therefore, assessing human rights conditions within a country has become crucial in helping businesses align their operations with ethical standards and mitigate risks associated with violence and instability. Metrics like the GRIP score by The University of Rhode Island, as well as Human Rights and Freedom Indices created by organizations like Freedom House and Amnesty International, evaluate a country's protection of human rights and freedoms and provide a crucial tool for businesses looking to expand. For example, on one end of the extreme lies Finland, with the most extensive human rights protections on the planet and laws encompassing everything from extensive paid time off for employees to legalized same-sex marriage. This has created an environment that, perhaps ironically, makes it extremely expensive and difficult for foreign businesses to operate within Finnish borders. Meanwhile, on the other end of the extreme lies Iran and Syria, with little to no human rights protections and severe civil instability, leading to a dangerously unstable environment for any local corporation and a massive disincentive for foreign investors. Only by accurately and diligently assessing the local human rights climate can businesses find the correct balance of these protections for their corporation's needs and values.

Measuring and understanding regional geopolitics is the only way for businesses to make informed decisions in a complex global environment. By measuring these factors, stakeholders can navigate geopolitical challenges, identify opportunities, and develop strategies for sustainable growth in the global marketplace. These metrics, when analyzed together, offer a comprehensive view of the geopolitical landscape, highlighting areas of risk, stability, conflict, and cooperation.

Geopolitics Within the TIGHT Framework

Geopolitics is fueled by a sense of competition, and thus, governments of the world all wish to be the strongest in key areas that signal their economic viability and political strength: namely, technology, infrastructure, and harnessed talent. In today's interconnected world, where economic competitiveness, national security, and strategic advantage hinge on such prowess, nations leverage geopolitical strategies to foster innovation, build critical infrastructure, and harness skilled human capital.

As in previous chapters, here we want to highlight the interrelationship that exists between the geopolitical driver and the other three with an emphasis on the impact geopolitics has on the other three drivers rather than the impact the other drivers have on geopolitics. Understanding these dynamics is crucial for navigating the complexities of global business environments and harnessing opportunities in an interconnected world driven by geopolitical imperatives.

Geopolitics and Technology

Geopolitics significantly influences the development, deployment, and governance of technology, with geopolitical considerations such as competitive pressures among nations often driving technological strategies, investments, and regulations. It shapes technological advancements by influencing research priorities, funding allocations, and regulatory frameworks. Countries vying for dominance in emerging fields such as artificial intelligence, quantum computing, and biotechnology strategically invest in research and development to gain an edge in global markets. This competitive drive not only spurs technological breakthroughs but also fosters collaboration and competition among businesses, universities, and research institutions across borders.

Most significantly, geopolitical considerations drive technology investment in emerging fields. A prime example is the ongoing race for supremacy in the field of 5G technology. Countries like the United States have heavily invested in developing and deploying 5G infrastructure, recognizing its potential to revolutionize industries through faster and more reliable communication networks. This technological race has spurred massive research and development efforts, with companies like Huawei and Qualcomm leading the charge in creating cutting-edge 5G solutions. The geopolitical stakes are high, as dominance in 5G not only promises substantial economic benefits because faster upload speeds nationwide would drastically increase productivity and efficiency but also ensures strategic control over critical communication infrastructures globally. This competition has accelerated innovation, leading to advancements in related technologies such as the Internet of Things (IoT), autonomous vehicles, and smart cities, illustrating how geopolitical ambitions can drive technological progress and innovation.

Second, geopolitics has also led to the implementation of export controls and sanctions on technology transfer, particularly for dual-use technologies that have both civilian and military applications. For instance, the U.S.-China tech rivalry encompasses areas like 5G, artificial intelligence (AI), and semiconductors. This competition is not just economic but deeply geopolitical, influencing global tech standards, data security practices, and technological sovereignty. In 2020, the US government restricted Semiconductor Manufacturing International Corporation (SMIC), China's largest semiconductor manufacturer, from accessing US technology, while earlier, in 2019, the US added Huawei and other Chinese tech firms to its Entity List, limiting their access to US technology over national security concerns.

Additionally, geopolitics significantly impacts technology in the context of cybersecurity and cyber warfare, with nations increasingly investing in cyber capabilities to protect their interests and assert power. For instance, Israel, a nation facing many regional conflicts, has become a global leader in cybersecurity, driven by the need to protect its national security and economic interests. As examples of Israel's cybersecurity industry, companies such as Check Point Software and CyberArk lead the global market in cyber solutions, while Israel's Unit 8200, the military's elite intelligence and cybersecurity division, serves as a recruitment and training ground for many of the country's top cyber talent. In addition to Israel, India, as one of the world's largest digital economies and with growing geopolitical aspirations, has also significantly ramped up its investment in cyber capabilities to protect its interests and assert its power on the global stage. The government has created agencies like the National Critical Information Infrastructure Protection Centre (NCIIPC) to safeguard vital sectors such as banking, telecommunications, and defense and has also gone on the offensive by implementing the Defense Cyber Agency, a military branch tasked to defend and deploy cyberattacks. In fact, globally, state-sponsored cyberattacks are a growing facet of geopolitical conflict, targeting critical infrastructure, political institutions, and commercial entities to disrupt, spy, or influence adversary nations. According to a report by Carbon Black in 2019, 79% of surveyed organizations worldwide reported increased cyberattacks, with many attributing this rise to geopolitical tensions. For example, Russia has become a major player in the realm of cyber warfare. The 2007 cyberattack on Estonia is a prominent instance where Estonia faced a massive and coordinated series of cyberattacks on its government, banking, and media websites, severely disrupting its digital infrastructure. Companies caught in the crossfire of this incident lost millions in damages and suffered severe disruptions in their operational capacity. This incident underscored the strategic use of cyber tools in geopolitical conflicts, prompting Estonia and other nations to bolster their cybersecurity measures and technological defenses (see Fig. 4.5). In response, Estonia established the NATO Cooperative Cyber Defence Centre of Excellence (CCDCOE) in Tallinn, advancing research, training, and innovation in cybersecurity. This situation illustrates how geopolitical tensions and conflicts drive technological advancements in cybersecurity, pushing nations to develop robust defenses and cyber capabilities to safeguard their digital sovereignty and maintain geopolitical stability.

Finally, geopolitics plays a critical role in shaping technology through data sovereignty and privacy regulations as countries strive to control data flows and protect citizens' privacy within their jurisdictions. While the most high-profile instance of this in recent news is perhaps the threatened US ban of Chinese company ByteDance's subsidiary TikTok, the European Union's General Data Protection Regulation (GDPR) serves as a larger, overarching example. Enacted in 2018, GDPR was driven by the EU's geopolitical aim to assert its regulatory influence globally and safeguard the data privacy of its citizens against foreign surveillance and exploitation. As of the end of 2020, GDPR fines reached over €272 million, affecting companies worldwide and

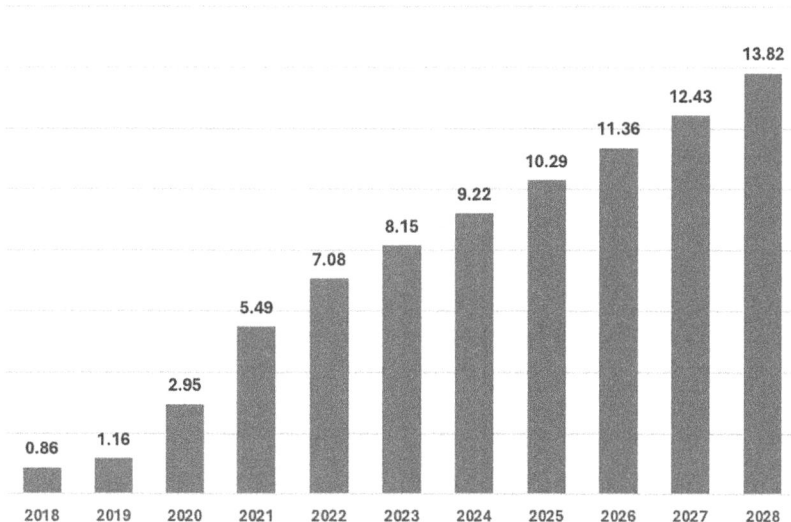

Fig. 4.5 Rise in cybercrime rates (*Source* Statista Data)

influencing global data management practices. This regulation has had far-reaching implications, compelling global technology companies to adhere to stringent data protection standards when operating within the EU. It has spurred innovation in data management technologies and privacy-enhancing tools as businesses worldwide strive to comply with these extensive regulations. GDPR's influence has also extended beyond Europe, inspiring similar legislative efforts in countries like Brazil with its General Data Protection Law (LGPD), thereby illustrating how geopolitical objectives and regional regulatory frameworks drive advancements in data privacy and security technologies globally.

These examples illustrate how geopolitics drives technological agendas, shaping global tech competition, cybersecurity landscapes, data governance policies, technology export controls, internet sovereignty efforts, and investment in emerging technologies. Geopolitical strategies significantly impact how technology is developed, deployed, and regulated worldwide, reflecting the intertwining of technological innovation and geopolitical ambitions.

Geopolitics and Infrastructure

Geopolitics significantly influences infrastructure development, with geopolitical considerations often driving or hindering infrastructure projects. For instance, geopolitical conflicts can divert government resources and attention away from infrastructure investment, as funds are often reallocated to military spending and conflict management. Instability such as wars, terrorist attacks, and violent riots deter foreign investment and disrupt the planning, construction, and maintenance of infrastructure projects. In Syria, for example, the civil war, which began in 2011, led to widespread destruction of the country's infrastructure. Once a developing nation with growing urban centers and modernizing infrastructure, Syria's roads, bridges, hospitals, power plants, and water systems have been severely damaged by years of conflict, and the ongoing war has diverted government resources toward military efforts, leaving little funding for infrastructure development or repairs. Due to this, in major Syrian cities, basic services such as electricity, healthcare, and clean water have become inaccessible to large segments of the population. Meanwhile, stable governments allow for longer-term infrastructure construction projects because peaceful transitions of power mean that a project can be passed from one administration to another without hindrance, creating stronger, more reliable infrastructure.

When President Biden announced the Build Back Better World initiative at the G7 meeting in Cornwall, UK, in 2021, it signaled the onset of a new era of infrastructure geopolitics. This move was largely seen as a direct response to China's Belt and Road Initiative (BRI), which has prioritized infrastructure as a core component of China's geopolitical strategy since its inception in 2013. The initiative aims to address the $40 trillion infrastructure gap in developing countries by 2035 by mobilizing private sector funding for quality infrastructure projects, focusing on climate, health and health security, digital technology, and gender equity and equality. Infrastructure development, both within a nation and between borders, is another cornerstone of geopolitical strategy and underpins economic growth and global connectivity. This impact is seen across various sectors beyond the more obvious use in military defense, including energy, transportation, digital infrastructure, and water resources. Major infrastructure projects such as transportation networks, energy pipelines, and digital communication highways are not only vital for domestic development but also serve as geopolitical instruments to enhance a nation's influence and connectivity within regions and beyond. Investment in infrastructure not only facilitates trade and logistics but also enhances resilience and geopolitical leverage in a rapidly evolving global economy.

Perhaps most relevant for supply chain and business operations, geopolitics plays a pivotal role in shaping energy infrastructure and global economics as countries navigate energy security issues, attempting to bolster their strategic positions by building new pipelines and distributing oil, natural gas, and other fuels as part of international trade. A prime example is the East Mediterranean Gas Forum (EMGF), established in 2019, which includes countries such as Egypt, Israel, Greece, Cyprus, and Italy. This coalition aims to harness the region's substantial natural gas reserves, driving investments in infrastructure like pipelines and liquefied natural gas (LNG) facilities. For businesses operating in these countries, the development of this energy infrastructure enhances energy security and reduces costs, providing a more reliable and affordable energy supply. It also opens new supply chain routes and markets, as the natural gas extracted and processed in the East Mediterranean can be exported to Europe and other regions. Companies involved in the construction, maintenance, and operation of these energy projects benefit from new business opportunities and partnerships. Furthermore, the improved energy infrastructure strengthens regional economic ties, facilitating smoother and more efficient trade and logistics operations across borders.

Additionally, geopolitics plays a crucial role in shaping transportation infrastructure because the strategic decisions made by nations and regional blocs to invest in transportation networks are often driven by geopolitical considerations, aiming to enhance connectivity, secure allies or trade routes, and boost economic integration. These investments can lead to the development of extensive infrastructure projects that not only facilitate the movement of goods and people but also promote economic growth and regional stability. The influence of geopolitics on transportation infrastructure is particularly evident in regions seeking to improve their competitive edge or comparative trade advantages and integrate more deeply into the global economy. A notable example of this is the African Union's African Continental Free Trade Area (AfCFTA), launched in 2021. This agreement aims to create a single continental market for goods and services, necessitating substantial investments in transportation infrastructure such as highways, railways, and ports. For businesses across Africa, improved transportation networks have been vital for reducing logistics costs, enhancing supply chain efficiency, and increasing market access. Companies benefit from faster and more reliable transit times, which facilitate just-in-time manufacturing and distribution models. Additionally, better transportation infrastructure attracts foreign direct investment (FDI) by providing a more predictable and robust framework for trade. For example, the Lamu Port-South Sudan-Ethiopia-Transport (LAPSSET) Corridor, part of AfCFTA's infrastructure development, aims to boost trade by connecting landlocked countries to international markets via Kenya's new deep-water port in Lamu. This geopolitical initiative significantly enhances the operational capabilities and competitiveness of businesses, making it easier to move goods across borders and integrate into global supply chains.

Third, geopolitics has also profoundly influenced the development and deployment of digital infrastructure, which is critical for the modern economy, affecting global economics, business operations, and supply chains. Nations recognize that control and innovation in digital infrastructure, such as broadband networks, data centers, and undersea cables, are essential for economic competitiveness and national security, and thus, geopolitical strategies often drive the creation of digital infrastructure to enhance connectivity, safeguard data sovereignty, and assert influence over global digital standards. A prime example is the European Union's effort to bolster its digital infrastructure through initiatives like the Digital Single Market (DSM) strategy. This geopolitical move aims to create a unified digital market across EU member states, fostering economic integration and competitiveness. A key component of this strategy is the deployment of the European High-Performance Computing Joint Undertaking (EuroHPC JU), which will see 32 European nations invest €7 billion between 2021 and 2027 to develop world-class supercomputing infrastructure. For businesses operating within the EU, this enhanced digital infrastructure means improved data processing capabilities, more reliable and faster internet connections, and robust cybersecurity measures. These advancements facilitate more efficient supply chain operations, enabling real-time data exchange, better inventory management, and optimized logistics. Furthermore, the strengthened digital infrastructure attracts tech companies and startups, boosting innovation and creating a dynamic digital economy. The EU's focus on digital infrastructure underscores the geopolitical drive to secure economic resilience and leadership in the global digital landscape, directly benefiting business operations and supply chains across the continent.

Fourth, because stable water flow is essential for agriculture, industry, and daily life, water resource infrastructure management has become a geopolitical priority for many nations. Control over water resources often dictates regional stability, economic development, and green energy generation, driving countries to invest heavily in infrastructure projects such as dams, irrigation systems, and water treatment plants. These investments not only ensure a reliable water supply but also enhance economic productivity, facilitate trade, and support industrial operations, thereby influencing global economic dynamics. A notable example is the Grand Ethiopian Renaissance Dam (GERD) on the Blue Nile River. This ambitious project, spearheaded by Ethiopia, aims to become Africa's largest hydroelectric power plant, which, upon completion, is expected to generate over 6000 MW of electricity and will significantly boost the country's energy supply and economic prospects. The GERD has profound implications for business operations and supply chains in the region. Reliable electricity generated from the dam will reduce energy costs for businesses, promote industrial growth, and attract foreign direct investment (FDI). Furthermore, improved water management will enhance agricultural productivity, ensuring stable food supplies and supporting agribusiness supply chains. However, the dam has also heightened geopolitical tensions with downstream countries like Egypt and Sudan, which rely on the Nile for their water needs. This geopolitical backdrop underscores how investments in water resource infrastructure can drive economic development while also reshaping regional power dynamics and supply chain dependencies. The GERD exemplifies how geopolitics influences water resource infrastructure, impacting business operations and the broader economic landscape in interconnected regions.

Finally, geopolitics also significantly influences infrastructure development in the context of environmental and climate resilience, as global economic strategies increasingly prioritize sustainable growth. Initiatives like the Paris Agreement illustrate this dynamic, driving countries to invest in renewable energy, flood defenses, and other climate resilience projects. The Green Climate Fund (GCF), which was created under the United Nations Framework Convention on Climate Change (UNFCCC), exemplifies the geopolitical commitment to addressing climate change. With $8.3 billion allocated to projects in developing countries, the GCF aims to support climate adaptation and mitigation efforts, encouraging investments in sustainable infrastructure that can guarantee a country's future economic viability and investment-worthiness in the face of climate change. This funding not only helps vulnerable nations enhance their resilience to climate impact and secure future FDI but also fosters international cooperation and economic stability by promoting green technologies and sustainable development practices that create jobs and increase human capital. Through such geopolitical initiatives, countries can collaborate on shared environmental goals, driving forward the global agenda for climate resilience and economic sustainability.

All in all, geopolitical considerations shape infrastructure development through strategic, economic, and security lenses, significantly impacting the planning, funding, and execution of infrastructure projects. The intersection of geopolitics and infrastructure underscores the importance of international relations in shaping the global infrastructure landscape.

Geopolitics and Harnessed Talent

Geopolitical considerations heavily influence the cultivation and mobilization of human talent critical to sustaining competitive advantage in global business. Nations invest in education, training, and immigration policies to attract and retain skilled professionals and entrepreneurs who drive innovation and economic growth. Geopolitical tensions and alliances shape global talent flows, influencing where expertise is concentrated and how it is leveraged across industries ranging from technology and finance to healthcare and manufacturing. Decisions, policies, and tensions can create opportunities, impose barriers, and shape the landscape for talent across various industries and academic fields. For example, post-Brexit immigration policies limited access to talent in sectors such as healthcare, technology, and education by restricting the free movement of workers from EU countries, limiting the number of foreign students able to study at UK universities, and decreasing the ability for British researchers to access EU-funded research programs, thus providing an excellent case study of the implications of geopolitics on human talent. Today's multinational companies must navigate geopolitics in their talent management strategies, adjusting their investment, location, and recruitment practices based on geopolitical stability, regulatory environments, and market access. In fact, a survey by Gartner found that 52% of HR leaders cite geopolitical instability as a top concern impacting their workforce strategy.

To begin with, geopolitics plays a critical role in shaping immigration policies, which are often influenced by a country's geopolitical stance, economic needs, and domestic political climate. These policies impact industries like technology and healthcare that rely on global talent to maintain competitiveness and innovation. Decisions around immigration can either facilitate or hinder the movement of human talent, affecting business operations, supply chains, and economic growth on a global scale. A clear example is the US H-1B visa program, which allows American companies to employ foreign workers in specialty occupations such as technology and engineering. This program is heavily influenced by geopolitical relations and domestic policy decisions. For instance, in 2020, the US government announced temporary restrictions on H-1B visas, affecting thousands of workers and companies (see Fig. 4.6). These restrictions were part of a broader geopolitical strategy and domestic policy shift, reflecting concerns over economic protectionism and national security. Such changes have direct repercussions for tech companies and other industries that depend on global talent to drive innovation and maintain competitive supply chains. When visa caps or restrictions are imposed, businesses face challenges in recruiting and retaining the skilled workforce necessary for their operations. This can lead to project delays, increased operational costs, and reduced competitiveness in the global market. The 2020 restrictions highlighted how geopolitical decisions could disrupt talent mobility, forcing companies to adapt their strategies and potentially relocate operations to other countries with more favorable immigration policies.

Additionally, geopolitics profoundly impacts education policies, particularly in the context of educational exchanges and international student mobility, which are critical for global talent development and economic growth. Educational exchanges foster cross-cultural understanding, innovation, and the transfer of knowledge, all of which are essential for economic competitiveness. The latest outbound student number for the United States reveals that over 190,000 students studied abroad, and 80% were bound for Europe and Latin America.

Geopolitical tensions and diplomatic relations between countries can significantly influence the flow of international students, affecting the availability of skilled talent and the dynamics of global supply chains. Changes in visa policies, bilateral relations, and political climates can either encourage or deter students from pursuing education abroad, thereby shaping the future workforce and talent pools for various industries. This is best exemplified by the decline in Chinese and Indian students studying in the US amidst rising

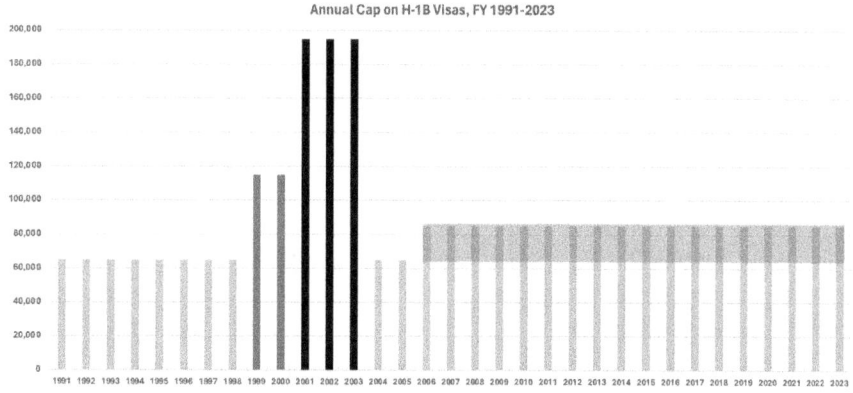

Fig. 4.6 The cap on H-1B visas (*Source* American Immigration Council)

US-Asia tensions and visa challenges. According to the Institute of International Education, the number of Chinese students in the US fell by 4.4% in the 2019–2020 academic year, marking the first drop in over a decade. These geopolitical frictions have direct implications for business operations and supply chains. For US universities and businesses, a reduction in international students means fewer skilled graduates entering the workforce, potentially leading to a talent shortage in critical sectors like technology, engineering, and research. Companies that rely on highly educated international talent to drive innovation and maintain competitive supply chains may face operational disruptions and increased recruitment costs (where sponsorship for an international student in America today can already cost tens of thousands of dollars).

Furthermore, along similar lines, geopolitics plays a pivotal role in the global phenomena of both "brain drain" and "brain gain," significantly influencing the distribution of human talent across the world. Political instability, economic crises, and conflicts in certain regions often drive highly skilled professionals to emigrate in search of better opportunities, leading to brain drain. Conversely, stable and prosperous countries benefit from brain gain, attracting talented individuals who contribute to economic growth and innovation. These geopolitical dynamics shape the availability and mobility of skilled talent, directly impacting where businesses choose to locate headquarters, establish supply chains, and conduct overall operations. A striking example of brain drain can be seen in Venezuela, where political instability and economic collapse have led to the mass emigration of skilled professionals. Since 2015, it is estimated that over 4 million Venezuelans have left the country, according to UN data, with many being university graduates and highly skilled workers. This exodus has significant implications for business operations and supply chains within Venezuela. The loss of educated and skilled professionals undermines local industries, stifles innovation, and disrupts the continuity of supply chains, leading to operational inefficiencies and increased costs for businesses trying to maintain productivity. On the other hand, countries receiving these professionals experience brain gain, enriching their talent pools and enhancing their competitive edge in various sectors. For instance, neighboring Colombia and other Latin American countries, as well as Spain and the US, have benefitted from an influx of Venezuelan talent, which supports local businesses, fuels economic growth, and strengthens the manufacturing industries within the area, making them more viable for global supply chain sourcing.

Finally, geopolitics places limitations on academia and research collaboration, influencing the flow of knowledge, talent, and funding across borders.

Political relations between countries can either foster or hinder international partnerships in scientific research and higher education, which are crucial for driving innovation and economic growth. Changes in geopolitical landscapes, such as shifts in alliances or the imposition of sanctions, can disrupt established research collaborations, affecting the development and dissemination of new technologies and knowledge. These disruptions have significant implications for business operations and economic competitiveness, as research and innovation are critical drivers of economic progress. A prominent example is the impact of Brexit on UK-based research projects and collaborations with the European Union. Before Brexit, UK universities were significant beneficiaries of EU research funding, receiving €1.3 billion between 2014 and 2018 (see Fig. 4.7). This funding supported numerous collaborative projects, facilitated talent exchange, and fostered innovation across various fields. Post-Brexit, the uncertainty surrounding EU research funding for UK institutions has posed challenges for academia and research collaboration. The potential loss of funding and restrictions on talent mobility can hinder the ability of UK-based researchers to participate in large-scale international projects, limiting access to cutting-edge research and technological advancements. For businesses, this geopolitical shift can lead to a slower pace of innovation, reduced competitiveness, and disruptions in supply chains that rely on academic research for new products and solutions.

Overall, geopolitics exerts influences on harnessed talent across various domains, shaping global economic landscapes and business operations in profound ways. From immigration policies that dictate the mobility of

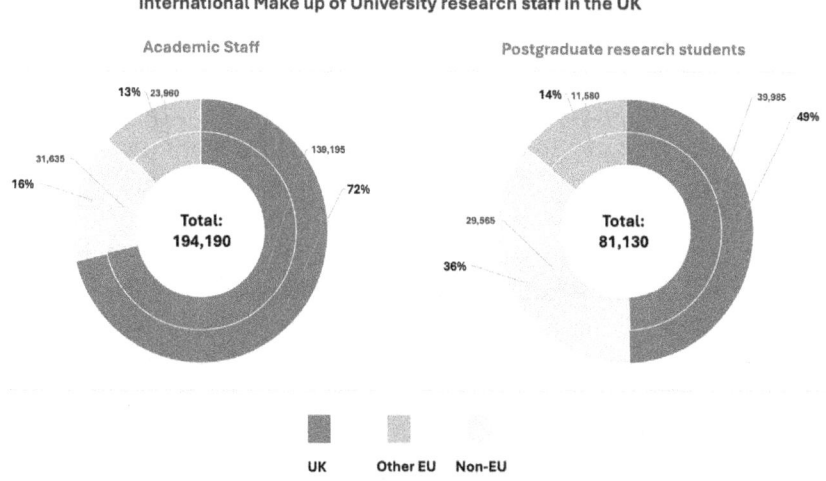

Fig. 4.7 Effect of Brexit on education (*Source* Statista)

skilled professionals to educational exchanges that foster cross-cultural knowledge transfer, geopolitical decisions impact the availability, movement, and utilization of talent worldwide. Understanding and navigating these geopolitical complexities are crucial for businesses seeking to leverage talent effectively, innovate consistently, and sustain growth in an interconnected global economy shaped by geopolitical imperatives.

Conclusion: Geopolitics Is the Matchbox That Incites All

In light of the TIGHT framework, geopolitics is the key motivation that drives forward development in all other drivers. Geopolitical strategies and tensions often dictate the direction of technological development and adoption, influence the development and prioritization of infrastructure projects—with nations investing in infrastructure to enhance their strategic position, access resources, or project power—and affect the global mobility and development of talent.

Geopolitical-driven investments in technology and infrastructure not only serve immediate strategic goals but also lay the groundwork for long-term economic and technological leadership. For example, dominance in 5G technology infrastructure can enable a country to set global standards and lead advancements in IoT, smart cities, and beyond. Meanwhile, strategic geopolitical infrastructure projects require a skilled workforce for their development, operation, and maintenance, and the creation of such infrastructure, in turn, attracts businesses and talent, fostering innovation ecosystems like tech hubs and smart cities that become magnets for global talent. Finally, national ambitions to lead in certain technological fields drive the development and attraction of specialized talent because initiatives to advance in AI or renewable energy technologies necessitate a skilled workforce, leading to investments in education and incentives to attract global talent.

In this perspective, geopolitics acts as the primary force orchestrating the development and interplay of technology, infrastructure, and talent. This interaction is crucial for nations seeking to enhance their global standing, economic competitiveness, and innovative capacity and shows the ways in which geopolitics molds the landscape of global development and innovation. For a company navigating today's global business environment, whether through its supply chains or its global expansion strategies, understanding national, regional, *and* global geopolitics is key to an efficient, profitable, and effective operation.

5

The Harnessed Talent Driver

Harnessed Talent: The Prerequisite for Success

In the global business landscape, talent has become the cornerstone of success. Skilled, adaptable, and innovative individuals drive the successful implementation of solutions and successfully navigate the complex global challenges and opportunities presented by today's rapidly evolving landscape. For instance, Satya Nadella, the CEO of Microsoft, has overseen a remarkable transformation of the company since taking the helm in 2014. Prior to his appointment, Microsoft was facing challenges related to a perceived lack of innovation and a declining market share in key areas like mobile devices and cloud computing. Nadella, a graduate of The University of Chicago's business school and a professional IT specialist before that, has revitalized Microsoft's culture and steered it toward a more mobile-first, cloud-first future. The company has experienced strong growth in revenue and market capitalization. Azure, Microsoft's cloud computing platform, has become a major competitor to AWS, and Office 365's suite of products has become the standard for offices worldwide. Thus, whether it's technological innovation, strategic expansion, or operational excellence, the right talent blends expertise and creativity to propel organizations forward, making human capital a key determinant in achieving competitive advantage and sustainable growth worldwide.

Harnessing Talent represents a holistic strategy that emphasizes the systematic and effective identification, development, utilization, and retention of individuals' skills and abilities to meet organizational needs. Organizations can more effectively harness talent by integrating various H.R. practices—such as talent acquisition, training and development, performance management, and career progression—to maximize employee contributions toward innovation, productivity, and competitiveness. For instance, Infosys, a global leader in consulting, technology services, and digital transformation, began implementing robust HR practices to maximize employee contributions toward innovation, productivity, and competitiveness. It recruits top talent through a rigorous selection process, provides its new recruits with an intensive 14-week training program, and has implemented consistent check-ins and evaluations. By integrating these HR practices seamlessly into their operations, Infosys has significantly enhanced employee engagement and loyalty, reduced turnover rates, and created high-quality solutions for clients, factors that have placed them steadily at the front of a highly competitive industry.

Due to diverse cultural, educational, and economic landscapes, developing the right talent globally poses unique challenges. In the modern business landscape, companies and organizations must navigate these complexities to build a skilled, adaptable workforce capable of driving global success, and only the company best able to achieve this comprehensive view will maintain a competitive edge and win in the new global economy.

Changes to Harnessed Talent: A New Digital Transformation

The way that harnessed talent is being used and obtained has changed rapidly in the past decade due to the complete redefinition of traditional office work. As a result of changing societal expectations, increasing globalization in the workforce, and technological advancements such as remote working platforms, this shift encompasses various aspects of how businesses operate, how employees work, and how workplaces are structured. The process of acquiring talent is more difficult than ever; according to the McKinsey Global Institute, tightening labor markets has been a trend across 30 advanced economies, and the number of job vacancies per unemployed person has increased more than 7 times in the U.S. between 2010 and 2023. In today's landscape, it has become crucial for executives to understand, implement, and adapt to this industry-wide change to operate effectively and bring their companies into modernity.

The most pressing theme in the shifting dialogue around Harnessed Talent is Digital Transformation. The adoption of digital technologies—such as artificial intelligence (A.I.), the Internet of Things (IoT), and cloud computing—has revolutionized business processes, enabling remote work, automating routine tasks, and facilitating data-driven decision-making. For instance, the widespread use of cloud services has allowed businesses to operate seamlessly across borders, with employees accessing shared resources and collaborating in real-time from anywhere in the world; in addition to increasing operational efficiency, this digital transformation has fundamentally reshaped the conversation around talent management. By integrating technologies like AI, IoT, and cloud computing, businesses have unlocked unprecedented opportunities to optimize workforce performance. For instance, global e-commerce companies like Amazon leverage AI-powered analytics to identify high-potential employees within its vast workforce. By analyzing performance metrics, customer feedback, and employee engagement data, Amazon pinpoints individuals with exceptional leadership qualities and provides them with tailored development programs. This data-driven talent identification and cultivation approach accelerates growth and strengthens its competitive advantage (see Fig. 5.1 for the growth of the US digital transformation market).

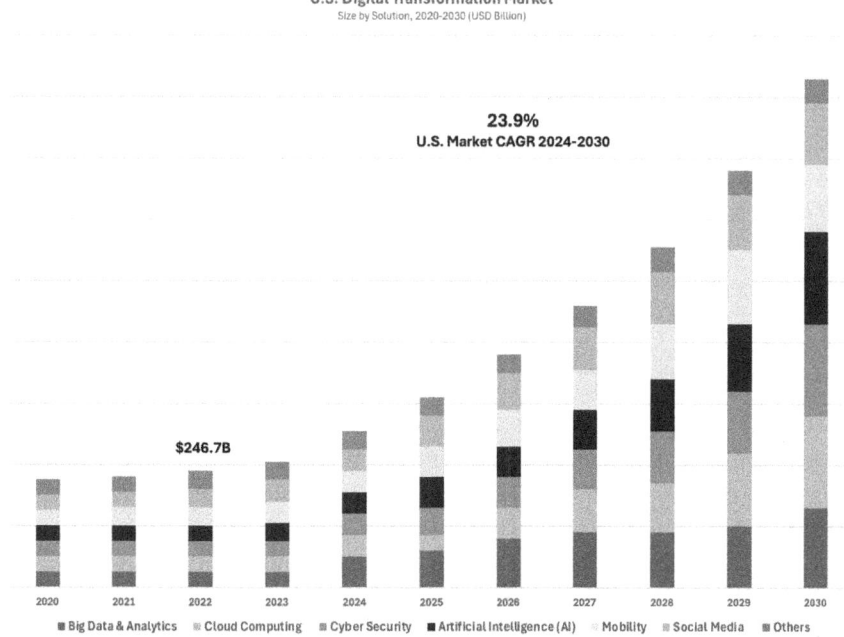

Fig. 5.1 US digital market growth YoY (*Source* Grand View Research)

Another crucial point in conversation lies around remote work and flexible employee schedules. The COVID-19 pandemic accelerated the trend toward remote work and proved that many jobs can be done effectively outside traditional office settings, and this shift has led to the adoption of more flexible work arrangements, balancing productivity with employee well-being. In fact, major tech companies like Twitter (now X) and Meta have announced permanent remote work policies, reflecting a broader acceptance of this model across industries. This ease of remote collaboration has enabled organizations to tap into global talent pools, hiring the best candidates regardless of geographical location. Companies are increasingly using platforms like Upwork and LinkedIn to hire freelancers and full-time employees worldwide, broadening their talent search beyond local markets, thus diversifying teams and bringing in varied perspectives. However, this also introduces challenges in managing cross-cultural, remote teams across different time zones and international work laws, requiring careful overseeing and effective communication strategies that can overcome language barriers, establish trust, and ensure alignment of goals. Companies able to navigate this scene gain access to top talent regardless of their geographic headquarters. They are proven to grow faster, be more responsive to shifting geopolitical challenges, and be more operationally effective at overseas product expansions.

Due to the same influences driving the growth of remote work, there is also now a large gig and freelancing economy. This growing trend toward freelance work and short-term contracts, driven by individuals seeking greater flexibility and autonomy, requires businesses to adapt their management and engagement strategies for a more transient workforce. For instance, the rise of marketplace platforms such as Uber, Airbnb, and Fiverr has enabled millions to find gig work and forced companies to rethink how they engage with and retain talent. On one hand, companies benefit from cost savings, increased scalability, access to specialized talent, and enhanced agility. By hiring freelancers on a project basis, businesses can reduce overhead costs, quickly adapt to changing demands, and tap into a global pool of experts. However, challenges include maintaining quality control, ensuring project commitment, protecting intellectual property, and building company culture. To effectively leverage freelance talent, companies must implement robust project management systems, develop talent acquisition and management strategies, and carefully balance freelancers with full-time employees.

Finally, the rapid pace of technological advancement necessitates a continuous focus on learning and upskilling to effectively harness talent. Companies are investing heavily in training programs and learning platforms to equip their workforce with in-demand skills. For example, Amazon's substantial investment in its Upskilling 2025 initiative demonstrates a commitment to developing employee capabilities in critical areas like software engineering and I.T. support, reflecting a broader industry trend toward prioritizing talent development and retention in addition to simple talent acquisition.

As part of this change in the approach to and use of harnessed talent, the workforce itself is undergoing a significant transformation. The demands of the goods and services market have changed, and, as such, the pool of human talent that will be harnessed in the future will have to shift. According to a McKinsey Global Institute report, in eight of the world's largest economies (China, France, Germany, India, Japan, Spain, the United Kingdom, and the United States), a projected one in sixteen workers may need to change occupations by 2030, a trend accelerated by the pandemic. Job growth is increasingly concentrated in high-skill areas like healthcare and STEM, while roles in sectors such as food service and office support are declining. Emerging industries like e-commerce and green energy are creating new opportunities for warehouse workers and wind turbine technicians; an aging population is driving demand for healthcare providers, while automation and technological advancements pose risks to certain jobs, such as retail clerks and administrative roles. Looking ahead over the next decade, STEP occupations are projected to grow faster than others (see Fig. 5.2).

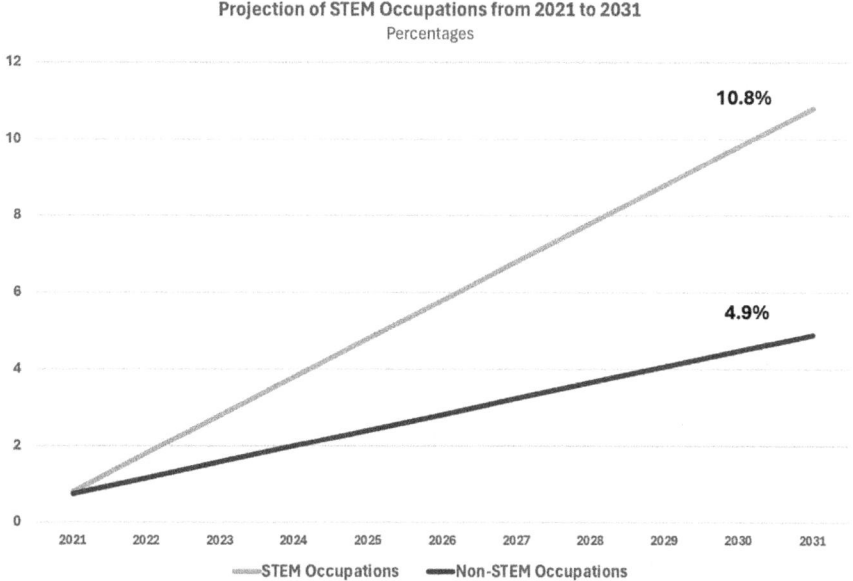

Fig. 5.2 Growth in STEM occupations (*Source* Bureau of Labor Statistics Projections)

Availability and the Challenge with Harnessed Talent

Over the past decade, sourcing human talent has become a critical problem for large corporations. According to McKinsey Research, many organizations are already grappling with a significant lack of essential talent, with 90% predicting substantial skill gaps in the near future. Concurrently, the rise of digitalization and automation is driving significant shifts in required skills, with around 40% of Americans and 34% of Western Europeans possibly needing to transition to different occupational groups by 2030 and with 40% of workers planning to leave their current jobs, employee turnover further complicates efforts to retain critical skills within organizations. As such, companies have begun to look abroad for human talent to harness, and in the near future, countries with the most cost-effective, highly skilled, and adaptable workforces will become our new global economic powerhouses.

However, sourcing and harnessing human talent internationally in the context of global business operations and international expansion involves significant cultural and educational challenges. One major challenge is the cultural differences in communication styles, work ethics, and leadership expectations, which can lead to misunderstandings and decreased team cohesion.

For instance, when IBM expanded into Japan, the company encountered challenges due to the stark contrast between Western and Japanese business cultures. Japanese employees often prioritize group consensus and long-term relationships, while IBM's American management style was more individualistic and results-oriented—a cultural clash that required IBM to adjust its management practices in Japan and emphasize relationship-building and consensus-driven decision-making in order to effectively harness local talent. Meanwhile, Uber's expansion into India highlighted the challenges of differing educational backgrounds and local knowledge. Many drivers in India lacked formal training in customer service and navigation, which are crucial in Uber's business model. Uber had to implement extensive training programs to ensure drivers met the company's service standards, addressed educational disparities, and adapted its operational model to suit the local context, including efforts to understand and integrate into India's unique cultural and regulatory environment to effectively manage and retain its driver-partners.

Skilled workers are the backbone of any economy, driving productivity, innovation, and competitiveness. Vocational and technical education contributes to economic development by creating a skilled labor force capable of supporting industry needs, attracting investment, and fostering entrepreneurship. As such, the importance of cultural, vocational, and technical education has surged in the new global business landscape, driven by rapid technological advancements, evolving job markets, and the need for company-specific specialized skills and communication methods. These educational pathways offer practical, skills-based learning designed to prepare individuals for specific trades, professions, and technical roles and help a nation align its human talent closely with the demands of modern economies and industries.

In many industries, especially those experiencing rapid growth and technological evolution, the skills gap presents the most significant challenge to effectively harnessing human talent. Vocational and technical education directly solves this problem by equipping students with the specific competencies that employers need. For example, sectors like IT, healthcare, and renewable energy are in constant need of workers who are not only knowledgeable but also possess hands-on experience. Vocational programs provide students with real-world training that ensures they are job-ready upon graduation, allowing companies to mitigate the skills gap that can hinder productivity and innovation. Countries with this type of education often see higher levels of FDI and international corporate expansion. For example, Germany's VET system serves as a model of the benefits of national vocational education. The system is structured as a dual program, where students from around the age of 15 split their time between classroom-based education and hands-on training at a company. This approach ensures that students not only acquire theoretical knowledge but also gain practical skills directly relevant to the workforce. Siemens AG, a global industrial manufacturing company headquartered in Germany, has long partnered with the German VET system to train its workforce, offering apprenticeships in engineering, mechatronics, and information technology and allowing students to work on real projects while learning. Siemens has benefited immensely from the VET system by developing a highly skilled workforce tailored to its operational needs. For instance, in its automation and digitalization divisions, Siemens relies on a continuous influx of skilled technicians and engineers who are proficient in the latest technologies and processes, so this collaboration has not only helped Siemens maintain its competitive edge in the global market but has also contributed to reducing youth unemployment in Germany.

In addition to decreasing unemployment, the availability of public vocational education helps a nation to experience rapid technological advancements that ensure its economic strength on the world stage. For instance, Singapore has made significant strides in its technological advancement by implementing the SkillsFuture initiative, which offers courses and certifications in cutting-edge technologies such as artificial intelligence, cybersecurity, and advanced manufacturing and ensures that the Singaporean workforce remains competitive in a rapidly evolving global market. As an example of corporate engagement and benefit from such national programs, Micron Technology, a leading global manufacturer of memory and storage solutions with a significant presence in Singapore, has partnered with local educational institutions and the SkillsFuture initiative to train its workforce in advanced semiconductor manufacturing and other high-tech fields. Micron's collaboration with Singapore's vocational education programs has allowed the company to tap into a highly skilled labor pool that is cost-efficient and geographically advantageous, which has been crucial for Micron as it continues to innovate and expand its operations in Asia.

Finally, by aligning educational outcomes with industry needs, vocational education not only empowers individuals but also plays a crucial role in driving forward national economies and enhancing global competitiveness. In Brazil, for example, the National Program for Access to Technical Education and Employment (PRONATEC) was launched in 2011 to expand access to vocational and technical education across the country. The program was particularly focused on reaching underserved populations, including rural residents and those who had previously dropped out of school, and offered vocational courses in fields such as manufacturing, construction, healthcare, and information technology, which are aligned with the needs of Brazil's growing industries. PRONATEC has been particularly successful in promoting social inclusion by reaching groups that are often marginalized in the job market, such as women, Afro-Brazilians, and young people from low-income families. Embraer, a leading aerospace company and one of Brazil's most prominent industrial players has partnered with PRONATEC to offer vocational training programs that prepare students for careers in the aerospace industry. This has diversified the workforce at Embraer and has supported the company's efforts to foster innovation and growth through new perspectives. Additionally, this partnership has enabled Embraer, which had previously encountered major challenges in hiring talent, to address its need for skilled technicians and engineers and develop a strong workforce essential for maintaining its competitiveness in the global market.

Measuring Harnessed Talent

Measuring a region's capacity for Harnessed Talent can help businesses discover new havens for talent acquisition and allow companies looking to expand overseas to narrow down their possible field of play. Metrics to evaluate a country's success in harnessing talent typically revolve around education, innovation, labor market efficiency, and technological readiness; these metrics provide a numerical approach to evaluating critical criteria for investors and CEOs alike and are listed here in order of relevance to the global business landscape.

Firstly, *Educational Attainment*. The most critical indicator of a region's potential for harnessed talent is the level of educational attainment within its population, particularly in fields that drive innovation and technology. Measuring the percentage of the population with tertiary education provides a snapshot of how equipped a workforce is with advanced knowledge and skills. For example, in South Korea, where, according to the OECD, nearly 70% of individuals aged 25–34 have completed tertiary education, there is a robust foundation for industries that rely on highly educated professionals. The country's focus on science, technology, engineering, and mathematics (STEM) fields, where, in 2022, according to the World Economic Forum, more than 30% of South Korean graduates graduated with a STEM degree (one of the highest ratios of STEM degrees in the world) signals its strong emphasis on fostering talent in industries like electronics, automotive, and biotechnology—a reason why South Korea leads sectors such as robotics, smartphone development, and medical automation. This commitment to STEM education, supported by government initiatives and investments in research and development, positions South Korea as an attractive destination for companies in knowledge-based industries seeking skilled professionals.

Secondly, *Labor Market Efficiency*. Labor market efficiency, a metric measuring the ability of workers to match their skills to appropriate employment opportunities quickly, plays a vital role in the success of companies looking to expand or operate within a new region. For example, Finland, ranked 15th out of 141 countries for labor market efficiency in the World Economic Forum's Global Competitiveness Report, exemplifies how a well-functioning labor market benefits businesses. Finland's adaptability in its workforce, combined with regulations that promote labor mobility and strong vocational training systems, enables companies to scale operations effectively. Whether it's filling specialized roles or adjusting to shifts in demand, businesses like the iconic Kone elevator company operating in Finland can rely on a steady flow of skilled workers, reducing hiring friction and maintaining efficient production processes. This level of labor market efficiency helps companies streamline operations, reduce costs, and remain agile in the global economy.

Thirdly, *R&D Investment as Innovation Capacity*. As with other drivers of the TIGHT Framework, for companies looking to enter new markets or expand their operations, a country's innovation capability is a key factor in determining its potential for long-term success. Innovation drives the creation of new products, technologies, and processes, enabling businesses to maintain a competitive edge in the global marketplace, and this capability is often evaluated by examining a country's research and development (R&D) investment and its output in terms of patents filed per capita. For example, according to the Swedish Institute, Sweden invests approximately 3% of its GDP in R&D, demonstrating a strong commitment to innovation. The country also ranks in the top 10 globally for patents per capita, signaling a vibrant innovation ecosystem that fosters the development of cutting-edge technologies. For companies operating in such an environment, this innovation-friendly infrastructure provides access to a wealth of new ideas, technologies, and collaborations, making Sweden an attractive hub for R&D-intensive industries such as pharmaceuticals, engineering, and information technology. By positioning themselves within a country with high innovation capability, businesses can enhance their ability to innovate, improve product offerings, and stay ahead in competitive markets.

Fourthly, *Digital Literacy*. As industries around the world undergo rapid digital transformation, the percentage of a population with digital literacy skills has become an increasingly vital metric for companies seeking to thrive in a tech-driven economy. For businesses, a workforce equipped with strong digital skills is essential for adopting new technologies, optimizing operations, and driving innovation. The availability of digitally skilled workers allows companies to integrate cutting-edge tools such as artificial intelligence, data analytics, and cloud computing into their processes. For example, in the Netherlands, surveys done by the government in 2023 reveal that 83% of Dutch people aged 16–75 have at least basic digital skills. With a workforce adept at navigating digital tools, companies in the Netherlands can more easily adapt to emerging technologies, scale digital initiatives, and remain agile in a rapidly evolving global market.

Finally, the *Global Talent Competitiveness Index (GTCI)*. The GTCI is a comprehensive measure that evaluates 134 of the world's countries' ability to grow, attract, and retain talent, making it a crucial metric for companies considering expansion or investment in new regions. A strong ranking on the GTCI indicates that a country has effective policies and infrastructure to support talent development and retention, which is vital for businesses seeking long-term success. For instance, Switzerland, Singapore, and the U.S. are the top three ranked countries for talent competitiveness. Ireland ranks 12th on the GTCI, reflecting its robust framework for fostering talent through education, professional development, and favorable immigration policies. Ireland's ability to attract international talent, supported by its high quality of life and competitive business environment, makes it an appealing destination for global companies. Firms operating in Ireland can benefit from a steady influx of skilled professionals while leveraging strong local talent pipelines. This talent competitiveness ensures that companies have access to the human capital necessary to drive growth, innovation, and operational excellence in an increasingly interconnected global economy.

In the modern global business landscape, a country's capacity to harness talent is pivotal for attracting investment and fostering economic growth. These metrics offer a multidimensional view of a country's readiness in the new global business landscape by evaluating its success in developing, attracting, and leveraging human capital. Evaluating educational attainment and the number of STEM graduates offers insights into the available foundational knowledge and technical expertise. Labor market efficiency reflects how well a country adapts to changes and meets business needs, while innovation capability highlights its potential for technological advancement and competitive edge. Digital skills among the population are crucial for thriving in a digital economy, and a strong Global Talent Competitiveness Index (GTCI) ranking signals effective policies for growing, attracting, and retaining talent. By examining these metrics, businesses can make informed decisions about where to expand and invest, choosing regions that offer a well-rounded and capable workforce. Countries like South Korea, Finland, Sweden, the Netherlands, and Ireland exemplify how strong performance across these areas can create attractive environments for global business, driving success and innovation in an interconnected world. Figure 5.3 illustrates how harnessed talent fits within the TIGHT framework.

Harnessed Talent Within the TIGHT Framework

Human talent, a region's most valuable asset, is pivotal in shaping technological advancements, infrastructure development, and geopolitical standing. A region's workforce's caliber, quantity, and diversity directly influence its ability to innovate, attract investment, and assert its influence on the global stage. From Silicon Valley's tech giants to emerging hubs in Asia, the correlation

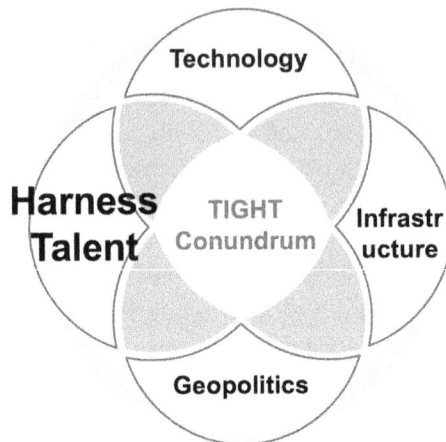

Fig. 5.3 Illustration of how harnessed talent fits within the TIGHT framework

between human capital and regional development is undeniable: a region's technological progress is directly linked to its human resources. Skilled engineers, scientists, and programmers drive innovation, creating new technologies and applications that fuel economic growth and social progress. A well-educated and adaptable workforce is essential for attracting and retaining foreign investment because businesses seek regions with large pools of talent to support their operations, and, in turn, these large foreign investments fund further technological growth.

Beyond technology, human capital also shapes a region's infrastructure development. A skilled workforce designs, constructs, and maintains essential infrastructure projects, such as transportation networks, energy systems, and communication networks, that ensure a region's operations run smoothly and connectedly. Finally, a region's ability to attract and retain human talent can influence its geopolitical standing. A strong talent pool can enhance a region's attractiveness to foreign investors, diplomats, and international organizations, strengthening its global influence and reputation.

Harnessed Talent and Technology

The effective harnessing of human talent is a key driver of technological advancement, fueling innovation, creativity, and interdisciplinary collaboration. When individuals with diverse skills and expertise come together, they generate groundbreaking ideas that propel new technologies forward; this collaboration unlocks unique solutions to complex challenges across fields like AI, healthcare, and renewable energy, where creative problem-solving and innovation are essential. By fostering an environment where talent is nurtured and deployed effectively, technological development not only progresses more rapidly but also becomes more robust, with high-quality and reliable solutions emerging from the combined efforts of skilled professionals.

Moreover, harnessing talent accelerates the pace of technological advancement and enhances a nation's global competitiveness. Skilled individuals streamline the development of cutting-edge technologies, such as the IoT, which is revolutionizing industries and reshaping economies worldwide; their expertise leads to faster, more efficient progress while ensuring that solutions are scalable and adaptable. Nations and regions that invest in developing and utilizing their talent pools are better positioned to lead in global markets, attracting investment and creating a technological edge that fosters long-term economic growth. Talent, therefore, is not just a catalyst for innovation but a vital resource for maintaining technological leadership and driving the A.I. revolution forward.

Most importantly for the Technology driver, harnessed talent fosters innovation and creativity, which is crucial for driving progress in industries such as I.T., biotechnology, and renewable energy. Silicon Valley is a prime example of how effectively harnessed talent can create a vibrant global business environment. As a leading hub for technological innovation, it attracts top talent worldwide, driving forward advancements that reshape industries and markets. Companies like Google, Apple, and Facebook have set benchmarks in innovation and technological development– Google's significant investment in employee development and research—spending $27.57 billion on R&D in 2020—demonstrates how nurturing talent can yield transformative results.

Secondly, effectively harnessed talent significantly boosts the speed of technological advancement by leveraging expertise, problem-solving skills, and collaborative efforts. Talented professionals can accelerate technological advancement through their expertise, problem-solving skills, and collaborative efforts. This allows businesses to rapidly adapt to and integrate emerging technologies like AI, blockchain, and quantum computing. India's I.T. and software services sector provides a compelling example of these advantages. The country's information technology (I.T.) and software services industry has grown exponentially, and the emphasis on education and skill development in STEM fields has created a large and highly skilled workforce with approximately 4.36 million employees and a contribution of around $177 billion to the economy in 2019. India's I.T. sector highlights the economic impact of a well-developed talent pool. For global investors and companies expanding internationally, tapping into markets with robust talent bases like

India can lead to accelerated technology development, smoother integration of new technologies, and a competitive edge in the global marketplace. This strategic approach not only enhances operational efficiency but also positions companies advantageously for future growth and innovation.

Additionally, harnessing highly skilled talent is crucial for ensuring quality and reliability in technological advancements. Skilled professionals contribute to producing high-quality outputs, minimizing errors, and enhancing the reliability of technological solutions and products, and their ability to address complex challenges with innovative solutions is particularly important in technology development. SpaceX's achievement in reusable rocket technology serves as a prime example. SpaceX has transformed space technology by developing rockets that significantly lower the cost of space travel—a breakthrough that was realized through the efforts of a talented team of engineers and scientists who pushed the boundaries of innovation. SpaceX's Falcon 9 rocket, which has successfully landed over 100 times since 2015, underscores the importance of harnessed talent in achieving technological milestones. Leveraging such talent not only drives technological progress but also provides a competitive edge by ensuring strong and innovative solutions in the global marketplace.

Fourthly, for companies seeking to expand into foreign markets, global competitiveness and workforce resilience are significant advantages provided by effectively harnessed talent. Nations or organizations that excel in leveraging their human capital attract investment, stimulate economic growth, and sustain a competitive edge in the global marketplace through technological advancements. Estonia exemplifies these benefits with its remarkable digital transformation. Known sometimes as "e-Estonia," the country has utilized its skilled workforce to become one of the most advanced digital societies worldwide. From digital governance to e-residency programs, the country has leveraged its tech-savvy workforce to implement innovative tech solutions. By focusing on developing digital skills and infrastructure, Estonia has enabled over 99% of public services to be accessible online 24/7. This extensive digital infrastructure not only highlights the societal impact of harnessed talent but also underscores the importance of workforce resilience because a continuously upskilled and adaptable workforce enhances industry resilience, allowing businesses to stay competitive and agile amid technological disruptions. For global investors and companies looking to enter new markets, the ability to tap into regions with high levels of digital sophistication and workforce agility can offer a substantial competitive advantage, ensuring that they can operate effectively, respond rapidly to technological changes, and secure their position in a dynamic global economy.

Finally, in the global race for artificial intelligence (AI) supremacy, the strategic harnessing of talent has become crucial for maintaining technological leadership. Countries like the United States, China, and the United Kingdom are making substantial investments in A.I. research and development, driven by the expertise of individuals in academia and the tech industry. This focus on talent is reflected in the anticipated global spending on A.I. systems, which is expected to reach $110 billion by 2024. As companies navigate this competitive landscape, staying ahead in tech talent acquisition has never been more important. According to a recent report by McKinsey Global Institute, job postings in fields related to 15 key technology trends grew by 15% between 2021 and 2022 despite an overall decrease in global job postings. Generative A.I., in particular, saw a 44% increase, illustrating the surging demand for specialized skills. For global investors and businesses, these insights underscore the value of investing in regions with deep pools of tech talent. The ability to access and leverage skilled professionals can drive significant technological advancements and offer a competitive edge, and as the tech landscape evolves, companies expanding into new markets must prioritize regions with a strong talent base to stay competitive and capitalize on emerging opportunities in AI and other key technologies. As noted in Fig. 5.4, the global AI market is expected to grow significantly.

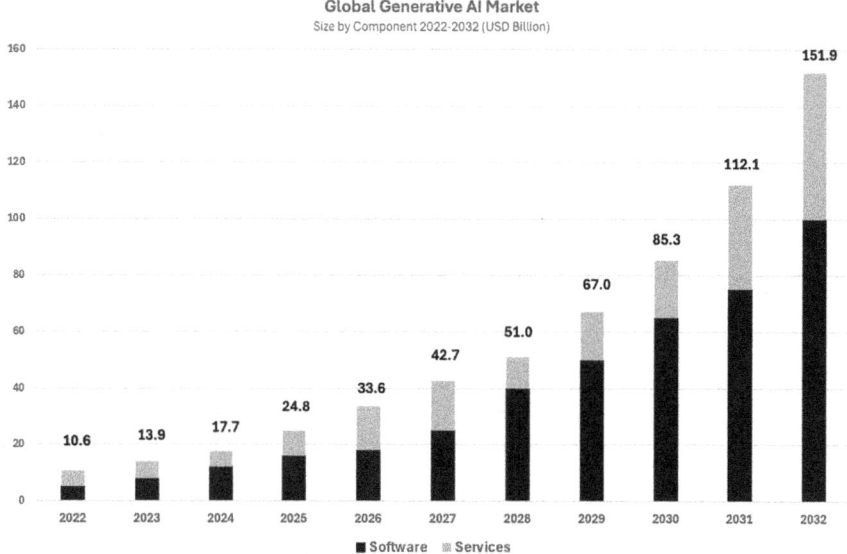

Fig. 5.4 Growth of generative AI (*Source* Market.us)

In summary, effectively harnessed talent is a critical driver of technological advancement, fostering innovation, creativity, and interdisciplinary collaboration. Skilled individuals not only accelerate the pace of technological development but also enhance a nation's global competitiveness through rapid adaptation to emerging technologies. From revolutionizing financial services to pioneering sustainable infrastructure and advancing smart city solutions, the impact of harnessed talent on technology is profound and far-reaching. By investing in and nurturing talent, businesses can position themselves at the forefront of technological progress, ensuring they remain competitive and agile in a dynamic global market.

Harnessed Talent and Infrastructure

Harnessing human talent is a precondition for infrastructure development, driving efficient project design and execution, improving sustainable development practices, and fostering innovation in infrastructure solutions. A skilled workforce is essential for creating and implementing comprehensive infrastructure plans that meet the needs of a growing population while minimizing environmental impact. By investing in education and training programs, regions can cultivate a pool of professionals with the expertise to design and construct sustainable infrastructure projects, such as transportation networks, energy systems, and water management facilities. A strong workforce can develop innovative solutions to address issues such as traffic congestion, housing shortages, and pollution, ensuring that cities remain sustainable and livable for future generations.

Most importantly, well-employed, harnessed talent plays a crucial role in the efficient design and effective execution of infrastructure projects, offering substantial benefits for global businesses and investors. Skilled professionals in engineering, architecture, and urban planning are essential for creating infrastructure that meets the needs of the population while optimizing costs and resources. The development of Kenya's M-Pesa mobile banking service provides a compelling example of this impact on digital infrastructure. Spearheaded by talented I.T. professionals, M-Pesa has revolutionized financial inclusion by delivering secure and accessible financial services via mobile infrastructure. With over 37 million active users and more than 11 billion transactions annually, M-Pesa has significantly enhanced Kenya's financial infrastructure and contributed to economic development while also streamlining business operations in the region by providing a reliable and widespread digital payment system, reducing the need for cash transactions, and improving the efficiency of financial exchanges. For global businesses and investors, the success of M-Pesa underscores the advantages of investing in regions with a highly skilled workforce capable of driving efficient project design and execution. By leveraging local talent, companies can ensure that infrastructure projects are both cost-effective and responsive to market needs, paving the way for successful expansion and investment in emerging markets.

Secondly, harnessed talent is pivotal in advancing sustainable development practices within infrastructure projects, offering significant benefits for global businesses and investors. Professionals trained in sustainable development can integrate green technologies and eco-friendly materials, promoting long-term environmental sustainability. For instance, Dubai, by leveraging the expertise of talented architects, engineers, and environmental specialists, has created the first net-zero energy development in The Emirates. This project features over 500 villas and a variety of amenities powered by renewable energy, achieving a 50% reduction in energy consumption compared to conventional developments. The Sustainable City has also attracted foreign businesses and foreign direct investment (FDI) to the region by showcasing Dubai's commitment to innovative and sustainable infrastructure, and for global investors, the success of The Sustainable City highlights the advantages of investing in regions with a strong focus on sustainable infrastructure. By harnessing local talent with expertise in green technologies, companies can contribute to environmental sustainability, enhance their market reputation, and align with global sustainability goals. This approach ensures that infrastructure investments are not only economically viable but also support long-term environmental and social benefits, making them more attractive to eco-conscious stakeholders and markets.

Thirdly, harnessing human talent is crucial for driving innovation in infrastructure solutions and addressing complex challenges such as developing smart cities, modern transportation networks, and resilient energy grids. The Netherlands exemplifies this impact with its advanced flood defense systems. By leveraging the expertise of hydraulic engineers, environmental scientists, and urban planners, the Netherlands has developed sophisticated infrastructure to protect its low-lying areas from flooding. The Maeslantkering, a massive movable barrier integral to the Delta Works project, showcases this innovation. This monumental system, which has cost over €5 billion, is renowned for its engineering prowess and environmental planning and has significantly improved business operations by reducing the risk of flood-related disruptions, thereby enhancing the overall economic prospects of the Netherlands. For global businesses and investors, the success of the Netherlands' flood defense systems illustrates the value of investing in regions with a strong talent base for infrastructure innovation. By harnessing local expertise, companies can benefit from cutting-edge solutions that enhance resilience and adaptability to future demand, thus mitigating the risks associated with environmental challenges and ensuring that infrastructure investments are forward-looking and capable of supporting long-term growth and stability.

Additionally, harnessing the right expertise significantly enhances the quality and durability of infrastructure projects, ensuring they are built to last and reduce the need for frequent repairs. This increases reliability and overall quality for essential infrastructure such as roads, bridges, buildings, and utilities. For instance, the Smart Nation Initiative, by leveraging talent across various sectors, has made significant technology-driven infrastructure improvements in Singapore's transport, healthcare, and public services. A notable project under this initiative is the development of the Smart Urban Mobility solution, which employs AI and IoT technologies to boost public transport efficiency. According to the Singaporean government, this initiative has resulted in a 10% improvement in public transport reliability, showcasing how expertly designed infrastructure can enhance the quality and functionality of urban systems. The Smart Urban Mobility solution has also improved business operations by increasing workplace efficiency, broadening access to the city's labor pool, and enhancing overall economic prospects. For global businesses and investors, Singapore's success highlights the advantages of investing in regions where talent drives infrastructure innovation because, by focusing on areas with a strong emphasis on quality and durability, companies can ensure their investments are supported by reliable and efficient infrastructure ultimately contributing to smoother operations and long-term economic benefits.

Finally, harnessing talent effectively allows nations and regions to respond swiftly to urbanization pressures by developing infrastructure that can accommodate growing populations. This includes expanding housing, transportation, water, and sanitation systems to meet increasing demands. China's high-speed rail network exemplifies this capability. As the largest network of its kind globally, it showcases China's engineering talent and its proficiency in executing large-scale infrastructure projects rapidly. Spanning over 37,900 kilometers as of 2021, with trains reaching speeds of up to 350 km/h, the network has dramatically reduced travel times between major cities and enhanced economic connectivity. The high-speed rail network has greatly benefited businesses operating in China by improving access to major markets, reducing logistics costs, and facilitating smoother supply chain operations. Additionally, it has better economic prospects for urban areas by boosting regional development, attracting investment, and stimulating local economies. The success of China's high-speed rail network underscores the benefits of investing in regions with a strong talent base capable of addressing urbanization challenges effectively; by supporting infrastructure projects that improve transportation efficiency and connectivity, companies can benefit from enhanced market access, streamlined logistics, and a more robust economic environment, paving the way for successful expansion and investment in rapidly urbanizing areas (Fig. 5.5).

Overall, harnessing human talent plays a pivotal role in transforming infrastructure development, offering significant benefits for businesses and investors globally. Skilled professionals drive innovation in project design and execution, leading to improved efficiency and functionality in infrastructure; integrating sustainable practices advances environmental goals and attracts investment by showcasing a commitment to green technologies; innovation in infrastructure solutions enhances economic resilience and operational efficiency; and effective responses to urbanization challenges improve market access and economic prospects for businesses. Collectively, these examples illustrate how effectively harnessed talent ensures that infrastructure projects are not only high-quality and durable but also adaptable and responsive to future demands. Leveraging regions with a strong talent base can enhance operational efficiency, economic growth, and a competitive edge in an increasingly interconnected and infrastructure-dependent world.

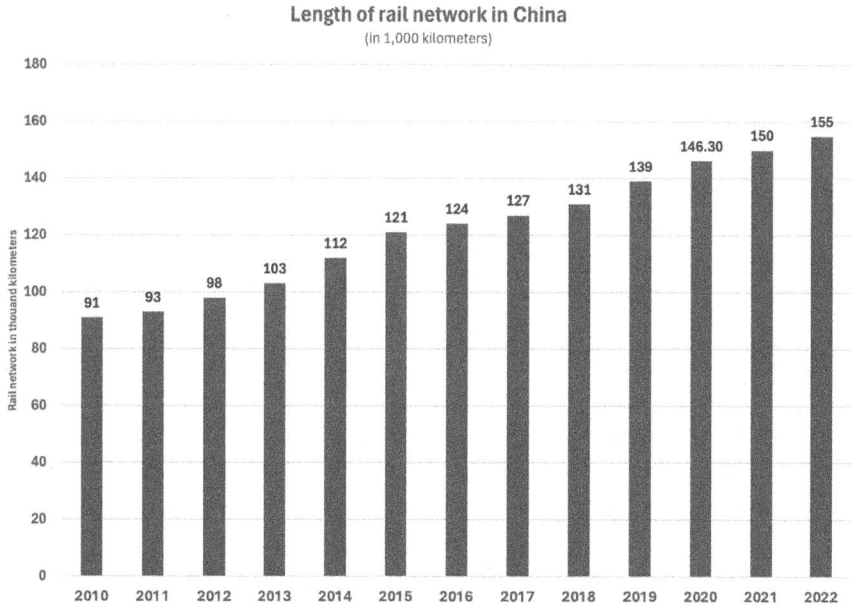

Fig. 5.5 The growth of Chinese railways (Source China Daily)

Harnessed Talent and Geopolitics

The effective harnessing of human talent is a critical factor in shaping a region's geopolitical standing. A well-educated and culturally diverse population can serve as a powerful tool for soft power and cultural diplomacy; by promoting cultural exchange and understanding, countries can strengthen their relationships with other nations and build a positive international image. Additionally, a skilled workforce is essential for maintaining national security and defense. A well-trained and motivated population can contribute to the development of strong military and intelligence capabilities, ensuring a country's sovereignty and protecting its interests.

Firstly, when a nation effectively harnesses its talent, it can achieve significant economic growth and technological advancements that elevate its geopolitical standing, creating an attractive environment for businesses to operate in. Countries with strong talent pools often lead in high-value industries, attract international investment, and shape global trade dynamics. This not only boosts their economic power but also strengthens their political influence on the world stage. Germany exemplifies this power dynamic—renowned for engineering excellence, Germany's robust technical and vocational education system produces highly skilled engineers and technicians, driving its export-oriented manufacturing sector. In 2019, the machinery and equipment sector alone contributed approximately €228 billion in revenue. This economic prowess not only supports business activity in Germany but also plays a role in its geopolitical influence.

A clear demonstration of Germany's geopolitical power occurred during the Greek financial crisis in the 2010s. As Europe's largest economy, Germany played a central role in shaping the European Union's response to the crisis, with economic strength having had a significant influence on bailout negotiations. Germany pushed for austerity measures and economic reforms in exchange for financial support—a pivotal moment for businesses operating in Europe, as Germany's leadership ensured the stabilization of the Eurozone, which was crucial for maintaining market confidence and economic continuity across the region. Germany's ability to wield such influence highlights how a nation's economic power, driven by effectively harnessed human talent, can have far-reaching impacts on geopolitical affairs. For businesses, this makes Germany an appealing location, not only due to its strong talent pool but also because of the economic and political stability it offers, which are vital for long-term strategic planning and investment.

Secondly, countries that excel in harnessing talent often become global leaders in technology and innovation, allowing them to set international standards, influence regulations, and gain strategic advantages in emerging technologies. This leadership can shift global power balances and significantly enhance a nation's geopolitical positioning, as it holds sway over critical sectors such as cybersecurity, artificial intelligence, and digital commerce. Businesses operating in these environments benefit from proximity to cutting-edge technology and the ability to influence global trends.

A prime example of this is the United States, where the concentration of tech talent in Silicon Valley has established the country as a dominant force in global technology. Silicon Valley, home to some of the world's most innovative companies, has played a pivotal role in advancing digital innovation, shaping international standards in areas such as data privacy, cybersecurity, and artificial intelligence. The U.S. Department of Commerce estimated that the digital economy accounted for 10% of the U.S. GDP in 2024, highlighting the immense economic impact of technological leadership driven by its skilled workforce. For businesses, this technological supremacy translates into opportunities for growth, innovation, and global influence. Companies operating in the U.S. benefit not only from access to top talent but also from being in a strategic position to influence the development of global standards and policies, giving them a competitive edge in international markets.

Skilled professionals in fields like the arts, media, and education not only contribute to a country's creative output but also help promote its values, ideals, and culture on the world stage. This enhanced cultural influence can improve diplomatic leverage, creating favorable conditions for international relations and cooperation. For businesses looking to operate in or invest in a region, a nation with strong, soft power can enhance the brand appeal and market penetration by associating with a globally admired culture; they can also create a more welcoming and collaborative environment, fostering trust and engagement with international partners in negotiations and collaborations, making them an attractive partner in global business ventures. South Korea's harnessing of talent through its cultural industries is a powerful example of how soft power can be achieved. The rise of the Korean Wave, or "Hallyu," has catapulted South Korean entertainment—such as K-pop, films, and television dramas—onto the global stage. The international success of K-pop groups like BTS and BLACKPINK, alongside critically acclaimed films like Parasite, which won the Academy Award for Best Picture in 2020, exemplifies South Korea's strategic investment in creative talent and cultural exports. This cultural diplomacy has significantly expanded South Korea's global cultural footprint, fostering positive perceptions of the country around the world. The shared experience of consuming South Korean culture has enhanced the nation's relationships with countries across Asia, the Americas, and Europe, enabling smoother diplomatic interactions and stronger bilateral ties. Economically, the Korean Wave has generated substantial revenue through increased tourism, product sales, and merchandise related to K-pop and Korean dramas, strengthening South Korea's economic standing.

Fourthly, effectively harnessing talent in national security and defense is crucial for bolstering a country's security apparatus. Skilled professionals in defense, intelligence, and cybersecurity contribute to advanced research and development, enhancing strategic capabilities and safeguarding national interests. This not only strengthens the country's ability to project power on the global stage but also improves geopolitical stability by ensuring it can respond to emerging threats and protect its assets. For businesses, operating in a country with strong national security can provide a more stable environment, fostering confidence for investment and expansion. For example, by investing heavily in cybersecurity and military technology, Israel has positioned itself as a global leader in these fields. Its talent pool has enabled the development of cutting-edge defense systems, significantly impacting international security policies and shaping global alliances. Israel's commitment to innovation is reflected in its R&D spending, which accounts for about 6% of its GDP, the highest ratio in the world as of 2023. A large portion of this investment is channeled into cybersecurity, fortifying Israel's geopolitical influence and ensuring the resilience of its defense infrastructure. For businesses, Israel's robust cybersecurity landscape offers opportunities for partnerships in defense technology. At the same time, the country's secure environment promotes stability for commercial operations, making it an attractive destination for investment in the technology and defense sectors.

Additionally, a highly skilled workforce plays a pivotal role in ensuring economic resilience and stability, which are vital components of a nation's geopolitical influence. Countries with diversified and robust economies can better withstand global economic fluctuations, maintain diplomatic engagement, and assert their economic power on the world stage. This stability not only reinforces their geopolitical position but also enhances their ability to shape global economic trends and policies. For businesses, initiatives for resilience create new opportunities for investment and collaboration in emerging industries, while the economic stability it fosters provides a favorable environment for long-term business operations and growth. For example, Saudi Arabia's Vision 2030 initiative seeks to diversify its economy and remove oil dependency. By investing in education and attracting global talent in sectors like renewable energy, tourism, and technology, Saudi Arabia is positioning itself as a key player in reshaping energy geopolitics and driving regional development. With plans to invest over $300 billion in its industrial and logistics sectors by 2030, Saudi Arabia is harnessing talent to build a more resilient and diversified economy.

Finally, talent-driven innovation and operational efficiency are key drivers of global competitiveness, which can significantly influence a region's trade relationships and geopolitical clout. Nations that harness talent effectively, especially in high-tech industries and advanced manufacturing, position themselves to secure favorable trade agreements, dominate global supply chains, and enhance their overall geopolitical leverage. By excelling in these areas, they boost their economic prospects and strengthen their ability to shape global trade dynamics. China's "Made in China 2025" initiative exemplifies this strategic approach. The country is channeling its vast pool of domestic talent, particularly in STEM fields, to transition from being the world's manufacturing hub to a global leader in high-tech industries like AI, electric vehicles, and renewable energy. With over 4.7 million STEM graduates produced annually, China is rapidly advancing in critical technologies, positioning itself for greater technological independence. For businesses, China's push toward technological leadership reshapes global supply chains and trade dynamics, creating new opportunities and competitive pressures across industries. The country's emphasis on innovation enhances its ability to negotiate favorable trade terms, making it a powerful force in the global marketplace. As noted in Fig. 5.6, China, India, and the U.S. lead the world in STEM graduates, with China far outnumbering all other countries.

Conclusion: Harnessed Talent Is the Driving Force Behind Corporate Expansion

In today's ever-shifting global economy, the effective harnessing of human talent has emerged as a crucial determinant of corporate expansion and investment strategies. As businesses seek to establish a foothold in new markets, regions that demonstrate a high capacity for nurturing and deploying skilled professionals become increasingly attractive. The ability to leverage local talent not only drives technological advancements but also shapes the infrastructure and geopolitical landscape in ways that significantly influence business decisions. Regions that excel in cultivating talent create a compelling value proposition for corporations looking to optimize their operations and achieve sustainable growth.

Harnessed talent is instrumental in fueling technological innovation, which in turn drives corporate expansion. Companies are drawn to regions

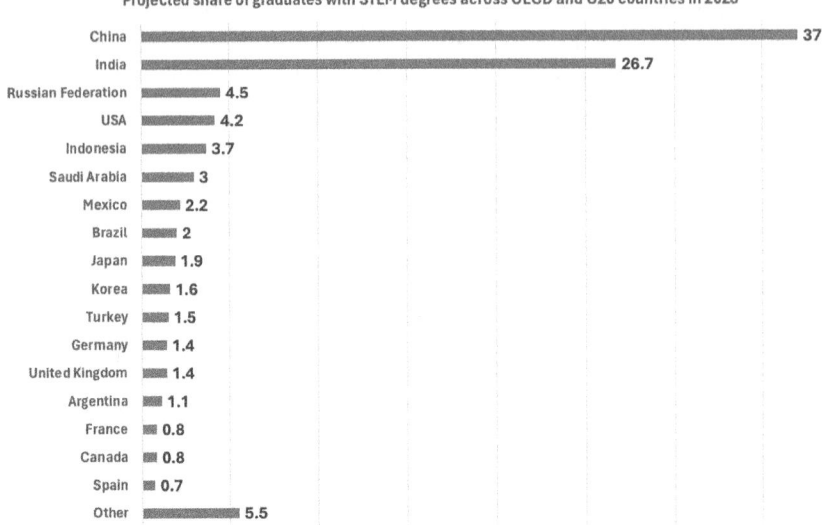

Fig. 5.6 Growth of talent across OECD and G20 (*Source* Statista)

where a diverse pool of skilled individuals can foster groundbreaking advancements and enhance competitive positioning. Whether through the development of cutting-edge technologies or the integration of emerging innovations, a well-developed talent pool accelerates progress and provides businesses with the tools needed to stay ahead in a rapidly evolving market. Regions such as Silicon Valley and India's I.T. sector exemplify how talent-driven technological prowess can attract global investments and shape industry standards, underscoring the critical role of human capital in driving technological leadership.

The impact of harnessed talent extends beyond technological innovation to influence infrastructure development, which is vital for business operations. Skilled professionals contribute to the design and execution of efficient, sustainable infrastructure projects that support economic activities and improve quality of life. For instance, Kenya's M-Pesa and Dubai's Sustainable City illustrate how local talent can revolutionize infrastructure and create environments conducive to business success. By investing in regions with robust infrastructure capabilities, companies benefit from enhanced operational efficiency, reduced costs, and better access to markets, reinforcing the link between talent and infrastructure in shaping strategic business decisions.

Finally, a region's ability to harness talent enhances its geopolitical influence, which can be a decisive factor in corporate expansion strategies. Countries that excel in leveraging human capital often emerge as leaders in global trade, technology, and cultural diplomacy, offering businesses a stable and influential operating environment. South Korea's cultural diplomacy and Israel's advancements in cybersecurity exemplify how talent-driven geopolitical power can influence trade dynamics and security considerations. For businesses, investing in or expanding into regions with strong geopolitical standings can provide strategic advantages and align with broader international goals, making talent a pivotal element in global business strategy.

In essence, the effective harnessing of human talent is not merely a factor in regional development but a fundamental driver of corporate expansion. Regions that excel in nurturing talent offer significant advantages across technology, infrastructure, and geopolitics, making them attractive destinations for investment and growth. For corporations, understanding and leveraging the talent landscape in potential markets can unlock new opportunities, optimize operational efficiency, and enhance strategic positioning, ultimately driving successful expansion and fostering long-term success in the global marketplace.

6

Case Studies

Introduction

Economic growth and social development of nations are critical topics for businesspeople; they are the needle in the gauge of market capacity.

The countries in this section are not global powers, but they are not a side show on the global stage. They are part of a group of rising middle powers that will have growing influence in international affairs in coming decades. Each has followed a different development path. Some approaches have worked. Others have failed. Some have stalled. That contrast makes them worth examining.

These cases highlight four useful elements for business decision-making:

First, the vital role of geopolitics.

Recent events and the country stories that follow highlight a frequent void in standard economic growth narratives. Most conventional economic models focus on demographic pressures, productivity gains, or losses resulting from advances or setbacks on investment in and human capital.

Geopolitics is often left out, even though it moves capital, goods, services, and people on a massive scale. Sometimes it does so in ways that appear irrational or random, to the uninformed.

Granted, geopolitics is unstable. A country can be cast and treated as a global pariah...until it isn't any more. It can be isolated one year and welcomed the next. The definition of ally or enemy can change because of an election, a court ruling, a coup, a religious decision, or a shift in leadership. This has less to do with institutions than with power and influence.

To global surprise, on December 8, 2024, rebel forces seized Damascus and toppled Syrian President Bashar al-Assad, ending 53 years of Assad family rule. The country quickly cut ties with Russia and Iran and aligned with rebel backers including the U.S., Turkey, Saudi Arabia, and others.

Business conditions can change overnight because of a domestic political move, a war, or the death of a leader, just as much as from shifts in economic policy instruments like exchange rate regimes or tax reforms. Geopolitics shapes who can move, what goods can be traded, and where capital can go—changing demographics, investment, production, and trade patterns along the way.

The stories that follow clearly show this instability, but they also reveal recurring patterns—some more stable and predictable than others. From Mexico to Vietnam, geopolitics has played a defining role in their economic trajectories, more than most economists or executives care to admit. In Vietnam's case, for example, it has been a main driver of foreign investment flows.

The TIGHT framework also shows that geographic location matters, but it's not enough for a country to be influential or to grow. Turkey gained an edge not just from where it is, but from how they've built infrastructure and logistics networks to take advantage of it. Since 2003, investors have committed over $250 billion to the country's transportation and logistics sectors through FDI, concessions, and other programs. This explains why Turkey has outperformed many of its neighbors—even if its long-time goal of joining the European Union is now out of reach.

Second, many widely accepted truths simply aren't.

Contrary to free-market intuition, Vietnam shows that under certain conditions, a centrally managed economy based on low-tech production can lift itself out of deep poverty faster than most market economies in the developing world.

Poland, far from the common narrative, is not Germany's cheap labor source. It has become a hub for European supply chains and defense—and is steadily stepping onto the global stage.

Mexico demonstrates that a complex web of production chains, migration, tourism, and managerial technology transfers has deeply integrated it with the U.S. and Canada. Headlines may suggest otherwise, but the underlying relationship is hard to unwind—for any of the three countries.

Saudi Arabia is a striking example of how personal power, carefully staged displays of opulence, and smart entrepreneurial moves have used

state and royal resources to buy influence far beyond what the country's size would suggest.

These cases should at least make it clear that, in the developing world, not everything works according to simple textbook models. China, for instance, defies the logic of market economies by permitting private property without enforcing property rights.

Third, this is mostly a tale of development.

This is a story about progress, not arrival. In 2023, Saudi Arabia—the richest country in this group of six—had a GDP per capita equal to just 39% of the U.S. level. Vietnam was at 5%. Nigeria was at 2%.

Scarcity and unmet needs remain widespread. In general, this section tries to present a data-backed perspective. The key takeaway is that business decisions must be based on hard data, not flashy headlines. If we want to understand what actually drives development, we need fewer superlatives and more numbers. Despite real progress, Silicon Valley is not relocating en masse to Istanbul or Hanoi anytime soon.

Nigeria is a good example. Serious development is unlikely to take off for at least another decade or two. This highly promising African country will remain on the sidelines of the global economy until its young population reaches household-forming age, finds reasons to stay in the country, and begins to invest. For now, oil revenues and existing political and social institutions do not seem not enough to trigger sustained growth. They would have to successfully contend with a daunting set of challenges: 43% of the population is under the age of 14, 91% live on less than $6.85 a day, and deep ethnic and religious divisions persist.

This section poses the basic question of how nations grow, but goes further. Through these examples, it tries to show how much infrastructure, technology, and human talent are required to build real material wealth, and how much developing countries must factor in political alliances, rivalries, wars, migrations, and cultural shifts into what might otherwise seem like a straightforward growth equation.

Fourth, 'economic miracles' never happen overnight.

There are no shortcuts. Each country analysis here uses 25 years of data to avoid drawing conclusions from the latest, single data point or from short-term policy changes. This long-term view reinforces a simple truth: growth and development are slow. Unless there's a catastrophe—like a war or natural disaster—progress is built over time.[1]

---

[1] The data used in our analysis extends mostly through 2023. Figures beyond the year mentioned in the following text are often unavailable due to the natural delays in data collection, verification,

* * *

No single framework explains everything, but these examples offer a clearer view of the forces shaping development today. This kind of analysis helps identify which countries are likely to grow—and which are not.

Mexico

In a multipolar world, some countries have opted for a unipolar path, fully embracing the advantages while confronting the challenges that come with this choice. Mexico is one of those countries. Mexico's $1.8 trillion economy ranks the 12th largest in the world. Over the past 25 years, its GDP per capita doubled from $6,500 to $13,800, which is clearly not enough to make it a growth miracle. However, this country holds the promise of fast economic convergence to the income level of its neighbor, the United States. Over the same period, Canada, the northern neighbor, has maintained a close trajectory and even surpassed the U.S.'s GDP per capita at certain points (see Fig. 6.1).

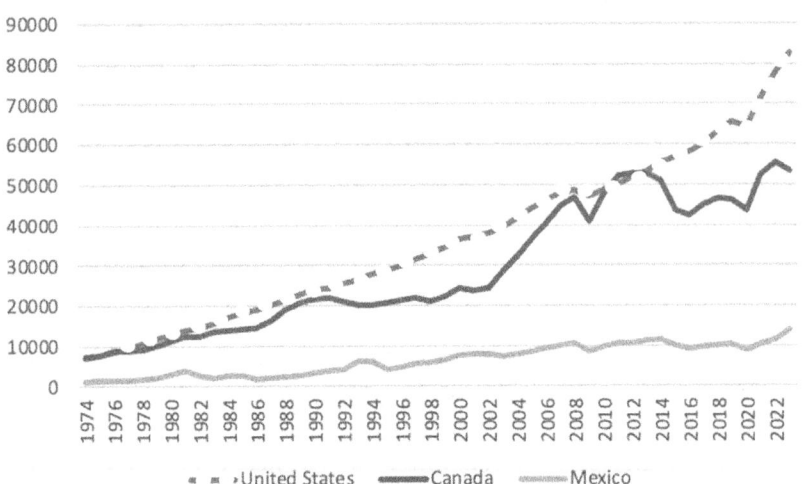

Fig. 6.1 Mexico and neighbors—GDP per capita (current $) (*Source* The World Bank)

---

and publication. Government agencies, research institutions, and academic sources typically take 1–3 years to compile, validate, and release comprehensive datasets—a timeline that prioritizes accuracy and reliability. More importantly, our charts and tables draw from 25 years of longitudinal data. This long-term perspective enables readers to identify consistent patterns and structural trends, rather than react to short-lived fluctuations. As a result, the insights presented throughout this report reflect enduring shifts rather than temporary anomalies, offering a more grounded basis for analysis.

Will Mexico be able to achieve convergence over the next 50 years? Based solely on its poor average annual GDP growth rate of 1.7% over the past 25 years, the answer would be a resounding no. But almost surely, this conclusion overlooks other critical factors and dynamics that influence Mexico's economic trajectory.

To begin with, Mexico's population stands at approximately 126 million, making it the 10th most populous nation globally, and its capital, Mexico City, is home to over 22 million people—the seventh largest worldwide. Economically, Mexico is classified as an upper-middle-income country.

The country is diversified, with major contributions from manufacturing, services, agriculture, and mining. Mexico is the world's largest exporter of avocados and silver and a major supplier of electronics and automobiles. Mexico ranked 13th globally in crude oil production, 21st in crude oil reserves, 16th in refining capacity, and fifth in logistics infrastructure.[2] The automotive sector—the world's 7th largest—is one of the most prominent, benefiting from proximity to the United States and the US-Mexico-Canada Agreement (USMCA), which governed trade across North America.

However, Mexico's economy struggles with informality, which employs nearly 56% of the labor force, and persistent poverty. In 2022, 22% of the population lived with less than $6.85 a day, a significant reduction from 50% in 2000, but very far from the 4.7% in Chile in 2022. Also, 1.2% live below the poverty line of $2.25 a day as of 2022.[3]

Demographically, Mexico is experiencing a gradual demographic transition. The fertility rate has dropped from 2.8 children per woman in 1999 to 1.8 in 2022, reflecting urbanization and increased access to education and healthcare. The population is relatively young, with a median age of 29.5 years, but it is aging rapidly; the median age was 21.5 in 1999. By 2050, it is projected that nearly a quarter of Mexicans will be over 60 years old, presenting challenges for healthcare and pension systems.

Socially, Mexico exhibits significant disparities. While life expectancy stands at 75 years, according to the World Health Organization, health outcomes are unevenly distributed, with indigenous and rural populations facing worse conditions. Mexico's education system has made strides in literacy, achieving a 95% literacy rate among individuals aged 15 and older, yet quality remains an issue. In the PISA assessments, Mexican students scored below the OECD average in reading, math, and science.

---

[2] U.S. International Trade Administration (2024) "Mexico Oil and gas" retrieved from: https://www.trade.gov/country-commercial-guides/mexico-oil-and-gas.

[3] At press time, no information beyond 2022 had been released.

It is common knowledge that Mexico faces significant security challenges, with organized crime and drug-related violence contributing to alarmingly high homicide rates. In 1999, the country reported 12,300 intentional homicides. By 2022, this number had surged to over 30,000, placing Mexico among the nations with the highest homicide rates globally. In 2022, the rate stood at 28 intentional homicides per 100,000 people, a stark contrast to the United States' rate of 7 per 100,000.

Mexico's strategic partnership with the United States, its largest trading partner, is the cornerstone of Mexico's economy and power. It was the United States' top goods trading partner in 2023, with a total two-way goods trade of $807 billion, surpassing China. In comparison, U.S. goods trade with Canada totaled $782 billion, while trade with China totaled $576 billion.[4] Mexico is a member of the G20, OECD, and the Pacific Alliance. It, however, has played an intermittently relevant role in regional integration initiatives and climate negotiations.

Legally, Mexico follows a civil law system. While reforms have modernized the legal framework, particularly with the introduction of oral trials in criminal cases, the judicial system remains plagued by inefficiencies and limited access to justice. Property rights enforcement and labor law compliance are inconsistent, discouraging some foreign investment. In parallel, corruption and impunity abound. Transparency International ranked Mexico 105th out of 180 countries in its most recent Corruption Perceptions Index, underscoring widespread governance issues.

A recent judicial reform mandates that all current state and federal judges, including Supreme Court justices, be replaced through popular elections. This change risks making the judiciary more dependent on political parties and severely threatens its independence.

Business Environment

Mexico's business environment is a complex mix of opportunities and challenges shaped by its geographic position, trade agreements, and internal structural issues. Financially, the country has developed a relatively stable macroeconomic framework, but growth remains uneven across sectors and regions. The financial sector, anchored by a sound banking system, has facilitated credit access for larger corporations but struggles to adequately serve small and micro, small, and medium-sized enterprises, which represent 92%

---

[4] U.S. Department of State (2024) "U.S. relations with Mexico" https://www.state.gov/u-s-relations-with-mexico/.

of all businesses. High borrowing costs and rigid lending criteria persist, with real interest rates hovering around 11% per annum, hindering the ability of SMEs to scale operations.

Mexico's trade environment has benefited significantly from its proximity to the United States, with whom it shares a 3145-kilometer border, and its membership in a North American trade treaty. The agreement has fortified Mexico's role in global supply chains, particularly in the automotive and electronics industries. Automotive exports alone generated $116 billion in 2023, accounting for nearly 26% of total exports. However, dependency on the U.S. market is a double-edged sword in that 81% of Mexican exports were directed to the United States in 2023, making the country vulnerable to fluctuations in U.S. demand, trade policies, and even domestic politics.[5] Despite these trade opportunities, legal and regulatory barriers pose challenges for both local and foreign firms. Complex tax regimes, bureaucratic inefficiencies, and widespread corruption remain significant obstacles.

Foreign direct investment (FDI) is a critical component of Mexico's economic performance. The country attracted $30.2 billion in FDI in 2023—the 9th largest recipient of FDI inflows in the world—largely driven by investments in manufacturing, retail, and renewable energy. However, inconsistent policy decisions, such as the nationalization of lithium production in 2022, have raised concerns among investors. The energy sector, once a major FDI magnet, has been hampered by government policies favoring state-owned enterprises like oil company PEMEX and the Federal Commission of Electricity (CFE). This has created fewer opportunities for private and foreign investors, especially in renewable energy, despite Mexico's vast solar and wind potential.

Nevertheless, certain sectors thrive amid these challenges. The aerospace industry has grown at a steady 14% per year over the past 15 years. It is the world's 12th largest in the industry and the 7th largest Mexican export to the United States. More than 350 firms create 60,000 jobs (0.1% of the total 59.9 million labor force) in 19 States. Most aerospace firms (79%) are manufacturers, 11% focus on design and engineering, and 10% provide Maintenance, Repairs, and Overhaul services.[5] The Bajío region, including Querétaro and Guanajuato, has become a hub for aerospace manufacturing, offering competitive labor costs and proximity to U.S. markets.

Similarly, the electronics sector has seen robust growth, with companies like Foxconn and Flex assembling components in Mexico for global markets.

---

[5] Intracen (2024) "Trade map" Retrieved from: https://www.trademap.org/.

In 2023, the electronics industry accounted for $40 billion in exports, making it the second-largest Mexican export category after automotive.[6]

Business operations in Mexico face regional disparities in infrastructure and security. While industrial hubs like Monterrey, Guadalajara, and Mexico City offer modern facilities and skilled labor, southern states such as Chiapas and Oaxaca lag significantly, with inadequate infrastructure and lower education levels. Security remains a pressing issue; More than 27% of the 38.6 million households in the country had at least one member being a victim of a crime. The figure, probably contrary to generalized perceptions, has gradually decreased. It is lower than the 35.6% peak in 2017.[7] In the business sector, insecurity disproportionately affects small businesses, which often lack resources to implement robust security measures, but has hit thriving, modern sectors like the avocado industry.

The legal framework for labor is another area of concern. Mexico's 2019 labor reform, aimed at improving worker rights and eliminating protectionist unions, created a more transparent labor environment. Improvement in the outcomes for Mexican labor can already be seen. For example, formal employment has continued to grow and is at historical highs, surpassing 26 million, not including workers in the service of the state and federal government. Furthermore, wages increased by 71% in Mexican pesos from 2021 to 2024. These factors have reduced the number of people in poverty by 23.7%.[8] The minimum wage rose by 20% in 2024 and by 12% in 2025 to $630 a month, improving worker incomes. However, some complain that compliance costs have increased for employers, particularly in manufacturing.

Technology

Despite notable strides in certain sectors, systemic challenges continue to impede Mexico's progress, and the country remains at a crossroads in addressing the digital divide and fostering technological advancement. The Mexican government has introduced various initiatives aimed at strengthening its digital infrastructure and fostering innovation. As of 2023, 81% of Mexico's population had internet access, up from 43% a decade earlier, reflecting significant growth but still lagging behind regional leaders such as Chile and Uruguay. The government's Internet for Everyone initiative,

---

[6] Intracen (2024) Op. Cit.

[7] Inegi (2024) "Encuesta nacional de victimización y percepción de seguridad pública" Retrieved from: https://inegi.org.mx/contenidos/programas/envipe/2024/doc/envipe2024_presentacion_nacional.pdf.

[8] Domínguez, Alfredo (2024) "Labor policy in Mexico and the USMCA" Brookings Insttution. Retrieved from: https://www.brookings.edu/articles/labor-policy-in-mexico-and-the-usmca/.

launched in collaboration with private companies, has focused on expanding broadband access in rural areas. However, progress remains uneven. While urban centers like Mexico City boast high-speed internet and advanced connectivity, rural areas often rely on outdated infrastructure, exacerbating economic and social inequalities. In 2023, there were 21 fixed broadband subscriptions per 100 people, not far from 22 in Brazil but lagging the OECD average (34) and the U.S. (38).[9]

Mexico used to be an undisputed leader in artificial intelligence applications. In 2018, Mexico was on the path to becoming a global pioneer in AI governance. Its Office for National Digital Strategy did devise a national plan for AI. At that moment, less than 10 countries worldwide had published one. The momentum halted with Andrés Manuel López Obrador, known as AMLO, coming into power, but its dismantling of AI leadership gave rise to the National Alliance on Artificial Intelligence (ANIA), which originated outside the central government and has become a prominent force in Mexico's AI governance landscape.[10]

AI has been adopted across industries, including healthcare, manufacturing, and finance. The 2024 AI Readiness Index, which measures AI preparation of companies, finds that 13% of Mexican companies are fully prepared, the same percentage reported as the global result, much less than the 25% in Brazil but more than 9% in Spain. Barriers to faster adoption include a lack of secure, scalable, adaptive IT infrastructure, skilled professionals, and limited access to high-quality data.[11] The IMF's AI Preparedness Index gave a score of 0.53 to Mexico, slightly better than 0.5 in Brazil and lower than 0.65 in Spain, 0.71 in Canada, and 0.77 in the United States.[12]

In the Internet of Things sector, Mexico has shown potential in leveraging its manufacturing base to integrate IoT solutions, particularly in the automotive and aerospace industries. Major automakers operating in Mexico, including General Motors and Volkswagen, have incorporated IoT technologies to optimize production lines and supply chains. The government's support for Industry 4.0 initiatives, such as the Prosoft program to develop software, has indirectly encouraged SMEs to adopt IoT and automation. Nonetheless, challenges persist, with only 22% of firms in Mexico employing

---

[9] The World Bank (2024) "World Development Indicators".
[10] Fuentes, Pablo (2024) "Beyond central government: How ANIA is shaping Mexico's AI landscape" Retrieved from: https://oxfordinsights.com/insights/beyond-central-government-how-ania-is-shaping-mexicos-ai-landscape/?utm_source=chatgpt.com.
[11] Cisco (2024) "Cisco AI Readines Index" Retrieved from: https://www.cisco.com/c/dam/m/en_us/solutions/ai/readiness-index/2024-m11/documents/cisco-ai-readiness-index-mx.pdf.
[12] IMF (2024) "AI Preparedness Index" Retrieved from: https://www.imf.org/.

IoT solutions in 2023, significantly lower than in countries like Germany or South Korea.

As for blockchain technology, it has seen limited adoption in Mexico, primarily in the financial sector. In 2023, the Bank of Mexico launched a pilot program to explore central bank digital currencies (CBDCs), aiming to enhance financial inclusion and reduce transaction costs. Startups such as Bitso, a cryptocurrency exchange, have gained traction, but regulatory constraints remains a significant barrier. The absence of a comprehensive legal framework for blockchain applications has deterred broader adoption across sectors, such as supply chain management and real estate.[13]

Big data and cloud computing represent areas of growing interest in Mexico. Companies recognize the value of data analytics in improving decision-making and customer engagement. For example, food giant Grupo Bimbo uses big data analytics to optimize distribution networks and forecast demand. The adoption of cloud computing has also accelerated, with public cloud spending in Mexico reaching $3.5 billion in 2023, a 25% increase from the previous year. However, concerns over data security and privacy, coupled with a shortage of skilled data scientists, continue to limit the full potential of these technologies.

Mexico faces several systemic challenges in its quest to become a technology leader. One such barrier is the country's low investment in R&D, which stood at 0.31% of GDP in 2023, well below the OECD average of 2.68%. Furthermore, the country's education system has struggled to produce a workforce with the skills needed for the digital economy.

Another pressing issue is the regulatory environment, which often lacks clarity and consistency. Businesses frequently cite bureaucratic hurdles and inadequate legal protections for intellectual property as significant obstacles to innovation. For example, Mexico's patent application process is notoriously slow, averaging four years for approval, compared to two years in the United States. Further integration of the North American market will probably offer opportunities to strengthen cross-border cooperation in tech development.

Despite these challenges, Mexico has made notable gains in specific areas. Per UNESCO, Mexico produces 113,944 engineering graduates annually, the seventh-highest percentage of STEM graduates among OECD nations. The country's aerospace industry has embraced advanced manufacturing techniques, including 3D printing and IoT, to maintain its position as one of the world's top exporters of aerospace components. Additionally, Mexico's fintech sector has experienced rapid growth, with over 770 startups operating

---

[13] Chambers and Partners (2024) "Blockchain Mexico" Retrieved from: https://practiceguides.chambers.com/practice-guides/blockchain-2024/mexico/trends-and-developments.

in 2023. The enactment of the Fintech Law in 2018, pioneering in Latin America provided a regulatory framework for crowdfunding and electronic payment systems, fostering innovation in financial services. Mexico is now home to eight unicorns and at least 38 startups that could soon reach this coveted status (Soonicorns).

In 2022, venture capital investments in Mexican startups were primarily focused on three sectors: fintech, e-commerce, and logistics/transportation. Fintech dominated, securing 57% of total venture capital, significantly boosting the banking industry through open finance and API technologies. The average investment in fintech startups was around $10 million. E-commerce received 37% of venture capital, and the remaining 12% was distributed among other sectors, showing a narrower focus on areas outside of these leading industries.

The world's reliance on advanced semiconductors is growing, with Western superpowers and major device makers shifting away from China, and also from Taiwan, which holds 60% of the global semiconductor market and 90% of the specialized chip market. This shift presents an opportunity for Mexico, especially in sectors like automobiles and aerospace, which rely on lower-end semiconductors. The electric vehicle market, in particular, is expanding rapidly, requiring more chips—1600 chips per electric vehicle compared to 700 in traditional fuel-powered vehicles.

Be that as it may, setting up a microprocessor factory can cost between $10 and $20 billion and can take up to a half-decade to begin producing chips. Leading experts also consider that establishing a semiconductor processing hub takes about 30 years, as it requires a highly-complex mix of skills and resources to develop. While Mexico is not ready to take on the complete process of chip fabrication, it can integrate itself into the value chain, offering adjacent activities such as testing, packaging, and bundling (like Vietnam). Also, Mexico could take on the manufacture of more basic chips used in everyday products.[14]

On the positive side, digital transformation presents significant opportunities. In 2024, México posted the world's largest growth rate of e-commerce and retail with a market valued at $33 billion.[15] Companies like Mercado Libre and Amazon have expanded their presence, tapping into a

---

[14] Gonzalez, Jorge (2024) "The future of semiconductor chip manufacturing: North America's opportunity with Mexico" Forbes, February 14.
[15] LLYC (2024) "Informe retail & ecommerce 2024 México" Retrieved from: https://llyc.global/ideas/informe-retail-ecommerce-2024-mexico/#:~:text=En%202024%2C%20M%C3%A9xico%20se%20posiciona,mil%20millones%20de%20pesos%20mexicanos.

growing middle-class market. However, logistics remains a challenge, particularly in rural areas where last-mile delivery infrastructure is underdeveloped.

Infrastructure

Mexico faces significant infrastructure challenges, with glaring gaps in critical areas such as transportation, energy, telecommunications, and water management. The statistics validate this claim. Mexico ranked 62nd out of 67 countries in the 2024 *Global Competitiveness Index* for infrastructure quality.[16] On the infrastructure pillar of the World Bank's Logistics Performance Index, Mexico scored 2.8, below Brazil's 3.2, U.S.'s 3.9, and less than Canada's 4.3 and the World's top performer Singapore's 4.6.[17]

Mexico's infrastructure spending averaged 3% of GDP per annum between 1996 and 2023, well below the recommended 5% for emerging economies.

Transportation infrastructure in Mexico suffers from uneven development and chronic underinvestment. Mexico's road network, which spans approximately 516,000 miles remains heavily concentrated along industrial corridors, leaving rural regions underserved. While highways like the México-Toluca toll road are critical for connecting major urban centers, 79% of country's roads are unpaved.[18]

Rail infrastructure, though experiencing modest growth, continues to be underutilized for freight. Projects like the Mayan Train, which aims to boost tourism and regional development, have faced cost overruns and severe environmental criticism. The government has announced a $7.8 billion investment to develop several major rail projects, including the AIFA-Pachuca and Mexico-Querétaro passenger trains, as well as the Saltillo-Nuevo Laredo and Querétaro-Irapuato sections. Additionally, the Maya Train will be converted into a freight railway system. These projects are expected to create 70,000 direct jobs and 140,000 indirect jobs. The goal is to build, with military engineers, more than 1864 miles of passenger railways.

Mexico's ports face challenges with congestion and, at times, outdated facilities. The Container Port Performance Index (CPPI) measures the time container ships spend in port and serves as an indicative measure of port performance. Among the ports analyzed by the World Bank, Lázaro Cárdenas

---

[16] IMD (2024) "World Competitiveness Ranking" Retrieved from: https://www.imd.org/centers/wcc/world-competitiveness-center/rankings/world-competitiveness-ranking/.
[17] The World Bank (2024) "Logistics Performance Index".
[18] Mexico Projects Hub (2024) "Highways and bridges" Retrieved from: https://www.proyectosmexico.gob.mx/en/how-mexican-infrastructure/investment-cycle/roads/.

ranked on the 51st position, but Veracruz ranked 214th, and Manzanillo was ranked 331st out of 405 ports.[19]

The Port of Manzanillo, Mexico's primary container gateway on the Pacific Coast, will grow its capacity to 10 million TEU, up from the present 3.5 million TEU capacity, making it the largest container port in Latin America, ahead of Panama's transshipment hub in Colon and Brazil's Santos Port from the top spots.[20]

However, more progress is needed to streamline trade and expedite border crossings. According to the World Bank's Logistics Performance Index, Mexico ranks 83rd out of 138 countries in terms of the efficiency of its customs clearance process. This is notably behind Canada, which ranks 4th, and the United States, which holds the 14th spot. Mexico's energy infrastructure requires significant investment in cleaner systems to meet new demands, especially with the growth of Nearshoring deals.

The country is heavily reliant on fossil fuels, with approximately 71% of its electricity generated from natural gas, while renewable sources contribute just 33%.[21] Hydroelectricity makes up 13%, with solar and wind growing to 11% and 7.3%, respectively. The government missed its goal of achieving 35% clean energy by 2024: it reached 22%.

Mexico's energy matrix will remain largely thermal, with combined-cycle plants meeting most of the demand. These plants are more efficient and less polluting, using natural gas as the primary fuel. In 2023, combined-cycle plants accounted for 60% of energy generation. However, Mexico imports nearly 70% of its natural gas from the U.S., exposing the Federal Electricity Commission (CFE) to risks such as supply shortages, price fluctuations, and exchange rate volatility. Over 65% of CFE's capacity depends on natural gas. To manage these risks, CFE introduced a Commodity Hedging Program, covering 45.8% of its gas needs, with plans to increase this coverage to 50%–60% depending on market conditions.[22]

Despite key renewable projects like the Villanueva solar park and Oaxaca wind farms facing regulatory challenges, Mexico's grid managed by CFE suffers from inefficiencies. Transmission losses averaged 11.4% from 2018 to

---

[19] The World Bank (2024) "The Container Port Performance Index 2023".

[20] Seatrade Maritime (2024) "Maxico's Manzanillo port to double container capacity" Retrieved from: https://www.seatrade-maritime.com/ports-logistics/mexico-s-manzanillo-port-to-expand-capacity.

[21] EIA (2024) "International, Electricity" Retrieved from: https://www.eia.gov/international/data/world/electricity/.

[22] Fitch (2024) "Fitch asigna calificaciones AAA(mex)" Retrieved from: https://www.fitchratings.com/research/es/corporate-finance/fitch-assigns-aaa-mex-to-cfe-new-cb-issuances-27-11-2024.

2022, compared to 5% in the U.S.[23] By 2024, losses were expected to exceed 10%. The national grid is vulnerable to disruptions, including thunderstorms and heat waves. In May 2024, for example, 20 out of 32 states experienced rolling power outages due to a surge in demand caused by unusually hot weather. These outages disproportionately affect rural areas, hindering efforts to attract industrial investment.

Mexico's oil production, a key economic sector, fell to less than 2 million barrels per day in 2024 from almost 3.5 million in 2004. Pemex also became the most indebted oil company in the world.

On Telecommunications and IT infrastructure, while internet penetration reached 72% in 2023, it remains below the regional average of 78%. Rural areas rely on outdated 3G technology or lack access altogether. Additionally, Mexico's IT infrastructure expenditure per capita is 41% lower than in OECD countries, limiting the digital transformation of businesses and public services.

Water and sanitation infrastructure remains one of Mexico's most pressing challenges. Across the world, demand for water is exceeding what's available. Mexico is classified by the World Resources Institute (WRRI) as one of 25 countries exposed to extremely high water stress, meaning they annually use over 80% of their renewable water supply for irrigation, livestock, industry, and domestic needs. Even a short-term drought puts these places in danger of running out of water. Efforts to improve water efficiency, such as constructing desalination plants in Baja, California, have seen limited success due to high operational costs and community opposition.

The challenges associated with infrastructure development in Mexico are compounded by governance issues. Bureaucratic inefficiencies, corruption, and regulatory uncertainty frequently delay projects and inflate costs. Mexico ranked 105th out of 180 countries in Transparency International's Corruption Perceptions Index in 2023, reflecting persistent concerns about the misuse of public funds. Additionally, the country's legal framework for public–private partnerships (PPPs), though improved in recent years, remains cumbersome, with lengthy approval processes deterring foreign investors.

The private sector has a crucial role to play in advancing Mexico's infrastructure agenda. Companies such as FEMSA and Cemex have invested in sustainable logistics and construction technologies, while international firms like Siemens have introduced smart grid solutions to improve energy efficiency. Encouraging greater private sector participation requires a stable regulatory environment. Additionally, there will be a gradual but steady

---

[23] CFE (2024) "Key operational and financial results, third qarter 2024" and EIA (2024) https://www.eia.gov/tools/faqs/faq.php?id=105&t=3.

transfer of technology as Mexican companies, such as Grupo México Transportes, consolidate their U.S. acquisitions, including the Florida East Coast Railway and Texas Pacific, or as Cemex—that divested its operations in Central America and the Caribbean—focuses on the U.S. market.

Geopolitics

When it comes to geopolitics, Carlos Salinas de Gortari, president of Mexico from 1988 to 1994, sought to establish a markedly autonomous trade agreement to spur economic growth and shield Mexico from global economic fluctuations. His first attempt focused on forging a free trade deal with Japan, a country he admired deeply. In fact, members of his family attended the Mexican-Japanese School in Mexico City. However, the 1990 stock market crash in Japan plunged this economy, at the time then the world's second largest, into a deep recession, rendering any trade agreement with the country impractical.

Salinas and his team explored a second option: a trade agreement with the European Community. However, economic problems in the region also undermined the feasibility of this plan. On the flight back from Europe, Salinas discussed alternatives with his team. As a result of this conversation, he instructed his advisors to draft a trade agreement with the United States as a sort of Plan C and to report back within a month.

One month later, Mexico entered discussions with the U.S. and Canada, which had signed the Canada-United States Free Trade Agreement in 1988. These negotiations eventually led to the creation of the North American Free Trade Agreement (NAFTA), signed in 1992.[24] Mexican geopolitics are now fully driven by its relations with the United States.

Mexico took positions against the U.S. in Ukraine and oftentimes has stood on the side of the Global South instead of Washington. Some analysts believe that this stance, typical of former president AMLO, played to domestic politics, leveraging a deep resentment against the U.S. This is not the case. Sentiment toward the U.S. swings dramatically, but it is far from being hostile. In 2017, at the start of Donald Trump's first term in office, only 29% of Mexicans had a favorable opinion of their northern neighbor. According to a 2024 Pew Research Center, 2024 61% of Mexicans had a

---

[24] Cardona, Diego (2004) "l'évolution de la notion de sécurité au Mexique" Institute de Hautes Etudes Internationales. University of Geneva, Switzerland.

favorable view of the U.S., a figure that climbs to 71% for Mexican adults under 30, a major element in a young country like Mexico.[25]

Mexicans feel North Americans, aspire to live like U.S. citizens: "Enjoy the same standard of living, but speak Spanish, pray to the Virgin of Guadalupe, and preserve their culture.[26]" Therefore, Mexico's independent stance is not about employing double-faced diplomacy—it represents a genuine difference that will mark their relationship. Mexico will do as Washington says, but it does not want to be bullied.

Trade: Mexico is highly dependent on the United States, with 80% of its exports going north. This reliance was even greater in 2004 when 89% of exports were directed to the U.S. While Mexico has increased its exports to Canada, these sales still align closely with U.S. demand cycles. The small share of exports to Canada (3%), China (2%), and Germany (1%) further underscores the unipolar world that Mexico inhabits (see Fig. 6.2).

On the flip side, the U.S. has increasingly relied on Mexico. In 2023, Mexico surpassed China to become the U.S.'s first-largest import source while also displacing Canada from second position in 2015. This trend is sustainable as the cost of labor in Mexico is now lower than in China.

The U.S.-China trade wars prompted many Chinese companies to invest in Mexico to circumvent tariffs and restrictions on entering the U.S. market.

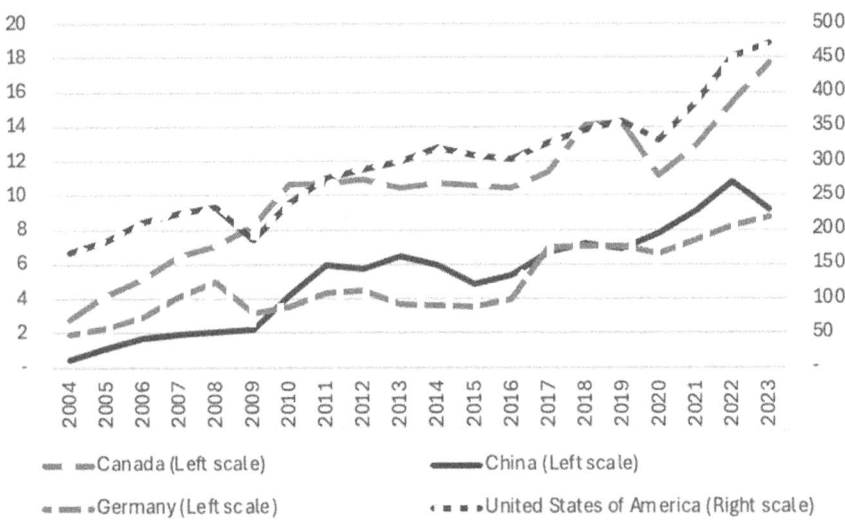

Fig. 6.2 Mexico—exports to the world ($ billion) (*Source* Intracen)

---

[25] Pew Research Center (2024) "How Mexicans and Americans view each other and their government's handling of the border" Retrieved from: https://www.pewresearch.org/short-reads/2024/.
[26] Cardona, Diego (2024) Op. Cit.

Chinese investments have indeed increased. In the first nine months of 2024, for example, China became the largest investor in Mexico's automobile sector, contributing $3.5 billion—18% of the total investment—followed by Germany, Japan and the U.S.[27] More recently, investment has come from European and other Asian countries. As for Mexico's imports from the U.S. have deepened the two economy's interdependence, see Fig. 6.3.

Location—like in Poland or Turkey—is an asset that has value only if it is supported by adequate infrastructure and by the right political agreements to facilitate the movement of resources. Infrastructure is a challenge for Mexico, but politics are now moving in the direction of the cohesion of the North American market, despite the rhetoric of confrontation, and despite that, demands from Washington, more than rules, will likely govern U.S. trade policy in the near future.[28]

Since his election in 2018, AMLO had implemented a nationalist agenda, emphasizing economic self-sufficiency and reducing dependence on foreign investment. His administration's decision to nationalize lithium resources in 2022 is emblematic of this shift. While this policy aims to secure strategic resources, it raised concerns among investors about Mexico's reliability as a destination for foreign direct investment.

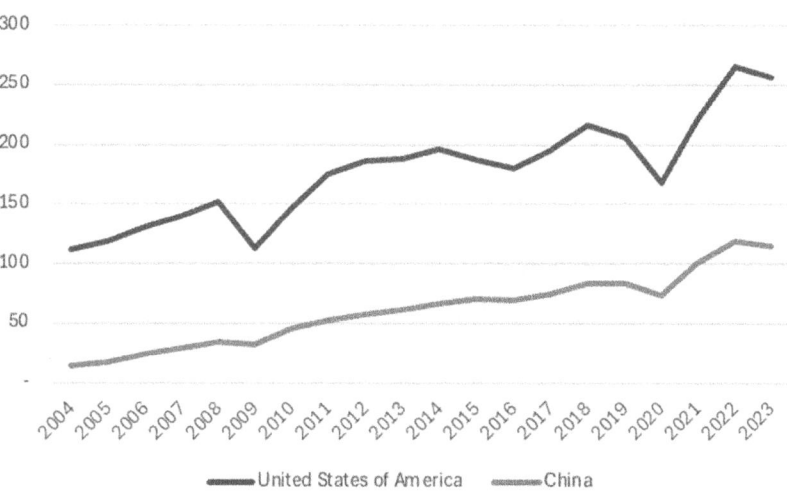

Fig. 6.3 Mexico—imports from the U.S. and China ($ billions) (*Source* Intracen)

---

[27] Energía Debate (2024) "Predominan inversiones chinas en el sector automotriz mexicano," November 25.
[28] Peterson Institute for International Economics (2024) "Expect Trump's demands, not rules, to govern US trade policy" Retrieved from: https://www.piie.com/search?search_api_fulltext=mexico.

Mexico's energy policies further fueled tensions, as AMLO prioritized strengthening the state-owned energy companies Pemex and the Federal Electricity Commission at the expense of private sector competition. This triggered disputes under the USMCA, as American and Canadian companies alleged violations of trade commitments. Independence is, and probably will be, a trait of Mexican foreign policy discourse, but complete interdependence is closer to the real state of affairs. AMLO, known for his reluctance to engage in foreign relations, made only 12 international trips during his presidency, five of which were to the U.S.

Under AMLO, Mexico's leadership role in Latin America diminished. For example, Mexico had previously played an active role in fostering trade agreements such as the Pacific Alliance and mediating peace efforts in Colombia. While his cooler relationship with Latin America may have long-term implications, it makes sense within Mexico's unipolar strategy to place its relations with the Latin American and Caribbean region in the background.

This North American approach is not only supported by the government but also by civil society and academia. In the 1980s, the Humanities Building at Mexico's largest university, UNAM, housed a two-and-a-half-story Latin American studies center. Today, two floors were overtaken by a North American studies center, reflecting the shifting focus.[29]

FDI. When it comes to foreign direct investment, both inward and outward, it will be crucial—perhaps more than anything else—to drive Mexico's economic convergence with developed nations. Macroeconomic investment in physical assets such as buildings, machinery, and other infrastructure is typically financed through domestic savings. When these savings fall short, foreign investment steps in, often through FDI, debt, or financial arrangements like concessions.

After a hard stop following the global financial crisis and the COVID-19 pandemic, investment surged above savings levels since 2008 and has remained around $300 billion annually, spiking to $450 billion in 2023 (see Fig. 6.4).

This increase was largely due to the North American Free Trade Agreement (NAFTA), which was implemented in 1999. The agreement, combined with significant investment in the automotive sector (comparable to that of Turkey), and occasional investment in the oil sector, fueled growth. Investment spiked again after July 2020, following the implementation of the USMCA.

---

[29] Cardona, Diego (2020) Op. Cit.

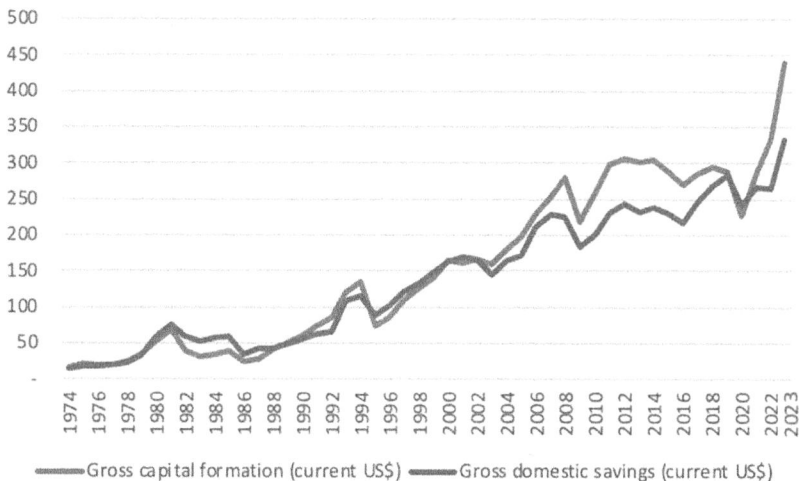

Fig. 6.4 Mexico—investment and savings (Gross capital formation and domestic savings—current $) (*Source* The World Bank)

FDI has played a key role in this investment growth. Between 1999 and 2012, FDI inflows averaged $20 to $30 billion annually. However, the administration of President Enrique Peña Nieto (2012–2018) introduced structural reforms under the Pact for Mexico, aiming to modernize key sectors of the economy. In response, FDI surged to over $50 billion in 2013, largely driven by the acquisition of Grupo Modelo, the Mexican brewer of Corona beer, by Belgium's Anheuser-Busch InBev for $20.1 billion (see Fig. 6.5).

Simultaneously, Mexico's 2013 energy reform opened the oil, gas, and electricity sectors to private and foreign investment, breaking the decades-long monopoly of state-run Pemex. This reform generated significant interest from foreign investors, though it was largely reversed by AMLO in 2018.

Despite the policy shifts, Mexico became the world's 11th-largest recipient of FDI in 2023. In that year, FDI inflows increased to $35 billion, spurred by new equity investment and reinvested earnings. The value of cross-border mergers and acquisitions rose to $8.2 billion (from under $1 billion in 2021), with the notable $4.8 billion acquisition of Grupo Televisa's content and production assets by U.S.'s Univision. Announcements of greenfield investment also more than doubled to $41 billion.[30]

Data on FDI stocks provide a clearer idea of investor interest and geopolitical stakes. In 2022, the stock of U.S. investments in Mexico reached $130.3 billion, led by manufacturing, non-bank holding companies, and finance and

---

[30] UNCTAD (2024) "World Investment Report 2023".

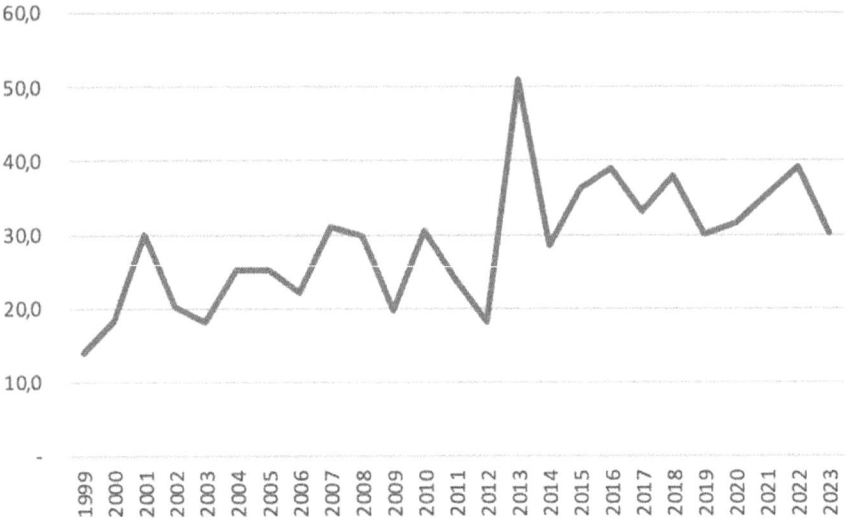

Fig. 6.5 Mexico—foreign direct investment inflows (Current $ billions) (*Source* The World Bank)

insurance. By comparison, U.S. investment stock in Canada stood at $438.8 billion, and in Brazil, it was $81.0 billion. On the other hand, the stock of Mexican FDI in the U.S. was only $33.8 billion, focused in manufacturing, wholesale trade, and real estate. For comparison, Canadian FDI in the U.S. was $589.3 billion, and Brazilian FDI stood at just $4.2 billion.[31]

The U.S. is increasingly countering large Chinese investments in Mexico. This mirrors the trade offensive against Japanese automakers under NAFTA. Tariffs and local content requirements prevented non-NAFTA carmakers from using Mexico as a platform to export cars into the U.S.

President Claudia Sheinbaum has already emphasized that while Mexico is open to Chinese investment, priority will be given to the U.S. and Canada. China's electric car giant BYD, for example, scrapped plans to build a major factory in Mexico due to geopolitical tensions. In contrast, projects aligned with U.S. interests, such as Taiwanese Foxconn's announcement to build the world's largest facility for assembling Nvidia's GB200 superchips, will receive full Mexican support.

There are limits to the relocation of U.S. plants to Mexico. For such relocations to be effective, technology must be compatible between the

---

[31] USTR (2024) "Countries and regions Western Hemisphere" Retrieved from: https://ustr.gov/countries-regions/americas/.

parent companies and their Mexican affiliates, meaning cutting-edge, sensitive sectors are unlikely to move. Additionally, large-scale manufacturing jobs will not relocate if it results in job losses in the U.S.

Drug trafficking. One cannot discuss trade without addressing narcotrafficking. The illicit drug trade adds another dimension to trade. If its value was included in the official trade figures, it was estimated to have increase the value of U.S. imports by 1.3% in 2017.[32]" The "Hugs Not Bullets" policy of the AMLO administration involved avoiding direct confrontation with drug cartels at the behest of the U.S. "We are not going to act as policemen for any foreign government," López Obrador stated in March 2024. However, U.S. pressure increased significantly due to the rising death toll from synthetic opioids like fentanyl—over 70,000 Americans die annually. This pressure is further fueled by evidence of Chinese involvement in the fentanyl trade. A U.S. House committee report suggested that Chinese companies supplying precursor chemicals and equipment are subsidized by the Chinese government and that China had become a major player in money laundering due to the booming fentanyl trade.[33]

President Donald Trump threatened with tariff increases on Mexican and Canadian imports unless both countries took stronger action to curb the flow of illegal drugs and immigrants. Mexico's response was swift, with the Sheinbaum administration abandoning the 'Hugs Not Bullets' policy. Recent actions include significant drug seizures, the detention of over 5000 people, and the relocation of the Secretary of Security to Sinaloa State, at the heart of the Sinaloa Cartel.

The intentional homicide rate in Mexico was 12.7 per 100,000 people in 1999 and climbed to 28 in 2022, compared to 7 in the United States. Primarily, the reason is that Mexico is home to some of the hemisphere's largest, most sophisticated, and most violent criminal organizations. The fall of drug bosses fragmented cartels into a large number of splinter groups, better armed, better trained, and more diversified. They now traffic in illegal drugs, contraband, arms, and humans and launder their proceeds through regional moneychangers and banks, real estate, and local economic projects.[34]

---

[32] Atkinson, Sarah (2020) "Toward developing estimates of U.S. imports of illegal drugs" BEA Working paper series. WP2020-2.

[33] NPR (2024) "U.S. goes after Mexican cartel leaders' drug profits in fight against fentanyl" Retrieved from: https://www.npr.org/2024/06/19/nx-s1-5011755/fentanyl-drug-cartel-sanctions-money-treasury-yellen-mexico-china.

[34] InSight Crime (2024) "Mexico Profile" Retrieved from: https://insightcrime.org/mexico-organized-crime-news/mexico/.

Far from President Sheinbaum's reach, the two largest Mexican cartels, the CJNG, and the Sinaloa Cartel, now compete in Ecuador for territory, allies, and routes; access to ports and the Panama Canal; buy from cocaine-production centers in Colombia; control cocaine warehouses and money-laundering in Ecuador, where the banking system operates in US dollars.[35]

Talent

Mexico has achieved universal coverage in primary education and near-universal coverage in secondary education, with 95% of adults aged 15 and older being literate. However, the quality of high school education remains a challenge. The latest results show that the performance of 15-year-olds in mathematics, science, and reading, as assessed by the PISA (Programme for International Student Assessment) scores, fell significantly below global benchmarks. Mexico's average score in mathematics was 395, trailing behind the OECD average of 472. In comparison, students in Turkey scored 453, while those in Vietnam reached 469.[36]

In contrast, at the university level, Mexico is making strides. The National Autonomous University of Mexico (UNAM), the country's largest public university, is ranked 94th globally and second in Latin America. With 269,000 students, it is also among the largest universities in the world. Meanwhile, the private, corporate-led Tecnológico de Monterrey is ranked 185th globally, showcasing the increasing competitiveness of higher education in the country.[37]

Mexico has a robust focus on engineering education, with approximately 580,000 students enrolled in engineering programs and 113,944 engineering graduates annually. It boasts one of the highest percentages of STEM graduates among OECD nations, highlighting a strong pipeline for technical talent.[38] However, obstacles remain in leveraging this talent effectively.

The Network Readiness Index, which evaluates a country's ability to harness technological assets, reveals gaps in Mexico's digital preparedness. On

---

[35] IISS (2024) "The expansion and diversification of Mexican cartels: Dynamic new actors and markets" Retrieved from: https://www.iiss.org/publications/armed-conflict-survey/2024/the-expansion-and-diversification-of-mexican-cartels-dynamic-new-actors-and-markets/.
[36] OECD (2023). *"Pisa 2022 Results"* https://gpseducation.oecd.org/IndicatorExplorer?plotter=h5&query=54.
[37] QS (2024) "QS Top Universities" https://www.topuniversities.com/world-university-rankings?countries=mx.
[38] UNESCO cited by Best Diplomats (2024) "Which country has the most Engineers?" Retrieved from: https://bestdiplomats.org/which-country-has-the-most-engineers/.

the "People" pillar, Mexico ranks 50th with a score of 45.2, slightly trailing Brazil (45.3) but far behind China (66.3) and global leader South Korea (79.3).[39]

Management, the labor market, remittances, and brain drain all greatly impact Mexico's quest to attract, retain, and improve the nation's talent base and capabilities.

Management. Effective management plays a critical role in driving economic growth. Mexico stands out in this area. According to the World Management Survey (WMS)—which assesses practices closely linked to strong firm performance, such as goal-setting and monitoring—Mexican managers ranked 11th out of 38 countries. A combination of solid academic training and sophisticated management practices in globally competitive firms like Cemex, Alfa, and Orbia, along with close ties to the United States through exports and business relationships, has made Mexican managers the best in Latin America. Interestingly, U.S. companies played an unexpected role in fostering these capabilities. During the 1970s and 1980s, many Mexican firms became global players as U.S. multinationals expanded their presence, challenging Mexican companies in their own markets.

Labor market. Average monthly earnings for Mexican employees doubled between 1999 and 2023, rising from $250 to $502, according to data from the International Labour Organization (ILO). At the core of the Mexican problem is the fact that these wage earnings represented 10% of those of a worker in the United States in 1999 and, again, only 11% twenty-five years later in 2023. Wage stagnation is a crucial element in defining the Mexican convergence problem.

The second major element of Mexico's situation is the relatively low labor force participation rate. Over the past 25 years, only 60% of Mexicans aged 15 and older participated in the labor market, compared to 64% in the U.S. and 66% in Canada, according to the World Bank. This limited participation—whether due to exclusion or self-exclusion—has contributed to Mexico's persistently low unemployment rate. In 2023, the unemployment rate stood at just 2.8%, with a 25-year average of 3.9%. By comparison, the U.S. averaged 5.7%, and Canada averaged 7.0% over the same period. While low unemployment might seem like a positive indicator, it also reflects fewer people actively seeking work, resulting in lower overall household income.

Remittances. They emerged as a lifeline for many Mexican households, particularly among lower-income families. In fact, more than 6.1 million

---

[39] Portulans (2024) "Network Readiness Index" Retrieved from: https://networkreadinessindex.org/analysis/#key-results.

people depended directly on these resources.⁴⁰ These financial flows surged tenfold, from $6.6 billion in 1999 to $66.5 billion in 2024, which will represent about 10% of total goods exports or 3.7% of the national GDP. From 2019 to 2024, remittances also represented a very large average of 17% of Mexico's total wage mass.⁴¹

For some households, remittances provide enough financial stability to opt out of employment altogether, lowering participation rates. Moreover, remittances act as a countercyclical economic buffer. During periods of high unemployment, remittances (and migration) typically increase. This mechanism has provided resilience for many Mexican households, particularly during economic downturns, but it makes the nation more vulnerable to conditions in the U.S. labor markets to sustain domestic consumption.

Brain drain. Mexico's migration pattern is, hence, a crucial factor influencing the economy. With an estimated 12.3 million Mexican migrants worldwide, Mexico is the second-largest country of origin for global migration, with 97% of these migrants residing in the United States. The peak of this migration flow occurred in 2019 when 12.4 million Mexicans migrated to the U.S. (see Fig. 6.6).

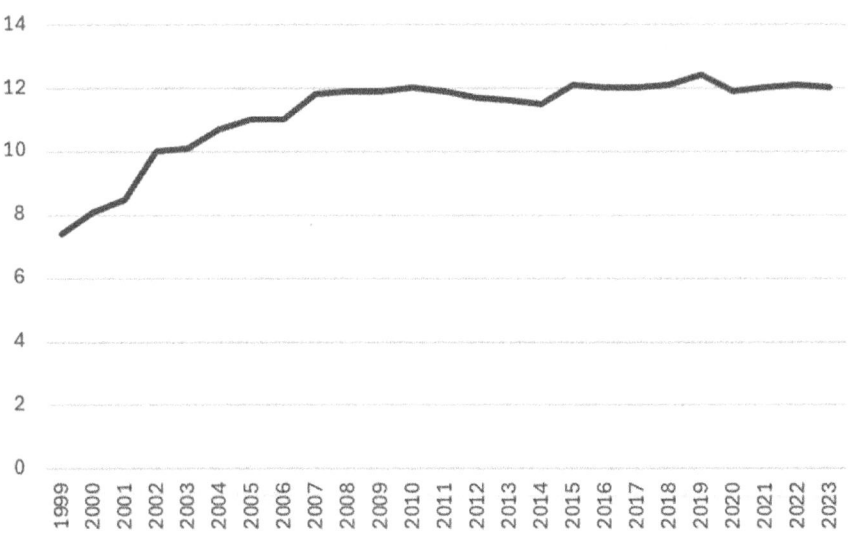

Fig. 6.6 Mexico—migrant population to the U.S. (millions) (*Source* BBVA Research)

---

⁴⁰ BBVA (2024) "Profile of Mexican migrants in the United States" Retrieved from: https://www.bbvaresearch.com/en/publicaciones/mexico-profile-of-mexican-migrants-in-the-united-states/.

⁴¹ IDB (2024) "Los salarios de las personas migrantes y las remesas a América Latina y el Caribe en 2023" Retrieved from: https://blogs.iadb.org/migracion/es/los-salarios-de-las-personas-migrantes-y-las-remesas-a-america-latina-y-el-caribe-en-2023/.

The 12 million Mexicans in the U.S. represent 20% of Mexico's labor force. Over one-third of these migrants were undocumented, with the majority being middle-aged (44–46 years old). While 46% have at least a high school education, 20% have only a primary education or less, and many work in sectors like construction and health services.[42] Although remittances help offset some of the loss in human capital, the overall impact becomes negative when migrants sever family ties, especially as children in Mexico graduate or marry. The return of Mexican migrants, including over 500,000 U.S.-born children between 2005 and 2018, creates an educational challenge. Mass deportations are not new; President Barack Obama deported three million undocumented immigrants. This often brings adults with enhanced skills back to Mexico, but U.S.-born children, while scoring slightly higher on PISA exams than their Mexican-born peers, still perform significantly worse than their U.S. counterparts,[43] indicating a sort of educational shock to reentry, where lessons learned are forgotten at the border.

Key Drivers

In today's multipolar world, Mexico effectively aligned itself with a single major partner: the United States. Far more than Poland, Mexico is tied to the U.S., and this relationship dictates that Mexico function as a low-cost supplier. While this is not a sustainable long-term strategy, it remains viable in the medium term, thanks to significant wage differentials.

This unipolar geopolitical stance—unspoken but evident in the numbers—creates a baseline equilibrium. Mexico must follow U.S. international moves while maintaining its dignity on the global stage. A neutral geopolitical stance benefits both the U.S. and Mexico, but it has limits. Mexico will, for instance, serve as the gateway for Chinese or European firms entering North America until circumstances necessitate closing that door.

Mexico's deepening ties with Latin American and the Caribbean is a nice-to-have in its political portfolio, but it is not essential. Mexico's primary identity is (and most Mexicans want it to be) North American, not Latin American.

The key to Mexico's long-term economic convergence with the Developed World will come from a larger, wealthier, and more educated middle class,

---

[42] BBVA (2024) "Profile of Mexican migrants in the United States" Retrieved from: https://www.bbvaresearch.com/en/publicaciones/mexico-profile-of-mexican-migrants-in-the-united-states/.
[43] Hoffmann, N.I. (2024) "Strangers in the Homeland? The Academic Performance of U.S.-Born Children of Return Migrants in Mexico." *Popul Res Policy Rev* 43, 40. https://doi.org/10.1007/s11113-024-09886-3.

that will spark domestic consumption and investment. Reduction of poverty becomes crucial. From 2018 to 2024, Mexico lifted 9.5 million people out of poverty through social programs and wage increases, with 2.2 million of them benefiting directly from remittances, according to the Inter-American Development Bank.

Curbing inequality is essential to maintaining long-term growth. While income inequality has improved slightly, it remains among the highest in the OECD. Mexico's Gini index for income dropped from 48.6 in 2016 to 43.1 in 2022. Reducing inequality does not imply the elementary idea of forced redistribution, but an arrangement of policy and business action that allow SMEs to grow and the population to receive more income and create more wealth.

Wealth inequality paints an even more telling picture. From 2000 to 2022, wealth per adult in Mexico grew at an impressive annual rate of 6.1%, almost fourfold the country's GDP growth. By the end of 2022, wealth per adult stood at $54,082 in Mexico, compared to $32,760 in Latin America as a whole. Yet, the Gini coefficient for wealth inequality remains very high, at 79.3 in 2022, showing that wealth is far more concentrated than income. By comparison, the U.S. has a wealth Gini of 83, and Canada's stands at 72.3.[44] This is a key task for domestic policy. The geopolitical alliance has largely been underused as a source of investment, yet it is the most effective way to drive growth. The examples of Poland, Vietnam, and local automotive industries demonstrate how to attract global investments to the North American region. These investments can provide the resources needed to address the country's challenges, including improving infrastructure and security.

Country Outlook

Despite the challenges and occasional controversies, the U.S. and Mexico share enough ties to make cooperation feasible. For decades, entrepreneurs from both nations have exchanged investments and ideas in formal meetings. Mexican business people have expanded their operations in the U.S. and are increasingly shareholders in American firms. Additionally, lawmakers from both countries have met regularly for the past 70 years.

The bottom line is this: the North American trade agreement is essential for both Mexico and the U.S., at least in the medium term. Mexico bears the greater burden in this relationship, dutifully following Washington's lead to ensure trade stability.

---

[44] UBS (2024) "Global wealth report 2024".

Technology will continue to follow the geopolitical contours of this relationship, with high-tech manufacturing staying in the U.S. and Taiwan while lower-end tasks move to Mexico. Cutting-edge semiconductor production won't be a short-term project—it takes decades and billions of dollars—but Mexico will take on related tasks like bundling Superchips and other technologies. This process will be complemented by substantial new investments and the acquisition of new scientific knowledge by Mexican multinationals. Mexico's highly skilled workforce is well-equipped to drive this forward.

Infrastructure development will be a major challenge for Mexico. To tackle the 'Mexico Cost'—which arises from issues like corruption, insecurity, and low productivity—improved infrastructure, especially in transportation and smart cities, is essential. Upgraded infrastructure will help address these internal issues and in opening new markets for Mexican manufacturers beyond the U.S. and Canada. The Global Infrastructure Hub estimates that Mexico needs to double its current infrastructure investment, which stands at 1.3% of GDP, to close the existing gap. An additional $544 billion is required by 2040 to address this shortfall.[45] While nearshoring could attract much-needed FDI, infrastructure development will need cooperation from the U.S., the EU, South Korea, or Saudi Arabia—countries that can provide the funds China is likely to stop offering.

Harnessing talent on both sides of the U.S.-Mexico border is feasible. The U.S. is likely to continue welcoming Mexican talent, from Nobel laureates teaching at American universities to entrepreneurs driving development in cities and infrastructure. It's also unlikely that low-skilled workers will stop filling jobs in U.S. agriculture.

It seems to be in both governments' best interest to organize migration flows. Like in Saudi Arabia, the U.S. increasingly depends on foreign workers to fill jobs that its own citizens are less willing to do. For Mexico, simultaneously, relying on low wages and low education levels is not a sustainable long-term strategy. U.S. and Canadian universities may become more open to Mexican students, particularly as restrictions on students from China, and Islamic countries increase. A North American version of the EU's Erasmus program could be part of the same plan.

In sum, going back to the initial question: will Mexico's unipolar choice accelerate its economic growth and bring its income levels closer to those of the U.S.? The answer isn't necessarily yes. But with more hugs and fewer bullets, more brains, and less inflammatory rhetoric, Mexico certainly has the potential to become a global success.

---

[45] PPIAF (2024) "Infrastructure market overview. Mexico" Retrieved from: https://www.gihub.org/countries/mexico/.

Nigeria

Africa is poised to play an increasingly significant role in driving global growth. According to the International Monetary Fund's (IMF) April 2025 World Economic Outlook, these markets are set for robust expansion, driven by demographic changes and a burgeoning consumer class.

Among the African nations, Ethiopia is forecasted to lead with an impressive 7.5% average annual growth rate in real GDP from 2024 to 2030. Following closely are Rwanda at 7.4%, Niger 6.9%, and Uganda at 6.8%, and then, Senegal at 5.6% and Mozambique 5.3%. These nations are expected to experience economic growth at rates more than double the global average, largely due to their rich natural resource deposits.

Yet, Nigeria is the crown jewel in Africa's emerging markets. With over 220 million inhabitants, Nigeria is Africa's most populous country and the sixth largest in the world. By 2050, it is expected to become the third largest globally, reaching a population of 400 million. Nigeria is also Africa's largest economy, with an estimated GDP of $370 billion in 2023.[46] Lagos, its largest city and commercial hub, is projected to rank among the world's ten largest megacities by 2035.

A notable feature of Nigeria's population is its youthful age distribution. Approximately 43% of the population is under the age of 14, and the median age is 19 years old.

Economically, Nigeria has achieved an impressive 4.9% average annual GDP growth over the past 25 years. This is notably higher than the 1.9% average for OECD countries during the same period. Income per capita has more than tripled, rising from $500 in 1999 to $1600 in 2023. While this performance elevated Nigeria from low-income to lower-middle-income status, significant challenges such as poverty, ethnic and religious conflicts, and corruption were not corrected.

Currently, 91% of the population lives on less than $6.85 a day, and 9% on less than $2.15 a day. Ethnic and religious divisions remain deep, exacerbated by Nigeria's colonial history, where arbitrary colonial borders brought together over 250 distinct ethnic groups, with the Hausa-Fulani, Yoruba, and Igbo being the largest. Since gaining independence from Britain in 1960, the country has struggled with tensions, particularly between the Islamic North and the Christian South.

Former U.S. Ambassador John Campbell described Nigeria as a country that has never functioned as a conventional nation-state. Instead, power

---

[46] The World Bank (2014) "World Development Indicators".

is decentralized, resting with traditional religious and local leaders rather than the federal government.[47] Richard Joseph, an Emeritus Professor at Northwestern University, noted that the country is comprised of "islands of authority surrounded by seas of ungoverned spaces. At the heart of the Nigerian paradox is the persistence of a state that generates enormous benefits for elites while the population grows ever poorer."

Nigeria's oil industry began in the 1950s, and by 1971, the country joined the Organization of the Petroleum Exporting Countries (OPEC). In 1999, it was the world's sixth-largest oil producer and held the 10th largest proven oil reserves globally, with daily production of 2 million barrels, reserves of 22 billion barrels, and gas reserves of 160 trillion cubic meters. However, as a commodity-dependent economy, Nigeria's growth has closely mirrored the international price of oil. The period from 1999 to 2010 saw robust economic expansion fueled by the oil price boom, economic reforms, and significant infrastructure investments.

From the early 2000s to 2008, rising global oil demand—particularly from China and India—drove oil prices upward. The influx of petrodollars provided over 80% of government revenues and 95% of export earnings, and the surge facilitated increased production and investments, particularly in the oil and gas sector (see Fig. 6.7).

Concurrently, Nigeria transitioned from military rule to a civilian government under President Olusegun Obasanjo in 1999. This shift boosted investor confidence and attracted foreign aid and investments. Economic reforms, such as deregulation, fiscal discipline, and anti-corruption measures, further stabilized the economy. Notable privatizations, particularly in telecommunications, energy, and banking, spurred growth.

Reforms and a more stable macroeconomic environment facilitated a major debt relief program from the Paris Club in 2005, which included an $18 billion write-off and aid packages. This allowed the government to allocate funds toward infrastructure projects, including roads, power, and education.

Agriculture, including fisheries, is Nigeria's most important industry, contributing 20–25% to the country's GDP. Over 60% of Nigerians work in these industries, primarily at the subsistence level. Notably, Nigeria is the world's largest yam producer, with a volume six times higher than Ghana, the second largest producing country, accounting for about 70% of global production. It is the number one cassava producer, accounting for about 20% of global production. It also ranks as the 4th largest producer of oil

---

[47] Campbell, John (2020) "Nigeria and the Nation-State: Rethinking Diplomacy with the Postcolonial World. Rowman & Littlefield.

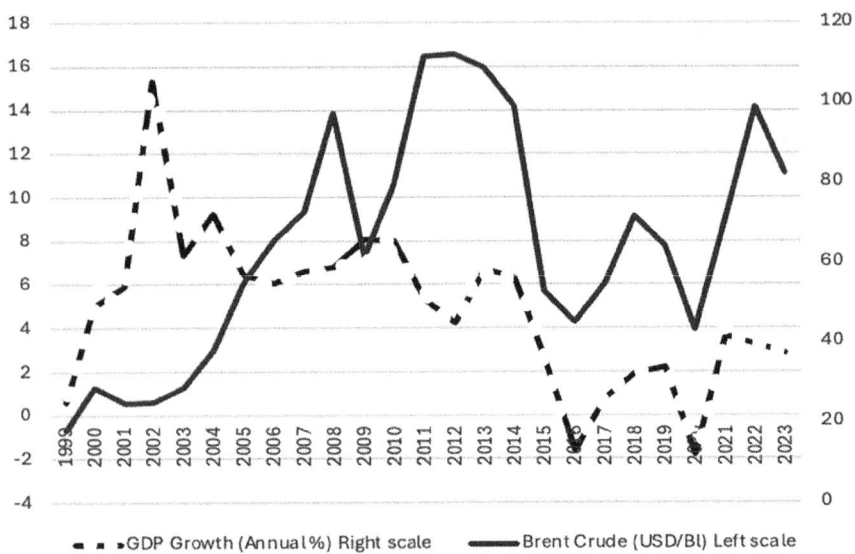

Fig. 6.7 Nigeria—price of oil and GDP growth (Current $ and %) (*Source* IMF, World Bank)

palm fruit, 12th in maize, and 13th in rice, and is among the largest fish consumers globally.[48]

However, according to FAO's latest data, performance in agricultural productivity has been mixed. Between 1999 and 2022, cassava yields declined by 37% and oil palm fruit fell 4%. However, maize yields increased by 40% over the same period.

During the oil-price boom period, remittances from Nigerians abroad surged from $2.3 billion in 2004 to $14.6 billion in 2005 and have remained around $20 billion annually since. This jump resulted from the Central Bank of Nigeria implementing policies to encourage remittance inflows through official channels. This included allowing dollar-denominated accounts and creating a regulatory environment conducive to foreign exchange flows. Previously, they were mostly sent through informal channels.

However, a sharp drop in oil prices starting in mid-2014—falling from over $100 per barrel to below $40 by 2016—significantly impacted Nigeria. Oil revenues, were close to 70% of government's revenues at the time. A sharp depletion of foreign exchange reserves forced the Central Bank of Nigeria

---

[48] FAO (2024) "FAO in Nigeria" Retrieved from: https://www.fao.org/nigeria/fao-in-nigeria/nigeria-at-a-glance/en/#:~:text=Nigeria%20has%2070.8%20million%20hectares,it%20famous%20for%20livestock%20keeping.

to devalue the naira, triggering inflation and higher costs for imports. Stiff capital controls disrupted business operations and investor confidence.

The economy entered a recession in 2016, with GDP contracting by 1.6%. Although growth returned in 2017, it remained weak at an average of 2% per year—below Nigeria's 2.5% population growth rate—leading to stagnating per-capita incomes and rising poverty. The COVID-19 pandemic exacerbated these challenges, causing a second recession in 2020.

Despite calls for economic diversification, Nigeria remains heavily reliant on oil, with limited progress in other sectors. Inadequate power supply, poor transportation, and weak digital infrastructure continue to hinder productivity.

Corruption and weak institutions further undermine progress. According to Transparency International's *Corruption Perceptions Index*, Nigeria ranked 145th out of 180 countries in 2023.[49] The 2023 earthquakes showed an unexpected cost of corruption in the construction industry. Poorly enforced building codes contributed to significant loss of life and property. These factors contributed to the decline of Nigeria's economy, causing it to fall from the 1st to the 4th position in Africa by 2023.

Examining the political landscape of the country, Nigeria operates as a federal republic with a multi-party system. It follows a presidential system of government with power divided among the executive, legislative, and judicial branches. President Bola Ahmed Tinubu assumed office as the 16th President of Nigeria in May 2023, succeeding Muhammadu Buhari, who served two terms.

The country's political framework is defined by a hard-to-maintain balance between federal governance and regional autonomy across its 36 states and the Federal Capital Territory, Abuja. However, political stability remains a significant challenge due to regional tensions, ethnic diversity, and security threats, including the Boko Haram insurgency in the northeast and secessionist movements in the southeast.

Security is a huge concern, as Nigeria faces profound security challenges that impact both domestic stability and its international relations. The Boko Haram insurgency, which began in 2009, has caused significant loss of lives and displacement of millions while destabilizing neighboring countries such as Chad, Niger, and Cameroon. The name Boko Haram roughly translates to "Western education is forbidden" or "Western education is sinful," reflecting the group's opposition to Western influence and its strict interpretation of Islamic principles.

---

[49] Transparency International (2024) "Corruption Perception Index 2023" Retrieved From: https://www.transparency.org/en/cpi/2023.

In addition to Boko Haram, criminal gangs in the northwest exacerbate insecurity through kidnappings, cattle theft, and armed robberies. In the Niger Delta, militancy linked to oil production has led to theft, sabotage, piracy, and attacks on infrastructure, significantly disrupting oil output. Groups such as the Movement for the Emancipation of the Niger Delta (MEND) and the Niger Delta Avengers (NDA) have attacked pipelines and installations to protest environmental degradation caused by oil extraction or to advocate for the rights of local communities. Despite government amnesty programs, the region remains volatile due to unresolved socio-economic grievances.

In assessing the current business environment, economic, legal, and resource issues loom large. To begin, inflation in Nigeria averaged 12% annually between 1999 and 2023, with several episodes of high inflation. The consumer price index reached a 28-year high of 34% in 2024. In contrast, inflation among OECD member countries stood at just over 4% in that year.

This price instability has been coupled with significant exchange rate volatility. Over 25 years, the Nigerian naira underwent a 35-fold nominal depreciation against the U.S. dollar, driven by high inflation, reliance on oil exports, and limited foreign reserves. Exchange rate volatility, measured by the standard deviation of the exchange rate, was 19% during this period, significantly higher than Mexico's 13% and Poland's 6%.

The volatility was exacerbated by capital controls, a managed float regime, and speculative pressures in the parallel market. Combined with inflation, this has created a high-interest-rate environment, further complicating business operations.

The African Continental Free Trade Agreement (AfCFTA) presents Nigeria with an opportunity to expand exports within Africa. Promising industries for regional trade include textiles, processed foods, and pharmaceuticals, but non-oil exports remain a small part of the economy. Trade barriers, such as port inefficiencies, customs delays, and inadequate logistics infrastructure, increase business costs. Smuggling and periodic border closures, implemented to curb illegal trade, further disrupt supply chains and complicate operations for legitimate businesses.

Legal environment. Nigeria's legal system is based on English common law, Islamic law (Sharia), and customary law. The judiciary is independent in theory but struggles with inefficiency, corruption, and delays. Businesses face challenges such as bureaucratic red tape, inconsistent enforcement of regulations, and limited access to justice.

Nigeria has a dual-faceted legal environment. On the positive side, it boasts robust commercial laws protecting intellectual property, contracts, and investments. Specialized courts like the Lagos State Arbitration Court provide faster resolutions for commercial disputes, making Nigeria an attractive investment destination. However, inconsistent enforcement of regulations, coupled with widespread corruption, poses significant risks. Businesses face unclear and overlapping policies at federal and state levels, resulting in delays and higher compliance costs. Foreign firms must also navigate uncertainties around taxation policies and profit repatriation.

Technology

Nigeria will have 230 million smartphone connections in 2030, nearly double South Africa's expected 140 million.[50] Mobile connectivity is often touted as one of Nigeria's technological strengths. However good, this statistic warrants a closer look.

In 2023, Nigeria recorded 224 million mobile cellular subscriptions, translating to 101 subscriptions per 100 people. While this figure seems impressive, it falls in line with global norms, where having more cellular subscriptions than inhabitants is common. For example, Poland has 131 subscriptions per 100 people, OECD member countries average 122, and Vietnam reaches 139. Despite financing options from e-commerce platforms, banks, and mobile operators, subscription growth in Nigeria has plateaued.

The advantage of cellular phone coverage loses its luster when paired with internet access data. In 2022, 76 million Nigerians were internet users, equivalent to 35% of the population. While Nigeria leads Africa in absolute numbers, surpassing Egypt's 82 million users, its internet penetration lags behind countries like Mexico (79%), Poland (87%), and the OECD average (90%).[51]

Broadband access paints a bleaker picture. In 2023, Nigeria had 117,000 fixed broadband subscriptions, equivalent to just 0.05 per 100 people. By comparison, Poland has 86 per 100, Mexico has 81, and the OECD average is 90. This data underscores that owning a smartphone doesn't necessarily translate to technological advancement or widespread digital adoption.

---

[50] GSMA Intelligence (2024) "The mobile economy Sub-Saharan Africa 2024" Retrieved from: https://data.gsmaintelligence.com/api-web/v2/research-file-download?id=88244676&file=111124-Mobile%20Economy-SSA-2024.pdf.
[51] The World Bank (2024) Op. Cit.

Nigeria's digital readiness is further illustrated by the IMF's AI Preparedness Index, which assesses countries' capabilities in leveraging artificial intelligence and managing its risks. In 2023, Nigeria ranked 139 out of 174 economies with a score of 0.35, close to the average for low-income countries (0.32) and below the 0.46 for emerging economies. Top-ranked Singapore scored 0.8.[52] The country's challenges are reflected in the low level of digital integration among firms; in 2021, only 22% of Nigerian firms had a website, compared to 41% in Mexico and over 70% in Europe.

As for startups, despite these challenges, Nigeria's startup ecosystem stands out in the region. Lagos, often dubbed with one of those rather kind marketing exaggerations as the "Silicon Valley of Africa," leads the tech scene, with the Yaba district emerging as a focal point for startups, incubators, and innovation hubs. Between 2015 and 2022 (latest available data), Nigeria attracted $2.1 billion in tech investments—more than double South Africa's $1 billion and Egypt's $0.8 billion.[53] Fintech dominates the ecosystem, comprising 36% of total startups in 2022.

In 2023, Nigeria accounted for $399.9 million in startup funding, representing 16.6% of Africa's total investment.[54] Notably, four out of Africa's seven unicorns originated in Nigeria, showcasing its entrepreneurial success. Initiatives like the Kite ICT park in Yaba and the 'Art of Technology Lagos' platform further drive innovation and attract international venture capital.[55]

E-governance is another area of progress, with initiatives like the National Identity Management Commission (NIMC) and Integrated Personnel and Payroll Information System (IPPIS) using digital tools to enhance transparency and efficiency. Innovations in agriculture, such as Afriscout, empower farmers by blending traditional and modern techniques, driving inclusivity and productivity. Regulatory framework.[56]

Technology is evolving but remains fragmented. Regulatory uncertainties in sectors such as fintech, blockchain, cybersecurity, and data privacy have discouraged foreign investment and slowed local innovation. Nevertheless, due to the sheer size of the country, Nigeria's tech sector is a promising destination for global investors.

---

[52] IMF (2024) "AI Preparedness Index" Retrieved from: https://www.imf.org/external/datamapper/.

[53] Natera, Alejandro, Dileep Nair, Javon Bethel, Roberto Reyes (2024) "An Assessment of the Key Drivers Shaping the New Business Landscape. Nigeria" Mimeo.

[54] Digital Cooperation Organization (2024) "Startup country guide 2024. The Republic of Nigeria" retrieved from: https://dco.org/wp-content/uploads/2024/08/Nigeria-Guide.pdf.

[55] Natera Op. Cit.

[56] Ibid.

Infrastructure[57]

"There is widespread consensus that inadequate infrastructure is one of the major constraints to sustained economic growth and development in Nigeria," reads the opening line of Nigeria's National Integrated Infrastructure Master Plan, the government's blueprint for infrastructure investment until 2025.

The statistics validate this claim. Nigeria ranked 66th out of 67 countries in the 2024 Global Competitiveness Index for infrastructure quality.[58] Similarly, the African Development Bank's Africa Infrastructure Development Index (AIDI) for 2022 placed Nigeria 24th out of 54 African nations.

The Logistics Performance Index, which assesses trade and transport infrastructure quality, rated Nigeria at 2.4 in 2022—barely matching its lower-middle-income counterparts. According to the Global Infrastructure Hub, Nigeria's infrastructure quality scored 40, significantly below the 57 average for lower-middle-income peers (on a scale 100). Infrastructure investment, at just 4% of GDP, also trails behind the 5.4% average for lower-middle-income. Rapid population growth and urbanization are set to further amplify the unmet demand for improved infrastructure. The Global Infrastructure Hub estimates that Nigeria requires $35 billion annually to meet its infrastructure needs, double the current investment levels. Given its heavy reliance on the volatile oil and gas sector for revenue, the government acknowledges the necessity of attracting private and foreign investments to fill this gap.

The government considers that infrastructure investment via Nigeria's sovereign fund and other tools is an efficient force to combat poverty and insecurity. "From the moment you start the construction of a railroad, you have to employ labor from those communities," explained Yusuf Maitama Tuggar, minister of Foreign Affairs, in a conference at the Woodrow Wilson Center in Washington D.C.

Just how is Nigeria faring across a wide spectrum of infrastructure?

Roads. Nigeria's road network spans approximately 200,000 kilometers, making it the 28th longest globally. However, only 30% of these roads are paved. Nigeria's road network is the primary mode of transport for goods and people, accounting for over 90% of passenger and freight movement.

---

[57] Sections on roads, railroads, ports and energy rely to an important degree on comments found in Natera, Alejandro, Dileep Nair, Javon Bethel, and Roberto Reyes (2024) Op. Cit.

[58] IMD (2024) "World Competitiveness Ranking" Retrieved from: https://www.imd.org/centers/wcc/world-competitiveness-center/rankings/world-competitiveness-ranking/.

However, the network suffers from poor design, poor maintenance, underinvestment, and weak regulatory enforcement.[59] According to the National Integrated Infrastructure Master Plan, Nigeria needs an investment of over $3 trillion to close its infrastructure gap, with a significant portion allocated to road upgrades.

The ongoing Lagos-Ibadan Expressway project, part of the Trans-African Highway network, is one of the most critical road infrastructure projects in Nigeria. This highway connects Lagos to significant cities and is a lifeline for freight transport. Similarly, the Abuja-Kaduna-Zaria-Kano Road, a 375 km expressway currently under reconstruction, will significantly reduce travel time and improve logistics between the north and south.

Private sector players like cement manufacturer Dangote Group have also invested in road infrastructure. In 2019, Dangote, in a joint venture with Brazilian construction company Andrade Gutierrez, completed the construction of the Obajana-Kabba road under a tax waiver scheme.

Railroads. Nigeria's rail system is undergoing a revival. The Nigerian Railway Corporation (NCR), the government agency responsible for rail transport, has overseen projects such as the Lagos-Ibadan Standard Gauge Railway, which was completed in 2021 by China Civil Engineering Construction Corporation (CCECC) as part of China's Belt and Road Initiative. This rail line is a critical link between Lagos, Nigeria's economic hub, and the industrial city of Ibadan. The line is expected to carry 4 million passengers and 2 million metric tons of freight annually, with a designed speed of 150 kilometers per hour.

The Abuja-Kaduna railway, another major line built by CCECC, was inaugurated in 2016. The total cost was $870 million. It connects the capital to northern regions. The NRC recently increased the number of train services on this route due to a perceived 22% increase in demand. These upgrades are part of the government's broader National Rail Infrastructure Master Plan, which aims to connect major economic hubs across Nigeria, reducing the burden on roadways and enhancing logistics efficiency.

Urban transportation. In 2024, Lagos—a city of 16 million and one of the fastest-growing in the world—is ranked as the worst globally for traffic congestion, according to the Numbeo Traffic Index. Commuters in Lagos often spend up to four hours daily in traffic. Additionally, the city is the 10th most polluted in the world.

---

[59] Leonard, Joel and Faith Abimaje (2024) "Optimizing Nigerian road reliability by defining poor road causes, maintenance strategies, and application" Engineering Science & Technology Journal, Volume 5, Issue 7, July 2024.

To address these issues, the Lagos Metropolitan Area Transport Authority (LAMATA) introduced the Bus Rapid Transit system in 2008. This system now transports approximately 4.5 million passengers annually and recently incorporated an AI platform to optimize its operations, aiming to improve efficiency and reduce delays.

LAMATA also launched the Lagos Rail Mass Transit project under a contract with the Chinese construction company CCECC. The second of five proposed lines of the 30-year plan was completed in 2024. The newly completed line is expected to carry over 1 million passengers per day, offering a vital solution to the city's mobility challenges.

Ports. Nigeria's ports handle 97% of exports and 80% of imports.[60] The Nigerian Ports Authority (NPA) manages major ports such as Apapa and Tin Can Island in Lagos, which account for most of Nigeria's maritime trade.

The country's first deep-sea port Lekki Port became operational in 2023. This facility is expected to ease any congestion at Apapa and Tin Can Island while enhancing the efficiency of imports and exports. Lekki Deep Sea Port—developed and controlled under the Belt and Road Initiative by the China Harbour Engineering Company (CHEC)—has a handling capacity of 2.7 million TEUs (twenty-foot equivalent units) per year.

Airports. In 2013, China Eximbank and the Nigerian government signed a $560 million preferential buyer's credit agreement to expand four major airport terminals in Abuja, Kano, Lagos, and Port Harcourt.[61] Remodeled Lagos Airport manages over 60% of the country's air cargo. The Murtala Muhammed Airport in Lagos and the Nnamdi Azikiwe International Airport in Abuja, the two busiest airports in Nigeria, handled 62% of the nation's total international aircraft movements in 2023.

The logistics and freight sector in Nigeria is further strengthened by companies such as Arik Air and Allied Air, which specialize in freight transport. These firms play a vital role in linking Nigeria to international markets, boosting trade capabilities, and supporting the country's economic growth.

Oil, gas, and energy infrastructure. As Africa's largest oil producer and an OPEC member, Nigeria's proven reserves and production levels are substantial but insufficient to influence global oil prices significantly. Years of failing to meet OPEC production quotas, combined with militancy, piracy, theft, and sabotage in the Niger Delta, undermine its reliability as a supplier. The Nigerian economy's vulnerability to oil prices also weakens its position even

---

[60] National Bureau of Statistics (NBS) "Foreign Trade in Goods".
[61] Aiddata (2013) "China Eximbank provides $500 million preferential buyer's credit for Nigeria Retrieved from: https://china.aiddata.org/projects/30341/.

more. Moreover, OPEC's influence has diminished due to increased U.S. production.

Nigeria's oil sector is heavily dependent on multinational oil corporations. This opens a new space for geopolitical bargaining. While major oil companies bring expertise, they have been criticized for prioritizing profits over environmental and social responsibilities. Oil spills, gas flaring, and environmental degradation in the Niger Delta have fueled tensions between local communities, the Nigerian government, and international firms.[62] More recently, the shift of multinationals to offshore operations creates opportunities for indigenous companies to become significant players in the global oil industry.

The Nigerian National Petroleum Company Limited (NNPC), a state-owned corporation, manages the country's oil and gas resources. The NNPC operates through joint venture agreements with international oil majors like Shell, Chevron, and ExxonMobil, typically holding a majority stake of 55–60%. It also employs production-sharing contracts for offshore exploration and licenses smaller independent operators. However, the NNPC has faced criticism for inefficiencies, corruption, and a lack of transparency, particularly regarding operational expenses, subsidies, and inadequate supervision of the industry.

Oil production in Nigeria declined 26% between 1994 and 2023, in stark contrast to a 39% increase in global production over the same period. This underperformance stems from underinvestment, mismanagement, and persistent issues such as oil theft and militancy in the Niger Delta. International oil companies have been divesting from carbon-intensive, problem-ridden onshore assets, and local independent firms have stepped in to acquire them. This will stabilize production to some extent[63] (Fig. 6.8).

Refining. Nigeria's limited refining capacity has necessitated heavy reliance on imported refined petroleum products, which have historically accounted for around 30% of its import bill. The Dangote Refinery, Africa's largest, began operations in January 2024. It sells gasoline, diesel, jet fuel, and other fuels through major traders like Vitol (Dutch), Trafigura (Singapore), and BP (UK), and also other inputs for the plastics industry.[64] The refinery was projected to save $10 billion annually in import costs, approximately half of the country's petroleum product imports in 2023.

---

[62] Natera, Alejandro et al. (2024) Op. Cit.
[63] Trade Commissioner Service (2024) "Oil and gas market in Nigeria" Retrieved from: https://www.tradecommissioner.gc.ca/nigeria/market-reports-etudes-de-marches/0007653.aspx?lang=eng.
[64] S&P Global (2024) "Nigeria's Dangote refinery to export first gasoline as local market struggles" Retrieved from: https://www.spglobal.com/commodityinsights/.

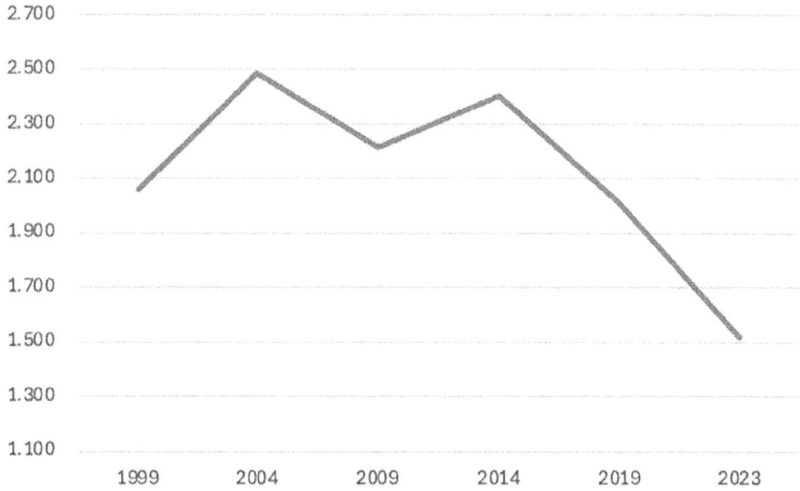

Fig. 6.8 Nigeria—production of petroleum and other liquids (thousands of barrels per day) (*Source* EIA)

The elimination of gasoline subsidies in May 2023 increased at-pump prices by 50%, which reduced local demand. Illicit imports have also cut the demand for Dangote products. In this scenario, Dangote will probably open export markets in regions like Ghana and the Caribbean Community CARICOM.[65]

The estimated cost of the refinery, at $19 billion, is significantly higher than the $10–16 billion typically required for refineries of similar capacity (600,000–700,000 bpd), which has raised concerns about its return on investment.

As for electricity, only 60% of Nigeria's population has access to electricity, leaving 88 million people without power—the highest globally. In rural areas, less than 30% of the population has access to electricity, highlighting a significant disparity in energy infrastructure.

Power outages are a persistent issue in Nigeria, largely due to inadequate investment in the energy sector. The national grid experienced 10 collapses in 2024, underscoring the system's fragility and the urgent need for reform.[66] An additional challenge is Nigeria's electricity generation and distribution capacity. Approximately 15% of the output is lost.

---

[65] Ibid.
[66] AP (2024) "Nigeria's major cities suffer blackouts as the power grid collapses yet again" Retrieved from: https://apnews.com/article/nigeria-nationwide-power-outage-electricity-3efa0ec13c42280d4a67d2d561a24322.

Beyond oil. Economic development requires building knowledge and skills in complex activities, products, and exports. According to the Economic Complexity Index, however, Nigeria is one of the world's least complex nations. It ranked 128 out of 133 countries in 2021.[67]

Nigeria will probably become more complex as it builds new non-oil industries. The telecommunications sector opened to private firms in 2001. Led by firms like MTN and Airtel, has driven digital transformation across the country. Agriculture, employing over 60% of the population, holds significant potential for value-added processing and export growth. Meanwhile, the entertainment industry, famously dubbed "Nollywood," is the second-largest film producer globally, generating substantial revenues and creating between 300,000 and 800,000 jobs. Its media and entertainment industry is among the fastest-growing creative sectors globally. With vast market size and rapid population growth, Nollywood might achieve an annual growth rate of 8.8%. In 2021, Nigeria's film industry alone contributed 2.3% to GDP and is projected to generate over $1 billion in export revenue. Combined, the motion picture and music industries added approximately $1.8 billion to the country's GDP in 2020.[68]

Infrastructure projects, especially in energy and transportation, present new investment opportunities. Public–private partnerships are increasingly financing these projects, attracting both local and international investors. One can expect to see the arrangements increase significantly in coming years.

Geopolitics

Despite its size, Nigeria plays a limited role in global affairs. The country receives some U.S. military support against Boko Haram, maintains deep ties and financial obligations with China for infrastructure development, is a banker for the UK, and serves as an oil supplier to Europe. However, this multipolar engagement is less a result of a deliberate non-aligned strategy and more a reflection of the general global irrelevance that most developing nations face.

Nigeria's geopolitical significance primarily arises from its participation in organizations like the African Union (AU), the Economic Community of West African States (ECOWAS), and the Organization of Petroleum Exporting Countries (OPEC). Its presence in the World Trade Organization's

---

[67] Growth Lab (2024) "Country and product complexity rankings" Retrieved from: https://atlas.cid.harvard.edu/rankings.
[68] U.S. International Trade Administration (2023) "Nigeria – Media and entertainment" Retrieved from: https://www.trade.gov/country-commercial-guides/.

General Directorate and recent efforts to secure representation for developing nations in the UN Security Council and G20 also reflect its concrete achievements and its aspirations for greater influence. However, internal challenges such as ethnic and religious divisions, corruption, and widespread insecurity limit its ability to exert meaningful influence regionally and globally.

In West Africa, Nigeria's population and economy position it as the dominant power. With a population larger than all other West African nations combined and the continent's largest economy, Nigeria is expected to play a significant role in shaping regional policies. As a founding member of ECOWAS, Nigeria has historically contributed to peacekeeping and conflict resolution in countries like Sierra Leone, Liberia, and Mali. However, ECOWAS has weakened in recent years, plagued by internal divisions, member withdrawals, and dwindling citizen support.

The region's lack of infrastructural connectivity further complicates Nigeria's role. According to the African Development Bank's Infrastructural Integration Index, Nigeria scores 0.252 (on a scale where one is best). Additionally, divergent colonial legacies and strategic alliances with external powers like France and the U.S. create tensions. While Francophone West African nations often align with France, Nigeria, an Anglophone country, is perceived as the leader of the Anglophone bloc.

Finally, President Tinubu's firm stance against military coups has deepened these divisions, prompting Mali, Burkina Faso, and Niger to withdraw from ECOWAS in January 2024, citing sanctions imposed by the Community as "inhumane."

When it comes to the geopolitical relations Nigeria maintains with both industrialized and emerging nations, global powers, and trading partners, Nigeria displays benefits from its posture of flexibility and pragmatism. To illustrate:

United States. The U.S. considered Nigeria a partner in counterinsurgency and regional stability. Despite concerns about corruption and human rights abuses, the U.S. viewed Nigeria as essential to maintaining stability in Africa against the growing expansion of Islam State's Boko Haram. It will also back the interest of its oil companies like Chevron and ExxonMobil. China's cutback on infrastructure financing might make Abuja turn to the United States for loans and aid.

China. China's engagement with Nigeria has expanded significantly over the past two decades, driven by the Chinese Belt and Road Initiative (BRI) and China's growing demand for resources. As one of Nigeria's largest trading partners, China has played a crucial role in financing and constructing infrastructure projects across the country.

However, this relationship has drawn criticism for its lack of transparency and the perceived neo-colonial nature of Chinese investments in Africa. Concerns have been raised about Nigeria's increasing reliance on Chinese financing and the implications for its sovereignty. Nigeria responds that China's financial terms for infrastructure projects remain more favorable than those offered by other international partners.

According to Nigeria's Minister of Foreign Affairs, Yusuf Maitama Tuggar, European firms often lose bids to Chinese companies on infrastructure projects due to less competitive financial conditions. He pointed out that "European export credit agencies shy away," creating a significant gap that Chinese institutions readily fill.

The Global South. Nigerians will strongly resent alliances, aid, or investment from countries that infantilize African nations, an attitude usually associated with the U.S. and European countries and some multilateral banks. "As if they do not know what is good for them. As if they need the protection of others," Minister Yusuf Tuggar remarked. Hence, alliances with BRICS and Global South organizations perceived as anti-imperialistic will likely be favored. In October 2024, Nigeria joined the BRICS bloc as a partner country, along with 12 other countries, and intends to join as a full member within two years.

Russia plays a quiet but notable role, particularly through its involvement in West African coups in Burkina Faso, Mali, and Niger. Russian advisors and the Wagner Group's presence in these regions reflect Moscow's efforts to counter U.S. and EU influence and circumvent economic sanctions.

Internal security. Nigeria faces significant security challenges. Boko Haram, which began its insurgency in 2009, seeks to establish an Islamic caliphate in northeastern Nigeria. The conflict killed thousands, displaced over 2 million people, and destabilized neighboring countries like Chad, Niger, and Cameroon. Boko Haram's allegiance to the Islamic State in 2015 transformed the group into the Islamic State in the West African Province (ISWAP), which now controls parts of northeastern Nigeria. Despite international support from the U.S. and EU, Nigeria's efforts to combat ISWAP have been undermined by corruption and poor coordination.

Trade. The European Union (primarily The Netherlands and Spain) accounts for one-third of Nigeria's exports, followed by India (14%), the U.S. (5%), China (3.2%), and the UK (2.7%). Small non-oil exports, including soybeans, cocoa, and citrus fruits, are produced in the tropical savannah climate of the Middle Belt and the humid rainforest zones of the southwest and south-south regions.[69] On the import side, China supplies nearly a quarter of Nigeria's imports (24%), followed by the EU (16%), India (9%), and the U.S. (7%).

Nigeria's growing population and economic potential ensure its global relevance will increase. As John Campbell noted, "With its already huge and rapidly growing population—estimated to become the third largest in the world by the end of the century—it is only going to become more, not less, important.[70]"

Talent

Simply put, Nigeria is a promise because it is a nation of children. Recapping, it is Africa's most populous country and the sixth largest globally; Nigeria has over 220 million inhabitants. By 2050, it is projected to become the world's third-largest country, with a population exceeding 400 million.

The nation's population is remarkably young, with 43% under the age of 14, 60% below 25, and a median age of just 19. Urbanization is happening at an extraordinary rate of 4% per year, with 54% of the population already living in cities as of 2023. Lagos, Nigeria's largest city, is on track to rank among the world's ten largest megacities by 2035.

For Nigeria, demographics are destiny. Over the next two decades, Nigeria will grapple with mounting pressures on its education and healthcare systems, as well as social and economic challenges, until its youthful population transitions into the household formation stage, potentially triggering a stabler, consumption-based growth trajectory.

Currently, education poses significant challenges in terms of both access and quality. According to UNESCO, only 62% of Nigerians aged 15 and older are literate. The nation's top universities, such as the University of Ibadan and the University of Lagos, are ranked below the world's top 1000.[71] Moreover, Nigeria's infrastructural shortcomings in electricity, transportation, and digital connectivity hinder talent development, making it difficult for individuals to pursue education and career opportunities.

Healthcare is another area of concern. The country's infant mortality is at 34 deaths per 1000 live births, compared to 5 in Poland and 4 in the UK.

---

[69] Intracen (2024) 2019 to 2023 averages with data from "Trade Maps" Retrieved from: https://www.trademap.org/Index.aspx.
[70] Ibid.
[71] QS (2024) "QS World University Rankings" Retrieved from: https://www.universityrankings.ch/results?ranking=QS&region=World&year=&q=Nigeria.

Additionally, Nigeria accounts for 27% of the global malaria burden, with 68 million cases and 194,000 deaths in 2021.[72] It has the world's second-highest burden of HIV/AIDS, with an estimated three million people living with the disease.[73]

Public health faces further challenges from drug trafficking and substance abuse. In 2017, around 14.3 million Nigerians, or 6.5% of the population, were reported to have used drugs.[74] This expanding market could attract international drug cartels, particularly as Nigeria transitions from being a transit point to a drug-producing area.

In addition to education and health, a large, young, and impoverished population is often linked to increased violence, gang activity, and insurgency. Groups like Boko Haram, with an estimated 15,000 members and criminal gangs, pose significant threats to stability and investment. These organizations often offer better financial incentives than legal employment, attracting vulnerable youth into their ranks.

Brain drain. "Japa," which translates to "run away" or "escape" in Yoruba, has become a cultural term reflecting the increasing wave of emigration from Nigeria. Poor healthcare, education, and security conditions have led to a significant brain drain, with many skilled professionals in healthcare, engineering, and technology seeking better opportunities abroad. This exodus weakens Nigeria's ability to retain talent and hampers growth in critical sectors.[75]

The trend is exacerbated by better air connectivity and by family ties with Nigeria's colossal diaspora, estimated at approximately 17 million people, or 8% of the population.[76] If accurate, this makes Nigeria's diaspora the second largest globally, surpassing Mexico (11.2 million) and second only to India (17.5 million).[77]

Unemployment. Odd as it might seem, Nigeria can be considered an economy with full employment. Its unemployment rate was 3% in 2023—lower than Egypt's 7.3% and South Africa's 28%—. Youth unemployment stood at 5.8%, compared to 19% in Egypt and 49% in South Africa. The

---

[72] WHO (2022) "Report on malaria in Nigeria 2022" Retrieved from: https://www.afro.who.int/countries/nigeria/publication/.
[73] Unicef (2024) "Nigeria" Retrieved from: https://www.unicef.org/nigeria/.
[74] UNDOC (2018) "Drug use in Nigeria" Retrieved from: https://www.unodc.org/.
[75] Natera, Alejandro et al. (2024) Op. Cit.
[76] IOM (2023) "2023 Annual report" Retrieved from: https://nigeria.iom.int/sites/g/files/tmzbdl1856/files/documents/2024-05/2023-iom-nigeria-annual-report.pdf. It is important.
[77] UN Population Division (2020) "International migrant stock 2020" Retrieved from: https://www.un.org/development/desa/pd/content/international-migrant-stock. This report places Nigeria's diaspora at 1.7 million.

real issue lies in the nature of employment. Wage-paying jobs are scarce, and a mismatch between academic training and business needs has led to higher unemployment rates among workers with post-secondary education compared to those with basic education.[78]

Nevertheless, enterprises like the Dangote Refinery, mentioned above, will require Nigerians to learn and deploy advanced capabilities. While it has relied on foreign expertise for design and construction, the refinery highlights the country's potential for new technological achievements. Indigenous companies in oil and gas are increasingly exploring modular refineries and gas-to-liquid technologies, diversifying Nigeria's industrial landscape.

Managerial talent. Nigeria faces significant challenges in this essential tool for development. The World Management Survey (WMS), which evaluates practices highly correlated with good firm performance, like target setting and monitoring, ranked Nigerian managers 28th out of 38 countries. This highlights significant weaknesses in managerial skills.

Nigeria's corporate structure also limits opportunities for developing advanced management experience. Over 75% of Nigerians work in establishments with fewer than five employees. These small-scale operations lack sophisticated management systems, reducing demand for skilled labor and stifling professional growth.[79]

To transfer business knowledge and practices, successful business owners in Nigeria's Islamic North often involve family members in their enterprises. Family structures are tightly knit, and trust within families is highly valued. This aligns with cultural and religious Islamic principles that encourages mutual family support.[80]

Where Nigeria's talent truly shines is in the arts. Nollywood, Nigeria's film industry, is the second largest globally in terms of output, producing an estimated 2500 films in 2022. These productions use English as the dominant language, but their topics and production quality limit their global appeal.

In music, Nigerian artists like Rema, Burna Boy, and Wizkid have brought Afrobeats to international prominence, solidifying Nigeria's global cultural influence. Additionally, the fashion industry, valued at $4.7 billion, accounts for 15% of Sub-Saharan Africa's total market value.

---

[78] Lain, Jonathan and Utz Pape (2024) "Why do so many Nigerian workers remain poor?" World Bank Blogs. https://blogs.worldbank.org/en/opendata/why-do-so-many-nigerian-workers-remain-poor-labor-force-surveys-may-have-answer.

[79] Pape, Utz and Jonathan Lain (2024) Op. Cit.

[80] Scur, Daniela et al. (2021) "The World Management Survey at 18: Lessons and the Way Forward". NBER Working Paper Series.

Key Drivers

Nigeria represents one of the world's most interesting economic growth stories, rich with hues and contradictions. It serves as a vital case study for understanding what happens when a big, resource-abundant nation goes poor, and to find the paths it should take to reignite progress.

Geopolitics stands out as the most significant factor driving growth. The country's oil wealth, international partnerships, and strategic regional role have historically formed the cornerstone of its economic trajectory. Infrastructure investment is a close second, gradually unlocking new opportunities. Meanwhile, technology and talent have played supporting roles but are poised to become critical as Nigerians grow older and diversify their economy.

From colony, to oil producer, to problem nation. Geopolitics is a major driver of capital importation into the country. Capital imports includes Foreign Direct Investment (FDI), portfolio investments, and other inflows like trade credit and other loans. To no surprise, between 2019 and 2022, the United Kingdom contributed between one-third and one-half of the total capital imported into its former colony, Nigeria. Additional significant investors, including South Africa, Singapore, and the United States, accounted for 20% to 35% of the total.[81]

Portfolio investments, rather than FDI, have dominated Nigeria's capital inflows, averaging 55% of total capital imports from 2014 to 2023. In contrast, FDI—a key driver of growth through skills transfer and local supplier development—accounted for only 10% (Fig. 6.9).

Foreign Direct Investment. FDI inflows into Nigeria from 1999 to 2003 were striking in dollar terms. On average, they equaled 6.6% of exports during that period—comparable to the value of Nigeria's top 10 non-oil exports combined and large relative to other African economies like Ghana, Kenya, Ethiopia, and South Africa.

Nigeria embarked on major economic reforms under President Olusegun Obasanjo's administration (1999–2007) through the National Economic Empowerment and Development Strategy (NEEDS). This reform package featured fairly standard, orthodox, fiscal and monetary tightening, debt reduction, anti-corruption measures, privatization, and financial sector reform.

In 2005, Nigeria negotiated a historic debt relief agreement with the Paris Club. Of its $36 billion debt, $18 billion was forgiven, and this new

---

[81] National Bureau of Statistics (2024) "Nigeria capital importation Q4 2023" Retrieved from: https://www.nigerianstat.gov.ng/elibrary/read/1241454.

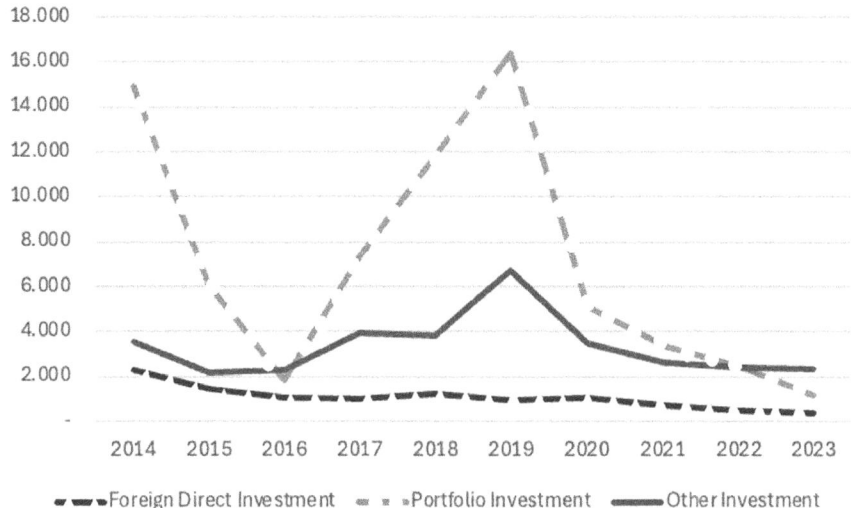

Fig. 6.9 Nigeria—capital imports (billions of $) (*Source* Nigeria's National Bureau of Statistics)

fiscal condition mobilized unprecedented FDI inflows in 2005 and 2006. However, the inflow largely failed to develop Nigeria's non-oil sectors.

Despite this initial boost, FDI inflows steadily declined after 2011, as falling global oil prices reduced government revenues, limiting infrastructure investment and macroeconomic stability (see Fig. 6.10). The oil price crash of 2014–2016, combined with the devaluation of the naira and rigid currency controls imposed by the Central Bank of Nigeria, further discouraged foreign investment. Growing insecurity, including Boko Haram insurgencies in the Northeast and militant activities, attacks on oil infrastructure, kidnappings, and banditry in the Niger Delta, further eroded investor confidence.

Confidence in Nigeria's oil sector returned with the passage of the Petroleum Industry Act in 2021. By 2023 and 2024, international oil majors announced plans for more than $17 billion in deep-water oil investments, marking a renewed commitment to Nigeria's energy future.

Nigeria has consistently attracted larger FDI inflows than most African peers, averaging $3.7 billion annually between 1999 and 2023, compared to $1.9 billion in Ghana and $1.5 billion in Ethiopia. However, the majority of this FDI has been concentrated in the oil and gas sector, primarily from the United States, the United Kingdom, and the Netherlands.

Simultaneously, adverse conditions prompted unusually high FDI outflows since 2008 compared to neighboring economies. Outflows represented 1.2% of exports on average from 1999 to 2003 (Fig. 6.11).

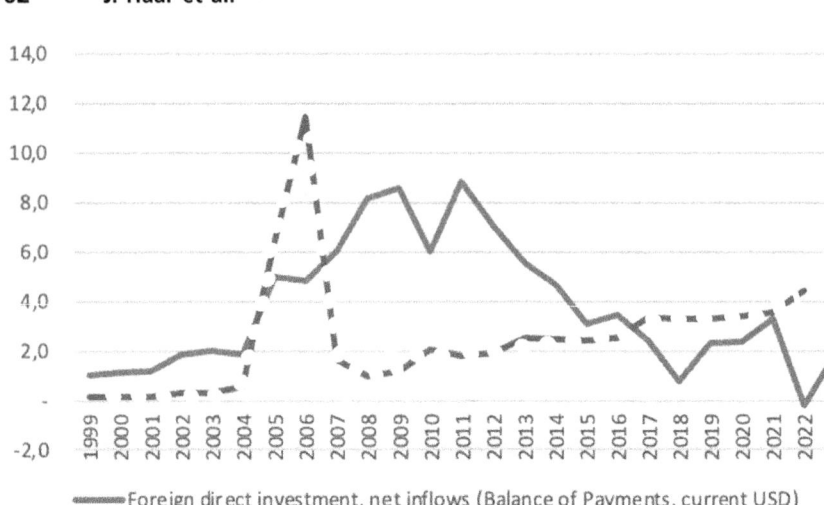

Fig. 6.10 Nigeria—foreign direct investment and Official Development Assistance and aid (Current billion $) (*Source* The World Bank)

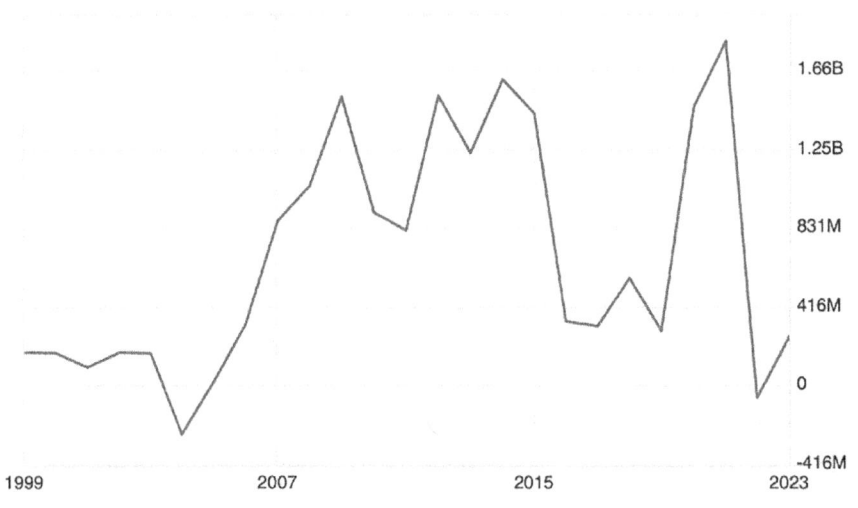

Fig. 6.11 Nigeria—foreign direct investment net outflows (Current $) (*Source* The World Bank)

Official Development Assistance (ODA): An overlooked growth factor. ODA has also played a significant role in Nigeria's economic development. Between 1999 and 2002, ODA was equivalent to 4.3% of exports, increasing from $102 million in 1999 to $4.4 billion in 2002, reaching almost the same value as total FDI inflows.

Much of the surge in 2005–2006 was tied to the Paris Club debt relief initiative. The global community, especially multilateral donors like the World Bank and IMF, supported these reform efforts with large aid packages and grants to ensure their success and sustainability.

In 2022, the World Bank Group emerged as Nigeria's largest donor, providing $2.1 billion in assistance, followed by the United States ($700 million). France fell far behind ($146 million). U.S. aid primarily targeted emergency response and health, particularly HIV/AIDS initiatives ($0.9 billion in 2023.)

International funds from both Foreign Direct Investment and Official Development Assistance went from $1.2 billion in 1999 to $4.3 billion in 2022, averaging 11% of Nigeria's exports during the period.

Infrastructure. Geopolitics has driven much of Nigeria's infrastructure development. During British colonial rule, infrastructure—as was typical across colonial settings—was primarily designed to extract resources and transport them to the colonial metropolis.

In contrast, China's Belt and Road Initiative introduced a new infrastructure paradigm, emphasizing connectivity between cities and countries. Projects like the Lekki Deep Sea Port, Lagos-Ibadan Railway, Abuja Metro Line, and Zungeru Hydropower Plant exemplify this strategy. Without this type of developments regional integration projects and ambitious initiatives like the African Continental Free Trade Area, will never become a reality.

However, China's approach to infrastructure in Africa is evolving. It shifted away from large, capital-intensive projects to focus on its "Small and Beautiful Projects" initiative. This new strategy emphasizes smaller, locally tailored projects such as rural roads, solar energy installations, water supply systems, agricultural processing plants, and health clinics.

Since Nigeria needs localized and also large-scale projects, the country is actively offering risk guarantees that complement credit insurance from investor countries to potential financiers in the United States and the European Union.[82] International politics will likely play a larger role in any new large investment than purely financial and political risk considerations. This is because Nigeria currently scores a low six on the OECD's 1-to-7 country risk scale (for comparison, China scores a 2).

For now, China maintains a significant advantage. It pledged $50 billion in financing for Africa from 2024 to 2028 and granted zero tariffs on imports from Nigeria and 32 other African countries, solidifying its economic influence in the region.

---

[82] Tuggar, Yusuf (2024).

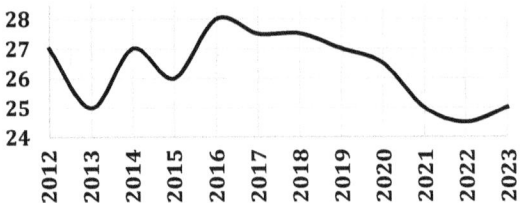

Fig. 6.12 Nigeria—Corruption Perception Index (2012–2023) (*Source* Transparency International)

On the oil and gas aspect of infrastructure, over the next decade, Nigerian oil companies will likely increase the country's reserves and production through field optimization, development of marginal fields, and enhanced theft control. The deep-water offshore initiatives led by major oil companies will also contribute significantly. If effectively implemented, investment in natural gas and gas-based industries could become a key growth driver.

The Nigeria Cost. Corruption is a significant impediment to Nigeria's economic growth. Transparency International's Corruption Perception Index (CPI) ranked Nigeria 145th out of 180 countries in 2023. Petty corruption alone cost Nigerians an estimated $1.3 billion in 2023, equivalent to 0.35% of GDP[83] (Fig. 6.12).

In 2023, Nigerians ranked corruption as the fourth most pressing issue facing the country, following the cost of living, insecurity, and unemployment. This underscores the widespread concern about corruption, surpassing other issues like education or housing. Public opinion surveys reveal that only 23% of Nigerians now consider bribery acceptable for expediting administrative processes, signaling a growing rejection of such practices. However, systemic issues remain, as 6 out of 10 successful candidates for public sector positions admitted to using nepotism, bribery, or both to improve their chances of recruitment.

While data on grand corruption is limited and imprecise, some estimates suggest its staggering scale. Transparency International has estimated that corruption accounts for around 20% of Nigeria's GDP, and PwC warned that Nigeria could lose up to 37% of its GDP to corruption by 2030 if decisive measures are not implemented.[84] Although these figures may be overestimates aimed at catalyzing policy action, there is evidence of large-scale

---

[83] UN (2024) "Corruption in Nigeria: Patterns and trends" Retrieved from: https://www.unodc.org/conig/uploads/documents/3rd_national_corruption_survey_report_2024_07_09.pdf.

[84] PwC (2024) "Impact of corruption on Nigeria's economy" Retrieved from: https://www.pwc.com/ng/en/press-room/impact-of-corruption-on-nigeria-s-economy.html.

mismanagement. For instance, in 2016, the Nigerian National Petroleum Corporation reportedly could not account for $16 billion.

Corruption's mirror image, illicit financial outflows, is equally alarming. The Nigeria Extractive Industries Transparency Initiative estimates these outflows to be between $15 billion and $18 billion annually, amounting to approximately 5% of GDP.[85] Oil theft, another partial manifestation of corruption, has been estimated to have peaked at 25% of the nation's oil production, which is equivalent to some 260,000 barrels per day, similar to the production of Congo.

The pervasive culture of bribery and petty corruption, combined with the misuse of power for personal enrichment on a grand scale, deters foreign direct investment and creates significant barriers for the poor, limiting their access to essential services like healthcare and education. Furthermore, nepotism, cronyism, and other forms of corruption exacerbate patterns of discrimination, fueling ethnic and religious tensions across the country.

A Note on Productivity. Productivity in Nigeria experienced significant growth from 1999 to 2012, interestingly driven by factors unrelated to the 2003–2009 oil price boom. Key contributors included privatizations, deregulation, investments in the energy grid, advancements in agricultural productivity, and the rapid penetration of mobile phone technology. These structural changes enhanced efficiency and output across multiple sectors of the economy (see Fig. 6.13).

Instead, the subsequent decline in productivity was compounded by falling oil prices, coupled with worsening security conditions, pervasive corruption, and deepening regional divisions. These challenges undermined the earlier gains and stifled further progress.

Labor productivity, on the other hand, has remained largely stagnant. This stagnation is attributed to limited access to capital, whether through FDI or ODA, and a persistent skills gap in the workforce. Current academic and vocational training programs appear insufficient to meet the country's productivity needs.

One example is the government's Digital Nigeria Skills Strategy, which aims to train 5 million Nigerians in digital skills by 2030. While commendable, this initiative is still a relatively small-scale effort compared to the nation's population and labor force challenges.

Agriculture, the largest employer in the country, holds substantial potential for driving productivity gains. The anticipated increase in fertilizer

---

[85] Obadare, Ebenezer (2022) "Nigeria's all too familiar corruption ranking begs broader questions around normative collapse" Council on Foreign Relations.

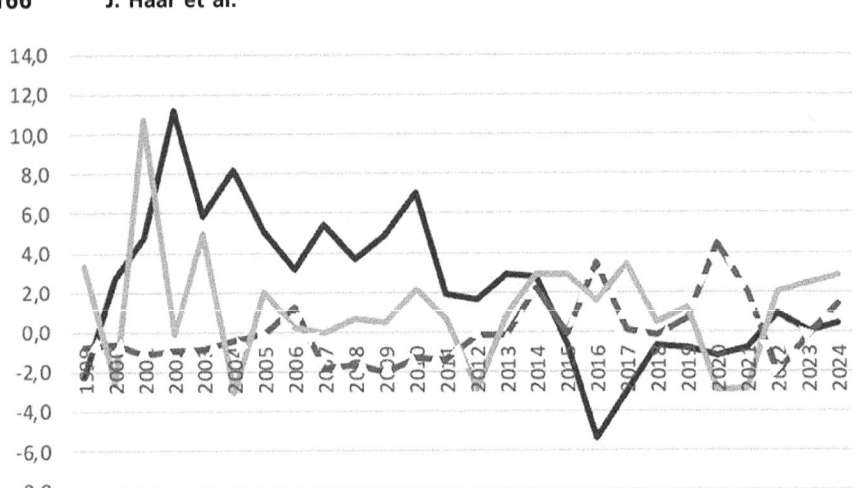

Fig. 6.13 Nigeria and Africa (select countries)—change in total factor productivity (%) (*Source* The Conference Board)

production, spurred by the operations of the new refinery and potential refurbishments of Nigeria's four, aging, refineries, has the capacity to transform the agricultural sector. Enhanced access to fertilizer and other agricultural inputs could result in significant improvements in crop yields and overall agricultural productivity.

The shift by oil majors to transfer onshore oil exploration and production to local companies while focusing on offshore operations should enhance productivity in Nigeria's vital oil industry. This move will also heighten the geopolitical stakes and interest in the country for global powers such as the U.S. (ExxonMobil and Chevron), the UK/Netherlands (Shell), France (Total), and Italy (Eni).

Country Outlook

Nigeria may need to wait a decade to fully unlock the potential of its two most significant resources: labor and oil.

Geopolitics will remain the number one factor shaping Nigeria's growth trajectory. It will determine the players behind the country's infrastructure development, the influence over religious movements in northern Nigeria, the parties arming or buying from rebels in the Niger Delta, the donors assisting its poor, and the tolerance for entrenched practices such as corruption.

Transforming Nigeria's challenging business environment to attract foreign investors will require substantial government intervention—a Herculean task, to say the least. Many investors exhibit "cold feet" when considering opportunities in the country due to these challenges.

For now, China and the oil industry's pressing needs will largely dictate Nigeria's infrastructure projects. Climate-related disasters could, unfortunately, further strain the country's resources and add to infrastructure demands.

In terms of technology, while Nigeria may see the emergence of some unicorn startups, widespread growth in this sector will likely be constrained by the limited availability of infrastructure, skills, and financing.

Talent will, in contrast, play a critical role. If geopolitical conditions do not change, Nigeria's primary export will soon be unskilled, young workers. Studies indicate that most young or skilled emigrants are unlikely to return. The country's growing and connected diaspora will facilitate further migration, amplifying this trend.

Internal migration will also shape Nigeria's future. Regional and religious conflicts will drive both expulsion and attraction of populations across different areas. Urbanization will continue to be a defining characteristic, with people not only crowding into Lagos but also moving to other emerging urban hubs that could gain relevance despite Nigeria's fragmented and dysfunctional federal system.

Additionally, resource conflicts driven by desertification in the north and land degradation in the south will trigger further internal migration. The agricultural sector, heavily reliant on climate-dependent practices, will also exacerbate these population shifts if employment opportunities decline.

A substantial surge in foreign direct investment may take several years, perhaps until Chinese investors decide to establish unsophisticated manufacturing plants for the domestic market or exports. Low labor costs (the minimum wage is currently $44 per month) will then kick in and start being the usual attractor. Perhaps investors from other countries who are not very concerned with human rights and domestic politics might join in.

Nigeria's challenges will not be resolved in a few years. However, as the next two decades unfold, patient observers will witness the tremendous opportunities emerging from the country's gradual progress. Accelerating this process will probably require a good deal of intent and aspiration. As Nobel laureate Wole Soyinka once remarked, the complexities rooted in Nigeria's colonial history do not make the country unviable. "I'm dreaming, in fact, of a

Nigeria that is impossible to achieve. That's not a pessimistic statement; it's an ambition.[86]"

Poland

Among the newer emerging markets, Poland is a stand-out. Economic liberalization, which began in 1989 after the end of Communist rule, rapidly transformed Poland into a Central European growth hub. Its per-capita income surged from nearly $1700 in 1990 to $22,100 in 2023. Over the same period, Poland's total GDP grew at an average annual rate of 3.7%, significantly outpacing the OECD average of 2.2% and the European Union's 1.7%.[87]

While Poland still has a way to go to catch up with neighboring Germany's per-capita income of $52,700 and the European Union's average of $40,800, its rise from a poor nation to a high-income economy in four decades is remarkable, and the path to prosperity has the momentum to support a bright economic future. It has been stated many times that Poland's per-capita income will surpass that of the UK as early as 2035.

With a population of 38 million and a GDP of $650 billion, Poland is the 19th largest economy in the world. Its central bank and its economic authorities have maintained a moderate inflation rate of around 4% and a 2.6% unemployment rate, one of the lowest in the European Union (EU). In comparison, the EU average inflation was 3%, and the unemployment rate was 6%.[88]

The country has a stable government revenue base compared with its peers, which is the main strength of Polish public finances. This stability reassures credit rating agencies, reducing concerns over a 5.5% GDP fiscal deficit or growing spending pressures. Current budgets reflect the government's commitment, based on electoral promises, to increase household disposable incomes, boost consumption, and build up defense spending.[89]

As is the case of many countries, domestic politics may hinder economic stability, not just emerging markets. As a democratic republic with a semi-presidential system, Poland's political environment is shaped by the interaction between the president and the prime minister, both of whom

---

[86] Wole Soyinka in an interview to Plus TV Africa 11 November, 2019.
[87] The World Bank (2024) World Development Indicators.
[88] Ibid.
[89] Fitch Ratings (2024) "Poland's 2025 Budget Proposal Highlights Fiscal Consolidation Challenges" Fitch Wire. Retrieved from https://www.fitchratings.com/.

hold significant power. This unique system of governance requires a careful balancing of responsibilities, which can influence policy direction and the effectiveness of government initiatives.

Today, the two dominant political forces in Poland are the Law and Justice Party (PiS) and the Civic Platform (PO), which represent conservative and liberal values, respectively. The Law and Justice Party, a right-wing, national-conservative party, lost power in 2023 after eight years in government. The Civic Platform, on the other hand, represents more centrist, pro-European, advocating for increased integration with the EU and promoting economic liberalization. These competing visions for Poland's future have created a political environment with sharp divisions between voters and escalated political tensions, which could pose risks to government effectiveness.

Since Civic Platform's Prime Minister Donald Tusk took office in December 2023, there have been repeated clashes between the new coalition government and the PiS party and its allies, which include President Andrzej Duda. Disagreements compound the difficult policy choices Tusk's government faces, such as restoring judicial independence. A judicial reform initially implemented by the PiS aimed at increasing government oversight over the judiciary. This reform drew significant criticism from the European Union, which viewed it as undermining the independence of the courts and threatening the rule of law. Realigning Poland with EU standards has been a challenging task due to political antagonisms.

Poland's fiscal stance is another important issue. The PO government promised to reduce the fiscal deficit but, at the same time, committed itself to new defense and social spending goals. As a result, the government debt-to-GDP ratio will likely increase to around 55% of GDP by 2025 from 49.3% at the end of 2022.[90] A lack of fiscal consolidation could negatively impact investor sentiment, especially if political controversies on this issue undermine the functioning of key institutions.

Unquestionably, one of Poland's greatest competitive advantages is its low-cost manufacturing hub for Germany. There are relevant cost considerations that make low-cost operations possible. In 2024, energy prices for non-household consumers in Poland were $0.22 per kilowatt-hour, compared to nearly $0.25 per kWh in Germany. The disparity in labor costs was more significant, with the monthly minimum wage in Poland at $1,085, while in Germany it was $2,327.[91]

---

[90] Fitch Ratings (2024) "Poland's Political Clashes Heighten Risks to Government Effectiveness" Fitchwire, Monday February 5.
[91] Eurostat website.

However, unlike Mexico's supplier relationship with the U.S., Poland's trade is not strictly tied to Germany. Around 20% of all Polish imports come from Germany, and 25% of its exports are sent to this country. Poland's production is sent largely to Europe, particularly to the Czech Republic, France, the UK, and Italy, and it has increasingly exported to Ukraine, especially in the form of fuel, energy generators, and weapons.[92]

Poland's leading exports include:

- **Electric batteries**: In 2022, Poland exported $9.55 billion worth of electric batteries.
- **Computers**: In 2022, Poland exported $6.73 billion worth of computers.
- **Electrical and electronic equipment**: In 2023, Poland exported $43.88 billion worth of electrical and electronic equipment.
- **Vehicles other than railway and tramway**: In 2023, Poland exported $37.99 billion worth of these vehicles.
- **Plastics**: In 2023, Poland exported $17.40 billion worth of plastics.
- **Furniture, lighting signs, and prefabricated buildings**: In 2023, Poland exported $11.89 billion worth of these goods.[93]

Among Poland's leading exporters are KGHM Polska Miedz (diversified metals, mining), Pgnig Group (oil, gas), Cimir Poland (seats, furniture parts), Nexter Automotive Poland S P Zoo (steering mechanisms, synchronous belts, goods transportation vehicles), and Tristone Flowtech Poland (tubes/pipes/hoses, latex, rubber transmission belts.

Polish manufacturing capacity, to a certain degree inherited from the Iron Curtain years, has steadily improved in quality, becoming more sophisticated and diversified. Beyond cost considerations, this has made Poland an attractive destination for foreign investors.

The balance of opportunities and challenges is heavily tilted toward Poland improving its economic conditions in the coming years and strengthening its current status as a middle power.[94]

In assessing Poland's current business environment, one may conclude that integrations and convergence with EU standards have been among the main reasons behind Poland's economic success and its improved business environment.

---

[92] ITC statistics.
[93] Trading Economics, OEC World.
[94] Middle Powers are nations that are not superpowers but still have significant regional or global influence due to their economic, political, military, or diplomatic strength. These countries often play important roles in international affairs, contributing to peacekeeping, mediation, and global governance.

Of the ten countries that joined the EU in May 2004, Poland has been one of those that benefited the most from the new membership. On one hand, Poland has been one of the largest recipients of EU funds. Since 2004, it has received approximately $178 billion after deducting EU fees. This is a sizeable sum compared to, for instance, the $53 billion that Portugal received during the same period. It might not sound like a game-changing figure, as it represents less than 40% of Poland's 2023 exports. Nonetheless, focused on infrastructure and talent, these funds became a potent engine for sustained growth.

On the other hand, low labor costs, unimpeded access to Europe, and convergence with EU law became a magnet for foreign direct investment (FDI). In 2023, Poland received net FDI inflows of $32 billion, making it the 11th-largest FDI recipient in the world, close to Italy and Spain, which received $33 billion each.[95] Poland also attracted nearly 45% of the $632 billion in foreign investment directed toward the eight countries in the Central and Eastern Europe region.[96] Foreign companies generally enjoy unrestricted access to the Polish market, but there are limits to foreign ownership of companies in selected strategic sectors and to the acquisition of real estate, especially agricultural and forest land.[97]

A successful strategy that shaped Poland's industrial organization differently from Russia and neighboring Eastern Europe nations was the pace of privatization. The construction of a market economy in the 1990s called for cutting subsidies and removing price controls. "Shock Therapy", as this policy package was known, was not accompanied by mass privatizations. Public sentiment in Poland favored a careful transition to avoid mass layoffs and economic shocks. The Polish government was mindful of maintaining social cohesion and avoiding a sudden surge in unemployment, which could lead to social unrest.

Regulatory frameworks and institutions to manage the privatization process effectively helped Poland avoid Russian-style, large-scale, voucher-based privatizations, which were often conducted without strong oversight. This rapid transfer of state assets to private hands in Russia frequently created economic oligarchs and resulted in significant wealth disparities.

Poland's Gini index—a measure of the extent to which income or consumption distribution deviates from perfect equality—, has steadily

---

[95] World Bank (2024) World Development Indicators. Retrieved from https://databank.worldbank.org.
[96] Le Monde (2024) "Twenty Years After Poland's succesful entry into the EU, its relationship has shifted" Retrieved from https://www.lemonde.fr/.
[97] U.S. Department of State (2024) "2024 Investment Climate Statements: Poland" Retrieved from https://www.state.gov/reports/.

declined since 2004, from 30 to around 28, much better than Germany's 32 and Russia's 35.[98]

Despite the slow pace, public sector participation decreased substantially. It went from approximately 8,000 state-owned enterprises in 1990 to around 16 large state companies operating in sectors such as energy, banking, chemicals, insurance, military, oil, and rail industries. Examples include PGE Polska Grupa Energetyczna S.A. in the energy sector and Polski Koncern Naftowy Orlen in the oil industry.

PKN Orlen is by far the largest company in Poland, serving as the country's biggest oil refiner and distributor. However, it is not oil but the services sector that is the largest component of Poland's economy, accounting for approximately 62% of GDP. The industrial sector—which includes manufacturing, mining, construction, and energy production—contributes about 34% of GDP. Poland has a robust manufacturing base, producing machinery, vehicles, electronics, and chemicals. Agriculture accounts for approximately 4% of GDP. Despite its smaller share, agriculture remains an important part of the economy, with Poland being a significant producer of cereals, fruits, vegetables, and dairy products.

Vehicles and parts account for more than 13% of all Polish exports. Other important export goods include computers, appliances, furniture, turbo-engines, meat, plastics, cigarettes, and pharmaceuticals. This short list shows the diversification of the country's productive base, which, in turn, is one of its greatest strengths.

Alongside EU funds and domestic investment, the government's development strategy has identified several goals for attracting investment, including improving the investment climate, stabilizing the macroeconomic and regulatory environment, and ensuring high-quality corporate governance, including in state-controlled companies. Interest from foreign investors has dwindled somewhat, but information such as the possibility that Poland might soon surpass the UK's per-capita income adds appeal to the country's value proposition.

A significant amount of foreign ownership is also present in the manufacturing and automotive industries due to multinational corporations establishing operations in the country. Nevertheless, as in previous years, the largest inflow of foreign direct investment to Poland in 2023 occurred in the service sector, especially in banking and retail, reflecting the change

---

[98] World Bank (2024) World Development Indicators.

of Poland's economy to a more service-oriented and less capital-intensive structure.[99]

A brief note on productivity. Coming from a low-productivity regime during the communist era, productivity growth in Poland has vastly outpaced that of most European countries since 1989. However, the rate of productivity increase has shown a downward trend, only temporarily interrupted by Poland's accession to the EU in 2004 (see Fig. 6.14).

The current challenge is that Polish firms may not be competitive on a global scale. They might primarily sell within the European market due to lower labor costs and high EU tariffs. The 2023 World Competitiveness Ranking provides evidence of this phenomenon, with Poland ranking 39th out of 64 countries, placing it at the lower end of the EU nations list—only surpassing Italy, Hungary, Romania, and Bulgaria.

To reach new markets, Poland needs more productive firms, especially considering that its Baltic ports are costly for goods to be transported to Asia or the Americas. Shipping a ton of cargo on a 20-foot container might cost

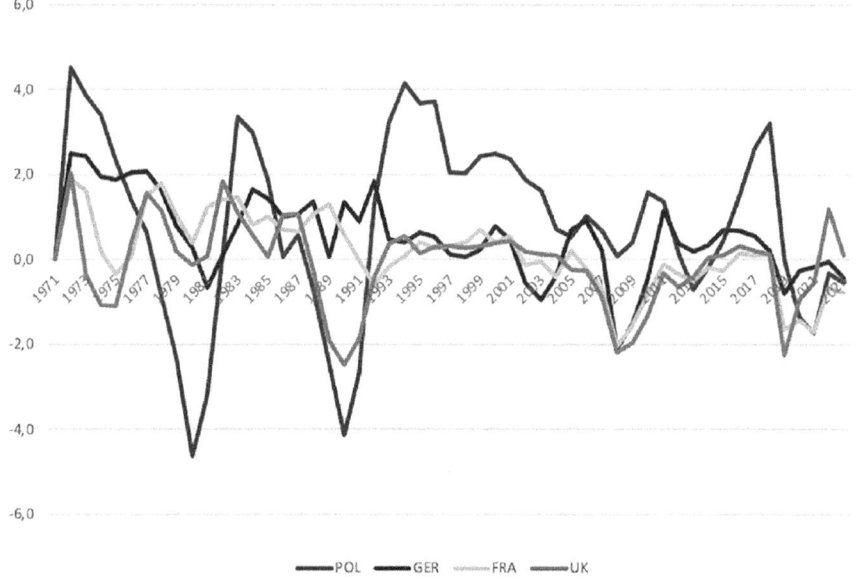

Fig. 6.14 Poland—growth of total factor productivity (%) (*Source* The Conference Board, https://www.conference-board.org/retrievefile.cfm?filename=TED_SummaryTables_Charts_may20241.pdf&type=subsite)

---

[99] U.S. Department of State (2024) "2024 Investment Climate Statements: Poland" Retrieved from https://www.state.gov/reports/.

$76 per ton from Gdańsk and $62 from Liverpool in the UK, 18% less—to ports in the U.S. East Coast.

In this scenario, Poland's diversified and increasingly sophisticated production could face significant challenges due to Europe's more permanent economic slowdown.

Moreover, relying on low labor costs follows the classic path to the middle-income trap. Countries aspiring to wealth must pay higher wages. However, as wages rise, competitiveness declines, causing the country to fall back into the middle-income bracket. Low productivity combined with low cost is a strategy that leads to a dead-end for progress.

If one were to name a remedy for dwindling productivity in emerging countries, it would almost always be increased investment in infrastructure, technology, and talent, whether domestic or foreign.[100]

Technology

Not long ago, Poland was considered a tech backwater. Investors came to the country to run their back offices, focusing on low-grade paperwork. Today, the country is moving up the value chain into semiconductors, cloud computing, and other cutting-edge services.[101]

Poland's information technology sector is expanding, with multinational corporations like Google, Microsoft, and IBM establishing operations and data centers in cities such as Kraków, Warsaw, and Wrocław. This will not be an easy, linear process. As an example, a setback occurred in 2024 when U.S. chipmaker Intel decided to delay the start of a chip plant in Poland for two years as part of a strict global cost-cutting program.

At the same time, Poland has to improve some good indicators, but perhaps not extraordinary ones. Warsaw is the only cluster in Poland ranked within the top 100 science and technology clusters in the 2024 Global Innovation Index. It filed 185 patent applications and published 8755 scientific articles per one million inhabitants over the last five years, placing it as the 90th largest science and technology cluster globally.[102]

---

[100] In the early 1970s, communist Poland implemented policies that encouraged investment in heavy industries, infrastructure, and technology. This induced the biggest, though short-lived, productivity spike in 50 years (see Fig. 1).

[101] CEPA (2024) "Polish Tech: Grand Ambitions on a Shaky Foundation" Retrieved from https://cepa.org/.

[102] WIPO (2024) "Science and Technology Cluster Ranking Report" Retrieved from https://www.wipo.int/.

Nonetheless, Poland is gaining recognition in certain tech areas. The country has a good reputation in software development and gaming technology. CD Projekt Red, a gaming company with $300 million in annual sales and creator of The Witcher, exemplifies Poland's technological growth.[103] Other notable gaming companies include Techland, Ten Square Games, and 11-bit studios.

Beyond software development, Poland has made significant strides in fintech, e-commerce, and cloud computing. The fintech sector, in particular, has thrived, with companies like PayU and Brainly emerging as major players in the European market.

Founded in 1999, Allegro is another success story. With nearly 20 million active buyers across six countries and over $14 billion in sales in 2023, Allegro is the largest e-commerce company of European origin. It has employed fintech strategies to achieve an 18% compound annual growth rate since 2017. In 2023, for example, 13% of its total annual sales were financed via its non-bank financial services arm, Allegro Pay.[104]

Cybersecurity has rapidly become world-class, as it has been forced to fend off a major threat. Since February 2022, following Russia's invasion of Ukraine, Poland became one of the most targeted EU countries for cyberattacks. These attacks targeted not only military and government sites but also private companies. Nearly 60% of firms reported at least one cybersecurity incident in 2022.[105] Attacks increased by an estimated 400% since then, but the damages have been mitigated by Poland's highly-rated cybersecurity defenses.[106]

Also defense-driven, "Aviation Valley" in southeastern Poland is a cluster comprising 190 companies that employ more than 35,000 engineers, designers, and technicians, generating $3.5 billion in annual sales. This cluster brings together aviation industry companies, scientific research centers, and educational and pilot training institutions.[107]

Access to high-speed internet has not been a significant issue. Private and public actions such as the Digital Poland Initiative have boosted technology adoption, even in rural areas.[108]

---

[103] CD Projekt Red. (2023). *Annual Report*. Retrieved from https://www.cdprojektred.com.
[104] Allegro (2024) "Introduction to Allegro" Retrieved from https://www.allegro.pl.
[105] U.S. International Trade Administration (2024) "Poland Country Guide" Retrieved from https://www.trade.gov.
[106] Warsaw Business Journal (2024) "Cyberattacks Surge in Poland" Retrieved from https:// https://wbj.pl.
[107] Aviation Valley (2024) Retrieved from https://www.dolinalotnicza.pl/en/about-us/.
[108] Ministry of Digital Affairs. (2019). *Digital Poland Initiative*. Retrieved from https://www.gov.pl/web/digital-poland.

At times, Poland's R&D spending has been highlighted as a challenge for technological improvement. In 2022, it accounted for only 1.5% of GDP, below the EU average of 2.3%. Low investment in R&D hampers domestic innovation and creates a reliance on foreign expertise. However, this figure represents progress from 2012, when R&D expenditure was just 0.9% of GDP. In fact, over the past decade, Poland has seen one of the most significant increases in R&D spending within the EU, alongside countries like Ireland, Croatia, Greece, and Belgium.[109]

Despite this progress, Poland faces notable challenges in digital adoption. Only 44% of the population possesses basic digital skills compared to the European average of 56%. Currently, only 61% of Polish companies have at least a basic level of digital intensity, whereas the EU aims for 90% of SMEs to reach this level by 2030 (currently at 64%). Furthermore, the digitization of public services could be improved; only 63% of users rely on e-government solutions, below the EU average of 74%. Advanced technology adoption by Polish companies remains limited, except for cloud technologies. Only 4% of companies have fully adopted AI, compared to the EU average of 8%, and only 19% use data analytics, against the EU average of 33%.[110]

Poland's tech sector primarily comprises smaller companies, and tech founders often cite access to qualified managerial talent as their top challenge. Other barriers include limited customer access for B2B companies, an unpredictable tax system, and inadequate legal frameworks.[111]

It is evident that the legal framework surrounding blockchain is underdeveloped. Similarly, while there have been efforts to regulate AI, data protection, and cybersecurity, the rapid evolution of these technologies requires Poland to quickly update and adapt its legal landscape. Depending on the political climate, this could be improved by adopting EU norms at a faster pace.

For instance, the Markets in Crypto-Assets (MiCA) regulation, currently being implemented, will establish a comprehensive legal framework for cryptoassets across EU member states. This regulation aims to standardize the rules for cryptoasset service providers, stablecoins, and other crypto industry aspects, which could significantly enhance Poland's regulatory environment.

In conclusion, Poland is not yet at the forefront of technological advancements, but it possesses the infrastructure, talent, and need to accelerate

---

[109] OECD (2024) "R&D Spending" Retrieved from https://ec.europa.eu/eurostat/statistics-explained/index.php?title=R%26D_expenditure&oldid=551418#Gross_domestic_expenditure_on_R.26D.

[110] U.S. International Trade Administration (2024) "Poland Digital Economy" Retrieved from https://www.trade.gov.

[111] Endeavor (2024) "Mapping Poland's Tech Sector" Retrieved from https://endeavor.org/wp-content/uploads/dlm_uploads/2024/03/Endeavor-Insight_Mapping-Polands-Tech-Sector.pdf.

development. As seen with R&D growth, Poland has built momentum that could bring it closer to Europe's leading tech and innovation hubs.

Infrastructure

Poland has made significant strides in improving its infrastructure, especially since joining the European Union in 2004, benefiting from EU Structural and Cohesion Funds aimed at narrowing the gap between richer and poorer EU regions. Poland's infrastructure advancement reflects its efforts to meet EU standards and integrate more fully into the region.

Poland's infrastructure development is at a critical juncture, with substantial progress in key areas such as transportation, energy, and digital infrastructure. However, challenges remain, particularly in terms of underinvestment, regulatory delays, and continued reliance on coal for energy generation. To address these challenges, the Polish government has implemented several strategic initiatives, including public–private partnerships, while leveraging support from the EU and multilateral financial institutions.

Transportation Infrastructure. Poland's transportation strategy emphasizes improved connectivity between major cities and neighboring countries. Notable progress has been made, especially in road and rail networks. The country boasts an extensive road network, including approximately 1300 miles of highways and 3807 miles of express roads. The General Directorate of National Roads and Motorways (GDDKiA) has utilized EU funding for many projects and plans to deploy it on other eligible roads.

For instance, Poland is constructing its national segment of the Via Carpatia, a north–south transnational highway network connecting the Baltic Sea in Lithuania with the Mediterranean in Greece, scheduled to begin operations in 2026. Additionally, Poland has developed 300 miles of the 540-mile Via Baltica highway, connecting Estonia to Poland via Latvia and Lithuania.

Nearly 400 miles of new roads were constructed in Poland between 2022 and 2023.[112] Infrastructure plans for the third decade of this century are valued at approximately $65.5 billion, including ring roads and local projects, many of which align with the EU's Trans-European Transport Networks (TEN-T).

Significant investments, mostly funded through the EU's Infrastructure and Environment Program, have been directed toward railway infrastructure. The 2030 National Railway Program aims to modernize 5592 miles of Poland's 12,000-mile rail network. This program focuses on improving cargo

---

[112] U.S. International Trade Administration (2024) Retrieved from https://www.trade.gov/.

routes and increasing train speeds, encompassing more than 230 projects, including the electrification of nearly 900 miles of rail lines and boosting train speeds on 5300 miles of track.

Challenges remain, such as the need for additional intermodal terminals and increasing cargo train speeds to meet EU averages.

Intelligent Transportation Systems. Poland is also investing in intelligent transportation systems, which serve as a technological layer atop road infrastructure. These systems include electronic toll collection, integrated photoradar connections, support for road maintenance processes, asset management, and real-time highway and road safety monitoring systems.

Plans are underway to technologically improve intermodal travel. One initiative involves developing a system that allows airline passengers to check in while boarding a train to the airport.

Airport Infrastructure. Poland's airport infrastructure has grown rapidly, with nearly 52 million passengers passing through Polish airports in 2023. Warsaw Chopin Airport remains the largest, but regional airports are also expanding. The most ambitious project is the Solidarity Transport Hub (STH), a new international airport expected to support 100 million passengers annually. This project, the most expensive infrastructure undertaking in post-communist Poland, is anticipated to face significant delays due to a lack of government support.[113]

Ports. The Port of Gdansk is the fastest-growing European port of the past decade, with a 167% increase over ten years. It is the ninth-largest European seaport by cargo tonnage and the largest in the Baltic Sea for container handling, moving 2.05 million TEUs in 2023.

Plans for new large-scale deep-water ports may encounter opposition due to environmental concerns, but state-owned ports in Gdansk and Gdynia are expected to improve efficiency and expand to meet rising demand. A $1.6 billion investment will enhance railway links between the seaports in Gdansk, Swinoujscie, and Gdynia.

Electricity. Poland's electricity grid remains a pressing concern as the country relies heavily on coal-powered plants. The Polish energy sector is the fifth largest in Europe, with an installed generation capacity reaching 55.216 GW in 2023.[114] The EU has committed to supporting Poland's transition to green energy.

While Poland has invested in renewable energy, particularly wind power, coal still accounts for about 70% of electricity generation. Transitioning to

---

[113] Ministry of Economic Development of Poland (2024) "A Record-Breaking Year for Polish Seaports" Retrieved from: https://www.trade.gov.pl/.
[114] IEA (2023) Retrieved from: https://www.iea.org/regions/europe.

renewable energy requires substantial investment in renewable sources and grid upgrades to accommodate these new energy forms.

For example, the government has invested in offshore wind farms in the Baltic Sea, targeting 10 GW of wind power by 2040. To support these renewable projects, Poland is modernizing its electrical grid to integrate variable renewable energy sources. Plans are also in place for the country's first nuclear power plant, set to be completed by 2033, to diversify its energy sources and reduce reliance on coal.

Digital Infrastructure. Poland's telecommunications sector is growing rapidly but still suffers from regional disparities in internet access, particularly in some rural areas.

Poland's national broadband plan aligns with the European Gigabit Society targets, aiming to provide 100 Mbps universal coverage, Gigabit connectivity to key institutions and businesses, uninterrupted 5G connectivity in urban areas and along major transport routes, and mobile data access everywhere. The European Funds for Digital Development 2021–2027 program provides funding for building a Gigabit Society in Poland and increasing access to fast broadband.[115]

Poland has also adopted a Nationwide Education Network program, providing all Polish schools with free 100-Mbps internet, advanced cybersecurity, and educational e-resources and tools.[116]

Poland's infrastructure progress over recent years highlights a country poised for growth but facing significant challenges. From comprehensive transportation networks and an expanding digital framework to ambitious energy transition goals, Poland is leveraging EU support and strategic initiatives to modernize and bolster its development. As Poland navigates its path forward, aligning with EU standards and expanding its innovative capacity will be crucial to securing long-term economic stability and further integrating into the European and global landscape.

Geopolitics

Poland is positioned at the intersection of major geopolitical tensions, including rising populism and the influence of Russian and Chinese expansionism. These dynamics have far-reaching implications for Poland's governance, economic stability, and ability to attract foreign investment.

---

[115] European Commission (2024) "Shaping Europe's Digital Future" Retrieved from https://digital-strategy.ec.europa.eu/.
[116] Ibid.

Poland's geopolitical significance. Poland's geographic location makes it particularly vulnerable to shifting geopolitical dynamics in both Eastern and Western Europe. Historically, it has served as a buffer state between Russia and Western Europe, shaping its political strategies and foreign relations. Today, Poland finds itself on the front lines of significant 21st-century geopolitical challenges, including the resurgence of Russian aggression and the rise of populism and nationalism across Europe.

The Ukrainian-Russian conflict dramatically altered regional security dynamics, reinforcing the mutual commitment between Poland and NATO. Poland emerged as one of Ukraine's strongest supporters, providing military aid and hosting millions of refugees. This support strengthened Poland's relationship with the United States and other NATO allies but also heightened tensions with Russia. Russian expansionism now poses a direct threat to Poland's security and economic interests.

In recent years, Russia has sought to reassert its influence in Eastern Europe through military interventions. Poland's proximity to Russia, combined with a historical mistrust of Moscow, has led it to advocate for stronger defenses on the alliance's eastern flank. However, this comes at a cost, as increased military spending has strained Poland's public finances.

Poland's defense budget is projected to rise steadily from $36.4 billion in 2024 to $39.9 billion in 2025 and is expected to remain at 4.3% of GDP until 2029, signaling a commitment to enhancing military readiness.[117]

Not included in these figures are the funds aimed at fending off potential Russian economic measures or cyberattacks against Poland, which remains a constant concern.

China's Influence. Alongside Russian expansionism, Poland faces challenges from China's growing influence in Central and Eastern Europe. China's Global Development Initiative (GDI) aims to expand Beijing's economic and political footprint across the region. While Poland has welcomed Chinese investment in its infrastructure projects, such as the expansion of rail and port networks, concerns about China's long-term strategic ambitions persist. Chinese investments often come with strings attached, requiring Poland to carefully balance the benefits of Chinese capital against potential national security risks.

This balancing act is complex. As an example, in August 2024, during the Ukraine-Russian war, equipment for the American army was scheduled to be unloaded at a dock near the Gdynia Container Terminal, owned

---

[117] Army Technology. (2023, October 17). *In data: Poland defence spending to match the US, outpacing NATO peers*. https://www.army-technology.com/news/in-data-poland-defence-spending-to-match-the-us-outpacing-nato-peers/.

by Chinese company CK Hutchison Holdings. "The ship's bow protruded about 50 meters into Hutchison's zone, and the company refused consent for unloading. The Gdynia port authorities attempted to intervene, but ultimately, the transshipment of military equipment was unsuccessful.[118]" Security concerns extend beyond Hutchison's control over port access to the port's proximity to key NATO and Polish military assets. The U.S. used a nearby dock to unload NATO and military equipment for northeastern Europe and materials bound for Ukraine.[119]

U.S.-China trade tensions have led many companies to consider nearshoring operations. Poland's well-developed infrastructure, access to the EU single market, and competitive labor costs make it an attractive option for multinational corporations seeking to relocate closer to Europe.

The Rise of Populism and Nationalism. Another key geopolitical challenge for Poland is the rise of populism and nationalism within its borders and across Europe. Poland's right-wing Law and Justice Party (PiS), which held office until 2023, promoted a nationalist-populist platform focused on protecting Polish sovereignty, restricting immigration, and upholding conservative social values. While this approach garnered domestic support, it created tensions with the European Union. The government was accused of undermining democratic institutions by exerting control over the judiciary and restricting media freedom. These actions led the European Commission to initiate legal proceedings against Poland, withholding billions in EU funds until the country complied with EU standards.

The pro-European administration of Prime Minister Donald Tusk has moved toward compliance with EU norms and regulations, prompting the release of EU funding and re-establishing Poland as a key component of European regional defense.

Regarding international trade, nationalism will likely seal borders and promote intra-alliance commerce, thus limiting Poland's ability to diversify trade away from its primary economic center of gravity in Europe.

Military Buildup. In 2022, Poland's military spending, as recorded by the World Bank, was $16 billion, placing it as the 18th largest military spender globally. With Russia's invasion of Ukraine, military spending was revised upwards. It climbed to a reported 4.3% of GDP in 2024, the highest percentage of any NATO member state. If military spending rises to 5% of

---

[118] Politico (2024) "Chinese Presence in a Polish Port Triggers Security Fears" Retrieved from: https://www.politico.eu/article/hong-kong-based-chinese-company-presence-polish-port-creates-security-worries-nato/.
[119] Ibid.

GDP, as some commentators predict, Poland would rank among the top five global spenders in comparison to the size of its economy.

Things are already in motion. The government announced plans to have the largest ground forces in Europe (and third largest in NATO). Additionally, the "Shield East" program aims to fortify Poland's borders with Russian-allied Belarus and Russia's Kaliningrad, incorporating physical barriers, modern surveillance systems, and other infrastructure. The government claims this is the most significant effort to strengthen Poland's eastern border and NATO's eastern flank since 1945.[120]

It may be an obvious remark, but many infrastructure projects not only facilitate the efficient operation of households and firms in peacetime but also serve military purposes. This is the case with the Via Carpatia and the TSH airport.

Despite the challenges posed by geopolitical tensions, Poland has several opportunities. Its close relationship with the United States and pivotal role in NATO makes it an attractive destination for defense contractors and military investment.

Poland's decision to build stronger bonds with the EU while maintaining a functional relationship with the United States and China has placed the country in good standing to profit from all three relationships. It is undoubtedly part of the European plan, but Poland can distance itself somewhat from Europe when dealing with the United States and China in a way that Germany, France, or even Italy cannot. The country's decision to build up its military beyond other European nations will also give it significantly more strength within NATO and other economic groups.

The idea of further strengthening its ties with the EU, particularly in trade and investment by replacing the local currency (złoty) with the euro, seems increasingly distant. Poland currently does not meet the requirements for inflation, fiscal deficit, public debt, and exchange rate stability needed to join the Eurozone,[121] and meeting these requirements will likely become more challenging with mounting pressures from increased infrastructure and defense spending.

Poland's Achilles' heel is, for the time being, its dependence on Russian energy, particularly oil. While the country has diversified its energy sources through investments in liquefied natural gas from the United States and

---

[120] Chancellery of the Prime Minister of Poland (2024) Retrieved from: https://www.gov.pl/.
[121] European Commission (2024) "Convergence Report Reviews Member States' Progress Toward Joining the Euro Area" Retrieved from: https://ec.europa.eu/commission/presscorner/detail/en/ip_24_3449.

renewables, it remains exposed to fluctuations in politically driven energy markets.

Geopolitical factors play a critical role in shaping Poland's economic landscape, with the country facing challenges from Russian expansionism, Chinese influence, and rising populism.

Talent

Harnessing talent refers to a country's ability to effectively utilize, develop, and direct the skills, potential, and abilities of its human resources in a purposeful and organized manner.

Poland has a relatively younger population compared to the rest of Europe. Its median age is 41, notably younger than the EU median of nearly 45. Although Poland is aging, with future implications for tax revenues and public service provision, it currently has a lower old-age dependency ratio than its neighbors. Old-age dependency is the ratio of people aged over 64 to those of working age (15–64). In 2023, Poland's dependency ratio was 19.9%, compared to the EU's 21.3%. This demographic advantage positions Poland well to leverage its talent pool for economic growth for at least one more decade.

This advantage is especially valuable, considering the demand conditions of the country's labor market. Despite having taken in nearly 1.6 million Ukrainian refugees who will not return to their homes, Poland's unemployment rate stood at a historically low 2.8% in 2023. It is one of the lowest in Europe. Such low unemployment might be somewhat surprising given that the minimum wage has tripled since 2004. But it is the result of robust economic growth, as well as a well-qualified labor force.

Poland performs well in most academic education indicators. Polish teenagers consistently rank in the top 10 in the OECD's Programme for International Student Assessment (PISA), which measures the performance of 15-year-olds in mathematics, science, and reading. Educational attainment is comparable to that of Germany. In 2022, 29.8% of the Polish population aged 25 and over had completed some form of tertiary education, while in Germany, this figure was 29.9%. In Poland, 28.6% had completed at least a Bachelor's degree, compared to 29.2% in Germany. Poland outperforms Germany in graduate studies, as 22.3% of Poles aged 25 and over held a Master's degree—almost double Germany's 12.3%.[122]

---

[122] World Bank (2024) World Development Indicators.

There are no precise figures on this, but Poland is reputed to have one of the largest engineering pools in Europe, and Polish software developers have also built a reputation as being among the best in the world. As an added characteristic, proficiency in English and German at a professional level is also common among Poland's office workforce.

Brain Gain. The brain drain, where highly skilled Polish professionals sought better opportunities abroad (especially in countries like Germany and the UK), has reversed over the past decade. Remittances, which are an indicator of the presence of nationals abroad, peaked in 2006 and have remained stable at around $7 billion from 2010 to 2023. Moreover, in 2023, Poland recorded its seventh consecutive year of positive migration, meaning more people settled in the country than left to live abroad.

International demand for Poles working remotely is now also a real option. For example, it is well known that engineers' fees are approximately 25–40% less than those of Scandinavian consultants with the same experience and expertise.[123] However, higher wages, low cost of living, a host of internationally respected employers, and a work standard that allows for better work-life balance are some of the reasons that drew Poles back to their home country. In addition, in 2022, Poland's Finance Ministry introduced the "Polish Deal," which offers returning citizens an exemption from income tax for their first four years back in the country, further incentivizing skilled professionals to return.

Management. Polish management is also a valuable asset. The World Management Survey assesses and benchmarks management practices across various countries and industries. It aims to understand how management quality impacts productivity and economic performance. It measures how effectively a company implements modern practices in operations management, performance monitoring, target setting, and talent management. The latest data includes 35 countries, and Poles rank 5th in the world alongside Mexican and Italian managers. This is a strong position, considering that managers from Great Britain and Singapore are tied for fourth place.

Family Firms. It is estimated that around 70% of all firms in Poland are family-owned or family-managed. Extensive research on family firms in Poland has confirmed several effects of this form of entrepreneurial arrangement. Unfortunately, the balance seems to lean toward the negative side.

It is not that these firms act in a completely different manner. For example, there is no significant difference in exit strategy preferences between family

---

[123] Emagine (2024) "Poland he IT hub of Europe?" Retrieved from: https://www.emagine.org/blogs/.

and non-family entrepreneurs from mature micro and small-sized firms. Both groups of entrepreneurs mostly opt for internal succession.[124] Family ties are even a key determinant of firm exports from Eastern Poland.[125] However, family businesses seem to go in a direction that does not favor improvement in business conditions. These firms in Poland perceive obstacles, such as overly complex bureaucratic procedures and requirements, as far less crucial than non-family businesses do. Family businesses also demonstrate a lower propensity to use real property as collateral for transactions.[126]

Furthermore, cluster formation and intra-sectoral collaboration are not of interest to most of them. Many are not familiar with the cluster concept, although some have experience operating within networks. "Family firms demonstrate a weak willingness to collaborate with other entities, as they highly value their autonomy and independence. They are generally not interested in influencing regional strategy, workforce transfer, or collaboration with academic and research centers. Factors essential to the essence of clusters are rejected by these firms.[127]" Perhaps modern management and a more internationally experienced labor force will, in the end, correct these managerial flaws.

In summary, Poland has an academically well-qualified workforce with superior practical skills, such as engineering and English proficiency, for problem-solving. Additionally, it has managed to establish a reputation for good quality at a low cost for its workers. These are major strengths that will help maintain the country's fast-growth trend over the next decade.

Key Drivers

Geopolitics and harnessed talent stand out as the main drivers of Poland's impressive growth in the past and will likely fuel and strongly influence its economic and social progress in the coming decades.

---

[124] Kołodkiewicz, Izabela and Marta Wojtyra-Perlejewska (2024) "Potential exit strategies of entrepreneurs operating micro and small family businesses and non-family businesses in Poland" Journal of Organizational Change Management.

[125] Gajewski, P., & Tchorek, G. (2017). What drives export performance of firms in Eastern and Western Poland? European Planning Studies, 25(12), 2250–2271. https://doi.org/10.1080/09654313.2017.1355890.

[126] Domańska, Ada and Robert Zajkowski (2021) "Barriers to gaining support: a prospect of entrepreneurial activity of family and non-family firms in Poland" In Equilibrium Quarterly Journal of Economics and Economic Policy.

[127] Staszewska, J., Smolarek, M., Foltys, J., Wotzka, D., & Frącz, P. (2024). The possibilities of cooperation among family firms within a cluster environment. European Research Studies Journal, 27(2), 132–154.

Poland was well-received into NATO in 1999. Its presence strengthened the alliance's eastern flank, reinforcing security and stability in the region. Simultaneously, for Poland, it marked the first step in a broader effort to integrate into Western political, economic, and security structures, which led to its accession to the EU in 2004.

Geopolitically driven, joining the EU was enormously significant for Poland. It instantly opened access to the world's third-largest economy—behind China and the US—which represents a market of 500 million consumers for Polish goods and people. It also allowed for a significant flow of assistance funds that were invested in infrastructure and education and facilitated the country's convergence with other European economies.

These elements combined unleashed the power of yet another force that has proven to be necessary for growth in emerging markets: Foreign Direct Investment (FDI). FDI is necessary when local savings are a scarce resource, as is often the case in developing nations and in Poland in the 1990s and early 2000s (see Figs. 6.15 and 6.16).

FDI responded positively to these geopolitical changes, peaking in 1999 and then rising consistently following Poland's entry into the EU in 2004. In 2023, for example, Poland attracted 4% of all foreign direct investment projects in Europe (229 out of 5694).

As has been proven time and again, FDI is important not only as a source of capital in a capital-thirsty economy but also as a source of knowledge and

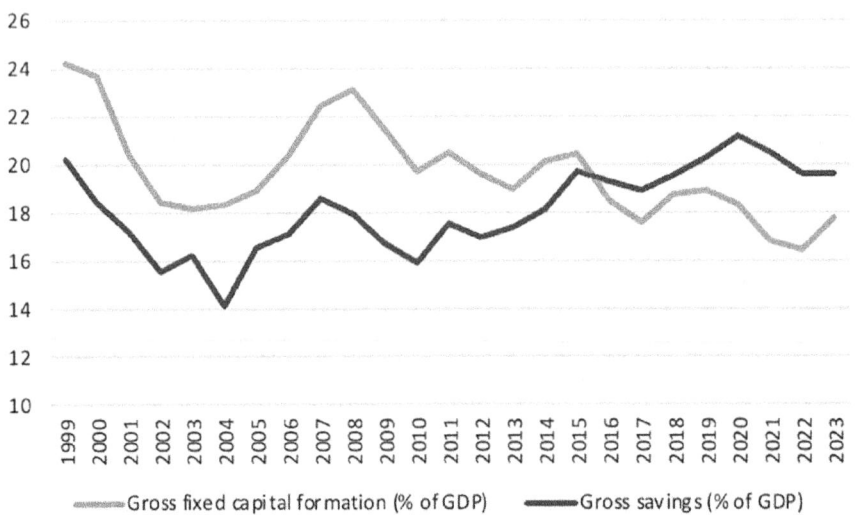

Fig. 6.15 Poland—savings and investment (% of GDP) (*Source* World Bank, https://databank.worldbank.org/source/world-development-indicators)

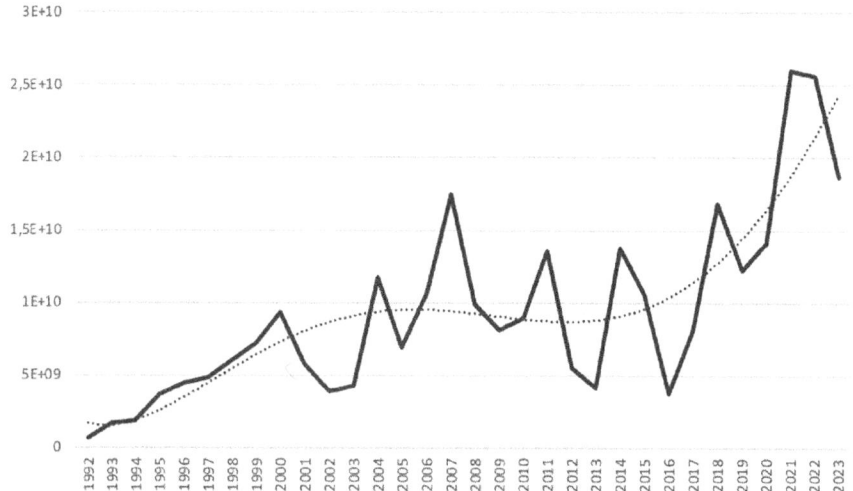

Fig. 6.16 Poland—foreign direct investment, net (BoP, current $ and trend) (*Source* World Bank, https://databank.worldbank.org/source/world-development-indicators)

best practices, and it is a determinant of exports. Foreign ownership in Poland has been proven to be a key factor in the export success of firms in Poland, even in the more backward Eastern part of the country.[128]

Exports grew at a very fast pace, becoming a major determinant of total GDP growth. This was the result of a virtuous combination of investment in infrastructure, in plant and equipment, and in workforce manufacturing skills, some of which were developed during the communist era (see Fig. 6.17).

Export growth has three very important features that set Poland apart from other emerging markets. First, Poland is not an exporter of natural resources. Second, it has a diversified portfolio of export products. Third, exports were not hindered by revaluations or by exchange rate volatility. This is, again, somewhat of an oddity in the emerging world, which often faces periodic crises ignited by exchange rate fluctuations (see Fig. 6.18).

Technological advances were, in turn, brought about by FDI and by talent readiness. Companies like Google, Boeing, Samsung, and Banco Santander contributed elements needed to develop technological hubs in Warsaw and new tech centers like Aviation Valley.

---

[128] Gajewski, P., & Tchorek, G. (2017).

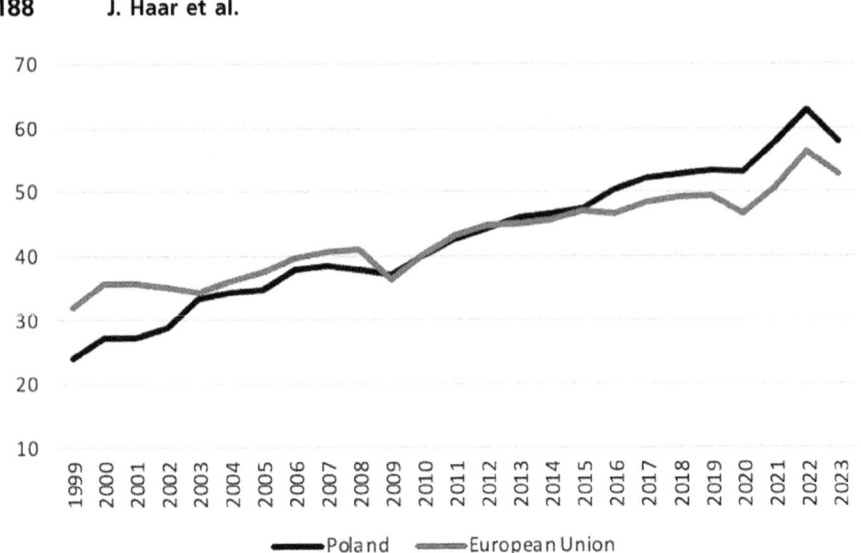

Fig. 6.17 Poland and EU—exports of goods and services (% of GDP) (*Source* World Bank, https://databank.worldbank.org/source/world-development-indicators)

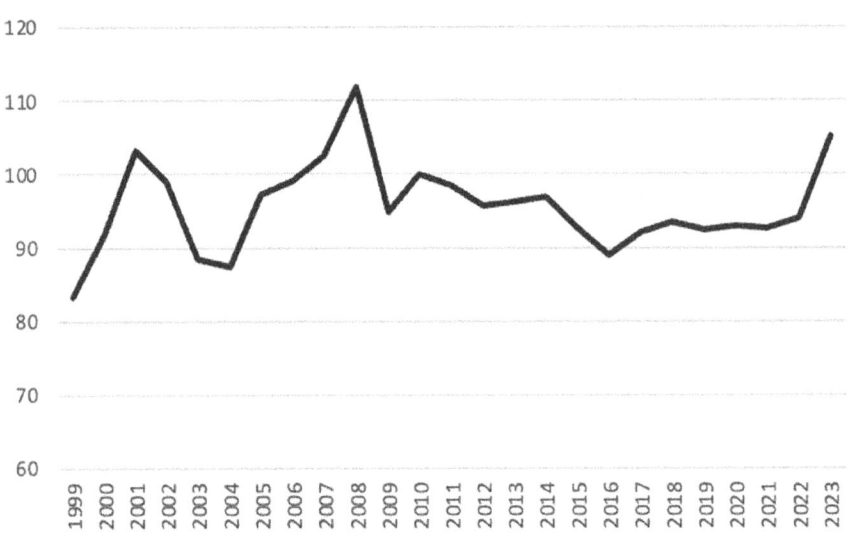

Fig. 6.18 Poland—real effective exchange rate index (2010 = 100) (*Source* World Bank, https://databank.worldbank.org/source/world-development-indicators)

Country Outlook

After three and a half decades of impressive income convergence with the developed world, Poland's growth model has achieved what is generally viewed as a small economic, social, and political miracle. It multiplied its per-capita income by 13, which, in a fairly egalitarian nation like Poland, is a good indicator of material wealth for all citizens. Its secret was to consistently invest EU and other funds in relevant infrastructure and talent, leveraging the traditional strengths of its labor force.

Exports, especially to the EU, played a significant role in Poland's success, but now, a grim European growth outlook and geoeconomic fragmentation—which present obstacles to penetrating new markets—cloud the future scenario. Additionally, low domestic savings weigh on investment, with an aging population posing a burden on the future size of the workforce.

There does not seem to be room for substantial increases in EU aid, which was another crucial factor in Poland's economic rise. Increases in this aid, potentially justified by arguments for community defense, are possible but uncertain.

Therefore, focusing on improving technology to be more competitive is a necessary strategy. The advantage of low labor costs should be replaced by advantages in processes and products.

There are many strategies for achieving this. These include partnering with European research centers, promoting innovation in military technology, or fostering innovation capacity through the influx of private equity and venture capital funds.

While building a substantial financial savings base, it is necessary to maintain the flow of foreign investment. To achieve this, a legal regime that protects citizens in the way European standards do more quickly than in other places and is more favorable to investment and innovation should be considered. This pragmatic approach is the most important element identified by companies to help Poland maintain its appeal.[129]

Poland received a strong favorable push from geopolitics and its talent base. Geopolitical uncertainties, which will likely be opportunistically capitalized upon, would probably need to be complemented with investments in productivity-inducing technologies to allow the country of the white-tailed eagle to finally rise to the status of a full-fledged global superpower.

Saudi Arabia

Saudi Arabia is one of the most promising new emerging markets. Over the past 25 years, Saudi Arabia's GDP has grown at an average annual rate of 3.2%, a seemingly moderate pace for a nation to be considered an emerging

---

[129] EY (2024) "Amid global competition for investment, what more can Europe do?" Retrieved from https://www.ey.com/en_gl/foreign-direct-investment-surveys/ey-europe-attractiveness-survey.

market growth star, but the country's per-capita income quadrupled over this period, increasing from $7,700 in 1999 to $28,900 in 2023, positioning it as the 41st richest country globally by this metric. Interestingly, there is only a marginal difference in per-capita income compared to Estonia ($29,800), a country not typically perceived as exceedingly wealthy.

The country was already classified as high-income before 1999. Its geopolitical influence, however, is substantial, amplified by its control of 17% of the world's oil reserves, its role as the custodian of Islam's two holiest cities, Mecca and Medina, and its strategic display of luxury and opulence, which contributes to the perception of immense wealth.

The Kingdom has made significant investments in high-profile projects such as the futuristic megacity Neom, lavish royal palaces, sponsoring major sports events and figures, and visible displays of wealth that reinforce Saudi Arabia's image as a financial giant.

Saudi Arabia is not poor, but not rich beyond limits. Its sovereign wealth fund, the Public Investment Fund (PIF), manages approximately $920 billion in assets, a figure that, though substantial, pales in comparison to the over $10 trillion managed by BlackRock, the world's largest fund. Nevertheless, PIF is comparable to sovereign wealth funds from the UAE ($1.1 trillion) and Kuwait ($980 billion), though smaller than Norway's ($1.8 trillion) and China's two major funds.

Saudi Arabia's primary source of wealth lies in its ownership of approximately 98% of Aramco. In 2024, Aramco reported revenues of $436 billion, positioning it among the world's largest companies by revenue, following Walmart, Amazon, and the State Grid Corporation of China. It remains the largest oil and gas company by revenue globally, ahead of Sinopec ($420.5 billion), PetroChina ($400.3 billion), and ExxonMobil ($349.6 billion). Aramco's market capitalization stood at approximately $1.74 trillion at the end of 2024, making it the sixth-largest company globally by market value, just behind Alphabet, which reached $1.9 trillion. In comparison, ExxonMobil's market capitalization was around $462.2 billion.

This vast wealth has not solved major challenges. Poverty persists. According to the United Nations, 13.6% of the population lived below the poverty line in 2021. While this is the highest rate among Gulf Cooperation Council (GCC) countries, it marks an improvement from 18.2% in 2010. Saudi Arabia has lifted 483,000 nationals out of poverty in this period.[130]

Inequality data is scarce, but the 2023 *Global Wealth Report* by Credit Suisse and UBS estimates a Gini index that measures wealth inequality is

---

[130] UNESCWA (2023) "Poverty in GCC countries: 2010–2021" Retrieved from: https://www.unescwa.org/publications/.

86.7 for Saudi Arabia, among the highest wealth inequalities globally. The top 1% of the population holds 37.6% of the nation's total wealth. This figure represents a slight improvement compared to earlier in the century.[131]

Unemployment is not a major problem. The unemployment rate has hovered around 4% and 6% over the past two decades, even compensating for a significant increase in male and female labor force participation. Male participation rose from 73% in 1999 to 83% in 2023, while female participation increased from 17 to 35%. Unemployment might eventually rise as more people enter the workforce since 63% of Saudis are under 30 years of age, and World Bank records show that one-fourth of the population are still children under 15 years old.

Business Environment

The current business environment is shaped by *Saudi Vision 2030*, a government program launched by Saudi Arabia that aims to achieve the goal of increased diversification economically, socially, and culturally, in line with the vision of Saudi Crown Prince and Prime Minister Mohammed bin Salman.

Originally a $7 trillion plan, it focuses on several key areas, including the development of non-oil industries, the privatization of state-owned enterprises, and the promotion of foreign investment. It also emphasizes the importance of creating jobs for the native Saudi population in the tourism, entertainment, and technology sectors. Additionally, the government has introduced various economic reforms to improve the business environment, including the easing of regulations, the introduction of a value-added tax, and the promotion of small and medium-sized enterprises.

The country's business environment reflects this transformative vision, characterized by substantial government initiatives, infrastructural advancements, a commitment to geopolitical stability, and a concerted effort to harness local and international talent. While there are challenges, particularly in navigating cultural and regulatory complexities, the plan is creating opportunities for growth and development.

Public Investment Fund (PIF). One of the most significant initiatives under *Vision 2030* is the development of the PIF. The stated goal is to make PIF the world's largest Sovereign Wealth Fund.

The PIF's investment portfolio is vast, with notable stakes in global companies such as Uber, in which the PIF invested $3.5 billion, representing one of the fund's largest technology investments. Additionally, it committed over

---

[131] Credit Suisse and UBS (2023) "Global Wealth Report 2023".

$1 billion to Lucid Motors, aiming to support the development of electric vehicle technology and manufacturing capacity. It took a strategic position in SoftBank's Vision Fund, contributing $45 billion to help drive global tech innovations in artificial intelligence, robotics, and renewable energy. These high-profile investments reflect Saudi Arabia's ambitions to diversify away from oil dependence and establish itself as a leader in cutting-edge industries.

Furthermore, the PIF has become increasingly involved with prominent U.S.-based companies. For example, the fund holds a significant stake in Live Nation, investing $500 million in the live entertainment giant to capitalize on the global entertainment and event sector. Additionally, it has a large investment in Meta, Disney, with over $2 billion invested, Boeing, with $714 million, and JPMorgan Chase, with $1.3 billion, further diversifying its reach into key industries, from entertainment to aerospace and finance.

State-Owned Enterprises (SOE). The Saudi government plays a central role in critical sectors, including water, power, oil, natural gas, petrochemicals, and transportation. Saudi Aramco, the world's largest oil company, is 94.5% government-owned. The Chairman of Aramco's Board also serves as the Managing Director of the PIF. In 2022, the government transferred 4% of Aramco's shares to the PIF to reinforce its role as a key financial driver of the Kingdom's Vision 2030 initiative.

Aramco significantly finances the government and PIF projects through substantial dividend payouts. In 2024, despite falling crude prices and weaker refining margins, Aramco maintained quarterly dividends of $31.1 billion, including a $10.8 billion performance-linked payout. To sustain these financial commitments, the company relied on acquiring debt. In addition to dividends, Aramco contributes to state revenues through royalties and taxes. Its royalty payments begin at 15% when Brent crude prices are below $70 per barrel, with higher rates applied as prices increase. The company also pays a 50% corporate tax on its taxable income, excluding specific exceptions for refining and gas-related activities.

In 2019, Aramco acquired from the PIF a 70% stake in SABIC, Saudi Arabia's largest petrochemical company and the fourth largest globally, for $69.1 billion. Beyond Aramco, the government wholly owns or holds controlling shares in several key companies, including the Saudi Electricity Company, Saudia Airlines, the Saline Water Conversion Company, Ma'aden, Saudi National Bank, and other prominent financial institutions.[132]

Over the past five years, Saudi Arabia has actively pursued privatization initiatives across various sectors as part of its economic diversification plan. In

---

[132] U.S. Department of State (2023) "2023 Investment climate statements: Saudi Arabia" Retrieved from: https://www.state.gov/reports/2023-investment-climate-statements/saudi-arabia/.

April 2023, the National Center for Privatization & PPP (NCP) announced a pipeline of 200 approved projects spanning 17 sectors, including transportation, health, education, and municipal affairs. These projects are open to local and foreign investors, aiming to enhance service quality and economic development. Notable privatization efforts include the sale of a 5% stake in the Saudi Telecom Company (STC) in December 2021, raising approximately $3.2 billion.

Challenges. Despite progress, concerns about transparency, legal protections, and the overall business environment remain critical barriers to sustained economic growth and diversification.

Transparency. While the Saudi government has taken steps to improve openness, particularly with the introduction of anti-corruption campaigns, investors remain cautious. The 2017 anti-corruption purge, which saw the detention of several prominent local business figures, raised concerns about the fairness and predictability of legal and regulatory enforcement. To address these concerns, the government has committed to more transparent governance measures, including the establishment of the National Center for Performance Measurement, which monitors the performance of government entities, and improvements in financial reporting standards for public and private companies. These efforts aim to build investor confidence by ensuring that businesses operate in a transparent, accountable environment.

Legal Protwctions. Another concern for foreign investors has been the perceived lack of robust legal protections, particularly regarding contract enforcement, intellectual property rights, and the overall legal framework. Contract disputes can be lengthy and unpredictable. To address these issues, the Saudi government has made reforms to the judicial system, including the creation of specialized commercial courts that handle business disputes more efficiently. Additionally, new bankruptcy and arbitration laws have been introduced to offer clearer legal recourse for businesses. The Saudi government is also working to align its intellectual property regulations with international standards, a critical factor in attracting investment in technology and innovation sectors.

Business Climate. While Saudi Arabia has made considerable progress in improving its business climate, bureaucracy and regulatory inefficiencies continue to hinder business operations, particularly for small and medium-sized enterprises. Additionally, foreign investors still express concerns over the unpredictability of regulatory changes, especially when it comes to labor and Saudization policies, which mandate hiring local workers. In response, the government has launched several initiatives to streamline regulations and make the country more business-friendly. These include the "Tayseer"

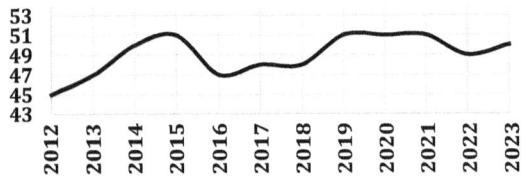

Fig. 6.19 Saudi Arabia—Corruption Perception Index 2012–2023 (Score 1 = poor, 100 = excellent) (*Source* Transparency International)

initiative, which is designed to simplify business procedures, reduce licensing timeframes, and promote private sector growth. Another effort is the establishment of the Saudi Center for Commercial Arbitration, aimed at offering a more accessible and reliable dispute resolution mechanism for businesses.

Despite these reforms, overcoming these long-standing issues will take time, and the success of Vision 2030 depends on the continued implementation of legal, regulatory, and business reforms.

Corruption. Saudi Arabia ranked 53 out of 180 countries in Transparency International's *Corruption Perceptions Index*, with a score of 52. Top-ranked Denmark has a score of 90, and neighbors Qatar 58 (ranked 40), and UAE 68 (ranked 26) (see Fig. 6.19).

Technology

With a strategically planned acquisition and partnerships plan, the Kingdom has obtained access to critical technological fields. These efforts provided opportunities for citizens and companies to benefit from these advancements while accelerating the development of technological proficiency necessary to drive further adoption and innovation.

Government Investment. The government has made substantial investments in digital infrastructure and emerging technologies, including artificial intelligence (AI), the Internet of Things (IoT), cloud computing, and blockchain. Key initiatives spearheaded by the Saudi Data and Artificial Intelligence Authority (SDAIA) and ambitious smart city projects are positioning the Kingdom as a regional technology hub. As of 2023, the Saudi Information and Communications Technology sector was the largest and fastest-growing in the MENA region. Valued at over $40.9 billion, it accounted for 4.1% of the Kingdom's GDP.[133]

---

[133] International Trade Administration (2024) "Saudi Arabia – Country Commercial Guide: Digital economy" Retrieved from https://www.trade.gov/country-commercial-guides/.

R&D Spending. Research and Development (R&D) spending is often considered a coarse indicator of technological progress, particularly in countries that are not yet at the frontier of innovation. Saudi Arabia has made notable strides. R&D expenditure rose significantly, from 0.06% of GDP in 1999 to 0.46% in 2022. Even more remarkable is the doubling of researchers within just two years, increasing from 435 researchers per million people in 2020 to 834 in 2022. However, Saudi Arabia still lags behind regional leaders like the UAE, which dedicates 1.5% of its GDP to R&D and boasts 2700 researchers per million inhabitants.

Artificial Intelligence. Saudi Arabia achieved significant progress in artificial intelligence, particularly when compared to its modest advancements in R&D. The country ranked 14th in the Global AI Index 2024 and earned the top spot globally for its "Government Strategy for AI" pillar. Additionally, Saudi Arabia ranked second in "Public Awareness of AI," as per Stanford University's AI Index Report,[134] and third globally in the number of AI policy publications, with over 57 policies.[135] On the corporate front, 17% of Saudi Arabian firms employing over 500 individuals are "fully AI prepared," compared to 7% in Europe and 15% in Asia. The AI sector is projected to contribute $135 billion to the Saudi economy by 2030, accounting for 12% of GDP.[136]

Saudi Arabia has actively sought to acquire technological know-how through acquisitions and partnerships. In 2016, the PIF's investment in Uber got the country a seat on its board of directors. In 2017, the PIF's commitment to the SoftBank Vision Fund, was meant to target startups using AI technologies—though the fund reported significant losses until 2022. A 2018 visit by Crown Prince Mohammed bin Salman to Silicon Valley spurred collaborations with Google and Apple. In 2024, Amazon Web Services announced a two-year $5.3 billion investment plan to launch data centers in Saudi Arabia. Furthermore, Google Cloud and PIF agreed to establish an AI hub in the Kingdom, leveraging Saudi Arabia's energy cost advantage, which offers power at approximately 13% less than the U.S. average.[137]

The AI talent pipeline will be constrained by security concerns. The Google-PIF collaboration, for instance, excludes model weight transfers or proprietary co-creation of AI technologies. Instead, it focuses on expanding

---

[134] Stanford University (2023) "AI Index Report".
[135] OECD (2024) "AI Policy Observatory".
[136] PwC (2024) "320 billion by 2030?" Retrieved from: https://www.pwc.com/m1/en/publications/potential-impact-artificial-intelligence-middle-east.html.
[137] Reuters (2024) https://www.reuters.com/breakingviews/gulfs-ai-strategy-is-built-more-than-sand-2024-11-13/.

Google's existing data centers and commercially available AI services without sharing proprietary elements.[138]

The Saudi startup scene has room to grow. Saudi unicorns Noon, STC Pay, Jahez, Tabby, Tamara, and Rasan represent various sectors, from e-commerce, fintech, insurance, to food delivery. Saudi Unicorns is a highly effective program expected to boost local startup ecosystems, helping more companies achieve high valuations.

5G technology. Saudi Arabia is a pioneer in 5G technology in the Middle East, with more than half the country covered by 5G networks. Urban hubs like Riyadh have emerged as some of the world's most connected cities. Additionally, Saudi Arabia's Communications and Information Technology Commission (CITC) announced that the Kingdom would dedicate the entire 6 GHz spectrum to unlicensed technology, allowing routers to access 150% more open airwaves than in any other country in the world.[139] This policy significantly bolsters the capacity of the new generation of Wi-Fi networks and cements the Kingdom's leadership in digital connectivity.

The Kingdom's infrastructure is complemented by the fact that it leads the UN's Global Cybersecurity Index,[140] and ranked sixth place globally in the UN's E-Government Development Index and first in the Open Government Data Index.

Tech for hire. In Saudi Arabia, 96% of the population uses the Internet, 97% of individuals own a mobile phone, and 99% of households have Internet access at home. It boasts 117% active mobile broadband subscriptions per 100 inhabitants. Saudi Arabia also retained its place as the 7th fastest country globally for mobile internet speeds in 2020 and 4th in the world for 5G internet speeds.[141] These conditions facilitate the preparation of the workforce for the demands of a digital economy. The pragmatic, 'buy skills' approach taken by the country will probably prove faster than waiting for its citizens to get academic degrees and relevant experience. For instance, in 2024, Saudi communications SOE, STC—64% owned by the PIF—acquired a 9.9% stake in Spain's Telefónica, becoming its largest shareholder. STC's partnership with Telefónica aims to foster the development of digital

---

[138] Soliman, Mohammed (2024) "Beyond Oil: Google's bet on Saudi Arabia's AI" Middle East Institute. Retrieved from: https://www.mei.edu/publications/beyond-oil-googles-big-bet-saudi-arabias-ai-future.

[139] U.S. International Trade Agency (2024) "Saudi Arabia enables 6 GHz Band".

[140] UN ITU (2024) "Global Cybersecurity Index".

[141] Saudi Arabia (2024) "Vision 2030: Digital Inclusion" Retrieved from: https://www.my.gov.sa/wps/portal/snp/careaboutyou/digitalinclusion/?lang=en.

cities in Saudi Arabia by importing technological know-how. Five Saudi cities are already among the top 100 smart cities worldwide.[142]

The Kingdom is also making strategic forays into Open Radio Access Network (RAN) technologies, which allow mobile operators to integrate equipment from multiple vendors, making cellular networks more flexible, cost-effective, and efficient. A notable step in this direction is Saudi Aramco's $1 billion investment in U.S.-based Open RAN software maker Mavenir, which aims to acquire both market access and expertise in this key technological domain.

Green Energy. Saudi Arabia's diversification strategy has increasingly focused on the production of green energy, such as hydrogen. In 2024, Aramco acquired 50% of Saudi Air Products Qudra's blue hydrogen industrial gases business. Projects like the 300-megawatt Sakaka solar farm and wind energy developments, such as the Dumat Al Jandal wind farm, reflect the Kingdom's intention to gradually reduce dependence on oil and gas. Collaborations with companies like Lucid Motors further emphasize the Kingdom's interest in advancing electric and autonomous vehicle technology as part of its broader energy innovation strategy.

Space and communications. The Saudi Space Agency, established in 2018, launched ambitious initiatives focused on satellite development and astronaut missions to the International Space Station (ISS). This program builds on Saudi Arabia's early space endeavors, notably the flight of Sultan bin Salman Al Saud aboard the Space Shuttle Discovery in 1985. In 2022, Ali AlQuarni and Rayyanah Barnawi, the first Saudi woman in space, participated in a mission to the ISS in collaboration with the private American company Axiom Space. With its growing focus on space exploration and technological advancements, this program is poised to gain further significance in the military and communication fields in the coming years.

Infrastructure

Infrastructure development is another key component of Vision 2030. Significant investments in energy, transportation, tourism, and urban development have made infrastructure central to the country's economic transformation. However, while these projects are intended to attract foreign direct investment, they have not yet achieved the expected levels of foreign capital inflows.

---

[142] IMD (2024) Smart City Index".

Saudi Arabia is also leveraging infrastructure projects to expand its presence in the global energy market, including initiatives in transition energy sectors such as natural gas.

Energy Infrastructure. Energy infrastructure remains the backbone of Saudi Arabia's economy, with Saudi Aramco at the center. Projects like the Sakaka Solar Power Plant and the Dumat Al Jandal Wind Farm are part of this effort. Despite these developments, renewable energy accounts for less than 1% of the kingdom's electricity consumption. The government aims to generate 50% of its energy from renewable sources by 2030. Saudi Arabia is also jockeying to position itself as a player in hydrogen production through initiatives like Saudi Air Products Qudra (APQ).

International Expansion. Saudi Arabia is also making significant investments in energy infrastructure abroad. In late 2024, Saudi Aramco and China's Sinopec began constructing a $9.8 billion refinery and petrochemical complex in southeast China. This is part of Aramco's strategy to expand its operations and supply one million barrels of crude oil per day to China for oil-to-chemical projects. Additionally, Aramco has entered the liquefied natural gas (LNG) market, acquiring a minority stake in MidOcean Energy for $500 million in 2023 and increasing its share to 49% in 2024. It has also agreed to source natural gas from the NextDecade Rio Grande LNG project in Texas.[143] These moves are in line with Aramco's strategy to diversify and tap into global energy markets. In partnership with U.S.-based BlackRock and KKR, Aramco acquired a 40% stake in a pipeline connecting the UAE to Saudi Arabia. BlackRock also partnered with Aramco in the AB4 pipeline, which links Bahrain's Sitra Refinery to Saudi Aramco's Abqaiq plant—the world's largest oil processing and stabilization facility. The fund bought a minority share from Bahrain's Bapco.[144]

Domestically, the King Salman Energy Park (SPARK) has attracted over $3 billion in investments from more than 60 companies as of September 2024. SPARK hosts seven operational factories, with 14 additional factories under construction. The park focuses on supporting the energy value chain, including manufacturing oil pipes, specialized cables, and chemicals.

Mining. To diversify away from oil, the country signed nine investment deals in metals and mining worth over $9.3 billion. Key projects include India's Vedanta constructing copper facilities, China's Zijin building a zinc smelter and a lithium extraction facility for battery production, and Australia's

---

[143] Reuters (2024) "Saudi Aramco wants to be major gas player" Retrieved from: https://www.reuters.com/business/energy/saudi-aramco-wants-be-major-lng-gas-player-gas-chief-says-2024-09-17/.

[144] Reuters (2024) "BlackRock managed fund buys stake in Saudi Barhain pipeline" https://www.reuters.com/markets/deals/blackrock-managed-fund-buys-stake-saudi-bahrain-pipeline-2024-09-11/.

Hastings Technology Metals establishing rare earth processing facilities. Additionally, Vancouver-based Platinum Group Metals is partnering with Ajlan & Bros Mining to build a platinum group metals smelter using materials from a South African mine.

Roads. Riyadh's Circular Roads Development Program aims to improve the city's road network with a $3.5 billion investment to meet future transportation needs. The program includes integrating advanced technologies, such as autonomous vehicles, with a target of achieving 15% autonomous public transport by 2030. This involves building smart road infrastructure and implementing the Saudi Highway Code to ensure road safety and efficiency.

Railways. Saudi Arabia is heavily investing in rail infrastructure, with total investments projected to exceed $40 billion. The Riyadh Metro Project, a central part of these efforts, involved a $22.5 billion investment to construct six metro lines spanning 109 miles with 85 stations. Additionally, the Saudi Railway Company (SAR) and the PIF are expanding intercity rail networks. The Landbridge Railway, a $7 billion project, will connect Jeddah on the Red Sea to Dammam on the Arabian Gulf via Riyadh, covering 590 miles. Construction is expected to begin in 2025 and be completed by 2030. It will be built by a consortium that includes SAR, China Civil Engineering Construction Company (CCECC), and Al-Ayuni Contracting as the local partner. Additional members comprise French, Canadian, and UK firms.

The Haramain High-Speed Railway, linking Mecca and Medina with speeds of up to 186 mph, is also set for expansion to accommodate growing numbers of pilgrims. The bullet train, manufactured by Spanish Talgo, currently runs 20 times a day on Chinese-built lines and has been adapted to tolerate the scorching heat.

Ports. Vision 2030 outlines extensive upgrades to port infrastructure to handle larger vessels, increase cargo volumes, and modernize operations. New logistics zones are being established to connect ports with industrial hubs such as Ras Al Khair, which focuses on mining exports. Saudi Arabia plans to double its annual container-handling capacity, rank among the top 25 countries in logistics performance, and increase transport and logistics' contribution to GDP from 6 to 10% by 2030.

The Jeddah Islamic Port on the Red Sea handles 65% of Saudi Arabia's imports and serves as the main port for the cities of Mecca and Medina. In 2022, Jeddah Islamic Port was ranked 44th among the largest ports in the world, handling approximately 5 million TEUs (twenty-foot equivalent units). The Red Sea Gateway Terminal (RSGT) company signed a 30-year agreement with the Saudi Ports Authority (Mawani) to build, operate, and transfer (BOT) the port. This agreement involves an investment of $1.7 billion in automation, infrastructure, and equipment, with completion expected by 2050. China's Cosco Shipping Ports Limited and Saudi Arabia's PIF each acquired a 20% equity stake in RSGT, totaling $280 million. The remaining 60% remained in the hands of Saudi SISCO and Xenel, a subsidiary of Malaysia's MMC Corporation Berhad.

Reports suggest that the port's current handling capacity increased to 6.6 million TEUs annually, with projections indicating a capacity of 9 million TEUs by 2050, surpassing the current throughput of Hamburg Port in Germany.[145] The port's strategic importance has grown due to ongoing U.S. and British military efforts to counter attacks by Yemen's Houthi forces on Red Sea shipping routes, reducing the relevance of Yemen's Hudaydah port for international shipping.

In 2023, Saudi Arabia hosted approximately 2 million Hajj pilgrims. The ongoing expansion of Jeddah Islamic Port aims to significantly enhance its capacity to receive pilgrims traveling by sea to perform Hajj in Mecca.

Airports. Major airport projects include the $37 billion Riyadh Air initiative, which aims to develop a new international airport in Riyadh to accommodate up to 120 million passengers annually by 2030, compared to the 28.5 million handled by King Khalid International Airport. The Riyadh terminal will serve as a base for the newly launched Riyadh Air airline. Expansion plans for King Abdulaziz International Airport in Jeddah are also underway, further supporting air traffic growth for religious tourism. By 2030, Saudi Arabia intends to increase total annual passenger capacity to 330 million through public funding, private sector participation, and airport privatization. Smart technologies and automation will enhance operations, positioning Saudi airports to compete with regional hubs like Dubai and Doha. The competition will be interesting to watch since in 2024, Doha–the base of the world's best airline, Qatar Airways–ranked first in the World Airport Awards by Skytrax.

Tourism Infrastructure. Tourism is an increasingly important part of Saudi Arabia's economic diversification strategy. Historically dominated by religious tourism for the Hajj and Umrah pilgrimages, the Kingdom is expanding its tourism offerings to include leisure, wellness, and cultural tourism. Projects such as Al-Ula focus on developing historical sites like the ancient Nabatean city of Hegra, while Amaala, a luxury, 3000-hotel-room wellness destination, aims to attract affluent tourists with yoga retreats and spa resorts. The Red Sea Project, spanning 28,000 square kilometers and

---

[145] World Shipping Council (2024) "The top 50 container ports" Retrieved from: https://www.worldshipping.org/top-50-ports.

featuring over 90 islands, emphasizes sustainability with plans to run entirely on renewable energy. The project includes luxury resorts, hotels, and residences, with the first phase completed in 2024 and full completion expected by 2025. Future tourism initiatives include hosting global events like the Asian Winter Games in 2029, the World Expo in 2030, and the FIFA World Cup in 2034, alongside efforts to double the number of Muslim pilgrims to Mecca and Medina.

Urban development and smart cities. Urban development is a significant aspect of Saudi Arabia's infrastructure transformation, often marked by stories of poor planning and financial difficulties. Neom envisioned as a futuristic city, stands out as a key initiative that integrates smart grids, autonomous transportation, and renewable energy to create a sustainable urban environment.

The Line, a central feature of Neom, is a 1600-foot tall structure initially planned to span 93 miles and accommodate 1.5 million residents. Initial cost estimates ranged from $100 billion to $200 billion, but some projections went as high as $1 trillion. Due to severe financial and planning setbacks, the Saudi government scaled back the project, extending the timeline to 50 years. The first segment, a 1.4-mile stretch, is now expected to be completed by 2030. Plans for a desalination plant to supply 30% of the city's water were halted in 2024 due to funding issues. The full large-scale project has faced criticism from human rights groups for the displacement of the Indigenous Howeitat people and from environmentalists who warn that the mirror façade would endanger migratory birds. Under financial strain, the government has now prioritized elements essential for hosting global sporting events, such as a stadium for the World Cup and Trojena, a planned mountain resort hosting the Asian Winter Games in 2029.[146]

Sindalah, a luxury island destination in the Red Sea, became the first Neom region to be completed. Meanwhile, Oxagon, another planned industrial city within Neom, is still under development.

Riyadh and Jeddah have focused on integrating intelligent infrastructure, such as metro lines and upgraded bus networks, and autonomous transport systems, including vehicles, drones, and public transit, which are integral to these urban development plans. In Jeddah, construction resumed in 2024 on the 3300-foot tall Jeddah Tower, which is set to become the tallest building in the world upon completion in 2028.

---

[146] Reuters (2024) "Saudi Arabia prioritizes sports" Retrieved from: Reuters https://www.reuters.com/world/middle-east/saudi-arabia-prioritizes-sports-neom-plans-costs-balloon-sources-say-2024-11-13/?utm_source=chatgpt.com.

The Mukaab, or Cube, is a downtown Riyadh project that broke ground in October 2024. This seven-square-mile development, inspired by the Kaaba, is one of 14 giga-projects being implemented as Saudi Arabia prepares to host the Riyadh World Expo 2030. The Qiddiyah Project in Riyadh as well, is an entertainment, sports, and cultural center, is close to completion.

King Abdullah Economic City. King Abdullah Economic City (KAEC) is another example of ideas that are having a hard time making into reality. Initially conceived as a $100 billion project and criticized as a vanity project of the late King Abdullah bin Abdulaziz, is now being reassessed under Vision 2030. Located between Jeddah and Medina, it was intended to host pilgrims traveling to Mecca and Medina. Initially planned to accommodate 2 million residents, the city housed only 7000 people in 2018, with 2024 projections reaching a maximum of 100,000. The project's developer recently entered a debt restructuring agreement, providing temporary financial relief.

Despite ongoing developments, Saudi Arabia faces financial challenges in realizing its infrastructure goals. Reliance on oil revenues has strained project funding, with rising costs and low oil prices delaying initiatives. Workforce shortages and regulatory obstacles further complicate progress. In 2024, the fiscal deficit was projected at 2.3% of GDP, a manageable figure, but insufficient to fund the scale of planned projects. Saudi Arabia would need significantly more than the $1 trillion available in its sovereign wealth fund to execute its ambitious plans. Simply stated, without FDI, the country doesn't have enough money.[147]

Geopolitics

Saudi Arabia's international strategy heavily emphasizes oil politics, contrasting its domestic policies that aim for gradual diversification away from oil dependency. Globally, the Kingdom seeks to amplify its influence in oil and petrochemical markets, using its resources and production capacity to strengthen its geopolitical position and economic power.

As the de-facto leader of OPEC since its inception in 1960, Saudi Arabia has shaped the organization's policies and strategies to a large degree. While OPEC remains a key player in global oil markets, its dominance has faced increasing challenges. The rise of non-OPEC producers, particularly the United States with its shale oil boom, and emerging players like Guyana, has reduced OPEC's ability to unilaterally dictate oil prices. The OPEC+ alliance,

---

[147] The Wall Street Journal (2024) "The big problem for Saudi Arabia's futuristic city" Retrieved from: https://www.wsj.com/world/middle-east/the-big-problem-for-saudi-arabias-futuristic-city-the-country-doesnt-have-enough-money-9b825a67?utm_source=chatgpt.com.

which includes Russia and other non-OPEC producers, reflects an attempt to maintain influence by coordinating production levels, particularly during economic downturns or geopolitical instability. Saudi Arabia, alongside the UAE and Russia, continues to leverage oil production as a tool of diplomacy and economic control, but internal divisions within OPEC threaten its cohesion.

Long-term challenges further complicate OPEC's future relevance. The global shift toward renewable energy, electric vehicles, and sustainability initiatives signals a weakening demand for oil, which could erode the organization's importance. While OPEC retains medium-term influence, its ability to remain a dominant force in the energy market faces significant pressure from ongoing energy transitions and geopolitical dynamics.

The close relationship between Saudi Crown Prince Mohammed bin Salman and the United States introduces another dimension to oil politics. This partnership could potentially consolidate control over global oil markets. This alignment suggests a possible shift in global oil dynamics, where Saudi-U.S. coordination plays a more dominant role in managing supply and prices.

Saudi Arabia's oil and petrochemical trade also remains central to its geopolitical strategy. Oil and oil products account for 89% of Saudi exports, which nearly tripled over the last two decades, growing from $126 billion in 2004 to $321 billion in 2023 (see Fig. 6.20).

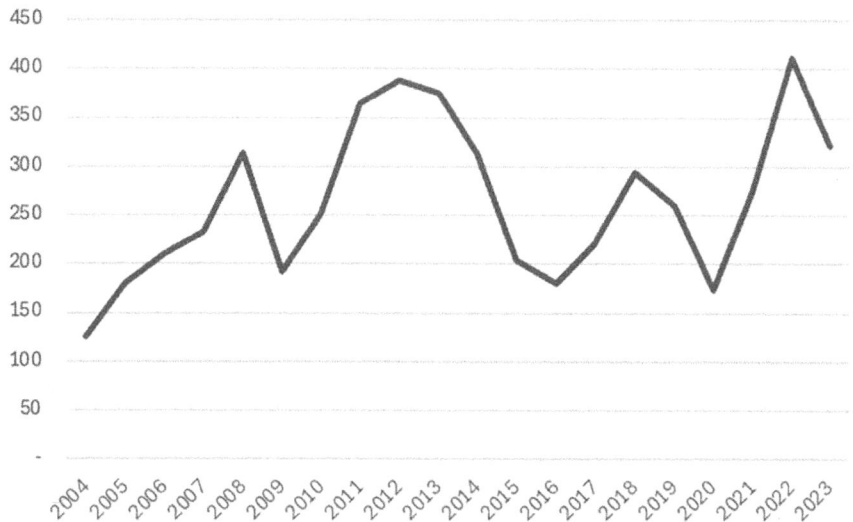

Fig. 6.20 Saudi Arabia—exports (Current billions $) (*Source* Intracen)

The geographic composition of these exports has changed significantly. A wide global distribution in 2004 transformed into a concentrated flow to key Asian markets in 2023. Saudi Arabia sends 16% of its exports to China, an additional 10% to Japan, and almost 10% to India. At the same time, these economies are growing dependent on Saudi oil. In 2023, Saudi Arabia ranked as China's 13th import partner, 6th for Japan, 5th for India, and 5th for South Korea (see Table 6.1).

Foreign direct investment. FDI inflows are critical for economic development in most fast-growing nations. In contrast, for Saudi Arabia, investments made abroad—foreign investment outflows (FDI-O)—are the critical element to accelerate growth and reduce the volatility associated with crude oil prices.

Indeed, FDI inflows will be important in the future. Right after the launch of Vision 2030, FDI inflows briefly spiked as reforms allowed 100% foreign ownership in key sectors and privatized assets like Saudi Aramco. Yet, despite these changes, inflows stagnated at approximately $25 billion annually, far below the $100 billion target set in Vision 2030.

Table 6.1 Saudi Arabia—exports by country (%)

	2004 (%)	2014 (%)	2023 (%)
China	0.7	2.3	16.6
Japan	0.2	0.3	10.1
India	0.4	1.2	9.6
Korea, Republic of	0.4	0.4	9.0
United Arab Emirates	1.6	2.0	5.2
United States of America	0.5	0.4	4.9
Bahrain	0.4	0.5	2.7
Taiwan	0.0	0.4	2.6
Malaysia	0.0	0.5	2.4
Singapore	0.5	1.2	2.4
Egypt	0.2	0.7	2.3
Poland	0.0	0.1	2.3
France	0.1	0.1	2.0
Oman	0.2	0.3	1.9
Thailand	0.1	0.2	1.6
Italy	0.2	0.3	1.5
Pakistan	0.2	0.1	1.5
Netherlands	0.3	0.1	1.4
Türkiye	0.1	0.7	1.3
Indonesia	0.1	0.2	1.2

Source Intracen

Foreign Direct Investment outflows, on the other hand, mirrored this cycle, also reaching $25 billion in 2023. The PIF had initially prioritized international markets through high-profile investments in sectors such as technology, renewable energy, sports, and entertainment, including stakes in Uber and the acquisition of Newcastle United Football Club (see Fig. 6.21).

In recent years, PIF shifted focus domestically, reducing foreign investments to 18–20% of its portfolio in 2024, down from 30%, while increasing domestic investments in areas such as artificial intelligence. This shift was meant to support local infrastructure and corporate development. Analysts worried that this domestic focus would weaken PIF's countercyclical nature as a Sovereign Wealth Fund. That is true, but major Saudi corporations Aramco and Saudi Basic Industries Corporation (SABIC) compensated the PIF's local concentration by expanding internationally through acquisitions and joint ventures to access new markets, technologies, and resources. For example, Aramco acquired a 10% stake in Horse Powertrain (owned by Renault and Geely) to develop efficient gasoline engines and hybrid systems, while SABIC ventured into China in projects such as the $6.4 billion plant with Fujian Fuhua Gulei Petrochemical and three other plants.

SABIC is one of the world's five largest producers of petrochemicals, including chemicals, fertilizers, and polymers. It's 70% owned by Aramco and 30% by the Saudi government. In 2023, SABIC posted revenues of $37.7 billion, while top-ranked Basf reported $72.4 billion.

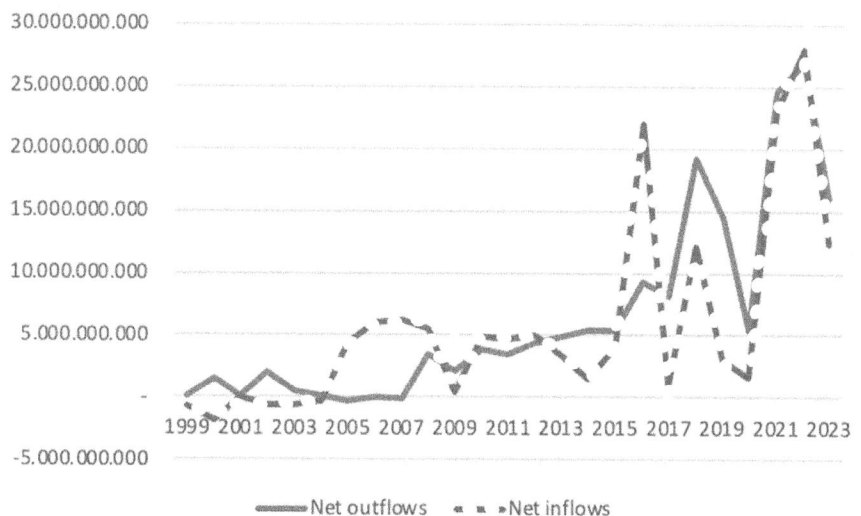

Fig. 6.21 Saudi Arabia—foreign direct investment inflows and outflows (Current $) (*Source* The World Bank)

Strategically, Saudi Arabia's corporate investments aimed at vertically integrating (SABIC's plants in China) is nothing less than a master move, as it will boost margins and reduce its dependence on the price of the fundamental commodity: crude oil.

FDI-O of Saudi corporates in clean energy abroad, position the Kingdom within sustainable value chains, fostering technology transfer, and supporting long-term industrial development. In the short term, they transfer the responsibility for environmental issues like plastic pollution away from Saudi Arabia to other producing nations. On a geopolitical level, FDI-O strengthens Saudi influence, particularly in Africa and Asia, through investments in energy and infrastructure projects. In macroeconomic terms, the final effect of corporate investments will be very hard to track, but it seems to be full of benefits.

Saudi Arabia has not always played a peacemaking role in the region. Instead, it has engaged in several direct and proxy conflicts as part of its strategy to counter perceived threats, primarily from Iran. The most prominent example is its 2015 military intervention in Yemen, where a Saudi-led coalition supported the Yemeni government against the Iran-backed Houthi rebels. The conflict led to a prolonged humanitarian crisis. In Syria, Saudi Arabia supported various rebel groups opposing the now-ousted, Russia-backed president Bashar al-Assad as part of its broader campaign to limit Iranian influence. Saudi Arabia has faced accusations of funding proxy groups in Iraq and Lebanon to challenge Iranian-backed militias and Hezbollah. In Libya, the Kingdom indirectly supported factions aligned with Khalifa Haftar's forces to counter Islamist groups.

The strategy sharply shifted in March 2023 when Saudi Arabia and Iran signed a China-brokered roadmap for the de-escalation of their conflict. This agreement marks a potential shift in Middle Eastern dynamics as Riyadh reduces its involvement in a costly standoff with Iran. The deal would allow Iran to re-establish economic ties with the Gulf Cooperation Council (GCC), easing some of the pressure from Western sanctions.[148] For the United States, this de-escalation creates an opportunity to apply pressure on Iran, potentially driving up oil prices that will benefit U.S. and OPEC producers without requiring Saudi involvement.

In 2022, Saudi Arabia also signed a truce with the Houthis in Yemen. The conflict had tarnished Saudi Arabia's international reputation and drained its

---

[148] Barnes-Dacey, Julien, and Cinzia Bianco (2024) "Mending fences: Europe's stake in the Saudi-Iran détente" European Council on Foreign Relations.

financial resources. Moreover, repeated Houthi attacks on Saudi infrastructure have undermined efforts to attract foreign investment and tourism,[149] further highlighting the economic toll of the war.

Saudi Arabia also engaged with the United States in efforts to normalize relations with Israel. The war in Gaza continues to complicate this process. However, if a resolution materializes, it would improve regional stability, facilitating investment and economic growth. Historical data from the World Bank shows that during intense regional conflicts, Middle Eastern countries experience a decline of about 2% in real GDP per capita within the first year of conflict, with losses reaching 10% over a decade. Saudi-led changes in the region are things that Stockholm will surely notice.

Military expenditure has been another tool that bolstered Saudi influence. Saudi Arabia ranks 23rd in the 2024 Military Strength Index,[150] right after Vietnam 22nd and Poland 21st. However, it is the second-largest arms importer globally, accounting for 8.4% of total arms imports from 2019 to 2023. It was the largest buyer of U.S. arms during this period, accounting for 15% of total U.S. arms exports. Additionally, Saudi Arabia topped the list of arms purchases in Spain (21% of its total sales), Canada (37%), and Belgium (38%), while being the second-largest buyer of Ukrainian arms (12%) after China. Although arms imports fell by 28% compared to 2014–2018 levels, the decline does not yet signal a meaningful shift toward domestic production.[151]

The General Authority for Military Industries (GAMI) aims to significantly increase military spending on local goods by 2030, with plans for a tenfold increase over current levels. In 2021, the Saudi government allocated $20 billion to its defense sector, with funds equally divided between general defense industry and research and development (R&D). GAMI's Industrial Participation Program requires the localization of supplier contracts through technology transfer and the development of domestic manufacturing. By partnering with equipment manufacturers, the program seeks to transfer technology and build local manufacturing capabilities. Additionally, GAMI has teamed up with Saudi universities to foster human capital, supporting the country's military R&D initiatives.[152]

---

[149] Arab Center for Research and Policy Studies (2024) "A fragile but enduring truce in Yemen" Retrieved from: https://arabcenterdc.org/resource/a-fragile-but-enduring-truce-in-yemen/.
[150] GFP (2024) "2024 Military Strength Index" Retrieved from: https://www.globalfirepower.com/.
[151] Sipri (2024) "Trends in international arms transfers, 2023" https://www.sipri.org.
[152] U.S. International Trade Administration (2024) "Saudi Arabia military industry" https://www.trade.gov/market-intelligence/saudi-arabia-military-industry.

Talent

Saudi Arabia has achieved near-universal enrollment rates at the primary and lower secondary levels. However, many young Saudis leave school without mastering the basic competencies required for future academic and professional success.[153]

The literacy rate for individuals aged 15 and older increased from 79% in 2000 to 98% in 2020, with high school enrollment reaching 97%. However, the performance of 15-year-olds in math, science, and reading, as measured by PISA scores, was significantly below international standards. In math, Saudi Arabia's average score was 389, 18% lower than the OECD average of 472. In comparison, students in Qatar scored 414, and in the UAE 431 in 2022. Additionally, 70% of Saudi students were classified as low performers in math (scoring below level 2 out of 6 levels), compared to 31% in OECD countries, 57% in Qatar, and 40% in the UAE.[154]

The reading scores follow a similar pattern: Saudi Arabia averaged 383, 20% below the OECD average of 476, while Qatar scored 419 and the UAE 417.

The proportion of individuals aged 25 and older with a Bachelor's degree or higher more than doubled, between 2004 and 2023, going from 15 to 31%. Saudi universities rank well globally, with King Fahd University of Petroleum and Minerals (KFUPM) placing 101 worldwide, and King Abdulaziz University 149. However, educational attainment drops significantly after completing undergraduate studies. Only 3.5% of the population aged 25 and older hold a Master's degree, compared to 2.2% in Qatar, 11% in the UAE, and 15% in Turkey.

In terms of employment, as is common in many countries, individuals with only basic education experience lower unemployment rates than the national average. In 2023, unemployment for those with basic education in Saudi Arabia was 1.3%, while the overall national rate stood at 4.9%. Interestingly, unemployment among those with advanced education was 5.9%, which is closer to the national rate than is typically seen in other countries. Saudi university graduates do find employment.

Despite this, unemployment in Saudi Arabia remains the highest in the GCC. In 2023, unemployment rates were 2.7% in the UAE, 1.5% in Oman, 1.2% in Bahrain, and 0.1% in Qatar. One contributing factor is a mismatch

---

[153] OECD (2020) "Education in Saudi Arabia" Retrieved from: https://www.oecd.org/en/publications/education-in-saudi-arabia_76df15a2-en.html.
[154] OECD. (2023). "*Pisa 2022 Results*" https://gpseducation.oecd.org/IndicatorExplorer?plotter=h5&query=54.

between student educational choices and the labor market needs, which emphasize infrastructure development and large-scale project management. According to OECD data, Saudi Arabia has one of the highest proportions of graduates in the arts and humanities among member and partner countries (17.7%, rank 3/45). Conversely, it has one of the lowest proportions of graduates in STEM fields (18.1%, rank 41/44), health and welfare (9.8%, rank 40/45), and services (0.6%, rank 41/44).

There are a number of other areas, presented below, where talent—its availability and relevance to competitiveness come into play:

Labor Costs. Saudi Arabia is not a low labor-cost country. In 2024, the minimum monthly wage is set at $1064. While this is significantly lower than the average earnings in the United States ($5330) or Germany ($4600), it remains higher than in countries like Turkey, where average monthly earnings are $608. As such, a cost-based development strategy will not be viable.

Saudization. Saudization (also known as Nitaqat) is a national policy launched in 2011 to reduce the reliance on foreign labor and increase employment among Saudi nationals in the private sector. Before its implementation, private sector employment was largely dominated by expatriate workers, primarily from India, Pakistan, the Philippines, Lebanon, and Egypt.

The program sets sector-specific quotas for employing Saudi nationals, with compliance offering incentives like streamlined visa processing for expatriates. The policy has evolved over time; for example, in 2024, the Ministry of Human Resources raised the Saudization quota for engineering roles from 20 to 25% for firms with five or more engineers. Official claims suggest that Saudization has increased female workforce participation, diversified the economy, and contributed to upskilling Saudi workers.

Oil and Gas. Despite Saudi Arabia's significant oil production, only a small portion of the workforce is employed in the oil and gas sector. Estimates place the number of workers at 250,000 out of a total labor force of 17 million. Saudi Aramco, the largest employer in the sector, has grown its workforce to 73,000 employees in 2023, up from 56,000 in 2011.

Under Vision 2030, there are plans to increase youth employment in the sector and improve working conditions. However, addressing these goals will require local firms to implement more effective performance management systems. Studies highlight a need for formal approaches to identifying and developing talent, improved training programs, and robust appraisal and feedback mechanisms.[155] These are not minor elements, as researchers have

---

[155] Alshehri, Abdullah, John Mulyata, et al. (2024) "The Effect of Talent Management in Saudi Oil and Gas MNCs: Strategies and Challenges" Journal of Human Resource and Sustainability Studies 12(3).

found poor satisfaction levels, and a lack of strong commitment among the young employees.[156]

Technology and Innovation. Saudi Arabia has made strides in attracting AI talent, moving up nine places to rank 15th globally in AI talent attraction relative to population size. The country has also demonstrated notable performance in cybersecurity and applied digital skills like animation and computer graphics. These efforts position Saudi Arabia as a growing hub for technology-focused professionals. Despite these advancements, language barriers are a significant issue, as Arabic is the dominant language outside business settings, complicating daily life for non-Arabic speakers. Cultural adjustments, including adhering to conservative dress codes and navigating gender-specific social norms, can also be difficult for expatriates.

Sectors like hospitality and tourism are expected to grow, offering new opportunities for employment. Currently, only 2% of the labor force works in hotels and restaurants. This figure should likely increase, aligning more closely with other Gulf countries such as Qatar at 4%, the UAE at 5%, and Oman at 7%. As these sectors expand, they will likely attract both local workers and immigrants. Saudi women, whose participation in the labor force currently stands at 34%, could particularly benefit from these openings.

Brawn gain. There are concerns that Saudi Arabia may struggle to secure enough workers to complete the large-scale infrastructure projects outlined in Vision 2030. However, workers will likely arrive, as the country already heavily relies on foreign labor—87.5% of employees in the construction industry, for instance.[157]

Saudi Arabia benefits from its location in a region that attracts significant migrant labor. According to the International Labour Organization (ILO), the Arab States region has become one of the top global destinations for migrant workers. The region also boasts the highest proportion of migrant workers relative to its local population. However, these workers are generally not highly skilled or academically trained. Many are low-income and low-skilled laborers, primarily employed in construction, hospitality, and domestic work.[158]

---

[156] Alanazi, Amal (2022) "The impact of talent management practices on employees' satisfaction and commitment in the Saudi Arabian oil and gas industry" International Journal of Advanced and Applied Sciences 9(3):46–55.
[157] Sinan, Mazen and Abdulaziz A. Bubshait (2021) "Challenges and opportunities in employing locals in the construction industry: Saudi Arabia case" Universal Journal of Management 9(No. 5):129–139.
[158] ILO (2024) "Labour migration" Retrieved from: https://www.ilo.org/regions-and-countries/ilo-arab-states/areas-work/labour-migration.

Family businesses. Family-owned enterprises dominate the private sector in Saudi Arabia, accounting for 95% of all firms. Ownership is tightly controlled, with 68% of these businesses operating as closed joint-stock companies. Family involvement extends beyond ownership into management, as 68% of these companies have a family member serving as CEO.

Family businesses in Saudi Arabia face unique challenges. While they benefit from centralized control, only one-third of them have a family charter, which often leads to governance issues. Compared to other countries, family businesses in Saudi Arabia are relatively young, having mostly been established during the 1960s. As a result, many have only gone through one succession, or none at all, which could present challenges in the future.[159]

Finally, sports have become a key tool for Saudi Arabia to engage its young population and enhance its soft power. The country has invested in high-profile sports initiatives, such as acquiring football teams, hosting professional golf tours, and sponsoring Formula One events. With 63% of its population under 30 and 25% under 15, sports play an important role in society. The Kingdom is expected to continue signing multi-million contracts with sports stars. While the immediate impact on local athletic performance has been limited—the Saudi Olympic team earned fewer medals in the 2024 Paris Olympics than in the 2000 Sydney Games—the country's strategy is paying off in other areas. Saudi Arabia's eSports team won the 2024 FIFAe World Cup in Rocket League, marking a notable achievement in digital sports.

Key Drivers

The usual diagnostic would go like this: Saudi Arabia's economic growth remains strongly tied to global energy markets, though diversification efforts are reducing this reliance. In 2024, the country's GDP was expected to grow by just 1.1%, while non-oil sectors was to expand at 4.6%. The oil sector's contraction is due to ongoing voluntary production cuts by OPEC, which are set to ease gradually through 2026. However, Saudi Arabia's GDP growth is expected to rise to an average of 4.7% in 2025–2026 as oil production recovers.

Diversification signs are already visible, with Saudi Arabia improving its position in the Economic Complexity Index—ranking 35th in 2024, up from 60th in 2000.[160] S&P Global has also upgraded the country's outlook to

---

[159] KPMG (2022) "Succession planning in family business" Retrieved from: https://kpmg.com/sa/en/home/insights/2023/03/succession-planning-in-family-businesses.html.

[160] Observatory of Economic Complexity (2024) "Economic Complexity Rankings" Retrieved from: https://oec.world/en/rankings/.

positive, citing strong non-oil growth and effective management of oil sector volatility. In this context, investments in infrastructure for non-oil industries are key to the nation's economic transformation.

All this is true, but there is a crucial element missing in this analysis: the personal influence of Crown Prince Mohammed bin Salman. Much like a family business, the Crown Prince controls all major national assets, including oil and mineral reserves, Aramco and state-owned enterprises, and manages as one, both personal and national wealth and influence. This dynamic transforms the analysis from that of a nation-state to that of a family-run multinational enterprise.

The estimates of Prince Mohammed bin Salman's net worth are absurdly inaccurate, ranging from $18 billion to $500 billion, reflecting the difficulty in distinguishing personal assets from state or royal family holdings, something typical of a family venture. As an aside, the 15,000-member Saudi royal family's wealth, equally hard to compute, is estimated at $1.4 trillion, dwarfing the wealth of Elon Musk ($488 billion) and Jeff Bezos ($233 billion).

The Crown Prince set the overarching strategy for the Saudi enterprise, Vision 2030: "…we will transform Aramco from an oil-producing company into a global industrial conglomerate. We will transform the Public Investment Fund into the world's largest sovereign wealth fund. We will encourage our major corporations to expand across borders and take their rightful place in global markets. As we continue to give our army the best possible machinery and equipment, we plan to manufacture half of our military needs within the Kingdom to create more job opportunities for citizens and keep more resources in our country."

To develop the strategy, the Crown Prince has three levers to maximize wealth and influence: government operations, investment portfolio management, and personal geopolitics.

Government operations serve as the first lever. As the owner of oil reserves and diplomatic authority, the Saudi government, under the Crown Prince's leadership, will manage OPEC and ties with the U.S. (and perhaps Russia) to maintain an iron grip over the oil market. It will also channel investments into infrastructure to boost religious and secular tourism. The government will attract foreign investments in the IT sector by offering strong financial incentives, leveraging the country's affordable energy, and promoting renewable energy projects. New IT players will train locals in advanced technologies. The government will invest in domestic startups. Furthermore, the multi-billion military budget will enhance the nation's capacity for domestic arms production.

The limits to this investment strategy will be set by the size of the fiscal deficit and by the risk of domestic asset price bubbles bursting.

Foreign direct investment inflows will likely continue, primarily targeting manufacturing, finance, insurance, construction, and wholesale and retail trade sectors. However, FDI will not necessarily be a pivotal driver of economic growth.

The Crown Prince will likely modify the goals, metrics, and standards of the plan at will. However, a robust project management infrastructure is in place to guide his decisions and assess the potential impacts of challenges.

Investment portfolio management is the second lever is. This lever revolves around the operations of entities such as Saudi Aramco, the Public Investment Fund (PIF), and the Crown Prince's personal wealth managers. Managers of this large pool of funds will focus on investing abroad in petrochemicals, prime real estate, sports, and other strategic sectors.

Personal geopolitics is the third lever. This refers to the strategic use of personal relationships to shape global geopolitics. For example, the Crown Prince's ties with figures such as U.S. President Donald Trump, his family,[161] and key leaders in the U.S. corporate world, including entities like Dell and BlackRock, pave the way for significant business deals. These relationships also reinforce U.S.-Saudi relations, transitioning from energy-based cooperation to include partnerships in technology and innovation.

The Crown Prince's relationship with Xi Jinping warmed China-Saudi ties. Chinese companies see promising investment opportunities in Saudi Arabia in areas such as renewables, construction, electric vehicles, and technology. Concurrently, Saudi firms have established joint ventures with Chinese firms in petrochemicals, while China is now heavily reliant on Saudi oil.

By withdrawing from armed conflicts with other Muslim countries, Saudi Arabia adopted a more moderate stance, which could enhance its influence within the Islamic world. The combination of religious, economic, and military capabilities may strengthen Saudi Arabia's position as a leading power among the 1.9 billion Muslims worldwide.

As with any complex, family-owned enterprise, the interplay between different areas of the organization is fluid. There are frequent overlaps and changes regarding the part of the organization that gets the deals, makes the profits, and meets goals. If foreign investors are reluctant to enter, personal connections will step in to support Saudi mega-projects. When opportunities

---

[161] BBC (2024) "Jared Kushner defends controversial $2 bn Saudi investment" https://www.bbc.com/news/world-us-canada-68296877 and Reuters (2024) "Trump Organization plans second Saudi Arabian tower in regional expansion" https://www.reuters.com/world/trump-organization-plans-second-saudi-arabian-tower-regional-expansion-2024-12-12/.

arise, Saudi investment portfolio managers are ready to negotiate and execute deals globally. In times of political tension, maximum-luxury diplomacy or coercion may be used to manage relationships with global leaders.

In summary, Saudi Arabia will become a global power driven by its ability to influence geopolitics. This influence is, in turn, powered by a combination of oil wealth, diversified portfolio investments, and a good group of friends. Ah, yes, the massive infrastructure building and technology adoption programs will most likely promote non-oil growth in the country.

A note on water: Saudi Arabia faces a severe water crisis. The country has just 67 cubic meters of renewable freshwater per person annually—the global threshold for absolute water scarcity is 500 cubic meters, and the European average is 5000 cubic meters per capita annually. Worse still, Saudi Arabia withdraws its renewable water resources at an unsustainable rate of 974%.

Saudi Arabia is focusing on expanding its leadership in desalination, which currently consumes 56 million MWh annually—more than the total electricity usage of many countries. To reduce energy use, more low-energy desalination plants are needed, and water efficiency in agriculture must improve. As temperatures rise and populations grow, combining innovation with smarter water use will be essential for securing Saudi Arabia's future.[162]

Country Outlook

Vision 2030 may need to scale back in certain areas, but progress is expected in infrastructure development, technology adoption, and tourism. Saudi Arabia is likely to advance in the global economic rankings, potentially becoming the 18th largest economy and possibly 17th place within five years.

Turkey

Turkey, a country straddling both Europe and Asia, is poised to become one of the world's leading global middle powers. This status is not only due to its economic strength in manufacturing and its role as a critical transit hub for energy products but also because, through a mix of strategic choices and fortuitous circumstances, it has adeptly navigated the challenges of sitting at the crossroads of competing global superpower strategies.

Turkey is the 18th most populous country in the world, with 85 million inhabitants. Its population is comparable in size to Germany's and about 25%

---

[162] The World Bank (2024) "The Gulf Economic Update".

bigger than that of the UK or France. The country, currently ranked as the 19th largest economy by GDP, is projected to climb to the 11th spot by 2050.[163] A member of the G20 since 1999, Turkey represents one of the most compelling examples of a middle power—a term used in international relations to describe large, successful emerging economies vying for influence in an increasingly multipolar world.

Over the past 25 years, Turkey's Gross Domestic Product (GDP) has grown at an average annual rate of 4.8%, outpacing the global average of 2.9%, the U.S.'s 2.2%, the U.K.'s 1.7%, and Germany's 1.2%. Income per capita rose from $4100 in 1999 to $12,980 in 2023, achieving an impressive average annual growth rate of 5.9%. While poverty has declined significantly, challenges remain. The percentage of people living on less than $6.85 per day fell from 10.3% in 2017 to 7.6% in 2021, compared to 1% in the U.S. and 0.7% in the U.K. during the same period.

In terms of demographics, Turkey is not an aging society as only 9% of its population is 65 or older, significantly lower than Japan (30%), Italy (24%), and most European countries (more than 20%). On the other end of the age spectrum, Turkey does not have a particularly young population either, with only 22% of its citizens being younger than 15 years old. In contrast, countries like Nigeria have more than 43% of their population in that age group. Consequently, Turkey's Age Dependency Ratio, which measures the proportion of people younger than 15 or older than 64 as a percentage of the working-age population, stands at a comfortable 46.9%. This figure is far lower than that of countries with the highest dependency rates, such as Niger and Somalia (around 100%).[164]

The working-age population in Turkey is large enough for the country to benefit from what is known as a demographic dividend, which arises when a larger portion of the population is actively saving and investing. This dividend is typically more significant when the population is well-educated. Higher education levels correlate with a rise in incomes, leading to increased savings and investments, even into retirement.

Turkey's age structure has remained relatively stable despite significant migratory flows from Afghanistan, Iran, and Iraq. Turkey has been only a temporary stop for migrants from on their way to Europe. However, the Syrian civil war of 2011 brought about a drastic change. Over 3.7 million Syrians arrived in Turkey between the beginning of the crisis and 2022. Currently, some 3.3 million Syrians live in legal limbo, not having refugee

---

[163] PWC (2017) "The world in 2050" Retrieved from: https://www.pwc.com/gx/en/world-2050/assets/pwc-the-world-in-2050-full-report-feb-2017.pdf.
[164] The World Bank (2024) "World Development Indicators".

or resident status, representing one of the largest populations in temporary exile worldwide.[165]

As a nation with a predominantly Muslim population, Turkey holds a relevant position in the Islamic world, often sharing—and occasionally competing for—influence with other rising powers. Additionally, Turkey's active diplomatic and military engagement over the past quarter-century in one of the world's most volatile regions has further bolstered its geopolitical influence.

Assessing the current business environment, investment—both local and foreign—has been the major driver of growth. Valued at 32% of GDP ($360 billion), investment has, in turn, driven exports, which amount to nearly $260 billion, and play a crucial role in the nation's economic development. Investment has helped build a diversified economy, built a manufacturing sector and a vital transit route for oil and gas between Asia and Europe, which is the core of Turkey's story of productive progress.

Manufacturing has been a major magnet for investment, increasing at 5.2% per year, and manufactured exports have grown at an impressive 6% annually on average. The country is the 6th largest exporter of apparel in the world, the 7th exporter of artificial filaments, the 17th of steel, and the 18th of footwear, to mention just a few items.

In 2023, the value added by manufacturing represented 19% of GDP, more than three times the contribution of agriculture (6%). Since 1996, the added manufacturing value has averaged 17% of GDP. Additionally, manufactured goods dominate Turkey's exports, accounting for nearly three-fourths of total merchandise exports (73% in 2023 and 78% on average over the last 25 years).

Approximately 50% of Turkey's manufacturing output stems from activities that could be categorized as low-tech. These include textiles, footwear, furniture, ceramics, glassware, processed foods, and some home appliances. Emphasis on this kind of manufacturer aligns with Turkey's labor cost advantage; the average monthly earnings of employees in Turkey was $608 in 2024, compared to $4700 in Germany.

Notably, sophisticated machinery and transport equipment account for another 20% of total manufacturing value added (18% on average over the past 25 years). Vehicles are Turkey's number one export, with the country ranking 18th globally among automobile exporters, selling mostly in the

---

[165] European Commission. (2023). "Türkiye Report 2023". From European Neighbourhood Policy and Enlargement Negotiations (DG NEAR).

highly competitive and demanding European market. Nevertheless, as indicated in Fig. 6.22, Turkey's GDP and manufacturing value add growth has been erratic in recent years.

Regardless of the unevenness of Turkey's manufacturing performance, economic development rooted in the manufacturing sector provides investors with a greater sense of security. There are distinct differences between emerging markets with strong manufacturing and service economies versus those reliant on commodity and raw material exports.Chief among these differences is volatility. Over the past 25 years, excluding a few outliers, there has been a clear inverse relationship between GDP volatility—measured by the standard deviation of GDP growth—and the share of manufacturing in total GDP. Economies centered on manufacturing tend to exhibit less volatility compared to commodity-dependent counterparts (see Fig. 6.23).

A strong domestic demand, an early entry of foreign firms to the Turkish market—especially in the automobile sector—, stable access to international financial markets, government incentives, the existence of a permanent portfolio of large infrastructure projects, and a high domestic savings have supported a strong investment flow. An element to highlight is the high savings rate, which is not usual in emerging economies. It reached a considerable 26% of GDP in 2023 and has never been below 20% of GDP in the past 25 years.

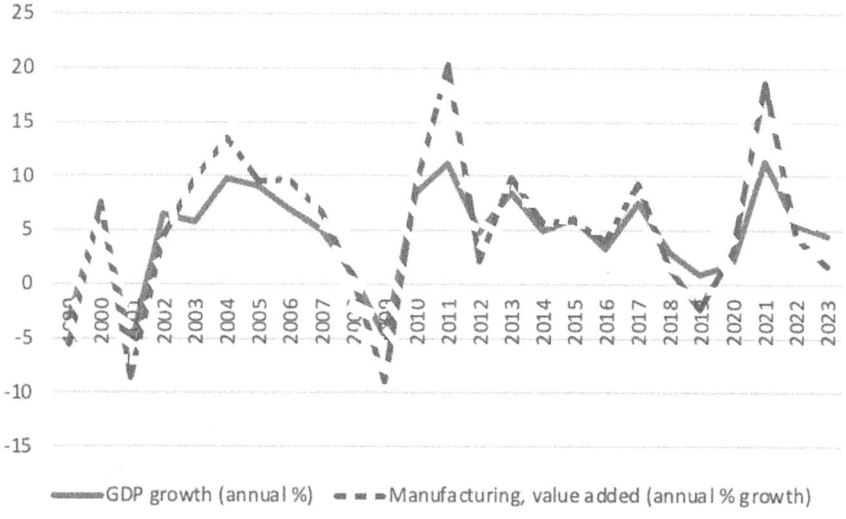

Fig. 6.22 Turkey—GDP and manufacturing value added growth 1999–2023 (Annual % growth) (*Source* World Bank, https://databank.worldbank.org/source/world-development-indicators)

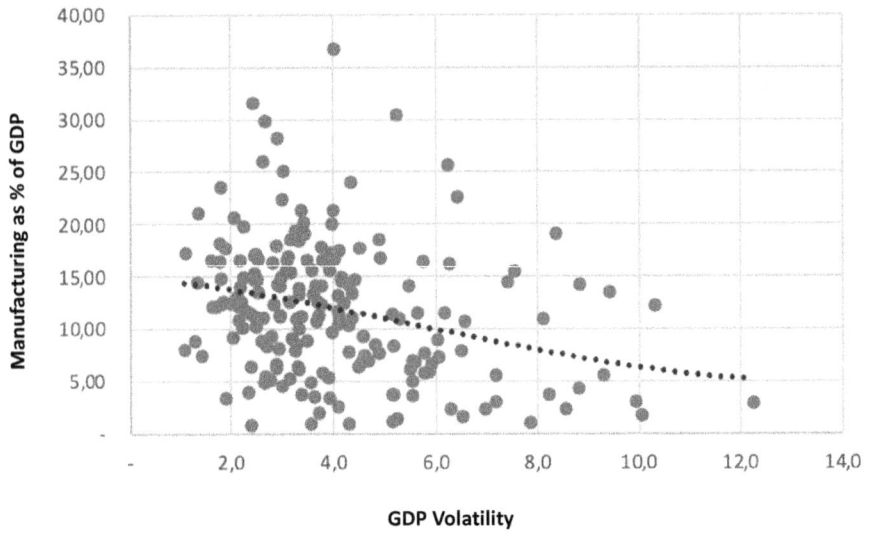

Fig. 6.23 World—GDP growth volatility (horizontal axis) and manufacturing value added as a percentage of GDP 1999 to 2023 (*Source* Latin Trade, The World Bank data, https://databank.worldbank.org/source/world-development-indicators)

This very favorable environment has compensated for problems that would have severely hindered the development of new investment projects elsewhere. Currency devaluation, inflation, and an estimated $150 billion or more in damage from the 2023 earthquakes could have left Turkey weak and very vulnerable to economic shocks.

Over the past decade, the Turkish lira lost 94% of its value against the U.S. dollar. The exchange rate went from approximately 2.2 liras per dollar in 2014 to 34.5 liras per dollar in 2024. Turkey's annual inflation peaked at 75.5% year over year in May 2024, and declined to more than 40% by year's end 2024, far above the OECD average of 5.7%.

Foreign direct investment has been a key to Turkey's growth, especially in recent years. Turkey's extensive investments in trade, energy, and transport infrastructure highlight its commitment to addressing both economic needs and geopolitical objectives, which have been game changers. Projects, such as the Trans-Anatolian Natural Gas Pipeline (TANAP) and TurkStream pipeline, along with significant investments in liquified natural gas facilities and the Sakarya gas field, position Turkey as a critical player in regional energy security. Moreover, the development of ports, road networks, and bridges underscores Turkey's strategic approach to becoming a key hub for global trade and energy transit. Turkey's Foreign Direct Investment Law of 2003 was a monumental breakthrough. It ensured equal treatment for foreign investors, removed restrictions, and streamlined the investment process. The results of this relevant institutional change produced a jump in investment.

Privatizations and mergers and acquisitions (M&A) also played significant roles in attracting FDI. Between 2005 and 2018, it drew more than $27 billion in just a few deals. The privatization of Türk Telekom, the country's primary telecommunications provider, to a Saudi-Lebanese consortium. British telecommunications company Vodafone then acquired Telsim, Turkey's second-largest mobile phone operator. Italy's UniCredit bought a 50% stake in Koç Financial Services, which owns Yapı Kredi, one of Turkey's largest banks. British private equity firm BC Partners acquired Migros, Turkey's largest supermarket chain. Spain's Banco BBVA acquired a 24.9% stake in Garanti Bank and bank Emirates NBD bought Denizbank from Russia's Sberbank, to name some relevant operations. Investments in the automobile industry, as mentioned previously, further reflect Turkey's ability to attract foreign capital.

Internal obstacles still pose a challenge to foreign investors. Although Turkey has one of the most liberal legal regimes for foreign investors among OECD members, foreign direct investment was only $10 billion in 2023, representing just 1% of GDP.[166] Foreign players encounter difficulties in government processes despite Turkey's adherence to European trade standards, including EU's Common External Tariff and zero customs duties and quantitative restrictions on bilateral trade with the EU.

Often, Turkey officials have a different interpretation of trade norms, and there are unexpected changes to import requirements, non-tariff barriers, and limited adjustment periods for businesses. Agricultural trade faces additional challenges due to tariff quotas and restrictive non-science-based requirements. Government procurement is also criticized for opacity, lengthy procedures, onerous conditions, and significant delays, all of which discourage effective participation.[167]

Turkey two main exports include Vehicles and vehicle parts—in 2024, Turkey's top export totaling $29.5 billion, and Refined petroleum.

Turkey is a leading producer of agricultural products, textiles, transportation equipment, construction materials, consumer electronics, and home appliances.[168] Turkey also possesses important iron ore reserves and sizeable

---

[166] U.S. Department of State (2024) "2024 Investment Climate Statements: Turkey" Retrieved from: https://www.state.gov/reports/.
[167] U.S. International Trade Administration (2024) "Trade barriers" Retrieved from: https://www.trade.gov/country-commercial-guides/turkey-trade-barriers.
[168] OEC World, Statista, World Bank.

cotton plantations, which make it a top global exporter of steel, textiles, and apparel.

Its geographic location—being near and between resource-producing nations and wealthy European consumers—has played a critical role in the country's economic growth.

Location should be treated almost as a factor of production, just as an oil well or a plot of fertile land. Contrary to intuition, location does not necessarily have a fixed value. It can be made more valuable with, for example, good infrastructure, or it can be devalued by signing treaties that close international markets.

A clear example of this strategic dynamic can be seen in the Turkish case. Although Turkey is a marginal oil and gas producer, the government and its partners have invested over $20 billion in pipelines that have transformed the country into a vital transit hub for hydrocarbons flowing from Asia to Europe. While the estimated financial return of this pipeline network is around $2 billion annually, its true value lies in the significant geopolitical leverage it provides. A similar dynamic plays out in Turkey's control of the Bosphorus and the Dardanelles—the critical Turkish Straits.

Technology

Turkey is gradually becoming an innovative, sophisticated manufacturing hub. In 2024, Turkey ranked 37th out of 132 countries in the Global Innovation Index, outperforming all other upper-middle-income economies in six of the seven main components of the index. Moreover, Istanbul and Ankara were classified as leading science and technology clusters, with Istanbul improving its position to 46th among the world's top science and technology clusters.[169]

The number of patents provides a telling, albeit imprecise, measure of innovative capacity. In 2022, Turkey registered 9119 patents, ranking 19th in the world. More significantly, it ranked #2 globally, after China, in the number of Industrial Design registrations.[170]

As we will discuss later, innovation and productive sophistication in Turkey are more the result of corporate action than that of strong collaboration with academia. The private sector, especially in industries like automotive, defense, and manufacturing, has played a significant role in advancing technology and

---

[169] WIPO. (2024). "Global Innovation Index 2024" Retrieved from: https://www.wipo.int/web-publications/global-innovation-index-2024/en/.

[170] WIPO. (2024) "World Intellectual Property Indicators 2023" Retrieved from: https://www.wipo.int/edocs/pubdocs/en/wipo-pub-941-2023-en-world-intellectual-property-indicators-2023.pdf.

innovation. The presence of foreign firms has also been a fundamental way to access technology.

Technology is not an independent sector but a competitive asset that is largely embedded in other key sectors. The examples below are illustrative.

Automobiles. Turkey's car making history dates back to Ford's establishment of its first plant in 1959, followed by Fiat (Tofaş) in 1968 and Renault in 1969. As the local workforce gained experience, more foreign entrants and plant expansions followed. In the 2000s, Toyota opened a plant in Adapazarı, Renault Oyak expanded its Bursa operations, and Fiat Tofaş expanded its facilities in Bursa. In the 2010s, Hyundai Assan expanded its plant in İzmit, Ford Otosan opened a plant in Yeniköy, and Mercedes-Benz Türk expanded its truck plant in Aksaray. Collectively, these investments totaled $3.1 billion over two decades.

A consequence (perhaps unintended) of technology transfer was the establishment in 2015 of the local Automobile Joint Venture Group (TOGG) to produce the country's first domestically manufactured electric car. The model, a Pininfarina-designed SUV, was launched in March 2023 and, by 2024, had already captured a 30% share of the domestic market. Notably, the plant, which has the capacity to produce up to 20 vehicles per hour, operates with an army of 250 robots, all under the full control of Turkish engineers.

There are additional success stories in the manufacture of transportation equipment. Affiliates of the state-owned Turkish State Railways have a longstanding tradition of manufacturing increasingly sophisticated locomotives, passenger cars, and freight wagons for the domestic railway system.

Defense and Aerospace. Turkey has developed a competitive defense and aerospace industry, particularly in a niche focusing on less technologically sophisticated products. In 2022, four Turkish firms—Aselsan, Baykar, Turkish Aerospace Industries (TAI), and Roketsan—were ranked among the top 100 arms-producing and military services companies in the world by revenue. That year, these firms collectively sold $5.5 billion worth of defense-related products.[171] Additionally, Turkey holds the 11th position globally as an arms exporter.[172]

War drones produced by Baykar and TAI are part of the arsenals of at least 33 countries. These drones have played pivotal roles in recent conflicts, including Ukraine's defense against Russia, as well as in other theaters, such as Libya and Nagorno-Karabakh.

---

[171] SIPRI (2023) "Rise in SIPRI Top 100 arms sales revenue delayed by production challenges and backlogs" Retrieved from: https://www.sipri.org/media/.
[172] Intracen (2024) Op. Cit.

Aselsan is recognized for its military electronics, producing advanced communication systems, radar, electronic warfare systems, and avionics. Meanwhile, TAI and Kale Aero specialize in manufacturing aerospace components, including aircraft parts, engines, and control systems, catering to both military and civilian aviation markets.

Renewable Energy. Local and multinational companies compete in Turkey's renewable energy sector. High-tech solar panels and wind turbines are manufactured by firms such as Turkish Zorlu Energy and Spanish-German Siemens Gamesa. Local companies such as Vestel and Aselsan provide smart grid solutions for electricity distribution.

Information and Communication Technology. In the information and communication technology sector, much of the market for mass-consumed telecom equipment is dominated by Chinese firms. Netaş, an affiliate of Chinese ZTE, and Huawei are leading providers of advanced telecommunication infrastructure, including 4G/5G network equipment and communication solutions.

Other Leading Areas. Advanced manufacturing, robotics, nanotechnology, and pharmaceuticals are additional higher-tech sectors in Turkey that are notable in their activity. For example, Durmazlar and Kuka Turkey operate industrial robot manufacturing facilities focused on automotive production and precision machining. Nanoksi specializes in nano-coatings and advanced materials for sectors such as automotive, electronics, and healthcare. In the pharmaceutical industry, companies like Abdi İbrahim and Deva Holding produce biotech drugs and advanced medical treatments. Turkey also demonstrates strong technological capabilities in the production of smart TVs, home appliances, and medical devices, particularly in medical imaging equipment and wearable health-tracking technologies.

National Space Program. In 2021, Turkey launched its National Space Program, which includes plans for lunar missions and the development of satellite and space technologies. Parts of the program probably have more hype than substance, but in 2024, at the cost of $55 million, the first Turkish astronaut, Alper Gezeravci, completed 14 experiments in a three-week mission to the International Space Station. Also, in 2024, Turkey applied to participate in the International Lunar Research Station, initiated by China and Russia. It will be the 10th nation—alongside unlikely space vanguardists like Nicaragua, Venezuela, and Somalia—to join the group that will attempt to place a station on the Moon.

In summary, technology-rich capital has been the driving force of Turkey's economic growth since the 2000s. More than from academia, the technology embodied in complex production lines has generated knowledge and skills in the Turkish labor force. This accumulated knowledge has been transferred to key firms and industries.

Infrastructure

International participation in infrastructure—much like the role of technology in manufacturing—has been a key driver of Turkey's economic growth. According to Turkey's Investment Office, the country attracted a total of $250 billion in investment for its transportation and logistics sectors between 2003 and 2022. These investments are not exclusively foreign direct investment (FDI); many were made through concessions and other structured programs.

Turkey's location has enabled its roads, bridges, and oil and gas pipelines to serve not only economic functions but also military and geopolitical aims. By positioning itself as both a civil and military transit hub, Turkey has used its infrastructure to amplify its global role—despite accounting for a small 1.1% of global exports. Among these assets, the country's oil and gas pipelines stand out as especially impactful in projecting influence across regions.

Oil and Gas. There are seven major chokepoints for global oil transport—narrow maritime passages essential to global energy security. One of them is the Turkish Straits, through which tankers transport approximately 460 million tons of oil each year. This accounts for about 4% of global maritime oil trade and 3.3% of the world's total oil supply. As a result, Turkey holds considerable geopolitical significance.[173]

Three pipelines, worth close to $20 billion, recently gave Turkey a central role in oil and gas distribution from Asia to Europe.

The Baku-Tbilisi-Ceyhan pipeline began operating in 2006, connecting Azerbaijan, Georgia, and the port of Ceyhan in Turkey. In 2023, the pipeline transported approximately 30.1 million tons of oil from these countries, as well as from Turkmenistan and Kazakhstan to the Mediterranean Sea and on to Europe. The construction, led by British Petroleum, brought in at least ten major international investors from Azerbaijan, the U.S., Norway, Italy, France, and Japan.

The Trans-Anatolian Natural Gas Pipeline (TANAP), completed in 2018, carries natural gas from Azerbaijan to Europe. The project was developed by a consortium led by state-owned enterprises from Azerbaijan and Turkey and

---

[173] EIA. (2024) "2024 World Oil Transit Chokepoints." Retrieved from https://www.eia.gov/international/.

British Petroleum. In 2023, it transported approximately 5.7 billion cubic meters (bcm) of natural gas to Turkey and 10.5 cm to European markets.

The TurkStream pipeline, operational since 2020, carries Russian gas to Turkey and southern Europe. In 2023, it transported approximately 16.2 bcm of natural gas. This pipeline is one of the routes through which Russian gas reaches Europe, bypassing U.S. trade restrictions imposed after the invasion of Ukraine. Turkey buys $37 billion worth of Russian oil and gas products annually, making it the second-largest client after China.[174]

Turkey is currently rushing to develop the Sakarya gas field, which was discovered in the Black Sea by the Turkish Petroleum Corporation (TPAO), along with a pipeline to bring gas to the mainland. The project carries a $10 billion price tag, but the field's estimated 540 billion cubic meters (bcm) of natural gas reserves offer substantial profit potential.[175] Once operational, it would place Turkey 27th in global gas reserves and could meet roughly 30% of the country's domestic gas demand. Currently, Turkey is almost entirely reliant on imported oil and gas—receiving over one-third of its natural gas and about a quarter of its oil from Russia.[176]

Roads. International involvement in land transportation has also been remarkable. Over the past decade, investments in urban mobility in Istanbul totaled $4.3 billion. A Turkish-Italian group completed the Yavuz Sultan Selim Bridge over the Bosphorus Strait. Turkish and South Korean companies constructed the Eurasia Tunnel, which connects the European and Asian sides of Istanbul beneath the Bosphorus.

Trade-related land transport also received an $8 billion boost. The Marmaray Tunnel under the Bosphorus integrates Turkey's domestic rail network with European and Asian systems and was largely financed and built by Japan. The Çanakkale 1915 Bridge, the longest suspension bridge in the world spanning the Dardanelles Strait, was completed in 2022 and built by a consortium of Turkish and South Korean companies.

The $6.3 billion Gebze-Orhangazi-İzmir Highway and the Osmangazi Bridge, completed in 2016 by a Turkish-Italian group, have dramatically reduced travel time between Istanbul and coastal İzmir. These projects are significant additions to the flows of capital that have fueled Turkey's growth and positioned it as a pivotal transit country for international trade and connectivity.

---

[174] Intracen (2024) "Total energy production 2022." https://www.eia.gov/international/rankings/.
[175] The gas field with the largest reserves in the world is the South Pars/North Dome Gas-Condensate field, shared between Iran and Qatar in the Persian Gulf. The field contains an estimated 35 trillion cubic meters of natural gas.
[176] European Commission (2023) "Türkiye Report 2023" Retrieved from https://neighbourhood-enlargement.ec.europa.eu/document/.

Nevertheless, there is still room for improvement. In 2022, Turkey ranked 42nd globally on the Logistics Performance Index, a measure of the quality of trade and transport-related infrastructure.

Ports. Turkey's maritime infrastructure has been critical to its trade. The Port of Ambarlı (Istanbul) handled 3.1 million TEUs in 2023, placing it as the 74th largest port globally.[177] The Port of Mersin (1.9 million TEUs) and the Port of İzmir (1.5 million TEUs) are also essential hubs for Turkey's seaborne trade.

Energy. Turkey's total energy supply in 2023 was generated from oil and coal (54%), natural gas (27%), and wind and solar (12%), a surprisingly high share of renewables.[178] To reduce dependency on fossil fuels, Turkey set a national energy plan calling for 7.2 GW of installed nuclear power capacity by 2035. The first reactor at the Akkuyu power plant became operational in April 2023. To the dismay of NATO members, the $20 billion, four-reactor, 4.8-GW project is being built with 99.2% investment from Russia's Rosatom.[179] Negotiations for a second Russian-built plant are underway, along with plans to construct 11 additional large-scale reactors across the country.

Airports and tourism. Turkey is also an internationally recognized builder of infrastructure projects, and the $12 billion Istanbul Airport (IST) demonstrates the prowess of local builders and financiers. IST opened in 2018 and quickly rose to become one of the world's largest aviation hubs. By 2023, it ranked as the seventh busiest airport globally, handling 76 million passengers—76% of them international.[180] The airport was constructed by a consortium of local firms (Cengiz, MAPA, Limak, Kolin, and Kalyon) and financed by a syndicate of six Turkish banks.

Turkish Airlines, the world's tenth-largest airline by revenue—reaching nearly $20 billion in 2023—played a central role in IST's rapid ascent. The airport's success is both a driver and a reflection of Turkey's booming tourism sector, which welcomed 51 million international visitors annually. In 2021, Turkey ranked as the world's fourth most-desired destination.[181]

Despite its well-known volatility, tourism in Turkey has attracted significant capital investment—an uncommon trend for a sector highly sensitive to climate, political shifts, and social unrest. For example, in the summer of

---

[177] The largest port in the World, Shanghai, handled more than 39 million TEUs in 2023.
[178] European Commission (2023) Op. Cit.
[179] Ibid.
[180] ACI. (2024, July 31). "Airports Council International, ACI" Retrieved from https://aci.aero/2024/04/14/.
[181] Invest Turkey (2024) *"Tourism."* Retrieved from https://www.invest.gov.tr/en/sectors/pages/tourism.aspx.

2024, Turkish hoteliers saw a drop in domestic tourism as a fast-track visa policy from Greece redirected travelers to its islands.

Over the past decade, billions of dollars have been funneled into Turkey's tourism industry, financing major projects such as the Belek Tourism Center, the expansion of the Istanbul Convention Centre, the Istanbul Sapphire skyscraper, the Istanbul Cruise Port, and the Turkish Riviera Yacht Tourism Initiative. Investments have also fueled the growth of high-end hotel chains including Maxx Royal Resorts, Rixos Hotels, and Marriott.

Geopolitics

On November 25, 1925, President Mustafa Kemal Atatürk banned the wearing of the fez in public, replacing the iconic Ottoman headwear with Western-style hats as part of his sweeping modernization reforms. Nearly a century later, on July 24, 2020, President Recep Tayyip Erdoğan led the first Muslim prayer at Istanbul's Hagia Sophia since its reconversion into a mosque—a symbolic reversal of Atatürk's 1934 decision to transform the former Byzantine cathedral into a museum. While Atatürk's move represented Turkey's embrace of secularism and Western orientation, Erdoğan's marked a clear pivot toward a more Eurasian, Islamic, and Global South alignment.

For decades, Turkey pursued a pro-European trajectory. It joined NATO in 1952, motivated by the shared threat of Soviet expansion, particularly along its eastern borders. In 1995, Turkey entered into a Customs Union Agreement with the European Union, removing tariffs on industrial goods and aligning regulatory standards. That same year, it became a member of the World Trade Organization. By 1999, Turkey had formally applied for EU membership, reinforcing its aspirations for Western integration.

However, EU accession talks repeatedly stalled. The European Commission cited concerns over human rights, unresolved issues surrounding the occupation of northern Cyprus, maritime disputes with Greece and Cyprus (both EU members), and past allegations of war crimes as ongoing obstacles to membership.

The failure to secure EU membership fueled Turkey's pivot toward the Muslim world and Eurasian alliances. The country's overwhelming Islamic Sunni majority (almost 90% of the population) elected Recep Tayyip Erdoğan president in 2014. Voters gladly backed his views about turning the secular, western-style state of his predecessors into a traditional Muslim state. In 2019, the European Parliament's vote to suspend Turkey's EU accession talks further cemented this geopolitical realignment.

Choosing sides. Turkey plays a complex and often contradictory geopolitical role. While maintaining critical trade relations with Europe and the U.S. (the country's first and second export markets), it has fostered closer ties with the Muslim world, the BRICS, and the China-Russia-led Shanghai Cooperation Organization.

Turkey has been seen as an unruly member of trade agreements and of NATO. The European Commission has criticized things, such as local content requirement practices, that are deemed to contradict the EU-Turkey Customs Union rules.[182]

In 2019, Turkey bought Russian S-400 long-range missile systems, an action that was considered a major breach of NATO protocols. It prompted the U.S. to cancel the plan to sell 100 F-35 aircraft and withdraw Turkish companies from the F-35 production program. More recently, the country's nuclear energy program has also been perceived as a step toward building a nuclear arsenal with Russia's help.

Turkey has pursued a confrontational foreign policy toward many of its neighbors. It has frequently threatened Greece, with whom it has a long-standing maritime border dispute. Between 2016 and 2019, Turkey launched multiple incursions into northern Syria to prevent the formation of an autonomous Kurdish region in Rojava that could support the Kurdistan Workers' Party (PKK) across the border—an organization designated as a terrorist group by Turkey, the EU, and the U.S. Further intervention in Syrian Kurdish territory remains a possibility.

Though Turkey has not formally declared war on any country, it conducted military operations in Cyprus and Syria, and has been involved in regional conflicts, such as supplying arms to Azerbaijan during its war with Armenia.

It took both sides in the Russia–Ukraine war. It sells weapons to Ukraine, has kept the Turkish Straits open for Ukrainian grain exports, and has blocked Russian warships from entering the Black Sea. At the same time, it continues to import Russian oil and gas and has welcomed Russian tourists and investments—moves that effectively bypassed U.S. and EU sanctions.

Turkey's assertive posture may complicate its ambitions to lead the Islamic world. That role is largely held by Saudi Arabia, a far wealthier nation, home to Islam's two holiest cities, Mecca and Medina, and perceived as a more neutral power in regional affairs.

Transit routes. Turkey's geographical location amplifies its influence, controlling vital energy transit routes. The importance of transit lines cannot be overstated. For example, the crude oil pipeline connecting the autonomous

---

[182] European Commission. (2023). "Türkiye Report 2023" Retrieved from: https://neighbourhood-enlargement.ec.europa.eu/document/.

Kurdistan Regional Government (KRG) to the Turkish port of Ceyhan serves as the sole export route for all oil from the KRG, accounting for 80% of its economy. By controlling the gate valves of this pipeline, Ankara wields tremendous influence over the fate of the KRG government. Similarly, the TurkStream pipeline transports substantial volumes of Russian gas to Europe, bypassing U.S. trade restrictions imposed after the invasion of Ukraine. This operation has Turkey as Russia's second-largest hydrocarbons client, after China.[183]

The Straits. The Kashagan oil field, located in Kazakhstan's Caspian Sea, is one of the largest offshore oil fields in the world. Crude from this field is transported to the Russian port of Novorossiysk on the Black Sea and then shipped via tankers through the Turkish Straits to global markets.

Turkey controls this critical waterway connecting the Black Sea to the Mediterranean. The 19-mile-long Bosphorus Strait links the Black Sea to the Sea of Marmara, while the 38-mile-long Dardanelles Strait connects the Sea of Marmara to the Aegean.

The Turkish Straits are the sole maritime passage for seaborne traffic to the Mediterranean from Russia, Ukraine, Georgia, Romania, and Bulgaria. They also serve as vital trade routes for companies operating along the Danube, Don, and Dnieper rivers, enabling access to global markets.

The passage through the Straits is governed by the 1936 Montreux Convention, which grants Turkey control of the straits under international oversight. The convention requires Turkey to guarantee free passage for civilian vessels during peacetime while restricting the transit of naval warships not belonging to Black Sea states. This agreement is so influential that it prevented the Russian navy from crossing the straits to support its invasion of Ukraine.

A silent water war. The headwaters of the Euphrates and Tigris rivers are located in Turkey. The rivers are critical sources of energy and, more importantly, water. The Euphrates supplies 85% of Syria's water needs, while together, the two rivers provide nearly 100% of Iraq's water supply. Upstream demand has driven Turkey and Iran to construct dams and diversions, significantly reducing water flows downstream and causing devastating water shortages in Syria and Iraq.[184]

This dependency underscores the transnational power Turkey wields over its neighbors and further elevates the strategic importance of its Kurdish region. If Turkey were to lose control of this region through autonomy or

---

[183] Intracen (2024) "Total energy production 2022." https://www.eia.gov/international/rankings/.

[184] Singh, Arushi (2023) "Tigris-Euphrates basin states must come together to address water crisis". The Strategist. ASPI.

independence, it would lose not only water and energy resources but also leverage over Syria and Iraq.

Military strength. Following a failed military coup in 2016, the Turkish government has relentlessly strengthened its armed forces. Between 1999 and 2020, an average of 2.4% of Turkey's labor force was engaged in the military, significantly higher than the global average of 1% and the 1.1% seen in high-income countries. By 2024, Turkey ranked 8th out of 145 countries on the Global Firepower Index,[185] which evaluates military capability based on factors such as manpower, equipment strength, logistics, and other metrics.

As previously mentioned, Turkey's arms and defense producers collectively export over $5 billion worth of products annually, making the country the world's 11th-largest arms exporter. This military buildup has bolstered Turkey's influence in a region marked by persistent conflicts.

At times, Turkey's military activities align closely with its soft power strategies. A notable example is its use of "drone diplomacy"—the sale of advanced drone technology to countries like Kuwait and Saudi Arabia, which has helped bolster diplomatic ties alongside defense cooperation.

Military power becomes even more pivotal for countries situated near conflict zones. In Turkey's case, proximity to Syria, Libya, Gaza, and Ukraine transforms risk into strategic advantage. This dynamic creates a paradox where closeness to instability—so-called "bad neighborhoods"—can yield greater geopolitical leverage. In this sense, "bad" becomes "better."

In summary, Turkey's political trajectory reflects a clear evolution from its 20th-century pro-European orientation to a more complex, multidirectional foreign policy. This emerging strategy seeks influence across multiple spheres—balancing long-standing alliances with Europe and the United States while simultaneously positioning Turkey as a leader in the Muslim world and as a strategic partner to Eurasia, the Global South, and BRICS nations.

Geography remains Turkey's greatest asset. Its control over critical transit corridors amplifies its geopolitical relevance. Yet, its confrontational approach, regional military interventions, and nuanced diplomacy also make Turkey—to its own disadvantage—, one of the more unpredictable actors on the global stage.

---

[185] GFP (2024) "2024 Military Strength Ranking" Retrieved from: https://globalfirepower.com/countries-listing.php.

Talent

The combination of low labor costs, a sizeable workforce, and favorable government policies made Turkey a competitive player in global manufacturing during the 2000s.

In 1994, Turkey was a low-cost labor economy, with an average monthly wage of just $32, compared to approximately $1800 in Germany. Following a sharp currency devaluation, Turkish wages dropped even further to $2.63 by 1999, while German wages rose to $2300. These low labor costs helped offset political and economic risks, solidifying Turkey's appeal as a destination for foreign investors and manufacturers seeking to cut production expenses through outsourcing.

Foreign investment fueled the growth of Turkey's export-oriented industries, particularly in textiles, apparel, and automotive components, sectors where relatively low skill levels sufficed. Yet, in 1999, 40% of Turkey's workforce was still employed in agriculture, underscoring the uneven distribution of skills across the labor market.

Turkey continues to be a low-wage economy. In 2023, the average monthly earnings per employee stood at $608, just 11% of the $5330 earned by an average U.S. worker, and significantly below Germany's $4600.

While access to education has expanded thanks to government incentives and the growth of academic institutions, the quality of education has not kept pace with these improvements.

Classrooms in need of change. Turkey has made notable strides in education, though significant challenges remain. Between 2002 and 2022, the performance of Turkish 15-year-olds in math, science, and reading, as measured by PISA scores, improved by approximately 8%. In contrast, scores in the United States remained flat, while France experienced a 4% decline over the same period.

Despite this progress, Turkey still ranks in the lower half of the global scale. In 2022, it placed 36th out of 81 countries, with an overall PISA score about 18% lower than that of top-ranked Singapore.[186]

The share of the population over age 25 with a university degree or higher rose significantly, from 7% in 2006 to 21% in 2022. However, the quality of higher education remains a concern. Even Turkey's best universities lag behind global standards. Middle East Technical University (METU) ranks

---

[186] OECD. (2023). *Pisa 2022 Results*. From OECD.org: https://www.oecd.org/en/publications/pisa-2022-results-volume-i_53f23881-en.html.

336th globally, Istanbul Technical University 404th, and Koç University 431st, with all other institutions ranked below 500th.[187]

Degrees of separation: education and employment. High unemployment is a structural feature of Turkey's economy. Over the past 25 years, the country's average unemployment rate has stood at 10.5%, well above the global average of 6.1%, and higher than rates in the United States (5.7%) and the United Kingdom (5.4%). In 2023, Turkey's unemployment rate was 9.4%, still high by international standards.

As in many emerging economies, Turkey's job market often rewards less-educated individuals more than those with vocational training or advanced degrees. Over the last quarter-century, individuals with only basic education have consistently had a lower unemployment rate (9.6%) than the national average. By contrast, those with higher education—such as short-cycle tertiary, bachelor's, master's, or doctoral degrees—have faced a slightly higher unemployment rate of 10.7%. The most affected group has been individuals with intermediate education (including upper secondary and vocational training), who have endured the highest unemployment rate at 12.5%.[188]

A clear causal relationship has been observed[189] between the rise in the number of graduates and increasing unemployment rates. Over the past 25 years, the number of graduates in Turkey has grown dramatically. Vocational school graduates increased from 74,000 in 1999 to 335,000 in 2023—a 4.5-fold rise. Bachelor's degree holders grew from 124,000 to 477,000 (3.8 times), Master's degree holders from 9000 to 81,000 (a ninefold increase), and Ph.D. holders from 2600 to 11,000 (a 4.2-fold increase).

This surge can be attributed to a range of incentives: free university tuition, subsidized dormitories, low-cost meals, and a sharp expansion in the number of higher education institutions—from just 29 universities in 1984 to 208 in 2023, a 7.2-fold increase.

As a result, Turkey now ranks fourth globally in the share of Ph.D. holders relative to its population. In 2022, 2.5% of the population held a doctoral degree—surpassed only by Switzerland, Slovenia, and Luxembourg.[190] The country also ranks 22nd in the world in the share of people with at least a Master's degree (22%).

---

[187] QS. (2024). *QS Top Universities*. From topuniversities.com: https://www.topuniversities.com/world-university-rankings/2024?countries=tr.
[188] The World Bank (2024) "World Development Indicators".
[189] Algul, Y. (2024). Higher Education and Unemployment in Turkey: Regional Panel Analysis with Undergraduate, Master's, and PhD Perspectives. Trends in Busines and Economics.
[190] The World Bank (2024) "World Development Indicators" Educational Attainment.

This trend likely reflects both a strategy to postpone entering a difficult job market and a belief in the growing demand for specialized skills. Whatever the motivation, the move toward higher educational attainment is likely to pay off in the medium term, as similar patterns in other.

Management and Family Business. Management skills can be acquired through formal education or on-the-job experience, particularly in firms that apply best-in-class practices. Managerial expertise is a vital complement to individual talent, and strong evidence shows that effective management is a key driver of firm performance. Studies consistently find that companies in the top deciles for management practices outperform their peers in productivity, profitability, growth, exports, R&D spending, and patent generation.

The World Management Survey (WMS) offers a standardized framework to measure these practices—such as lean operations, performance monitoring, target setting, and continuous improvement—as likely causal factors in organizational success.[191]

According to WMS results, the highest management scores are found in the United States (3.3), Germany (3.2), Sweden, and Japan. In contrast, Turkey ranks 18th out of 35 countries with a score of 2.7. This performance gap could be avoided given that modern management practices are globally accessible and can be adopted by hiring professionals with experience in multinational or large domestic corporations.[192]

However, family-owned businesses—which make up about 95% of Turkish firms[193]—often hinder the adoption of these practices. Many of these companies place less emphasis on merit-based management. In fact, 45% of Turkish firms surveyed reported that top leadership roles were filled by relatives or friends rather than professionals selected for their qualifications.[194]

In large companies, senior managers may be professionals, but boards are typically composed of family members. Strategic decisions often rest with the eldest member of the owning family, even when professional managers are in place.[195] This structure limits merit-based progression and dampens

---

[191] Scur, Daniela et al. (2021) "The World Management Survey at 18: Lessons and the Way Forward". NBER Working Paper Series.
[192] WMS scores vary directly with firm size. Companies with more than 1,000 workers score better than smaller firms.
[193] Silantieva, Tatiana (2023) "Cultural Specificity of the Turkish Family Business Model: Comparative and Axiological Analysis" SSRN.
[194] Bloom, Nicholas; Lemos, Renata et al. (2024) "WMS" Retrieved from: https://worldmanagementsurvey.org/data/wms-data/download-public-data/.
[195] Silantieva (2024) Op. Cit.

the returns on managerial education, slowing the diffusion of best practices across the economy.

In summary, while universities have contributed to skill development, Turkey's persistent low wages and high unemployment among the highly educated suggest that the most effective way to build a skilled manufacturing workforce lies within firms themselves. These companies must integrate advanced technologies and managerial systems—not just academic knowledge—to enhance productivity and global competitiveness.

Key Drivers

In 1999, Turkey's GDP per capita stood at $4000, just 21% of the European Union's $18,500. By 2023, it had risen to $13,000, narrowing the gap to 31% of the EU's $40,800. While this may seem like small progress, its implications are significant. Over the same period, life expectancy in Turkey rose from 70 to 78 years, marking notable social development.

Several factors fueled this growth. Turkey's abundant, skilled, and low-cost labor force, combined with its geographic proximity to Europe and a pro-investment policy environment, attracted substantial foreign investment. Low-tech manufacturing industries such as apparel, footwear, and automotive components thrived, and drove export-oriented strategies. Between 1999 and 2008, exports soared from $48 billion to $182 billion, increasing their share of GDP from 19 to 24%, even though exports were not the dominant engine of economic expansion.[196]

Geopolitics played a pivotal role in Turkey's initial industrialization, as Western organizations like the WTO, NATO, and the European Union welcomed Turkey into their ranks.

Turkey's strategic location has long been a driver of economic growth. Positioned between resource-rich Asian countries and wealthy European consumer markets, it serves as a critical transit hub for energy and goods flowing between continents. Over time, this corridor has evolved to meet shifting economic and geopolitical needs.

Importantly, geography is not a static asset. Like a natural resource or a piece of infrastructure, the value of location can rise with targeted investments—such as roads, pipelines, and ports—or fall when shifting alliances and trade disruptions limit access to key markets. In Turkey's case, its ability to capitalize on its geography has been a key differentiator in its development trajectory.

---

[196] The World Bank (2024) "World Development Indicators".

Economic growth in Turkey has been fueled by infrastructure investment and rising exports, which in turn attracted additional capital, particularly in manufacturing and logistics. However, progress in social infrastructure has lagged, and the country's digital infrastructure remains largely under the control of foreign entities.

Technology has also played an important, especially through innovations embedded in complex manufacturing processes. These advances have significantly enhanced workforce skills, largely independent of formal academic institutions. On-the-job training—driven by both local entrepreneurs and multinational companies—has enabled the emergence of world-class industries, including electric vehicles and a booming tourism sector.

Despite these gains, inefficiencies persist, particularly in management practices among family-owned firms, where leadership often prioritizes kinship ties over professional qualifications.

Turkey's evolving industrial landscape is reflected in its ranking on the Economic Complexity Index (ECI), where it stands as the 41st most complex economy in the world (see Fig. 6.24).

While exports have flourished, Turkey is not a full-fledged export economy. In 2023, the country exported $376 billion, representing 32% of its GDP.

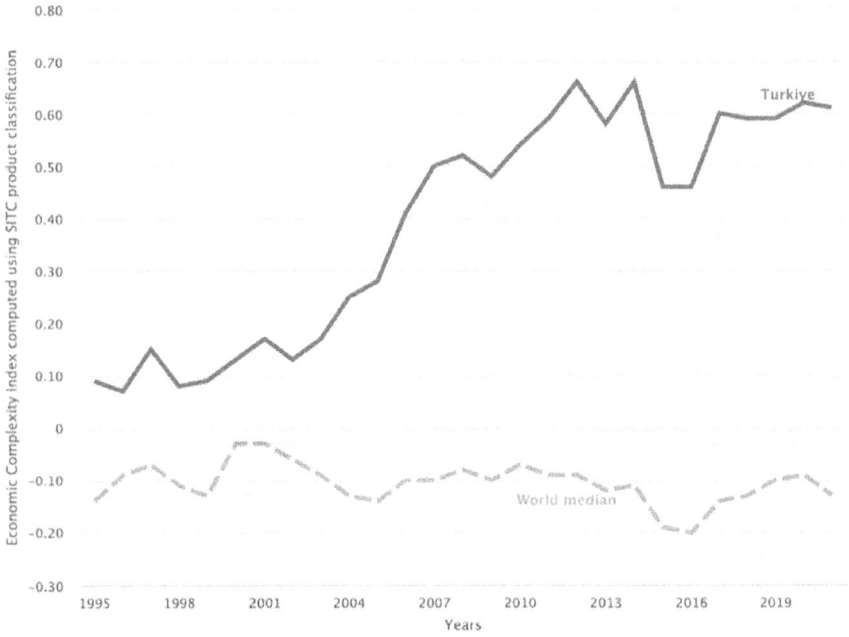

Fig. 6.24 Turkey—Economic Complexity Index (*Source* Harvard Growth Lab, https://atlas.cid.harvard.edu/rankings)

For comparison, exports account for 94% of GDP in Vietnam and 52% in the European Union.

Turkey's exports are well-diversified, mirroring its geopolitical alliances and strategic interests. In 2023, 29% of exports went to Europe, 6% to the U.S., 5% to Iraq, 5% to the UK, 4% to Russia, and 3% to the United Arab Emirates (UAE). Imports followed a similarly broad pattern, with 24% originating from the EU, 13% from Russia, 12% from China, 4% from the U.S., and 3% from the UAE.

Over the past 25 years, geopolitical decisions have played a defining role in shaping Turkey's development. These choices enabled foreign investment in manufacturing geared toward European markets and supported the construction of pipelines, dams, and other strategic infrastructure. Today, geopolitical considerations increasingly influence Turkey's arms exports and are likely to bolster the growth of its nuclear energy sector.

Turkey has leveraged its geography to maximum advantage. Despite being a relatively minor oil and gas producer, the country has invested over $20 billion alongside its partners, in pipeline infrastructure that positions it as a vital transit hub for energy flowing from Asia to Europe. While the pipeline network generates approximately $2 billion in annual revenue, its geopolitical value is far greater, affording Turkey significant strategic influence. This logic also applies to the Turkish Straits, a key maritime transit route with global importance.

A note on productivity. Turkey's Total Factor Productivity (TFP) growth between 1996 and 2024 showed significant volatility, averaging close to zero over the period[197] (Fig. 6.25).

GDP growth is driven by two primary factors: increasing the quantity of inputs such as capital, labor, and natural resources, and improving the efficiency with which these inputs are used. This efficiency component is captured by Total Factor Productivity (TFP), which reflects gains from technological innovation, better management practices, enhanced labor skills, economies of scale, improved infrastructure, and a supportive regulatory and institutional environment. These elements allow for greater output without requiring more inputs.

Among these, technological progress—measured through TFP—is widely recognized as the most important driver of long-term economic growth. As economists often emphasize, "Sustained economic growth ultimately requires

---

[197] With data from The Conference Board, TFP average was -0.01, and volatility, measured by the standard deviation of TFP 3.33.

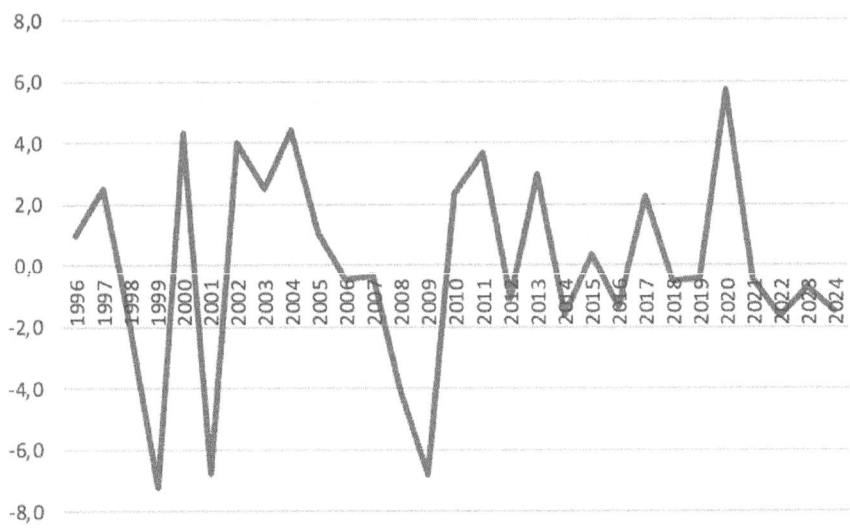

Fig. 6.25 Turkey—Total Factor Productivity (TFP) 1996–2024. Change in the natural log (*Source* The Conference Board, https://www.conference-board.org/retrievefile.cfm?filename=TED_SummaryTables_Charts_may20241.pdf&type=subsite)

technological progress and higher TFP, since growth cannot rely indefinitely on simply expanding the quantity of inputs.[198]"

Zero average TFP growth would typically be associated with low GDP growth rates. However, Turkey defies this expectation, revealing two important characteristics of its economic development that are common to many emerging markets.

First, Turkey's growth was not driven by population expansion—the most common input in production—which grew at a modest average of 0.4% per year. Instead, growth was fueled by consistent capital inflows—another input in production.

Second, while technology did improve in Turkey over time, periods of technological progress, such as those in 2003–2004 and 2010–2011, were arithmetically counterbalanced by recurrent crises—an all-too-familiar pattern in emerging economies. These crises offset the gains from technological booms, resulting in zero average TFP growth.

Comparing Turkey's TFP and GDP growth suggests an interesting policy insight: in the medium term, factor-led growth (as opposed to technology-led growth) can be a viable strategy for emerging economies. This pattern is evident in Turkey and in countries such as Vietnam, Mexico, and Poland.

---

[198] Dieppe, Alistair, Ed. (2021) "Global productivity: trends, drivers and policies" Washington, D.C., World Bank Pg. 42.

Certainly, zero TFP growth will eventually impact GDP growth. Over the long term, relying solely on labor growth or capital investment is unsustainable due to diminishing returns, which inherently limit the ability of any single input to drive growth indefinitely. Nevertheless, it is evident that 25 years of consistent fixed capital inflows were sufficient to sustain economic growth in Turkey during this period.

In the short term, factor-driven growth fosters valuable virtuous cycles. Foreign capital introduces embodied technologies, enabling the workforce to acquire new skills and produce a wider variety of sophisticated goods, thereby increasing economic complexity. Unlike TFP, knowledge and skills are much less affected by economic downturns. While knowledge tends to grow during expansions, it rarely diminishes during recessions. People retain what they have learned, allowing technical skills to accumulate and compound over time—for instance, a physician mastering advanced robotic surgery systems retains that expertise regardless of economic fluctuations.

Country Outlook

Excluding the impact of wars or natural disasters, Turkey will maintain a strong growth trajectory over the next decade and will climb to be the world's 11th-largest economy by 2050.

Geopolitics will continue to be a driving force behind Turkey's economic growth. Strong views about global dominance, paired with a complex and sometimes contradictory network of alliances and rivalries, will both open and close opportunities for foreign investors and local exporters.

Turkey's large and increasingly affluent domestic market, along with well-established operations, will remain attractive for investment. Emerging and increasingly sophisticated industries in tourism, manufacturing, defense, and technology will leverage the academically overqualified labor force, creating further demand for improvements in trade infrastructure.

Addressing issues such as corruption and environmental protection could help attract foreign investment. Simultaneously, domestic savings will act as a buffer against potential declines in FDI. Over the past 25 years, Turkey has stood out among emerging markets by maintaining a consistently high savings rate—around 25% of GDP. This stability has provided a strong foundation for financing investment. During the same period, capital formation averaged 26% of GDP, just one percentage point above the savings rate, highlighting a healthy alignment between domestic savings and investment needs.

Geopolitical risks, including protectionist policies, restrictions on the flow of goods and capital, and the potential for local or regional armed conflicts in Turkey's delicate neighborhood, remain pressing concerns. However, Turkey's strategic position allows it to play its Arab, Asian and European alliances to its advantage. To ensure internal political stability, which is no minor matter given ethnic differences and external pressures, Turkey will probably place greater emphasis on building social infrastructure that promotes upward mobility where Turkey lags significantly.

Vietnam

Vietnam's economic transformation has captivated global attention, positioning it as a rising star in Southeast Asia. Vietnam has emerged as one of the region's most dynamic economies in the past three decades. With a population of 100 million people, Vietnam boasts a rich cultural history. It has rapidly transformed its economy, transitioning from one of the poorest agrarian societies to an increasingly diversified, middle-income, export-driven industrial economy. After decades of recovery from the devastation of the Vietnam War that ended in 1975, a reunified North and South nation has not only rebounded but has positioned itself as a key player in global manufacturing and trade.

The transformation can be summarized in one statistic: per-capita income experienced a more than tenfold increase, climbing from $367 in 1999 to $4300 in 2023 (see Fig. 6.26).

Responsible for the dramatic improvement was the introduction of the Đổi Mới ('Rejuvenation') reforms in 1986. They marked a crucial moment in Vietnam's business history as they instituted liberal, market-oriented measures. It dismantled the largely planned economy, opened a closed market to international trade, and started pro-business reforms. At the same time, it focused its social policy on improving access to education and electricity.[199]

These reforms, in practical terms, also pulled Vietnam out of the Soviet communist orbit, to which it had firmly belonged since 1978, and helped spark significant foreign investment, which drove rapid industrialization.

Vietnam is a highly disciplined society where the common good takes precedence over individual wants. Its hierarchical social and political institutions have united its large population in fulfilling the promise of transforming a poor country into a middle-income economy within one generation.

---

[199] IMF (2019) "Vietnam's Development Success Story an Unfinished SDG Agenda" Working Paper WP/20/31.

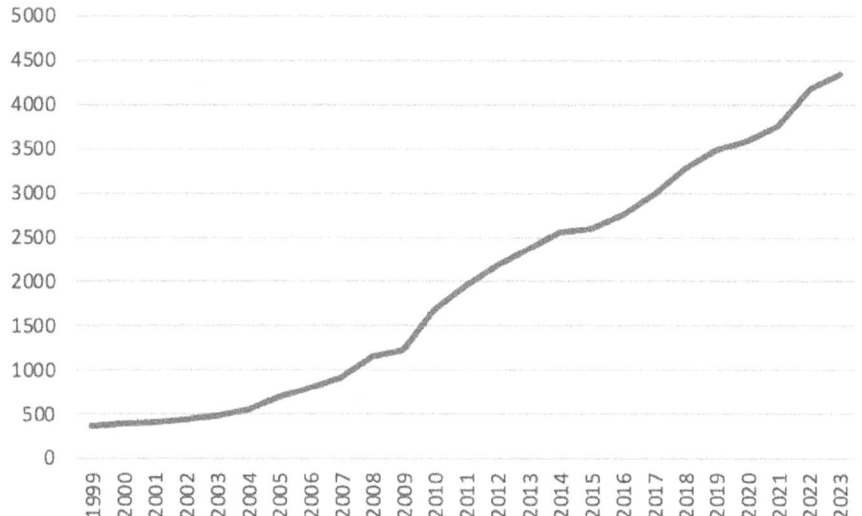

Fig. 6.26 Vietnam—GDP per capita (Current US$) (*Source* World Bank, https://databank.worldbank.org/source/world-development-indicators)

Vietnam now aspires to become a high-income country by 2045, and it is well positioned to achieve that goal.

Politically, Vietnam is a one-party state led by the Communist Party of Vietnam (CPV). Its geopolitical positioning in Southeast Asia makes it a critical player in regional affairs, particularly in relation to China, with which it shares both strong economic ties and territorial disputes. In 1979, for example, China invaded Vietnam, and currently, there are stark disagreements over territorial rights in the South China Sea. As Vietnam seeks to balance these regional tensions with its economic ambitions, it also strengthened its relations with other powers, such as Japan, which views Vietnam as a strategic ally in the Indo-Pacific. The U.S. recently changed its attitude from being a staunch ally to place it as a threat to its balance of payments balance.

Today, Vietnam's prospects for continued growth remain buoyed by its stern social discipline, low-cost labor, an expanding middle class, increased urbanization, and rising global interest in its manufacturing sector.

Vietnam's economy experienced outstanding growth over the past quarter-century, with an average GDP growth rate of 6.2% annually. This made Vietnam the 17th fastest-growing economy in the world during this period. This feat was achieved with a combination of favorable regulation, low labor costs, and integration into global supply chains that positioned Vietnam as a key manufacturing hub, especially in electronics and textiles.

In 2007, Đổi Mới's focus on infrastructure development remained strong. That year, Vietnam joined the World Trade Organization, and the government implemented incentives and policies to attract foreign investment, such as tax breaks, simplified regulations, and land concessions.

In that year, the average hourly earnings of Vietnamese employees was $0.45, just 2% of the approximately $22 per hour prevalent in the United States. Investors recognized an opportunity to relocate part of their manufacturing facilities to major Vietnamese cities. Foreign Direct Investment (FDI) surged from almost nothing to $10 billion in 2007, representing 10% of Vietnam's GDP. With some fluctuations, FDI continued to grow, reaching a net inflow of more than $20 billion in 2023. Exports soared from $14 billion in 1999 to an unbelievable $385 billion in 2022. In 2023, the country was the world's 15th largest exporter.[200] Exports, in turn, facilitated additional investments in infrastructure, significantly improving roads, ports, and telecommunications networks. The World Bank's Logistics Performance Index summarizes logistics professionals' perceptions of a country's trade and transport-related infrastructure (e.g., ports, railroads, roads, information technology) on a scale ranging from 1 (very low) to 5 (very high). Vietnam improved its score from a modest 2.5 in 2007 to a much stronger 3.2 in 2022. For comparison, the UK scored 3.7 in 2022.

Major cities like Hanoi and Ho Chi Minh City (HCMC) saw substantial investment in urban infrastructure, while rural areas continued to benefit from improved access to electricity and clean water. Foreign firms integrated Vietnam into their global trade networks, significantly strengthening the nation's global economic footprint. Samsung Electronics, Intel, Nokia, LG Electronics, Bridgestone, and Panasonic were among the multinational corporations that invested heavily in plants and equipment between 2007 and 2012.

This strategy yielded tangible benefits. Although unemployment has not been a major issue over the past quarter-century, the average unemployment rate declined from 2.3% between 1999 and 2010 to what now appears to be a stable full-employment 1.5% figure. More importantly, as a result of this progress, Vietnam lifted nearly half of its population out of poverty. In 2002, approximately 72 million people lived on less than $6.85 per day (90% of the total population). By 2022, this figure had dropped to 19 million. (Fig. 6.27).

Vietnam's major exports include:

---

[200] ITC (2024) "Trade Map" Retrieved from: https://www.trademap.org/.

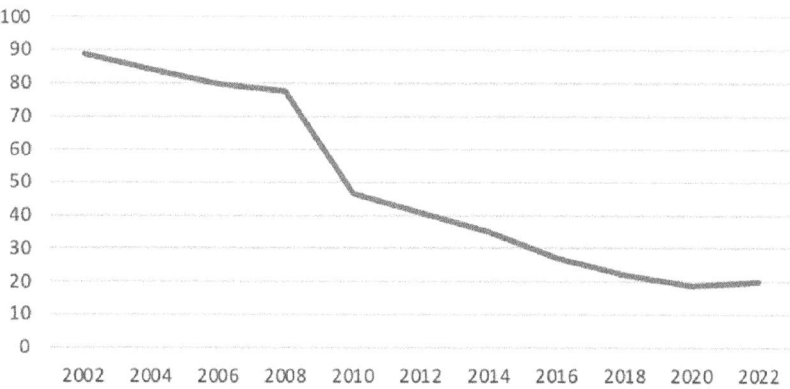

Fig. 6.27 Vietnam—Poverty headcount. Poverty headcount ratio at $6.85 a day (2017 PPP) (% of population) (*Source* The World Bank, https://databank.worldbank.org/source/world-development-indicators)

- **Electronics**: In 2023, Vietnam's electronics, computers, and components exports were worth about $57.3 billion.
- **Phones**: In 2023, Vietnam's phones and related components exports were worth about $52.4 billion.
- **Machinery**: In 2023, Vietnam's machinery exports were worth about $43.13 billion.
- **Textiles**: Textiles make up about 12% of Vietnam's total exports.
- **Footwear**: Footwear makes up about 7% of Vietnam's total exports.[201]

Vietnam's main export partners are the United States, China, Japan, South Korea, Hong Kong, and The Netherlands. Vietnam's economy is primarily made up of 27.5% agriculture, 33.4% industry, and 39% services. Vietnam's most important crop is rice, which is grown in the Mekong and Red River deltas. Other major food crops include sugarcane, cassava, corn, sweet potatoes, and nuts.

Vietnam's business landscape has changed dramatically over the past 25 years. The country has steadily become more urbanized. In 1999, less than 25% of its population lived in urban centers, but by 2023, this figure had risen to 40%.

Urbanization is likely to continue as coastal regions and urban centers like Hanoi and HCMC have experienced significant economic advancements.

---

[201] Trading Economics; U.S. Department of Commerce.

These areas have seen improvements in GDP per capita and life expectancy, further driving Vietnam's economic dynamism.

At the same time, a sharp increase in FDI in manufacturing reshaped Vietnam's productive structure, reducing the size of the agricultural sector while increasing manufacturing.

Large firms—mostly in the foreign-invested sector—now account for about 30% of employment in Vietnam's enterprise sector and 70% of total exports. Notably, Vietnam is heavily concentrated in labor-intensive and final assembly stages of global value chains—particularly in apparel, footwear, and mobile phones—limiting the extent of technological spillovers to domestic firms.[202]

Foreign firms remain largely disconnected from Vietnam's domestic private sector—particularly small and medium-sized enterprises (SMEs), which make up 96% of all businesses. Despite their numbers, SMEs are highly unproductive: they employ 47% of the workforce but generate only 36% of national value added—well below the OECD averages of 70% and 60%, respectively.

Foreign firms have done little to create demand for local inputs, transfer technology, or diffuse managerial expertise. At the same time, most domestic firms appear ill-equipped to meet international standards, limiting their ability to integrate into global value chains. In this context, FDI has fostered a kind of enclave economy. "The domestic private sector lacks the scale, business sophistication, and technology needed to boost productivity for market expansion. Only 20% of domestic enterprises export." This is reflected in low domestic value addition and a weak domestic supplier base. "Vietnamese firms are mostly concentrated in the third-tier supplier industry, characterized by the production of low value-added inputs and/or tasks such as basic materials and packaging.[203]"

Studies have consistently highlighted weaknesses in the operating business environment, as well as internal constraints that hinder the development of firms' capabilities. Key external factors include the regulatory environment, access to finance, infrastructure, and the lack of a level playing field. On the other hand, the state-owned enterprise (SOE) sector remains a dominant player in Vietnam's economy but suffer from low productivity. While their number has significantly decreased, their importance has not. In 1989, there were 12,000 SOEs in operation. By 2017, the number had fallen to 2600, representing just 0.5% of enterprises in the country but producing nearly

---

[202] The World Bank (2021) "Vietnam: Science, Technology and Innovation Report" Retrieved from: https://documents1.worldbank.org/curated/en/929681629871018154/pdf/Vietnam-Science-Technology-and-Innovation-Report.pdf.

[203] Ibid.

30% of GDP, compared to less than 10% of GDP generated by the formally registered domestic private sector.[204]

While the private firm Samsung Electronics is the largest company by revenue in Vietnam, the list of top revenue generators is dominated by SOEs such as Vietnam Oil and Gas Group (PetroVietnam), Vietnam National Petroleum Group (Petrolimex), Vietnam Bank for Agriculture and Rural Development (Agribank), Bank for Investment and Development of Vietnam (BIDV), Viettel Group, Vietnam JSC Bank for Industry and Trade (VietinBank), and Vietnam National Coal and Mineral Industries Group (Vinacomin). The state maintains a strong presence in key sectors such as oil and gas, electricity, telecommunications, and rice, among others.

There have been restructuring plans to improve the productivity of SOEs, but these are not necessarily robust. In general, such plans "contain information relating to past achievements and some future intentions designed to achieve whatever outcomes the SOE believes will be acceptable to its owners and the government, rather than being based on commercially sound assumptions.[205]"

A key risk to their operation is that SOE management has prioritized the preservation of state capital over increasing its value. For example, Fitch Ratings expects the return on equity (ROE) of Vietnam Electricity (EVN) to remain low, averaging 0.2%-2% from 2024 to 2027. EVN sets tariffs charged to its distribution affiliates with the goal of providing them with modest profits.[206] However, this socially well-intentioned strategy has led to underinvestment in new power plants and delays in updating the country's electricity grid.

Given the significant share of assets held by SOEs, successful reform of inefficient SOEs could lead to a considerable increase in the overall productivity and competitiveness of the economy. While the government aims to privatize SOEs on a large scale, the number of equitized Vietnamese enterprises to date remains far below expectations.

Trade agreements are another important element of the business environment. The 2001 U.S.–Vietnam Bilateral Trade Agreement (BTA) largely modified the bilateral commercial relationship between the two nations. Trade increased from $2.9 billion in 2002 to over $139 billion in 2022, making Vietnam the sixth-largest source of U.S. imports and the 28th-largest

---

[204] ADB (2020) "Reforms, Opportunities and Challenges for State-Owned Enterprises" https://www.adb.org/sites/default/files/publication/618761/reforms-opportunities-challenges-state-owned-enterprises.pdf.
[205] ADB (2020) Op. Cit.
[206] Fitch Ratings (2024) "Fitch Affirms Vietnam's Five Power Corporations at 'BB+': Outlook Stable" Press release.

destination for U.S. exports.[207] The BTA is currently in the process of being revised.

Vietnam has made significant progress in advancing free trade agreements to enhance its attractiveness to foreign investors by providing better market access for Vietnamese exports and by adopting market-friendly reforms. The EU-Vietnam Free Trade Agreement came into force on August 1, 2020. The UK-Vietnam Free Trade Agreement followed on May 1, 2021. The Regional Comprehensive Economic Partnership entered into force on January 1, 2022, for 10 countries, including Vietnam. These agreements benefit companies operating in Vietnam by reducing barriers to importing inputs and exporting goods to participating countries. Vietnam is also a founding member and active participant in the ongoing Indo-Pacific Economic Framework for Prosperity (IPEF) negotiations involving 14 partners.

Vietnam's evolving legal and regulatory framework has addressed some critical issues, including land use, real estate, banking, telecommunications, and environmental protection, laying the groundwork for sustainable growth. The Investment Law (2020) and Public–Private Partnership Law (2020) incentivize foreign investment in large infrastructure projects, reducing the financial burden on the government and fostering public–private partnerships. In 2021, during the 13th Party Congress of the Communist Party of Vietnam (CPV), the government approved a 10-year economic strategy aimed at shifting foreign investment toward high-tech industries and implementing stricter environmental standards. The Securities Law (2021) eliminated foreign ownership caps in most industries. The Labor Code (2021) introduced greater labor flexibility, expanded workforce recognition, and allowed the formation of independent worker organizations.[208]

Vietnam's financial landscape is also undergoing significant changes. The government has implemented reforms to improve the banking sector and capital markets, yet challenges persist, including high non-performing loans and limited credit access for small and medium enterprises.[209] This strong economic foundation is further supported by the Socio-Economic Development Strategy for 2021–2030, which seeks to achieve upper-middle-income status. Vietnam's favorable business environment benefits from strategic financial, trade, and legal frameworks, although companies still feel that they have to carefully navigate associated challenges to succeed.

---

[207] U.S. International Trade Administration (2024) "Vietnam. Market Overview" Retrieved from: https://www.trade.gov/.

[208] U.S. Department of State (2024) "2024 Investment Climate Statements: Vietnam" Retrieved from https://www.state.gov/reports/2024-investment-climate-statements/.

[209] Asian Development Bank. (2022). Vietnam: Key Indicators for Asia and the Pacific. ADB.

Technology

Vietnam is an active player in the region, embracing digital transformation across various sectors, including finance, manufacturing, and public services. The government's "National Digital Transformation Program," approved in 2020, aims to develop a digital government, economy, and society by 2025. The program focuses on enhancing digital infrastructure, promoting digital enterprises, and fostering innovation across multiple sectors. The initiative emphasizes efforts such as increased adoption of cashless electronic payment systems, expanded broadband fiber-optic cable coverage for households and communes, and digital platforms for businesses in industrial parks and export processing zones.[210] It also promotes the use of artificial intelligence (AI), robotics, and the Internet of Things (IoT), particularly in manufacturing sectors.

Although digital transformation is still a work in progress, Vietnam's General Statistics Office reports that the digital economy accounted for over 12% of GDP in 2023. In the ASEAN region, Vietnam is in a similar range to Thailand and is behind only Singapore and Malaysia. Moreover, the growth rate of Vietnam's digital economy has outpaced that of other ASEAN member states in recent years, with a compounded annual growth rate of 19% in 2023.[211]

Unsurprisingly, Vietnam's private sector stakeholders, particularly in key sectors such as aviation, banking, energy, healthcare, broadcasting, telecommunications, and urban infrastructure management, are increasingly adopting advanced ICT solutions to enhance operational efficiency and support sustainable growth.

In contrast, in terms of R&D and technological investment, Vietnam ranks below its regional peers. The country's R&D spending is approximately 0.4% of GDP, significantly lower than China (2.4%), Singapore (2.2%), and Malaysia (1.0%).[212] Most of this expenditure is still funded by the public sector, which accounts for about 49% of R&D spending, in contrast to the private-sector-driven models in countries like China and Singapore. This lower level of investment reflects Vietnam's emerging status, though the government is committed to increasing private sector involvement in technology adoption to enhance its competitive standing in the region.

---

[210] U.S. International Trade Administration (2024) "Vietnam Digital Economy". Retrieved from: https://www.trade.gov/.
[211] U.S. International Trade Administration (2024) Op. Cit.
[212] The World Bank (2024) "World Development Indicators".

A key foundation for innovation in the coming years is the "Science, Technology, and Innovation (STI) Strategy for 2021–2030," launched in 2022. This strategy prioritizes the development of science, technology, and innovation as national priorities to drive economic growth, competitiveness, and sustainable development.

Vietnam has also made significant strides in fostering an ecosystem that supports startups and entrepreneurial ventures, particularly in the tech sector. Vietnam has become a notable hub for tech startups, with venture capital investments in Vietnamese tech companies steadily increasing. The government actively encourages international collaboration to bolster its technological capabilities. Partnerships with global tech companies such as Google, Microsoft, and IBM have transferred technological expertise to Vietnam, particularly in areas like AI, cybersecurity, and cloud computing.

Homegrown technology development remains a slow process, requiring more than government initiatives. For example, the "Make in Vietnam" strategy, launched in 2016, aims to attract FDI and promote domestic manufacturing. It encourages companies to establish production facilities in Vietnam.

The startup ecosystem in Vietnam is still nascent. Funding for many of the top 25 startups has only reached a few million dollars, with the largest companies securing around $300 million after multiple rounds—[213] far below the hefty figures seen in other markets.

Smart cities may also drive innovation. HCMC and Hanoi have launched smart city initiatives incorporating technologies such as IoT, big data, and AI to improve urban management, enhance public services, and promote sustainability.[214] These projects focus on areas such as traffic management, public safety, waste management, and environmental monitoring.

Vietnam's e-commerce market is another area of technological growth. With a rapidly expanding middle class and increasing internet penetration, the e-commerce industry has flourished. Technologies like mobile payment systems, AI-driven customer service platforms, and blockchain are being integrated into e-commerce operations, allowing Vietnamese businesses to compete globally.

Vietnam has also prioritized the development of AI and big data applications. These technologies are increasingly being used in sectors like healthcare, agriculture, and finance. For example, AI is powering smart healthcare solutions, while big data analytics is supporting decision-making in agriculture.

---

[213] Failory (2024) "Top 25 startups in Vietnam in 2024". Retrieved from www.failory.com.

[214] OECD. (2022). *Unleashing strong, digital, and green growth in Viet Nam.* https://www.oecd.org/en/publications/unleashing-strong-digital-and-green-growth-in-viet-nam_78bcbbcd-en.html.

Some examples of companies in Vietnam that are at the forefront of AI technology are Saigon Technology, Vinova, Synodus, and Kyanon Digital.

However, Vietnam's education system is struggling to keep up with the pace of technological change, and there is a growing demand for skilled professionals in these areas. The government has launched public–private partnerships to address this gap and foster AI talent.

Vietnam has also emerged as a place for blockchain innovation, particularly in the FinTech sector. The government is encouraging the adoption of blockchain to enhance transparency and security in digital transactions. Startups in the FinTech space are growing, with blockchain being used for payment solutions, supply chain management, and digital banking.[215]

However, regulatory uncertainties pose significant challenges. The lack of a comprehensive regulatory framework for blockchain technology creates uncertainty for businesses and investors, potentially hindering broader adoption.

Regulatory restrictions on technologies like IoT, cloud computing, and blockchain may gradually align with those of more open economies. For instance, foreign firms providing cross-border services in specific categories are required to store user data in Vietnam upon government request. Faster technological transformation will likely require adjustments to such regulations in the future.

Despite its promise, Vietnam faces challenges in becoming a technology leader. The talent gap is a significant issue. The 'Skills' pillar of the UN's 'Frontier Technology Readiness Index,' which measures relevant skills for adopting and adapting frontier technologies, consistently scores Vietnam at 0.3—below Nigeria's 0.4 and Poland's 0.7 and far below the 0.8 achieved by United States, UK, and Ireland.

Infrastructure

In 1986, Vietnam prioritized investments in physical infrastructure to improve access to electricity. This strategy has gradually delivered results. For example, in 2008, firms in Vietnam experienced an average of one power outage per month. By 2015, this improved to one outage every five months, but the system is far from perfect. In May and June 2023, droughts severely limited hydropower supply. Factories in some areas could not operate for

---

[215] McKinsey & Company. (2023). "Vietnam's economic transformation: Capturing emerging opportunities."

hours multiple times a week, and the World Bank estimated that these outages cost Vietnam 0.3% of its GDP.[216]

The initial drive on infrastructure has only strengthened. Vietnam stands out in the ASEAN region by investing approximately 6% of its GDP in infrastructure, significantly higher than the regional average of 2.3%.[217]

According to available information, some of the largest infrastructure projects currently underway in Vietnam include the North–South Expressway, the Long Thanh International Airport (set to be the largest airport in Vietnam), additional metro lines in Hanoi and HCMC, and a planned high-speed rail network connecting the northern and southern regions of the country, estimated to cost around $67 billion.

These investments should improve infrastructure quality indicators, like the one published by the World Economic Forum, which ranked Vietnam 77th out of 141 countries in 2019.[218] Still, as of 2024, Vietnam faces an annual infrastructure investment gap of $4 billion, with needs estimated at $22 billion annually and current spending trends at $18 billion.[219]

This gap is not due to a lack of savings. Vietnamese households and businesses are notably frugal, with gross domestic savings reaching $149 billion in 2022. Over the past 25 years, savings have averaged 30% of GDP and peaked at an impressive 36% in 2022. By comparison, savings represent just 18% of GDP in the United States, 23% in OECD countries, and 19% in peer lower-middle-income economies.

Vietnam could likely invest more through borrowing, and its fiscal position supports this. General government debt stands at 34% of GDP—well below the 53% median for countries with similar credit ratings (BB+). It also remains under the national target of keeping total public debt, including government-guaranteed and sub-national debt, below 60% of GDP by 2030.[220]

Still, borrowing is not always the optimal strategy. Decisions must weigh the risks, returns, and long-term sustainability of debt-financed investments.

Vietnam's infrastructure plans are ambitious and cut across many sectors.

---

[216] VN Express (2023) "Power outages cost Vietnam $1.4 billion: World Bank" August 10. https://e.vnexpress.net/news/economy/power-outages-cost-vietnam-1-4b-world-bank-4640388.html?utm_source=chatgpt.com.

[217] Vietnam Briefing. (2022). *Why Vietnam's Infrastructure is Crucial for Economic Growth.* https://www.vietnam-briefing.com/news/why-vietnams-infrastructure-crucial-for-economic-growth.html/.

[218] Open Development. (2022). *Open Development Vietnam.* https://vietnam.opendevelopmentmekong.net/topics/infrastructure/.

[219] G20 (2024) "Global Infrastructure Outlook" Retrieved from: https://outlook.gihub.org/countries/Vietnam.

[220] Fitch Ratings (2024) "Fitch Affirms Vietnam at 'BB+" Press release.

Road, water, and rail. Vietnam's infrastructure plans are ambitious. The country's road network, spanning over 570,000 kilometers, is the primary mode of transport for passengers and freight. Motorbikes dominate transportation, accounting for 85% of all vehicles. In 2019, Vietnam, with 61.3 million motorcycles, was the fourth-largest motorcycle market globally, following China, India, and Indonesia. However, traffic congestion remains a critical challenge, particularly in urban centers like HCMC and Hanoi.[221]

Roads are essential to logistics, but only 20% are paved. Large-scale projects are underway, such as the 1800-km HCMC-Hanoi Expressway and the expansion of national highways. By 2030, these projects aim to extend Vietnam's highway network from 1290 km to 5000 km.[222]

Vietnam's inland waterways, particularly in regions like the Mekong Delta and Red River Delta, account for 18% of freight but receive limited investment and remain underutilized. The government aims to increase the share of maritime and inland waterway transport to 50%, reducing logistics costs and road congestion.

The railway infrastructure remains underdeveloped. Diesel-fueled freight trains operate at 50–60 kilometers per hour, and passenger trains at 80–90 kph—far below the 150–200 kph speeds seen in developed countries. The government plans to build a $67 billion high-speed north–south railway linking Hanoi and Ho Chi Minh City, with speeds of up to 350 kph. Construction is expected to begin in 2026 and finish by 2035. The government has indicated a preference for using domestic funds and technology to reduce reliance on foreign capital and loans.

Seaports and Aviation. Seaports are vital to Vietnam's economy. In 2024, Vietnam ranked 8th in the UNCTAD Liner Shipping Connectivity Index, reflecting strong ties to global shipping routes.[223] Connectivity improvements have reduced costs, improved reliability, and attracted more service providers. Vietnam also saw the highest increase (199%) in this index since 2006, surpassing China (66%) and South Korea (50%). Growth will continue under the Seaport Master Plan, which aims to handle 46–54 million TEU of container cargo annually by 2030, up from 18.5 million TEU in 2023. For context, the port of Shanghai, the world's largest, handles 49.2 million TEU annually.[224]

---

[221] Open Development (2022) Op. Cit.
[222] Vietnam Briefing (2022) Op. Cit.
[223] UNCTAD (2024) "Review of maritime transport 2024" Retrieved from: https://unctad.org/.
[224] World Shipping Council (2024) "The Top 50 Container Ports" Retrieved from: https://www.worldshipping.org/top-50-ports.

The plan is ambitious but feasible. For example, the Vietnam Maritime Administration (VINAMARINE) informed that 30 of Vietnam's 34 port systems are already equipped to handle the largest ships in the world, attracting operations from major international shipping lines.

Vietnam's aviation sector has also expanded significantly, with 22 civil airports, including 12 international hubs. The largest project, the $16 billion Long Thành Airport, is being built in three phases. The first phase includes one runway and a terminal capable of handling 25 million passengers per year, up from the country's current 15 million passengers annually. Expected to open in 2026,[225] the airport is being developed on land donated by local residents. The national airport development plan envisions 30 airports by 2030 (14 international and 16 domestic).

Energy Infrastructure. Vietnam's energy demands are surging, with annual electricity consumption expected to maintain growth rates of 12%. The Power Development Plan (PDP8), approved in 2023, aims to increase generating capacity from 80 to 150 GW by 2030. The plan carries a $134 billion price tag, but financing remains uncertain.

The heavy reliance on coal (57%) and hydropower (19%) raises sustainability concerns. Coal-fired power deters foreign investors who prioritize clean energy, while hydropower is vulnerable to climate change impacts such as droughts and unpredictable rainfall. Frequent power outages in recent years have affected production and reduced Vietnam's competitive advantage, shifting investor interest toward countries like Indonesia and Malaysia.

The government is working to diversify energy sources by increasing investments in solar and wind power, which now account for 14% of the energy generation mix. However, this transition has not been without challenges. Prominent European firms such as Equinor and Ørsted have withdrawn from wind energy projects, citing issues related to pricing and regulatory uncertainty.

In 2024, the government announced plans to amend PDP8 to include more renewables and reintroduce nuclear energy. Talks with officials from South Korea, Canada, and Russia are underway to explore installing small nuclear reactors.

Digital Infrastructure. Vietnam's digital infrastructure has expanded rapidly but has only reached 78% of the population with internet access. The National Digital Infrastructure Strategy aims to provide high-speed internet to 99% of the population and nationwide 5G coverage by 2030.

---

[225] Việt Nam News (2024) "PM requests launch of emulation drive to complete Long Thành airport project by 2025" September 24.

Nonetheless, progress is evident. The UN's Frontier Technology Readiness Index measures the level of ICT infrastructure for using, adopting, and adapting frontier technologies. Indicators included in the index are, for instance, the number of internet users and broadband speed, much better than China's 0.4 and close to Saudi Arabia's 0.7 and the UK's 0.8.[226]

Public–private partnerships (PPPs) have been crucial in addressing infrastructure financing gaps, particularly in transport and energy projects, and are expected to remain vital. One of the largest public–private partnership (PPP) projects in Vietnam is the North–South Expressway, with a significant portion of the investment coming from private investors through a Build-Operate-Transfer (BOT) model, particularly in the Lang Son Province section managed by a joint venture led by the private Vietnamese Deoca Group; this project is expected to significantly boost economic development and regional trade within Vietnam and with neighboring countries like China. Other notable PPP projects in Vietnam are Lach Huyen Port in Hai Phong that brought in Japanese investment; Long Thanh International Airport, one of the biggest infrastructure developments in Vietnam, and several projects utilizing renewable energy sources.

Geopolitics

To achieve high-income status by 2045, Vietnam requires advanced technologies from the United States, investment from Japan, clean energy generation methods from Europe, infrastructure support from China, and nuclear energy—and potentially more military equipment—from Russia. Remarkably, it appears to have access to all of them.

This access stems from Vietnam's "Bamboo Diplomacy," a term coined in 2016 by Communist Party General Secretary Nguyen Phu Trong. It describes Vietnam's foreign policy using the imagery of strong roots, a sturdy trunk, and flexible branches as the core traits of its diplomacy. This approach reflects adaptability and flexibility in responding to external pressures while maintaining steel-like resilience.

Adaptability is underpinned by a commitment to non-alignment and the "Four No's" policy: no military alliances, no siding with one country against another, no foreign military bases, and no use of force or threats in international relations. Trong believed these principles would foster "more friends, fewer foes."

---

[226] United Nations (2024) "Technology and Innovation Report 2023" Retrieved from: https://unctad.org/tir2023.

Vietnam's non-aligned stance has enabled it to skillfully navigate relationships with major powers. A testament to the success of this policy is that in September 2023, U.S. President Joe Biden, in December 2023, China's President Xi Jinping, and in June 2024, Russia's President Vladimir Putin visited Hanoi—an achievement no other country can claim.

However, beneath the diplomatic discourse, ambiguity and a frail memory of historical grievances are crucial to advancing this strategy. This nuanced balancing act is one of Vietnam's most potent lessons in managing a multipolar and antagonistic world.

An overview of Vietnam's challenges in a multipolar world is as follows:

China. Vietnam's northern neighbor, sharing a 1200-kilometer border, China is Vietnam's largest source of imports and its second-largest export market. The two countries share a similar ideological framework as single-party communist states. The 1979 Chinese invasion of Vietnam fading into oblivion, their relationship remains strained by territorial disputes in the South China Sea, particularly over the Spratly and Paracel Islands, regions believed to be rich in hydrocarbons.

In 2012, China heightened tensions by establishing Sansha City to administer these islands, and in 2014, the deployment of a Chinese oil rig in Vietnam's exclusive economic zone sparked anti-China protests within Vietnam.

Despite such disputes, economic and diplomatic ties have strengthened. During President Xi Jinping's December 2023 visit to Vietnam, the two nations reaffirmed their commitment to a "comprehensive cooperative strategic partnership," underpinned by substantial Chinese investments in infrastructure, including the Kunming-Haiphong railway link. These projects align with Vietnam's growth goals while deepening regional integration. Promised Chinese investments span green technology, new energy, ICT, and e-commerce logistics. Xi Jinpin returned to Vietnam on April 2025, as a response to the U.S. threat to rise tariffs on imports from Vietnam to 46%. The Chinese leader offered Hanoi its backing for infrastructure-led growth.

United States. Another major former adversary, the United States, signaled interest in collaborating with Vietnam on higher-tech initiatives, including semiconductor manufacturing. While Vietnam's semiconductor production grew steadily, the country largely focused on the lower end of technological sophistication: assembly, testing, and packaging (ATP) processes. Experts suggest that developing a true semiconductor hub like Taiwan could take up to 30 years.

Although Vietnam belongs to the little leagues in the semiconductor industry, it has emerged as the third-largest Asian semiconductor exporter to the U.S., with prospects for further growth. However, now the path is full of challenges. In 2023, Intel postponed a $3.3 billion expansion plan, citing concerns over power stability and bureaucratic hurdles. Vietnam's Ministry of Planning and Investment stated that Intel had requested "cash support" equivalent to 15% of the investment. The government's refusal prompted Intel to explore alternatives in Poland, though global market conditions ultimately delayed the expansion altogether.

The U.S. partnership serves Vietnam to counterbalance China's influence. As one observer put it, "There is nowhere on earth more fearful of Chinese hegemony than Vietnam.[227]" In 2023, Vietnam elevated its diplomatic relationship with the U.S. to a "Comprehensive Strategic Partnership," the highest level of engagement in its foreign policy framework. The tariff war proposed by the U.S. to balance its trade deficit, will probably take into consideration that Vietnam is still a strong candidate for "friendshoring" manufacturing operations away from China, and that Vietnam is crucial to maintaining U.S. influence in Southeast Asia and countering China's maritime dominance. Compensations to the trade imbalance will probably involve increasing the participation U.S. business in oil and mining resources in Vietnam.

Russia. Not an enemy but a long-time supporter, Vietnam's historical ties to Russia trace back to Soviet support during the Cambodia-Vietnam conflict in 1979. The Soviet Union provided military aid, and today, more than 80% of Vietnam's military equipment is Soviet- or Russian-made.[228]

Vietnam continues to engage Russia diplomatically, refraining from condemning the invasion of Ukraine and voting against suspending Russia from the U.N. Human Rights Council. In return, Russia has committed to investments in Vietnam, including nuclear energy projects.

Global agreements. Global protectionism presents a substantial risk to Vietnam's export-driven economic model. Vietnam has crafted a network of free trade agreements to ensure open export markets. Membership in ASEAN and agreements with the U.S., EU, and Japan, as well as participation in the Comprehensive and Progressive Agreement for Trans-Pacific Partnership (CPTPP), might sustain diversified trade relationships. Vietnam is also a key player in the Regional Comprehensive Economic Partnership (RCEP).

Strategic assets. Vietnam possesses distinctive features that are likely to attract global attention. Vietnam's strategic assets include its role in global

---

[227] CSIS (2024) "An indispensable upgrade: The U.S.-Vietnam Comprehensive Strategic Partnership" Retrieved from: https://www.csis.org/analysis/indispensable-upgrade-us-vietnam-comprehensive-strategic-partnership.
[228] CIS (2024) Op. Cit.

transit routes, significant oil and gas reserves, and the world's second-largest rare earth reserves.

Transit. The South China Sea is a critical global trade route. In 2023, 10 billion barrels of petroleum and petroleum products, as well as 6.7 trillion cubic feet of liquefied natural gas (LNG), passed through this maritime corridor. This underscores Vietnam's strategic importance in facilitating international commerce.[229]

Oil and Gas. Offshore exploration significantly bolstered Vietnam's proven crude oil reserves, which expanded from 0.6 billion barrels in 2011 to 4.4 billion barrels in 2012. These reserves have remained at 4.4 billion barrels through 2024, as Vietnam's waters remain largely underexplored. Vietnam currently ranks 25th globally and is the third-largest holder of crude oil reserves in Asia, following China and India.[230]

Rare Earths. Rare-earth elements are among the planet's most valuable resources. These 17 metallic elements—including Scandium, Yttrium, Lanthanum, and Neodymium—have unique magnetic, conductive, and fluorescent properties. They are critical for manufacturing smartphones, other "smart" devices, and some advanced technology applications. Vietnam holds the world's second-largest reserves of rare earths, estimated at 22 million tons, trailing only China's 44 million tons. Commercial deposits are found along Vietnam's northwestern border with China and its eastern coastline.

The need for independence. The success of Vietnam's "Bamboo Diplomacy" lies in its ability to maintain a delicate balance in foreign relations, ensuring it avoids over-reliance on any single country for investment, trade, or political alliances. This is a strategy that Vietnam has skillfully navigated.

Foreign Direct Investment (FDI). In the first nine months of 2024, 148 countries and territories invested in Vietnam. South Korea ranked first with a total registered capital of nearly $88.3 billion, accounting for 18% of the total. Singapore followed with $81.1 billion (16.5%), Japan at 16%, China at 14%, and Taiwan at 8%. These rankings were maintained in 2023: South Korea (18%), Singapore (16%), Japan (16%), China (13%), and Taiwan (8%).[231]

Trade. Vietnam's trade is more concentrated than that of FDI sources. From 2018 to 2023, China accounted for less than a third (31%) of all imports, followed by South Korea (18%), Japan (7%), Taiwan (6%), and

---

[229] U.S. Energy Information Administration (2024) "South China Sea" Retrieved from: https://www.eia.gov/.

[230] EIA (2024) "Vietnam" Retrieved from: https://www.eia.gov/international/analysis/country/VNM.

[231] Ministry of Planning and Investment of Vietnam (2024) "FDI attraction situation in Vietnam". Deveral reports retrieved from: https://www.mpi.gov.vn/.

the United States (5%). On the export side, the United States absorbed 26% of all Vietnamese exports, followed by China (20%), South Korea and Japan (7% each), and the Netherlands (3%).[232]

Economic and geopolitical dynamics. In dollars and cents, loyalties and interests are straightforward to calculate. South Korea, Singapore, Japan, China, and the United States are pivotal contributors to Vietnam's growth through FDI and trade. These partners benefit from Vietnam's low-cost labor force and other natural and 'soft' assets, and Vietnam will likely strive to keep these relationships thriving. While Vietnam continues to champion its 'Bamboo Diplomacy,' beyond the slogan lies the constant task of adding and subtracting costs and benefits to decide how much to engage and with whom.

Talent

Vietnam has successfully capitalized on low labor costs for over three decades, fueling sustained economic growth. Labor remains highly competitive compared to other regions: as of 2024, the minimum monthly wage is just $196 in Hanoi and Ho Chi Minh City, and $137 in rural areas. For comparison, China's minimum wage stands at $370, Mexico's at $440, and New York City's at $2600.[233]

Unemployment is remarkably low—just 2.2% in 2024—with a steady labor force participation rate of around 70%, signaling a strong labor market.

Vietnam's demographic profile supports continued growth. Half the population is under 35, ensuring a robust labor supply for years ahead. Each year, about 1.2 million new job seekers enter the workforce, driving the country's expanding economy.

However, youth unemployment remains a presssing issue, especially in urban areas: it is 7.8%, well above the national average. Underemployment affects 2.7% of young workers, many of whom hold jobs in informal sectors like retail and hospitality, which are below their skill level and offer limited stability and few benefits.[234]

These discrepancies highlight a key challenge for policymakers: ensuring that young entrants to the labor market acquire the skills needed for growing opportunities in the job market. Reports indicate that 65% of employers in Vietnam cite finding skilled talent as their top hiring barrier. They also feel

---

[232] Intracen (2024) "ITC Trade Map" Retrieved from: https://www.trademap.org/.
[233] Le, Dahlia (2024) "Vietnam's workforce" Retrieved from: https://vietnam.incorp.asia/.
[234] Vietnam General Statistics Office (2024) Retrieved from: https://www.gso.gov.vn/en/.

that many recent graduates lack the technical skills and practical experience required for entry-level roles.[235]

Vietnam has made notable progress in building human capital through formal education. Adult literacy is high at 97%, yet educational attainment remains modest compared to other emerging economies. Only 14% of the population aged 25 and over has completed at least a short formal training course—far below Poland's 29%. Likewise, just 12% hold a Bachelor's degree (compared to 29% in Poland), and a mere 0.6% have earned a Master's degree (versus 22% in Poland).

These weaknesses are not due to government inaction. Vietnam prioritized infrastructure improvement, institutional reform, and human resource development. To prove its commitment, Vietnam allocated 17–18% of its annual budget to education from 2011 to 2020 (although the figure dropped to 15% in 2022).[236] This spending level exceeds that of the United States (13%) and is set to reach 20%, aligning with peers like Indonesia (18%) and Singapore (20%).

In absolute terms, education spending in Vietnam remains low. In 2020, the country allocated $11.3 billion to education—similar to Singapore's $11 billion, despite having ten times its population—and significantly less than Mexico's $56 billion.[237] The country's age structure, with 22% of the population under 14 years old, requires sustained investments in basic education, which limits funding for reskilling and upskilling programs for working-age individuals, which are critical for Vietnam's ambition to become a high-tech hub. The UN's Frontier Technology Readiness Index, which measures relevant skills for using, adopting, and adapting frontier technologies, highlights this gap. Vietnam has consistently scored 0.3 since 2008, lagging behind Nigeria and China (0.4) and far behind Poland (0.7) and the US and UK (0.8).

To address this—once again through active government intervention—Vietnam's Prime Minister has set a target of training 50,000 semiconductor engineers by 2030, up from just over 5000 today, to better integrate the country into global manufacturing value chains.[238] The government has

---

[235] World Economic Forum (2023) "Putting skills first: a framework for action" Retrieved from: https://www.pwc.com/gx/en/issues/upskilling/.

[236] U.S. International Trade Administration (2024) "Market intelligence: Vietnam" Retrieved from https://www.trade.gov.

[237] UNESCO (2024) "Government expenditure on education" Retrieved from: https://data.uis.unesco.org/.

[238] Hanoi Times (2024) "Developing Vietnam's semiconductor workforce" https://hanoitimes.vn/developing-vietnams-semiconductor-workforce-depends-on-a-collaborative-strategy-327268.html.

also liberalized private sector involvement and actively encouraged foreign participation in education and training.

Vietnam's young workforce represents a significant opportunity for economic growth, but it is essential to ensure these workers are equipped with the skills for a tech-driven economy. By investing in vocational training, fostering public–private partnerships, and enhancing STEM education, Vietnam is making strides in bridging the skills gap.

By 2023, Vietnam had established over 1900 vocational training institutions nationwide. The goal for 2030 is to attract 50–55% of high school students to the vocational education system. Additionally, 50% of the workforce will be retrained through continuous education programs, with a target of 90% proficiency in IT skills.

Case studies show successful of collaborations between the government and foreign companies. Samsung's "High-Tech Academy" trains hundreds of workers annually in fields like electrical engineering and robotics, enabling them to transition from general factory roles to technical positions. Similarly, Intel has developed in-house programs to train employees in machine learning, AI, and advanced manufacturing. Local tech firms like VinGroup also invest heavily in R&D.

STEM education has become a cornerstone of Vietnam's strategy to create a tech-savvy workforce. As part of the National Strategy for Industry 4.0, Vietnam has introduced new curricula at secondary and tertiary levels to build competencies in science, technology, engineering, and mathematics.[239] These efforts have led to a sharp increase in STEM graduates, who now comprise 35% of total university enrollments.[240]

Regardless of individual talent, effective management is essential to enterprise performance. The World Management Survey (WMS) provides a structured evaluation of organizational management practices and links them to firm performance. Vietnam scores 2.6 on the survey, placing it in the lower half of the 35 countries evaluated. In comparison, top performers like the United States score 3.3, and emerging economies such as Mexico and Poland both score 2.9. The WMS also reveals a dual structure within Vietnam: while multinational corporations operate with advanced managerial practices, domestic firms private and State-run, lag behind.

---

[239] Nguyen, PL (2024) "Vietnam's STEM Education Landscape: Evolution, Challenges, and Policy Interventions" Vietnam Journal of Education. Vol 8, Issue.
[240] UNESCO. (2022). "STEM education in Asia: Vietnam's growing talent pool." https://www.unesco.org.

A recent study confirmed the limited quality of management practices in Vietnamese firms.[241] It also confirmed that key metrics like more sales volume, larger payrolls, and higher investment in physical and human capital are all associated with better managerial practices.

Key Drivers

Vietnam experienced remarkable economic growth by transitioning a large pool of unskilled workers from subsistence activities to manufacturing and service occupations. The country capitalized on its strengths, focusing on labor-intensive production, such as apparel and footwear, alongside agriculture.

In the economic development literature, the Đổi Mới reforms and the subsequent surge in Foreign Direct Investment in manufacturing are rightly credited as the key catalysts behind Vietnam's impressive economic transformation.

It is important to realize that the Đổi Mới reforms were born out of geopolitical realignment. Vietnam's heavy reliance on aid from the Soviet Union became unsustainable as the Soviet state faced severe economic challenges in the 1980s. Internally, Vietnam grappled with economic stagnation, hyperinflation (which peaked at 700% in the mid-1980s), and widespread poverty—much of it stemming from inefficiencies in the centrally planned economic system modeled after the Soviet Union and the lingering economic consequences of the war against the U.S. These internal crises, coupled with the withdrawal of Soviet support, made exploring new avenues of economic growth imperative.

Vietnam's isolation from Western markets due to sanctions imposed after the Vietnam War and its military intervention in Cambodia further highlighted the need for diplomatic pragmatism to diversify trade partners and integrate into the global economy.

Before 1986, small-scale experiments with market-oriented policies, such as Contract Farming where farmers were incentivized to exceed quotas, showed early success and laid the groundwork for broader reforms.

Vietnam's reform model was inspired by China's Reform and Opening-Up policy, introduced by Deng Xiaoping in 1978. This approach combined market-oriented reforms with continued one-party rule, offering a roadmap that Vietnam adapted to its unique context.

---

[241] Nguyen Tuan Kiet, Hu Huu Phuong Chi, and Trinh Cong Duc, "Management practices of firms: A Study of the Vietnam Delta," Managerial and Decision Economics, September 2021.

The Đổi Mới reforms liberalized trade, encouraged private sector participation, and opened the economy to foreign investors. Major multinational companies, such as Samsung, Intel, and LG Electronics, invested heavily in Vietnam, creating jobs, boosting exports, and integrating the country into global supply chains.

Enter infrastructure. From the outset of Đổi Mới in 1986, the government prioritized infrastructure development and human capital improvement to sustain FDI and export-driven growth. Vietnam's geographic location and low-cost labor—strategic geopolitical advantages—spurred the development of a robust network of free trade agreements, including membership in the CPTPP and RCEP. These agreements, coupled with improved infrastructure, created a competitive edge and became a barrier to entry for other low-cost producers vying for inclusion in global value chains.

Technology adoption remains gradual, but state programs and foreign firms have facilitated advancements in this area, which will continue to evolve over time.

This version of Vietnam's economic history, however, overlooks an essential element that broadens the scope and significance of the 'Harnessed Talent' concept: the role of its cohesive, disciplined, and community-oriented culture. Vietnam has relied on its frugal, hardworking, and hierarchical society to implement and sustain its development strategies. While low-cost, unskilled labor is a valuable resource globally, labor unified by a collective purpose is an even greater asset.[242]

Emerging from tremendous collective struggles, Vietnamese society has strengthened its cultural and religious sense of unity and mutual assistance. It is rare to find a nation with such diversity—comprising 54 ethnic groups—working together to overcome adversity, demonstrating a communal mindset over individualism.

Self-restraint, reinforced by cultural norms, religion, and possibly authoritarian governance, has maintained social and family progress as a central priority, often at the expense of individual gain. Exposure to international perspectives has further strengthened this collective spirit, steering the country away from internal disputes.

This disciplined collective talent also underpins Vietnam's ability to execute its economic plans effectively. The Vietnamese government has shown exceptional capacity to implement medium- and long-term strategies, particularly in areas like economic reforms, infrastructure development, and poverty alleviation.

---

[242] Thanks to international consultant Pilar Larreamendy for her generous insights on this topic. December 2024.

Discipline and restrained individualism will continue to be critical assets as Vietnam strives to achieve its ambitious goals of attaining upper-middle-income status by 2030 and high-income status by 2045.

A brief note on productivity. The Vietnamese story revolves around low-cost goods, carefully manufactured by low-paid workers. But, is this sustainable? Probably yes, for at least another decade.

Vietnam is gradually becoming more expensive than some of its neighbors. Vietnamese workers earn an average monthly wage of $330, compared to $263 in Cambodia, $178 in Laos, and $156 in Myanmar. However, Vietnam's wages remain just 23% of China's average monthly wage of $1385. Figure 6.28 illustrates Vietnam's performance in terms of the growth of total factor productivity.

Vietnam consistently prioritizes infrastructure—investing around 6% of GDP annually—which has yielded significant results. The country's superior trade infrastructure often compensates for wage differences, making Vietnam an attractive manufacturing hub.

If current trends in FDI, exports, and investment in infrastructure and human capital continue, productivity is likely to increase at a faster pace than in China or South Korea. This progress will provide the foundation for wage growth and an eventual exit from the low-cost model.

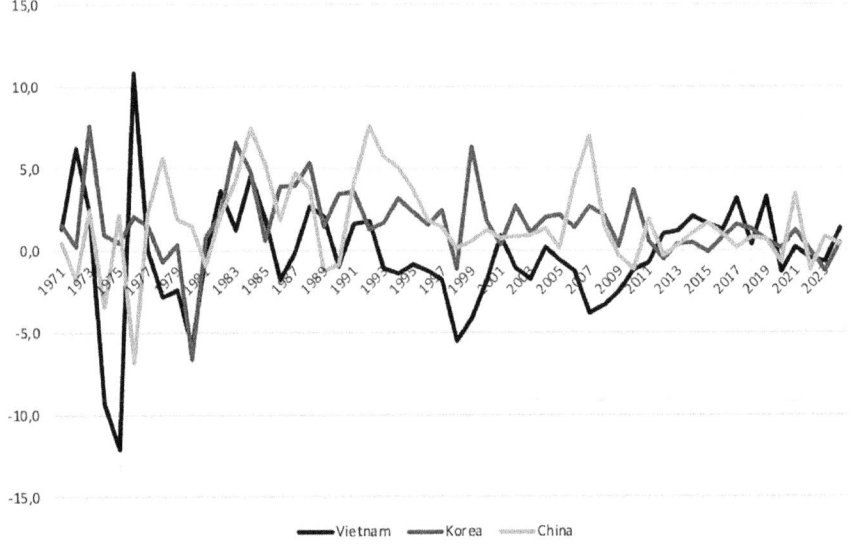

Fig. 6.28 Vietnam—Total Factor Productivity (TFP) 1971–2024. Change in the natural log (*Source* The Conference Board, https://www.conference-board.org/retrievefile.cfm?filename=TED_SummaryTables_Charts_may20241.pdf&type=subsite)

However, opportunities to improve productivity exist today. Reforms in State-Owned Enterprises (SOEs), better integration of low-productivity domestic firms into global value chains, and focused skill development for workers could all significantly boost productivity.

Finally, when it comes to resource traps. Vietnam faces difficult choices in sectors like coffee farming. In the 1980s, coffee farmers benefited from support by the World Bank and other international agencies, alongside favorable domestic policies—such as subsidies, concessional loans, and land reforms. By the late 1990s, Vietnam had emerged as the world's second-largest coffee producer.

Today, the sector supports around 600,000 households—roughly 3% of the population—and generates $4.6 billion annually, accounting for about 1% of total exports. With average yields of 2.9 tons per hectare, Vietnam ranks among the world's most productive coffee-growing nations.

Yet, despite this success, coffee farmers earn between $2000 and $3500 per year. Since most famers cultivate less than one hectare, their incomes tend to fall at the lower end of this range. In contrast, even basic urban jobs typically pay around $3600 per year, offering more predictability and stability.

Coffee producers also face mounting headwinds: volatile and inflexible commodity prices, unpredictable weather, tariffs on value-added products like roasted or ground coffee, and more recently, elevated freight costs.

The story above—so common across developing countries—is basically saying that 3% of the population is trapped in a low-income pocket. These kinds of traps negatively skew income distribution and keep whole groups from sharing in the economic gains happening elsewhere. Just something to ponder over coffee.

Country Outlook

Vietnam is on track to become a high-middle-income country within the next decade. Its combination of strategic infrastructure investments, talent development, and a politically neutral, business-friendly environment is likely to sustain Foreign Direct Investment (FDI) inflows and export growth over this period.

Achieving the ambitious goal of high-income status by 2045 will require enhanced investment in the productivity of both public and private firms, a strong commitment to combating corruption, and a focus on fostering environmental and social sustainability to keep its markets open.

7

Conclusion

The worldwide pandemic and its aftermath have altered the business landscape broadly and profoundly. However, the seeds of change were planted before the global health crisis. During the last decade, the geography of accelerated economic growth potential has changed and is moving forward at an even faster pace and will continue to do so over the next ten years. Geopolitics has overtaken purely economic issues, as witnessed by the conflict between Russia and Ukraine, ethnic-religious tensions in India, the rise of populism and authoritarianism in many regions of the world, increased inflation and fiscal deficits, public safety and anti-foreigner manifestations in South Africa are impacting nations, the public and private sectors, and consumers and citizens at large.

Four key drivers, shown in Fig. 7.1, are altering today's global business landscape—technology, infrastructure, geopolitics, and harnessed talent. The acronym we apply here is TIGHT (technology, infrastructure, geopolitics, and harnessed talent), and we refer to it as the TIGHT Framework. Individually and collectively, they are producing dramatic impacts on how nations and companies compete. To illustrate, geopolitics in the form of deteriorating U.S.-China relations are motivating American companies that operate in and source from China to consider nearshoring. New technologies in artificial intelligence and machine learning are accelerating innovation and productivity in both manufacturing and service firms. Public–private partnerships in infrastructure, such as ports and roadways, are producing efficient and cost-effective solutions to both domestic and foreign commerce, while the quest for talent presents an overwhelming and continuous challenge for corporations of all sizes.

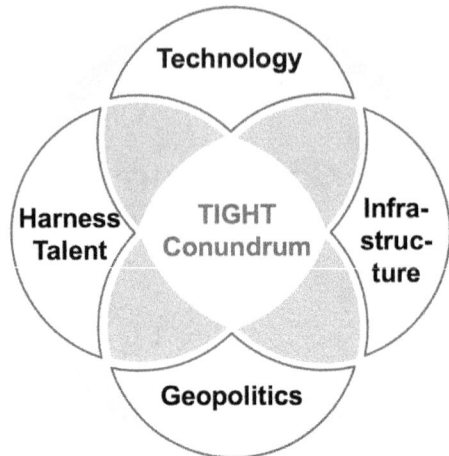

Fig. 7.1 The TIGHT conundrum and four key drivers

The aim of our book was twofold: (1) assess how the TIGHT Framework is altering today's global business landscape and (2) examine how one important "living laboratory"—new emerging markets—is faring vis-à-vis the framework.

In the first instance, we presented a deep dive into each driver and presented the challenges and impediments, opportunities and prospects, and evaluation to date of how, when, and where each driver is achieving results. Their interdependence is the most critical part of our focus and message, for it is the dynamic nature of the interrelationship that makes a difference. In the second instance, we intended to zero in on 6 of the new emerging markets to render a verdict on our assessment of the TIGHT Framework as applied to the most important and fastest-growing segment of global commerce—the new emerging markets.[1]

From our extensive research and case analysis, what lessons did we learn from analyzing technology, infrastructure, geopolitics, and human capital and their relevance and application to other emerging markets?

To begin with, there is the ***technology driver***. The application, effects, and impacts of technology are ubiquitous, encompassing both our private lives and today's geopolitical and business landscape. As they pertain to the

---

[1] In referring to "emerging markets" one tends to immediately think of the BRICS—an acronym for five leading emerging economies: Brazil, Russia, India, China, and South Africa. The first four were initially grouped as "BRIC" (or "the BRICs") in 2001 by Goldman Sachs economist Jim O'Neill, who coined the term to describe fast-growing economies that would collectively dominate the global economy by 2050. The "new" emerging markets are the next wave, especially since the original BRICs, except for India, have not been faring well.

business world, these are artificial intelligence (AI), information technology, green energy technology, financial technology, and the Internet of Things (IoT). These technologies have significantly reshaped borders and international policy and also altered the business landscape by having a dramatic impact on operations, customer engagement, and competition.

With regard to artificial intelligence, its potential in the business world is immense, given its ability to boost operational efficiency and productivity. Automating routine tasks, language, and mathematical programs allows a company's human resources to be deployed to more strategic and creative endeavors. The results are cost savings and improved competitiveness. Early adoption of AI in the supply chain arena has resulted in a decrease of more than 15% in logistics costs. Another important benefit is that AI-driven personalization vastly improves customer experiences by tailoring products and services, thereby producing greater customer loyalty and increased revenue.

As for information technology (IT), this covers the gamut of computer software, networks, storage, retrieval, and a host of electronic devices. With enterprise software systems, communication networks, and cloud computing services, businesses of a range of sizes—but large firms especially—can streamline their operations, boost efficiency, enhance customer communication, and lower costs. One should note that IT provides the advantage of enabling companies to facilitate communication and collaboration among employees, customers, and stakeholders, irrespective of physical location. This, in turn, fosters greater agility and responsiveness to market dynamics.

The investment required to achieve all of this is significant. Global IT spending at present approaches $5 trillion.

Another technology driver is green energy technology. This refers to renewable energy sources and sustainable practices that lessen the impact on the environment while fulfilling energy needs. Some good examples are NextEra Energy, with regard to wind and solar, and General Electric, with fuel and energy-efficient engines. Including solar, wind, hydroelectric, biomass, and geothermal, the renewable energy market surpasses $2 trillion worldwide.

Given the contemporary socio-political landscape, renewable energy does more than mitigate the risks associated with climate change; it strengthens a firm's brand reputation and appeals to consumers and investors who are environmentally conscious. Firms such as Apple, Unilever, Disney, Microsoft, and Ford are exemplary in reducing their carbon footprint. At the same time, green technologies open a space for lucrative opportunities for innovation and market expansion. Airbus, for example, is spending nearly one billion dollars to create a zero-emission hydrogen-powered plane engine within the next decade.

Another technology shaping the business landscape is financial technology (FinTech) FinTech, with firms such as Venmo and PayPal in the vanguard of the financial technology sector. It encompasses a wide range of financial tools, platforms, and systems, from mobile banking, digital payment systems, and blockchain applications such as cryptocurrencies to peer-to-peer payment services, robot advisors, and trading platforms. Fintech can help consumers do much more than access their bank accounts; it can help customers optimize cash flow and investment opportunities. For companies in particular, technology platforms like QuickBooks enable firms to reallocate resources and focus on core competencies.

Finally, the fifth technology shaper is the Internet of Things (IoT). It is a vast network of everyday objects embedded with sensors, software, and internet connectivity. These are smart devices that include thermostats, factory robots, Google Home, and Amazon Alexa devices, among others. IoT data offers a deeper understanding of customer behavior and preferences, with the ability to personalize experiences and develop targeted marketing strategies. The retailer Target provides an excellent example.

To reiterate, artificial intelligence, financial technology, green energy, information technology, and the Internet of Things have individually and collectively altered the business landscape in the twenty-first century. From supply chain management to advanced manufacturing, workflow processes, and customer service, these technologies have boosted efficiency, productivity, and consumer responsiveness.

In addition to technology per se, this driver has also had an impact on infrastructure, geopolitics, and harnessed talent—the three other features of the TIGHT paradigm. To begin with, the relationship between technology and infrastructure is a circular one. Technology has a major impact on the planning, design, construction, and operation of infrastructure. Infrastructure development offers the foundation and support for using and disseminating various technologies. For example, China has developed new bridge-building methods that allow cities to construct overlapping and interconnected highways and overpasses, resulting in improved transportation speed and efficiency. Industrialized nations benefit from the marriage of telecom and infrastructure, for example, with 5G technology—a technology that enhances mobile internet speed and reliability. This, in turn, enables new applications in remote work, telemedicine, and IoT.

Another area where technology and infrastructure come together is Smart Cities, such as Singapore, Amsterdam, and Dubai. Modular construction, 3D printing, and robotics dramatically advance the process of construction and lead to faster, cost-effective, and environmentally sound projects while IoT improves the popularity of Smart Cities worldwide.

Moving on, the nexus between technology and geopolitics is another feature of the TIGHT paradigm. A perfect example that centers on global power dynamics, national security, and economic competitiveness is Israel's deployment of the "Iron Dome." Developed by Rafael Advanced Defense Systems and Israel Aerospace Industries, the system is designed to intercept and destroy short-range rockets and artillery shells fired from distances of 4–70 kilometers (2–43 mi) away and whose trajectory would take them to an Israeli-populated area.

As technology advances, it becomes a key shaper of the geopolitical landscape, allowing nations to leverage technological innovations, manifest dominance, project strength, and negotiate international relations. Technology can surely drive geopolitical change. E-commerce and the digital economy have disrupted trade patterns and opened up new opportunities for emerging markets, especially such as India, Mexico, and Vietnam. As for the major powers, the competition for technological leadership in areas like semiconductors and AI is linked to economic prosperity, military power, and global influence.

At the corporate level, especially for businesses seeking to expand their operations overseas, the digital economy poses threats as well as opportunities. Questions of privacy, data security, and electronic surveillance loom large and pose enormous problems potentially for companies and workers. The rise of digital currencies and blockchain can also disrupt the competitive landscape of the business world.

Finally, the relationship between technology and harnessed talent provides an additional dimension to the TIGHT paradigm. Without a steady supply of skilled people, businesses—and the technology ecosystem itself—cannot drive societal progress, economic growth, and competitiveness. The nexus between technology and harnessed talent permeates all aspects of economic and business growth and drives innovation in all sectors and industries. As a catalyst for the growth of human capital and harnessed talent, technology provides online learning platforms that equip individuals with the skillsets they need to further develop their capabilities and improve their performance. Technology also democratizes access to information, while unequal access to technology worsens existing inequalities.

The epitome of technology and harnessed talent is the explosion of telecommunications and cloud-based solutions. The rapid growth and expansion of call centers and back-office operations in Asia, Latin America, the Caribbean, and Central Europe are illustrative. This outsourcing gives companies leverage in their competitiveness. Firms like Microsoft, Google, and Amazon invest heavily in employee training programs to respond to the necessity of human capital for outsourcing operations. The global IT training market, currently a $69 billion operation, is expected to grow 5% annually.

Within the TIGHT framework, technology is instrumental in further shaping the domain of geopolitics, infrastructure development, and talent acquisition. For example, in the geopolitical sphere, energy, space, critical minerals, and environmental management are important areas in which the U.S. and Canada cooperate and collaborate. Advancements in AI and automation are improving infrastructure development, as in the case of companies like Germany's Siemens, which utilizes digital twins to optimize construction projects. When it comes to technology and human capital, communication tools allow decentralized and diversified work teams to collaborate the world over.

Technology is, indeed, a vital catalyst in today's business landscape and will continue to be so for the foreseeable future.

Infrastructure is the second driver in the TIGHT framework, and it encompasses a range of physical and non-physical building blocks that serve as enablers of economic growth and business competitiveness. The infrastructure driver can be thought of as "hardware," whereas technology may be considered the "software." For companies seeking to invest or expand overseas, understanding, measuring, and assessing international infrastructure is a key determinant of success.

Physical infrastructure entails transportation networks, energy, water, and digital infrastructure. The apex of competitive infrastructure is "smart cities," such as Singapore, Helsinki, Zurich, and New York. Social infrastructure—often overlooked—entails facilities and services that enhance the quality of life for both people and communities. This included education, healthcare, cultural activities, and public safety. Social infrastructure is essential for the development of a skilled and engaged workforce. Finland and Singapore are good examples of countries with very well-developed social infrastructure. According to the OECD, among 15 countries, France, Finland, and Belgium are nations with the highest social spending, whereas South Korea, Turkey, and Mexico spend the lowest.

Infrastructure can best be thought of as "the great connector" and one of the pillars of the World Bank's Global Competitiveness Index. In the transportation sector alone, logistics and trade costs are nearly 9% lower in low-income countries. An example is Vietnam's expansion of deep-water seaports, which can now handle large container ships, allowing the nation to compete better in global markets. When it comes to digital infrastructure, including high-speed internet and telecom networks, cloud computing and big data analytics have emerged as powerful tools to bolster competitiveness. Digital connectivity has also allowed businesses to utilize remote work for their workforce—to greater and lesser degrees—with firm-level benefits such as greater productivity, in many instances, and social benefits such as lower levels of pollution due to less-crowded highways. Connectivity has also made it possible for companies operating or manufacturing in emerging markets to enhance their supply chain resistance. Maersk is a good example of how its integrated advanced tracking and forecasting technologies bring benefits to logistics in both industrial and emerging markets.

Infrastructure that supports research and innovation is yet another example of driving business and fostering new business development and process improvements. Laboratories, online databases, and other educational and training enhancements have allowed companies to improve their workforce by closing the skills gap and expanding knowledge capabilities within their enterprises.

The role of infrastructure in the new global business landscape transcends efficiency and cost-effectiveness. Morocco's Noor Solar Plant plays a major role in reducing reliance on fossil fuels, and the Port of Rotterdam's smart infrastructure integrates IoT sensors, AI, and data analytics to optimize logistics and reduce carbon emissions.

Measuring the infrastructure driver within a region is of major importance as it allows businesses to make informed decisions regarding supply chain sourcing, operational expansion, and future investment. Several key metrics deserve attention. First is high road density and public transport accessibility. These are key to hundreds of industries, including natural resources, restaurants, and commodity markets. Without reliable roads and transportation networks, a nation's economy can stagnate. Zambia and the Congo are good examples, as they have huge copper deposits, but they are very difficult to retrieve. For businesses considering entering a new market, road density is a major factor. A lack of access to public transportation limits the talent pool that companies can draw upon during the hiring process and exacerbates employee turnover.

The electrification rate is another key infrastructure factor. Without a well-developed and reliable electrical system, productivity will suffer, especially due to delays, disruptions, and lost data. Worldwide, there is great variation in electrification infrastructure, from a rate of 100% in the U.S. to 15.3% in Tanzania. Internet penetration rates and average upload speed are other critically important features, as they facilitate communication and enable key operations like data analysis and e-commerce.

Hospital beds and clean water availability are other important infrastructure metrics. Healthcare, water, and sanitation infrastructure are crucial to the attainment and maintenance of a healthy, skilled workforce for any industry. According to the World Economic Forum, healthier workers are more productive and generate higher returns for their employers. To illustrate, Anglo American, a British multinational mining company faced with the impacts of HIV/AIDS and tuberculosis, partnered with local healthcare providers to deliver services on-site. This action reduced absenteeism, increased productivity, and enhanced workplace safety.

Still, another important indicator pertains to second and tertiary degrees and national literary rates. Educational infrastructure is the launchpad for a nation's workforce. More and more jobs require critical reasoning, problem-solving skills, and learning capacity to contend with the ever more complex technologies and infuse the global landscape. A particularly important feature of educational infrastructure is the relationship between a country's minimum wage, productivity per capita, and average educational level. As one can imagine, the variation is huge. Whereas half of all people in the Netherlands have a college degree, in El Salvador, only 82% of children make it to the 8th grade; yet we know that higher education fosters a talent pool that will help businesses increase their productivity, fuel innovation, and produce higher returns and revenue.

To recap, these metrics measure the five key infrastructure factors that cover transportation, electricity, digital, sanitation, and education. An assessment by region and country can provide indispensable information for companies in their foreign investment planning and operations.

As for the relationship between infrastructure and the other three drivers in the TIGHT framework, technology is of special importance. Reliable power grids, robust communication networks, and data storage facilities power public and private sector growth. Upgrades and expansion in technology, such as 5G networks, provide a backbone for deploying operations to increase efficiency, sustainability, and resilience. China's high-speed rail network is a good example. At the consumer level, a good example is Netflix, which leveraged cloud storage via Amazon Web Services (AWS) to store and analyze huge amounts of customer data. The result was better algorithms for the firm, personalized content offerings, and improved user engagement—all leading to higher subscription retention rates and growth in its worldwide user base.

When it comes to geopolitics, infrastructure, and geopolitics are deeply intertwined and reflect geopolitical strategies, power dynamics, and the economic relationships among countries. Infrastructure can act as a tool for countries to manifest their influence, secure their interests, and cooperate (and compete) in the global space. Control over key infrastructure assets, such as Panama's control of the canal, can provide a nation with leverage in international relations. The competition for leadership between the U.S. and China in AI, quantum computing, semiconductor manufacturing, and biotechnology are several examples. Other examples of the interface between infrastructure and geopolitics are the highly controversial Nord Stream 2 project transporting natural gas from Russia directly to Germany and China's Belt and Road Initiative (BRI), a huge infrastructure development project financed by China in which that endeavor helps China secure energy supplied by building pipelines and ports to facilitate resource transportation while meeting the PRC's political, economic, and strategic objectives both in and beyond their spheres of influence.

Finally, when it comes to infrastructure and harnessed talent, this relationship is foundational to economic development, innovation, and societal progress. First-rate infrastructure allows nations and companies to attract and retain high-quality talent, thereby improving the well-being not just of the enterprise but society as well. Countries like Finland, Singapore, Israel, and Switzerland consistently score at the top of global education rankings. Singapore invests 20% of its national budget in education, and Northern Europe scores extremely high in innovation year after year.

In sum, the cyclical relationship between infrastructure and each of the drivers highlights infrastructure's role in the TIGHT framework.

Moving to the third driver, *geopolitics*, the last two decades have seen a significant increase in the influence and impact of geopolitical forces and factors in shaping the global business environment. Among industry leaders, geopolitical risk ranks as the highest concern, with geopolitical hedging gaining increased prominence. With the world in considerable turmoil yet more interconnected than ever before, multinational firms especially must pursue plans and strategies to overcome serious challenges. They must institute financial and operational hedging by diversifying investments and operations across multiple regions. In doing so, they hope to mitigate risks from political instability, build flexible supply chains, establish partnerships in politically stable countries, and leverage regional trade agreements.

Geopolitical factors encompass the influences that geography and politics have on international relations, global dynamics, and strategic decisions within states and across regions. This intersection influences political decisions among nation-states. The decision of Great Britain to exit the EU, the U.S. to support Ukraine's accession to NATO, and China's launch of a Belt and Road Initiatives all have major impacts on the business landscape and geopolitical configuration of the countries involved. Tariff policies, especially, produce widespread repercussions, as witnessed by the tariffs imposed by both the U.S. and China during the 2018 trade war. These tariffs impacted the $450 billion bilateral trade relationship and prompted companies to rethink their supply chain strategies. As an example, China moved some of its production bound for the U.S. to Vietnam. Samsung and Nike also followed suit.

Beyond trade, the digital economy—including cybersecurity and information exchange—impacts international commerce. From a geopolitical perspective, state-sponsored cyberattacks are of particular concern since they can target infrastructure and corporate data. Corporate espionage and international sabotage are very much active in the global arena.

"Governability," a key feature of geopolitics and the visible hand of government policies and regulatory frameworks, influences a nation's ability to leverage globalization for economic growth and development. This is especially true in nations where natural resources play a major role, be these resources abundant or scarce. Countries rich in natural resources, such as Saudi Arabia and Guyana, have enormous streams of wealth derived from these resources but are also subject to a "resource curse" whereby government upheaval, instability, and poor rule of law produce widespread negative impacts.

There are five key geopolitical factors. The first is political stability, where high political stability within operating countries is crucial for business efficacy, a consistent revenue stream, and quality long-term investments. A case of utter failure along this dimension is Venezuela, with its political instability, dramatic economic decline, widespread corruption, hyperinflation, and surging crime. Thousands of businesses have gone bankrupt, and foreign investors have fled (except for oil and gas). Singapore, with its strong governance, rule of law, free market policies, and pro-foreign investment stance, is the polar opposite.

A second factor is *trade dependency and economic sanctions*. A country's level of trade dependency conveys its potential economic reliance on global markets that make it vulnerable to geopolitical changes and trade disruptions. Countries with a high dependency on trade can be vulnerable to domestic and international tensions (including disputes and sanctions) as they can impact supply chains, market access, and overall economic stability. Yet another factor is *peace and military spending*. Nations that are peaceful and stable are prone to having strong institutions, effective governance, and sound regulatory frameworks, thereby instilling investor confidence, which, in turn, allows for long-term planning. To understand the importance of geopolitical peace for global business, one needs to compare Syria and Japan. During the Assad period, Syria experienced a halt in industrial production, a decline in investment, and economic contraction. GDP per capita hovered around $420 only. With Japan, it has been the exact opposite. The nation registers the fourth largest GDP in the world, has a solid legal, financial, manufacturing, and social system, and is home to scores of global firms such as Toyota, Sony, and Mitsubishi.

A fourth factor to consider is *foreign direct investment*. Reviewing the global business landscape, one notes that FDI flows indicate whether or not there is investor confidence (and how much) in a region. Nations with high influxes of foreign capital, such as China, Mexico, Brazil, Singapore, and India, signal favorable market conditions, a sound legal framework, a healthy pool of talent, and strong consumer demand. Finally, *human rights protection* is the fifth geopolitical factor that should be measured. No company wants to be boycotted or sanctioned and see their names plastered all over the front page of major newspapers. Companies must be extremely vigilant to ensure that their company's health and safety, human rights, and human resources policies are pristine and their implementation impeccable. At the country level, countries that pursue policies akin to Cuba, Nicaragua, Iran, Afghanistan, and Yemen will continue to see foreign companies shun them like the plague.

Geopolitics and technology are critically important starting points within the TIGHT framework. Geopolitics plays a major role in the development, deployment, and governance of technology. The competitive pressure among nations drives technology investments, strategies, and regulations, especially in high-priority areas such as AI, 5G technology, quantum computing, and semiconductors. Firms like Qualcomm, Huawei, Nvidia, and TSMC strive for global dominance.

Related to the relationship between geopolitics and technology, technology is impacted significantly by geopolitics in the context of cybersecurity and cyber warfare. For example, Israel became a global leader in cybersecurity, given its need to protect its national security and economic interests. Examples included companies such as Check Point Software and CyberArk. India has also ramped up its cyber capabilities and created agencies such as the National Critical Information Infrastructure Protection Centre (NCIIPC) to safeguard telecom, defense, and financial services. Geopolitics is also shaping technology through data sovereignty and privacy regulations as nations seek to control data flows and protect citizens. The threatened US ban on Chinese firm ByteDance's subsidiary TikTok and the EU's General Data Protection Regulation (GDPR) are good examples.

As for geopolitics and infrastructure, geopolitical conflicts can divert a nation's attention away from investment in infrastructure, with funds reallocated to military spending. The Middle East is a prime example, with gross underinvestment in healthcare, education, sanitation, and electricity. Interestingly, when former President Biden announced his "Build Back Better" initiative in 2021, it shined the light on a new era of infrastructure geopolitics. Understandably, it was a geopolitical response to China's "Belt and Road Initiative." Domestically and internationally, infrastructure politics plays a major role politically, economically, and socially. The US, Canada, Sweden, Germany, and other nations finance infrastructure in emerging markets through loans, grants, and other forms of technical assistance. In essence, the geopolitics of infrastructure is a tool of statecraft and a vehicle to exert cooperation, power, and influence in the global ecosystem of development.

Finally, there is the nexus between geopolitics and harnessed talent. Geopolitical factors heavily influence the development and mobilization of human talent, which is vital to sustaining the competitive advantages of global businesses. Nations invest in education, training, and immigration policies to woo and maintain skilled professionals and entrepreneurs who power innovation and economic growth. A clear example is the U.S. H-1B visa program, which permits American firms to employ foreign workers in STEM specialty occupations (science, technology, engineering, and math). The H-1B program is heavily influenced by international relations, geopolitics, and domestic labor policy decisions. For example, in 2020, the US government announced temporary restrictions on the visa program, which affected thousands of workers and companies. The policy shift was driven by economic protectionism and national security. Recognizably, when visa caps are imposed, businesses face great challenges in recruiting and retaining skilled workers in specific job categories.

When it comes to human capital, geopolitical tensions and diplomatic relations can greatly impact international student flows, affecting the availability of skilled labor and the functioning of global supply chains. On need of note is the decline in recent years in Chinese and Indian students, given the rise of U.S.-China tensions in particular. Political instability, economic crises, and conflicts in various regions of the world fuel a brain drain whereby many of the brightest students from countries such as Venezuela and Ukraine emigrate from their homelands. Geopolitics also places limitations on research collaboration across a wide spectrum of disciplines in science, engineering, the social sciences, and humanities. The impact of Brexit on UK-based research projects is a prime example.

In essence, within the TIGHT framework, geopolitics is the prime motivation that drives the development of all other drivers forward. As a result, it dictates the technological development of a nation, its national security, and its competitiveness going forward.

The fourth pillar of the tight framework is **harnessed talent**. Talent has become the cornerstone of success in the global business landscape. Individuals with skills, adaptability, and an innovative mindset successfully confront the constantly challenging environment of international business. An excellent personification of those traits is Satya Nadella, the CEO of Microsoft. A University of Chicago business school graduate and professional IT specialist, he has revitalized Microsoft's culture and steered it toward a more mobile-first, cloud-first future.

Harnessing talent represents a holistic strategy that emphasizes the systematic and effective identification, development, utilization, and retention of individuals' skills and abilities to meet organizational needs. Organizations can more effectively harness talent through HR practices of talent acquisition, training, development, performance management, and career progression. These aim to maximize employee contributions toward innovation, productivity, and competitiveness. Infosys, a global leader in consulting, embodies these practices, especially in the sphere of training new recruits.

How harnessed talent is being utilized and obtained in a way that completely redefines traditional office work. Technological advancements such as remote working platforms have dramatically changed how employees work and how workplaces are structured. Within the human resources space, talent acquisition is increasingly difficult. Tightening labor markets has been a characteristic of personnel recruitment in over 30 advanced economies, and in the U.S. alone, the number of job vacancies has increased by a factor of 7 in recent years. The adoption of digital technologies has contributed hugely to this trend. Related to this is the conversation surrounding remote work and flexible employee schedules. COVID-19 accelerated the trend toward remote work, and one major result is that companies found that many in-office tasks could be performed outside the office, leading to the movement toward flexible working arrangements. Companies are now increasingly using platforms like Upwork and Linkedin to hire freelancers and full-time employees worldwide. The result has been a broader talent search and a diversification of teams.

The rapid proliferation of technology necessitated a continuous focus on learning and upskilling in order to harness the talent necessary for both public and private sector organizations. Companies invest heavily in training programs and learning platforms to equip their workforce with in-demand skills. Talent development, retention, and recruitment in software engineering and IT support, in particular, have become a higher priority for companies of all sizes, and job growth in healthcare and STEM shows no sign of abating. McKinsey Research reports that many organizations are facing a significant lack of essential talent, with 90% predicting substantial skill gaps in the near future.

In many industries, the demand for harnessing talent is being alleviated by vocational and technical education. For example, Germany's VET system manifests the benefits of vocational education at the national level. In essence, it is a structured system where students from the age of 15 split their time between classroom-based education and hands-on training at a company. The advantage of a public vocational education initiative is that it helps at the national level to capture rapid technological advancements to compete on the global stage. Singapore's SkillsFuture undertaking offers courses and certifications in AI, cybersecurity, and advanced manufacturing. In order to align educational outcomes with industry needs, Brazil launched PRONATEC (National Program for Access to Technical Education and Employment) in 2011, and it focused especially on reaching underserved populations.

When it comes to measuring harnessed talent, metrics to assess a country's success in harnessing talent usually revolve around education, innovation, labor market efficiency, and technological readiness. To begin with, educational attainment is the most critical indicator of a region's potential for harnessed talent. Measuring the percentage of the population with a university education is a good indicator of how skilled the workforce is with respect to advanced knowledge. South Korea provides a good example of its superior achievement within OECD countries, with 70% of individuals 25–34 having completed tertiary education. Labor market efficiency is another important metric as it measures the ability of workers to match their skills to appropriate employment opportunities quickly. Finland's adaptability in its workforce enables its companies to scale operations effectively.

R&S investment as innovation capacity is yet another key metric, for it is a key factor in determining its potential for long-term success. Innovation drives the creation of new products, technologies, and processes, enabling firms to have a competitive advantage in the global marketplace. Digital literacy is another indispensable metric for gauging a nation and a firm's competitiveness. The availability of digitally skilled workers allows firms to integrate cutting-edge tools such as AI, data analytics, and cloud computing into their processes. The Netherlands ranks very high in that regard, with 83% of Dutch people aged 16–75 possessing those skills.

Finally, there is the metric of the *Global Talent Competitiveness Index*. This index assesses 134 nations' ability to grow, attract, and retain talent. Switzerland, Singapore, and the U.S. are the top three countries in terms of talent competitiveness.

When it comes to harnessed talent within the TIGHT framework, the tie between harnessed talent and technology is most notable since harnessing talent accelerates the pace of technological advancement and enhances a nation's global competitiveness. IT, biotechnology, and renewable energy are prime areas where recruitment and retention of highly skilled workers have fueled the economic and technological growth and advancement of knowledge clusters such as Silicon Valley, Bangalore, Osaka, Boston, Tel-Aviv, and Hangzhou.

As for harnessed talent and infrastructure, harnessing human talent is a precondition for infrastructure development, driving efficient project design and execution, strengthening sustainable development practices, and advancing innovation in infrastructure solutions. Well-employed, harnessed talent is essential in the efficient design and effective execution of infrastructure projects. An excellent example is the development of Kenya's M-Pesa mobile banking service, which provides a compelling example of this impact on digital infrastructure. M-Pesa revolutionized financial inclusion by delivering secure and accessible financial services. At the big picture level, harnessing human talent is essential for driving innovation in infrastructure solutions and addressing complex challenges such as building smart cities with their state-of-the-art transportation networks and resilient energy grids.

The relationship between harnessed talent and geopolitics may not seem obvious, but the effective harnessing of human talent is a critical factor in positioning a region's geopolitical standing. A population that is well-educated, culturally diverse, and aware of the world around them can serve as a powerful tool for soft power and cultural diplomacy. By harnessing talent, a country can attain significant economic growth, technological prowess, and competitiveness. Germany is an excellent example. As Europe's largest economy, Germany demonstrated its geopolitical during the Green financial crisis of the 2010s by playing a central role in the EU's response. Germany insisted on austerity measures and economic reforms in exchange for financial support and ensured stabilization in the Eurozone.

Finally, there is the issue of talent recruitment and national security. Skilled professionals in defense, intelligence, cryptography, and cybersecurity contribute to advanced research and development and safeguard national interests. Not only does this allow a nation to project power on the global stage, but it improves geopolitical stability by achieving a response to emerging threats and protecting its assets.

In sum, effectively harnessing human talent is more than a major factor in regional development; it is a basic drive of corporate resilience, agility, and company expansion. Regions that excel in cultivating talent possess significant advantages across technology, infrastructure, and geopolitics, making them magnets for investment and growth.

Index

A

Africa 142
African Continental Free Trade Area (AfCFTA) 81, 163
agriculture 6, 18, 82
   Nigeria and 144, 165
Amazon 19, 36, 38, 92, 266, 268
   Amazon Web Services (AWS) 43, 55, 89, 195, 270
Andrés Manuel López Obrador (AMLO) 123, 129, 131–132, 133, 135
Apple 19, 36, 37, 74, 101, 265
   Nigeria and 157
   Saudi Arabia and 195
   Vietnam and 258
Aramco 190, 192, 197–198, 204–205, 209, 212–213
Artificial Intelligence (AI) 18–19, 25, 263–265, 266, 267–268. *See also* technology
   geopolitics and 33
   harnessed talent and 102–104
   human capital and 38–39
   infrastructure and 63
   Mexico and 123–124
   Nigeria and 148
   Saudi Arabia and 195–197
   TIGHT framework and 277, 268, 270, 273
Atatürk, Mustafa Kemal 226
automation 15, 16

B

Baku-Tbilisi-Ceyhan pipeline 223
Bamboo Diplomacy 251, 254–255
Belt and Road Initiative 3, 58–59, 60, 63, 270–272, 274
   Nigeria and 150–151, 155, 156, 163
   US Build Back Better initiative and 80
bin Salman, Mohammed 191, 195, 197, 203, 212–213
blockchain 33, 34–36
   Mexico and 124
Boko Haram 145, 146, 154, 155–156, 158, 161
Bosphorus Strait 228

Index

BP (British Petroleum) 72
brain drain 86, 137, 138, 158, 184, 274
   Nigeria and 158
   Poland's brain gain reverse of 184
   Saudi brawn gain and 210
Brexit 66, 84, 86–88, 274
Build Back Better World initiative 80, 274

C

cellular coverage 147
China 2–3. *See also* Belt and Road Initiative
   contraries to commonly held truths about 116
   COVID-19 and 5
   e-commerce in 24
   Nigeria and 155–156
   Poland and 181
   "Small and Beautiful Projects" initiative 163
   US relations and 77, 130, 181, 263, 274
   US trade war with 66–67, 70
   Vietnam and 252, 258
Civic Platform (PO) 168–169
climate change 1, 20, 83, 250, 265
closed circuit TV cameras 34
cloud-based technologies 37
cloud storage 55
communism 238–239, 244, 251–252. *See also* Vietnam
corruption
   Mexico and 128
   Nigeria and 145, 164–165
   Saudi Arabia and 194
COVID-19 Pandemic 4–6, 275
   technology and 24
cryptocurrencies 34–35
   Mexico and 124
   MiCA regulation and 176
cultural difference 94

cybersecurity 10–11, 25, 27, 34, 36, 78
   harnessed talent and 100–111, 112
   hedging and 10–11
   Poland and 175
   TIGHT framework and 271
   trade and 68

D

Dangote Refinery 153, 159
data sovereignty 78–79
de-globalization 1, 3
democratization of entrepreneurship 24
demographic dividend 215
development 113, 117
   aid to Nigeria and 162, 163
digital infrastructure 46–47, 55–56. *See also* infrastructure
   digital transformation and 90–91
   geopolitics and 82–83
   Poland and 179
   Saudi Arabia and 197
   Vietnam and 251
digital literacy 98
Digital Nigeria Skills Strategy 165
Digital Silk Road 58–59
Đổi Mới ('Rejuvenation') reforms 238, 240, 258–259
drug trafficking 134–135
dual-use technologies (military and civilian) 77
Duda, Andrzej 169

E

East Mediterranean Gas Forum (EMGF) 81
e-commerce 26
economic miracles 117
ECOWAS (Economic Community of West African States) 155

education 50–52, 270
　geopolitics and 85–88
　harnessed talent and 60–61,
　　94–96, 99–109
　Nigeria and 157
　Saudi Arabia and 208–209
　Turkey and 230–231
　vocational-technical skills and
　　94–98
efficiency *vs.* effectiveness 15
e-governance 148
electrification 49, 269
　Nigeria and 153
energy infrastructure. *See also*
　　infrastructure
　Mexico and 127
　Nigeria and 151–154
　renewable energy and 54–55
　Saudi Arabia and 198
　Turkey and 225
　Vietnam and 250
Erdoğan, Recep Tayyip 226
Estonia 78, 102
European Union (EU) 170,
　　181–182. *See also* Poland
　Digital Single Market (DSM)
　　strategy in 82
　General Data Protection
　　Regulation (GDPR) 78–79
　Horizon 2020 program 63
　Turkey and 226–228

family firms 184–185, 211
　Turkey and 232–233
financial technology (FinTech)
　　21–23, 266
　Mexico and 124–125
Finland 75–76
5G 29–30, 55–56, 88
　geopolitics and 76–78, 88
　infrastructure and 63
　Saudi Arabia and 196

Ford, Henry 14, 28
foreign direct investment (FDI) 273
　flow of 74–75
　Mexico and 118, 131–136
　Nigeria and 160–161, 167
　Saudi Arabia and 203–205
　Vietnam and 241–243
friendshoring 65–67. *See also*
　　nearshoring
frontier economies 47, 64

General Data Protection Regulation
　　(GDPR) 78–79
geographical location 116, 131
geopolitics 13, 87–88, 115–116,
　　273–275. *See also* TIGHT
　　(technology, infrastructure,
　　geopolitics, and harnessed
　　talent) framework
　bamboo diplomacy and 254
　Bosphorus Strait and 228
　foreign direct investment and
　　74–75
　governability and 68–70
　harnessed talent and 84–88,
　　100–111
　hedging against 65–66, 271
　human rights protections and
　　75–76
　immigration and 84–85, 87
　infrastructure and 57, 59–62,
　　76–82
　Mexico and 128–131
　Nigeria and 154–156, 160, 166
　peace/military spending and
　　73–74
　personal forms of 213
　Poland and 179–180, 181–183
　political stability and 71–73
　research collaboration and 86–87
　rise of populist nationalism and
　　181

risk hedging and 10–11
Saudi Arabia and 202–206, 207
Saudi proxy groups and 206
stable water flow 82–83
technological workforce and 86–88
technology and 33–36, 76–79
TIGHT framework and 266–267, 271–274
trade and 66–68
Turkey and 225–230
Vietnam and 250–253, 254–255
Germany 57, 108, 183, 277
mobilizing harnessed talent and 108
Polish trade with 169–170
gig economy 92
Global Competitiveness Index 44, 98–99, 277
globalism 1, 3, 6
globalization 3–5, 43, 68–69, 71, 90, 272
globalism and 1–3, 6
Globalization, Competitiveness, and Governability (Haar et al?) 4, 68
Global Peace Index (GPI) 74
Global South 156
Google 24, 43, 46, 101, 266, 268
harnessed talent and 37–39
internet of things and 23
Poland and 174, 188
Saudi Arabia and 195
Vietnam and 245
governability 68–70, 272
Grand Ethiopian Renaissance Dam (GERD) 83
Greek financial crisis 108
Green Climate Fund (GCF) 83
green energy 19–21, 23, 56, 265. *See also* renewable energy
infrastructure and 31
Saudi Arabia and 197
Grupo Bimbo 47, 124, 129, 133

H

H-1B visa program 84–85, 274
harnessed talent 13, 89–90, 274, 278. *See also* TIGHT (technology, infrastructure, geopolitics, and harnessed talent) framework
AI and 103–104
available workforce and 94–96
corporate expansion and 111–113
digital transformation and 90–93
educational attainment and 97
education in Turkey and 230–232
geopolitics and 84–86, 100–111
Global Talent Competitiveness Index and 98–99
infrastructure and 60–63, 104–107
innovation capacity and 97
labor market efficiency and 97
Mexico and 135–139
Nigeria and 156–159, 167
Poland and 183–185
regional development and 112–113
research collaboration and 86–87
Saudi Arabia and 208–211
technology and 36–39, 100–103
TIGHT framework and 99, 267–268, 271, 275
Turkey and 229, 231–233
Vietnam and 255–258
health care 270, 276
harnessed talent and 60–61
hospital beds and 50–51, 270
infrastructure and 50–51
Nigeria and 157–158
hedging 9
geopolitical forms of 63–64, 271
HIV/AIDS 50
hospital beds 50–51, 270
human rights 75–76, 155, 167, 226, 253, 273
Saudi Arabia and 202

IBM 94
IKEA 21, 30
immigration 84–85, 87
   Mexico-US relationship and 141
inequality 5, 37, 123, 140, 190, 267
Inflation Reduction Act 19
informal economy 119, 255
information technology (IT) 19, 265
Infosys 90
infrastructure 13. *See also* TIGHT (technology, infrastructure, geopolitics, and harnessed talent) framework
   Belt and Road Initiative 58–59
   connector 44–47
   education and 50–51
   electrification and 49
   geopolitics and 57, 59, 80–84
   governability and 68
   green energy technology and 31–32
   harnessed talent and 60–63, 104
   health and 50–51
   internet and 48–49
   Mexico and 126–129, 141
   Nigeria and 148–150, 164
   physical infrastructure and 42
   Poland and 177–178
   Saudi Arabia and 198
   social infrastructure and 43–44
   technology and 26–29, 31–32, 53–55
   technology deployment and 55–57
   TIGHT framework and 52, 63–64, 266, 268–270
   transportation and 48
   transportation in Nigeria and 149–151
   Turkey and 223–226
   two main types of 41–43
   Vietnam and 247–250, 258–259
   Vietnam's digital infrastructure and 250
innovation capacity 98
internal migration 167
International Space Station (ISS) 197
Internet for Everyone initiative 122
Internet of Things (IoT) 23–24, 266. *See also* technology
   5G and 27
   Mexico and 123
internet penetration 46, 49–50, 128, 147, 246, 269
investment portfolio management 213
Iran 206
Islamic State in the West African Province (ISWAP) 156
Israel 7–8
   cybersecurity and 77–78, 110
   "Iron Dome" and 267
   Saudi Arabia and 207

Japan 74

King Abdullah Economic City (KAEC) 202
King Salman Energy Park (SPARK) 198
Kroger 18, 19
Kurdistan Regional Government (KRG) 228

labor market efficiency 97–99, 276
Lagos-Ibadan Expressway Project 150
Lagos-Ibadan Railway 150, 163

Lagos Metropolitan Area Transport Authority (LAMATA) 151
Latin America 132
Law and Justice Party (PiS) 168–169, 181
literacy 51–52. *See also* education
Low Earth Orbit (LEO) satellite networks 29

M

Made in China 2025 initiative 111
Maersk 46, 68, 269
"Make in Vietnam" strategy 246
management. *See also* harnessed talent
   Mexico and 137
   Nigeria and 159
   Poland and 184
   Turkey and 231–233
Markets in Crypto-Assets (MiCA) regulation 176
Meta (Facebook) 19, 92
Mexico 118–120, 140–141
   brain drain and 138–139
   business environment in 120–122
   contraries to commonly held truths about 116
   drug trafficking and 135–136
   education and 137
   FDI and 132–135
   geopolitics and 129–130
   infrastructure and 126–129
   labor market and 137
   technology and 122–126
   trade and 130–132
   United States and 139–140
Microsoft 38, 43, 89, 275
Middle East 8, 65, 70, 274. *See also* Saudi Arabia; Turkey
mining 198
M-Pesa mobile banking service 104–105, 277
Musk, Elon 21, 212

N

Nadella, Satya 89, 275
National Autonomous University of Mexico (UNAM) 136
nationalism 181
National Program for Access to Technical Education and Employment (PRONATEC) 96, 276
NATO (North Atlantic Treaty Organization) 7, 180–182, 186, 271
   Turkey and 225, 226–227, 233
natural resources 70, 269, 272
nearshoring 3, 66, 67, 127, 141
   US-China relations and 181, 263
Neom, Saudi Arabia 190, 201
Netflix 55
Netherlands flood defense system 105
new emerging markets (NEM) 3, 13, 74, 105. *See also* Mexico; Nigeria; Poland; Saudi Arabia; Turkey; Vietnam
   infrastructure and 44, 46
   TIGHT paradigm and 16, 264, 268, 274
Nigeria 142–145, 165–168
   brain drain and 158
   business environment and 146
   corruption and 164–165
   development and 117
   energy infrastructure and 151–153
   FDI and 160–161
   geopolitics and 154–156, 160
   healthcare and 157–158
   infrastructure and 164
   legal environment and 146–147
   managerial talent and 159
   political landscape of 145
   productivity and 165–166
   technology and 147–148
   youth and 158–159

Nigerian National Petroleum
    Company Limited (NNPC)
    152
Nollywood 154, 159
Nord Stream pipeline 57–58
North American Free Trade
    Agreement (NAFTA) 129,
    132, 140
North Atlantic Treaty Organization
    (NATO) 78
NotPetya cyberattack 68

Obasanjo, Olusegan 143, 160
Official Development Assistance
    (ODA) 162, 163
oil production 197–199, 202–204,
    206, 272. See also energy
    infrastructure
  FDI and 160–161
  indigenous companies and 159
  Nigeria and 143–146, 149,
    151–154, 164–167
  Saudi Arabia and 189–192,
    211–212, 213, 216
  Turkey and 216, 219, 223–225,
    227–228
  US counterinsurgency policy and
    155
  Vietnam and 243, 252, 253–254
OPEC (Organization of the
    Petroleum Exporting
    Countries) 202, 206, 211–212
  Nigeria and 143, 151, 154
OpenAI 18, 38
Open Radio Access Network (RAN)
    197

patent applications 25
peace spending 73–74, 272
Pemex 121, 128, 132–134

Peña Nieto, Enrique 132–133
Peru 70
physical infrastructure 39, 42, 46,
    47, 53, 54
  smart cities as epitome of 268
  TIGHT framework and 268
  Vietnam and 247
PKN Orlen 172
platform-based business models 24
Poland 168–170, 171–175, 187–189
  contraries to commonly held
    truths about 116
  EU membership and 171
  FDI 186–187
  geopolitics and 179–181
  infrastructure 177–179
  military buildup and 181–183
  productivity and 172–174
  technology 175–177
political stability 272
  Nigeria and 71–72, 145
populism 179–181, 183, 263
Port of Manzanillo, Mexico 127
post-communist economic
    liberalization 168, 172–174,
    178, 187. See also communism
privacy 34–35, 109, 124, 148, 267,
    273
  data sovereignty and 78–79
privatization 143, 160, 219
  Saudi Arabia and 191, 192, 200
  shock therapy as 171
  Turkey and 218–219
public investment fund (PIF) 190,
    191–192

QuickBooks 22

Remote Container Management
    (RCM) system 46

remote work 24, 92
renewable energy 54–55, 265. *See also* energy infrastructure; green energy
   infrastructure and 63
   Turkey and 222
research and development (R&D) 25, 69. *See also* technology
   harnessed talent and 98
resilience 3, 10, 46, 110, 277
   hedging and 10
resource traps 261
rising middle powers 115
risk. *See* hedging
roads 52
   high road density and 48
Russia 33, 263, 264, 271. *See also* Ukraine
   cyberattacks by 78
   Nigeria and 156
   Poland and 171, 175, 179–180, 181–183
   Ukraine conflict and 6, 68, 180, 181
   Vietnam and 253

S

Salinas de Gortari, Carlos 129
Samsung 240, 243, 257, 259, 272
sanctions 272
Saudi Arabia 189–191, 192–194, 211–214
   contraries to commonly held truths about 116
   FDI and 203–206
   geopolitics and 203–204, 206–207
   infrastructure and 197–200
   key drivers in 211–214
   public investment fund and 191–192
   talent and 208–210
   technology and 194–197
   urban development and 201–202
Saudi Basic Industries Corporation (SABIC) 192, 205–206
Saudi Vision 2030 initiative 192, 197–198, 202, 202–204, 209–210, 212
   harnessed talent and 110
   public investment fund and 191–192
Saudization 209
secondary and tertiary degrees 51–52
semiconductors 33, 36, 39, 43, 96
   Mexico and 125
   Semiconductor Manufacturing International Corporation restrictions and 77
Sheinbaum, Claudia 136
Shield East defense program 182
Silicon Valley 28, 112, 117, 277
   harnessed talent and 99, 109
   Nigeria and 147
   Saudi Arabia and 195
Singapore 61, 68, 71–72
Skills Future initiative 96
smart cities 27, 31–32, 42, 266, 268, 277
   Saudi Arabia and 200–202
   smart water management and 30
Smart Urban Mobility solution 106
social infrastructure 43–44, 47, 61, 234, 238, 268
South Korea 69
   Korean Wave of culture from 109
   STEM education and 97
Soyinka, Wole 167
space exploration 59, 60
SpaceX 102
sports 211
state-owned enterprises (SOE) 192–193
   Vietnam and 242–244
STEM (science, technology, engineering, and mathematics) 97, 99, 101, 111, 274, 276

growth in 93
Mexico and 136
Saudi Arabia and 209
Vietnam and 257
Stockholm International Peace Research Institute 74
supply chains 26, 34–36, 37
surveillance technologies 34, 78, 182, 267
sustainability initiatives 47, 203
Sustainable City (Dubai) 105
Syria 73, 227–229
    Turkey and 215
    war's effect on infrastructure in 80

talent. *See* harnessed talent
technology 12, 17, 38–39, 264–267. *See also* TIGHT (technology, infrastructure, geopolitics, and harnessed talent) framework
    adoption and integration of 26
    AI and 18–19
    COVID-19 pandemic and 24
    FinTech and 21–22
    geopolitics and 33–35, 76–79
    green energy and 19–21
    green energy and 31
    harnessed talent and 36–39, 100–101, 267
    information technology and 19–20
    infrastructure and 26–29, 31, 53
    measuring status of 25–26
    Mexico and 122–126, 140
    Nigeria and 147–148, 167
    Poland and 175–177
    Saudi Arabia and 194–197, 210
    TIGHT framework and 27–28, 32, 270, 273
    Turkey and 220–223, 236
    Vietnam and 245–247

telecommunications 28–29, 266–268, 273
    cloud-based technologies and 36
Tesla 21, 38
TIGHT (technology, infrastructure, geopolitics, and harnessed talent) framework 12, 265–270, 273, 275, 277
    as conundrum 14, 263
    geographic location and 116
    geopolitics and 76–77, 87
    harnessed talent and 99
    infrastructure and 52, 63–64
    new emerging markets and 12, 16, 264, 274, 277
    technology and 27, 28, 32, 39
    utilizing 14
Tinubu, Bola Ahmed 145, 155
trade dependency 72, 272
Trans-Anatolian Natural Gas Pipeline (TANAP) 218, 223
transparency 36, 58, 247
    Mexico and 120, 122, 128
    Nigeria and 145, 148, 152, 155, 164–165
    Saudi Arabia and 193–194
transportation
    geopolitics and 81–82
    harnessed talent and 60–62
    harnessed talent and 106
    intelligent systems for 177–179
    Nigeria and 149–151
    Poland and 177–178
    Saudi Arabia and 199–200
    Vietnam and 248–250
Tuberculosis (TB) 50
Turkey 214–216, 233, 235–238
    economic growth and 234–235
    FDI and 218–220
    GDP and 216–217
    geopolitical importance of Bosporus Strait and 228
    geopolitics and 226–228, 229
    infrastructure and 223–226

talent and 230–233
technology and 220–223
Turkstream pipeline 218, 224, 228
Tusk, Donald 169, 181

U

Uber 94
Ukraine 33, 73, 129, 263, 271, 274
  Israel and 15
  Poland and 170, 177, 179–181, 183
  Russian conflict and 6, 68, 224, 227–228
  Saudia Arabia and 207
  Turkey and 221
  Vietnam and 253
United States 2, 5, 274
  bin Salman and 203
  China relations and 67, 70, 77, 130, 181, 263
  COVID-19 and 5
  FDI in Mexico and 135
  H-1B visa program and 84–85, 274
  Mexican's perceptions 129–130
  Mexico's convergence with 118–119
  Mexico and 119, 139–141
  Nigeria and 155
  TIGHT Conundrum and 14
  trade with Mexico and 120–121
  Vietnam and 252
upload speeds 49
upskilling 92
urbanization 106–107
  Saudi Arabia and 200–202
US-Mexico-Canada Agreement (USMCA) 3, 119, 131–132
U.S.- Vietnam Bilateral Trade Agreement (BTA) 243

V

Venezuela 71
  brain drain and 86
VET system 95
Vietnam 241–244, 261
  China and 252
  contraries to commonly held truths about 116
  deep-water seaport expansion in 44
  digital infrastructure and 250
  economic transformation of 238–240
  energy infrastructure and 250
  geopolitics and 251–255
  infrastructure and 247–250
  key business drivers and 258–260
  productivity and 260–261
  talent and 255–258
  technology and 245–247
  US and 252
vocational training programs 46–47
Volatile, Uncertain, Complex, and Ambiguous(VUCA) 11

W

waste management 30–31, 42, 47, 246
water 30–31, 42, 270
  infrastructure and 53
  Saudi Arabia water crisis and 214
  stable water flow and 83
  Turkey's geopolitical influence and 228–229
  water availability and 50–51
West Africa 154
World Bank World Development Indicators dataset 71–72

Y

Yemen 206–207

GPSR Compliance

The European Union's (EU) General Product Safety Regulation (GPSR) is a set of rules that requires consumer products to be safe and our obligations to ensure this.

If you have any concerns about our products, you can contact us on

ProductSafety@springernature.com

In case Publisher is established outside the EU, the EU authorized representative is:

Springer Nature Customer Service Center GmbH
Europaplatz 3
69115 Heidelberg, Germany

www.ingramcontent.com/pod-product-compliance
Lightning Source LLC
LaVergne TN
LVHW010337260326
834688LV00036B/753